AF342223

Acting for the Common Good

Acting for the Common Good

Social Justice in the Light of Catholic Social Teaching

MICHAEL J. McGRATH

CASCADE *Books* · Eugene, Oregon

Cascade Books
An Imprint of Wipf and Stock Publishers
199 W. 8th Ave., Suite 3
Eugene, OR 97401

www.wipfandstock.com

PAPERBACK ISBN: 978-1-5326-1774-4
HARDCOVER ISBN: 978-1-4982-4266-0
EBOOK ISBN: 978-1-4982-4265-3

Cataloguing-in-Publication data:

Names: McGrath, Michael J., author.

Title: Acting for the common good : social justice in the light of catholic social teaching / Michael J. McGrath.

Description: Eugene, OR: Cascade Books, 2023. | Includes bibliographical references and index.

Identifiers: ISBN 978-1-5326-1774-4 (paperback). | ISBN 978-1-4982-4266-0 (hardcover) | ISBN 978-1-4982-4265-3 (ebook).

Subjects: LCSH: Common good—Religious aspects—Catholic Church. | Social Justice—Religious aspects—Catholic Church. | Virtue. | Catholic Church—Doctrines—Papal documents. | Christian sociology—Catholic Church. | Economics—Religious aspects—Catholic Church. | Human ecology—Religious aspects—Catholic Church.

Classification: BX1795.S62 M60 2023 (print). | BX1795.S62 (epub).

08/03/23

For Tycie

Colin and John Michael

whose love and encouragement made writing this book
not only possible but joyful

Contents

Preface

The goodness of life, the beauty of creation, the love in a family, the joy of friend-ship, the harmony of health, the delight of food, the thrill of competitive games, the excitement of learning, the satisfaction of work, the order and stability of society, the rectitude of justice, the peace of prayer—all are goods that give meaning to our lives, goods that motivate us to endeavor to attain them in their fullness, goods that we see as constituting happiness. When we fail to achieve these goods in our lives, we prop-erly see and understand our failure only in the light of the good that we have failed to reach. Any therapeutic response on our part to remedy the failure must be planned and executed in the light of the good that is lacking. Our success in achieving the good depends on our being sufficiently moved by the value of the good in our lives to the degree that we are motivated to undertake the struggle to realize the good. The good is primary. All that is failure, deficiency, or limitation must be seen and can be remedied only in the light of the good.

Our study concerns the good of justice, particularly justice that pertains to the good of the whole, whether this be the whole of a society, the whole of the global order of societies, or the environmental good of Earth itself. Justice as a norm can be applied variously to the relations between individuals (say, fairness in the market-place), to relations between the government and its citizens regarding the fairness of the government's distribution of the society's goods (distributive justice), and more broadly to the interrelationships that make up the whole (society, the global order, the earth) and to the cooperative effort required on the part of all to realize the good of the whole. Here the justice that is sought in and through the interrelationships that constitute the whole is the common good of the whole. Acting for the common good, then, defines this third form of justice, termed *social justice* to distinguish it from individual justice and distributive justice. The good of social justice—acting for the common good—this is the focus of our study.

The understanding of the common good that we will employ has its origin in the philosophy of Aristotle, who lived in Athens in the fourth century BCE, its philosophical-theological articulation in the medieval theology of Thomas Aquinas in the thirteenth century, and its modern-day articulation in Catholic social thought and in the authoritative social teaching of the Roman Catholic Church: the conciliar documents of Vatican II, the pastoral statements of the Catholic bishops, and the papal social encyclicals from Pope Leo XIII in the late nineteenth century to Pope Francis in the present day (Chapter 2). This tradition brings a distinct viewpoint to social issues, one that sees social justice in the context of the interrelationship of peoples, whether local, national, or global, and more widely in the context of the interrelationship of all creatures of the earth. This tradition stands in tension with and thus provides an alternative viewpoint to the tradition of social justice that prevails in the West, one that is rooted in the philosophical tradition of the seventeenth- and eighteenth-century Enlightenment. The intent of our study is to bring these two traditions of social justice into dialogue with one another, and also to bring both traditions into dialogue with the viewpoints of the main social institutions that structure society, particularly government, the economy, and religion—this for the purpose of achieving a clearer understanding of the issues of social justice that confront us as a people and the motivation to respond to these social issues in effective ways through collective action.

As the norm of social justice, the common good is abstract, a universal concept that functions as a guide or an ideal to the acts of social justice. The common good gains specificity only in the concrete acts of justice that realize the common good. Accordingly, our study of the common good will proceed inductively by observing social justice at work in two different ways: first, by considering social justice conceptually as the moral norm that guides social institutions and as the moral virtue that disposes us to act justly (Chapter 3), and then by defining the common good as the norm of social justice, not in abstraction, but in terms of the interplay of the main social institutions that structure society (Chapter 4); and secondly, by observing empirically the present-day struggle to realize the common good, this in terms of four extended examples: the 2008 financial crisis in the United States and worldwide (Chapter 1), gender inequality in the family and in the workplace (Chapter 3), raising the minimum wage (Chapter 4), and the environmental threat of climate change (Chapter 5). This inductive approach, both conceptual and empirical, enables us to see and understand the common good in concrete terms. Our study ends, however, not at the point of understanding the common good, but with the call to act for the common good. The common good as the norm of social justice becomes concrete and thus actual only in and through our acting for the common good, this both individually and collectively, in social settings that range in scope from the local to the national and global, and more widely in the ecological setting of planet Earth (Chapter 5). What guides our study of social justice throughout is the premise that the good is primary as the end or purpose of all human action, but this with the realization that the good exists and is observable only in and through its embodiments. Thus, we begin our study of social justice by considering the primary embodiment of social justice—the good of being a community (Chapter 1).

Chapter 1

The Good of Being a Community

THE QUESTION:
WHAT IS THE GOOD OF BEING A COMMUNITY?

"Nothing draws your love but what is good." These words, written in the fifth century by the Christian theologian Augustine, intend to draw our mind to the Good itself, the "goodness of every good," which is God. In this light we see and delight in every good. What is good? Augustine answers:

> Good is earth with its lofty mountains, its gentle hills, its level plains. Good is the beauteous and fertile land, good the well-built house with its symmetry, its spaciousness and light. Good are the bodies of living things, good is the temperate and wholesome air, good is the pleasant and healthful food, good is health itself free from pain and weariness. Good is the human face with its regular features, its cheerful expression, its lively colouring; good is the heart of a friend whose comradeship is sweet and whose love is loyal; good is a righteous man, good is wealth for the things that it can enable us to do, good is the sky with its sun, moon, and stars, good are the angels of holy obedience; good is the speech that instructs the hearer winningly and counsels him appropriately, good is the poem of musical rhythm and profound thought.[1]

Let us add to Augustine's words: good is the society that has order and stability, the society that ensures that all people within its domain breathe clean air, drink pure water, eat healthful food, live healthy lives, and engage in productive work. Good is the society where friendship flourishes, where love forms families in which parents nurture their children, where citizens participate fully and freely in the decisions that govern their society. Good is the community of nations that respect one another's autonomy, trade fairly in one another's goods, cooperatively care for the earth, and

---

1. Augustine, *Trinity* 8.4.

coexist in peace. Whether as a local community, a national community, or the global community, good is being a community.

Pollution, poverty, hunger, disease, illiteracy, marginalization, war—these are the privation of good. The Latin word that Augustine used to name the ills of humanity was *privatio*, which refers to the lack of what ought to be. The word articulates his understanding of the nature of evil: it is the absence of good. This insight enabled him to break free from the hold that Manichaeism had on him in his youth. The Manichees were a religious sect who saw the world as made up of two forces, the good (the Kingdom of Light) and evil (the Kingdom of Darkness): the Kingdom of Light was passive and at rest, and the Kingdom of Darkness was active, an invader. The world's ongoing struggle between good and evil is the result of this invasion on the part of evil. The plight of the good in this tragic mingling is to be passive, to suffer.[2] In the *Confessions* Augustine offers the reason for the seductive power of Manichaeism on him: "while actually receding from the truth, I thought I was moving toward it. The reason was that I did not know that evil is only the privation of a good, even to the point of complete nonentity."[3] Augustine came to see that evil is not something; it is nothing.

Understanding evil in this way changed Augustine's understanding of the mingling of good and evil in the world. Here the term of agency is reversed. Good is active; evil is passive. Good is the creation or generation of that which is good. Evil then is understood to be "a kind of noncreation, a draining away from that which is."[4] Good is action; evil is inaction. With regard to all efforts to realize the good, evil is inert. Realizing the good necessarily requires thoughtfulness and responsibility. Evil, the absence of good, is the result of thoughtlessness and recklessness. Good is generative in that it brings into being that which is genuinely new. Evil by contrast is habituation, repetition, mimesis.[5]

The Moral Good

Insofar as evil is the absence of good, judging something as evil implies, however vague, a conception of the good. Indeed, the judgment of evil impels the consideration of what is good. Responding to evil requires acting for the good. "Nothing draws your love but what is good." What draws our love; what is good? Provoked by an encounter with evil, the question heightens our awareness of what is evil and guides our response. When human beings suffer social evils, what they suffer is the loss or the diminishment of what constitutes the good of society—the good of being a community. If we as a society are to address adequately the ills that beset our society, we must ask this fundamental question: what is the good of being a community? But, is

2. Brown, *Augustine of Hippo*, 52.

3. Augustine, *Confessions* 3.7.

4. Elshtain, *Augustine and the Limits of Politics*, 81.

5. Elshtain, *Augustine and the Limits of Politics*, 81–87.

this a question that we can even answer? If it is answerable, how must we begin? What terms must we employ in order to pursue the question?

The philosopher William Frankena, in his consideration of the various senses of the word "good," points to a basic distinction that we must make as we enter into a discussion of the good, which is the distinction between moral and nonmoral good. The difference can be seen at a glance by considering the difference between these two statements: we might say about a person that this person "led a good life," or that this person "had a good life." What distinguishes the one statement from the other are the different grounds or reasons on which each statement is based. The statement that one had a good life is based on objective criteria that we judge to be necessary for constituting the good life. In our judgment that this person had a good life, we are commending certain facts of this life without necessarily prescribing that these facts ought to be realized by others. Here we are considering the good life as a nonmoral good. In saying that a person led a good life, on the other hand, we are pointing not to factual aspects of the person's life but to their moral purposes and to the will and ability to realize these purposes. Fulfilling these moral purposes, moreover, is prescriptive: a person ought to lead his or her life in this manner. Here we have the moral good.[6]

The difference between moral and nonmoral good we see expressed in Augustine's rhapsody concerning what is good. The beauty of the earth, the comeliness of the human face, the health of our bodies, the joy of friendship, the art of rhetoric, the pleasure of poetry—these are nonmoral goods that make up the good life. The "righteousness" of a person (Augustine uses the Latin word *justus*, which means being just) and the "holy obedience" of the angels, however, are moral goods. Portraying the good of a community in terms of its order and stability or in terms of its ability to provide for basic human needs is to depict the nonmoral good of the community. The shared intention within a society to be a community, on the other hand, is a moral good. What being just, being obedient to the will of God, and being a community have in common is moral agency. Each demonstrates the will to realize a moral purpose. Each is expressed in actions that seek to bring about the moral good. The distinction between nonmoral and moral good is significant because it shows us that the question that we are asking—what is the good of being a community—is not solely a question about an objective state of affairs. It is at root a moral question.

The Social Nature of the Moral Good

Moral agency—both the will and the ability to bring about the good—is readily apparent in the lives of individuals. But can a collectivity of people, whatever size that this collectivity might be, demonstrate moral agency as well? What must be present in a group (whether a family or circle of close friends, a corporation or a university, a

6. Frankena, *Ethics*, 62, 80–83.

city or a nation-state, or the assemblage of nation-states) to enable the group to demonstrate moral purpose? The sociologist Philip Selznick poses this question. "Here sociology touches a special branch of moral theory: how collective and individual responsibility are distinguished and related." Agency, he notes, involves competence (ability), intentionality (will), and accountability. But "to be a *moral* agent, something more is required. There must be values in play beyond technical excellence, efficiency, or effectiveness"[7] (values—what draws our love, what is good). Moral agency, then, requires the ability and the will to realize the good. Accountability in this case becomes moral responsibility (our commitment to realize the good and be answerable for the outcome).[8] Can moral agency be attributed to groups? Yes, the sociologist answers, but this affirmation requires that we understand the distinctive nature of social behavior in contrast to individual behavior, that is, individuals acting in and through groups.

An overall definition of a group, in the view of sociology, is this: "a number of individuals who interact recurrently according to some pattern of social organization."[9] Whether the group is small, such as a family, or large, such as a nation-state, the actions of individuals in the group are shaped by the pattern of social organization that constitutes the group. An aggregate of people waiting at a bus stop is not a group as such precisely because no ongoing structure of social organization binds them together. In light of this definition of a social group, we cannot think of a group as being something other than the individuals (their decisions and actions) that make up the group. At the same time, we cannot think of group behavior as being simply the aggregate of the individual decisions and actions of those in the group, because these individual decisions and actions are being shaped by the group's pattern of social organization. The pattern of social organization, moreover, is the product of human decisions and actions that created it and that maintain it, and thus the social organization of a group implies agency. Insofar as a group's behavior is purposive, its decisions and actions demonstrate moral agency.[10]

Consider, for example, the decision-making structure of a corporation: a corporate decision is a collective outcome, involving a variety of actors in specific roles and reflecting the established policies and practices of the corporation. This is its pattern of social organization. Yet, individuals acting in and through the corporation's structure of social organization, which is itself the product of human decisions and actions, make the corporation's decisions. Insofar as a corporate decision is purposive, that is, seeks to realize an outcome that will be judged not only efficient and effective but also good, the decision implies moral agency. The good that this decision intends defines its moral purpose.[11]

7. Selznick, *Moral Commonwealth*, 238.

8. Selznick, *Moral Commonwealth*, 345.

9. DeFleur et al., *Sociology*, 33.

10. See May, *Morality of Groups*, chs. 1–4.

11. Selznick, *Moral Commonwealth*, 242–43.

Seeing group behavior as something wholly other than individual behavior, or seeing group decisions or actions as no more than the sum of individual decisions and actions eliminates from our understanding of groups any sense of their moral purpose. Both views of group behavior (that a group behaves as it does apart from the individuals within it, or that a group behaves as it does because of the individuals within it) restrict the sphere of morality to individual behavior alone: the first view by picturing a social group as an entity apart from the individuals that make it up and thus as outside the sphere of morality; the second view by picturing morality as pertaining only to an individual's decisions and actions and thus not to group behavior. Groups demonstrate moral purpose by acting for the good, but this purpose is enacted by the individuals within the group in and through the pattern of social organization that structures the group. Groups, like individuals, act to bring about the moral good. Selznick concludes: "The moral logic we apply to institutions is in important respects the same as that we apply to persons . . . The logic of moral action governs all moral actors, collectivities and persons alike."[12]

But, can collectivities that are composed of many and diverse groups demonstrate moral purpose? A village, town, or city, for example, is a collectivity that is made up of a multitude of varied groups: families, businesses, schools, civic organizations, hospitals, churches, and so forth. Each group within the collectivity demonstrates a distinct purpose; each seeks to realize a specific good. Yet, the collectivity is more than the aggregate of these groups. A village, town, or city provides the pattern of social organization that integrates these groups and their specific purposes. Distinct to this pattern of social organization is place in the sense that geographical location defines a village, town, or city. But place does not fully define this type of collectivity. The purpose of this pattern of social organization is to be "an *integrative social system* that ties together the activities of the various groups of which it is composed."[13] The interaction of those persons and groups that make up the collectivity is the nonmoral good that this pattern of social organization seeks to realize. That this interaction intends human flourishing, seen as a value, is its moral good. The name that sociologists give to this type of social organization is community. Being a community, insofar as this form of social cooperation intends human flourishing, is a moral good.

Being a Community

Spatial location is a customary criterion, used by sociology, to designate a community. Selznick, however, proposes to extend the idea of community to refer to social groups not delimited by place. Although common residence, such as in a village, town, or city, is conducive to the type of social interaction that constitutes community, it is not a necessary requirement for being a community. The union of nations that make up

12. Selznick, *Moral Commonwealth*, 244.

13. DeFleur et al., *Sociology*, 79–80.

the European Union, for example, may be thought of as a community of nations. The Catholic Church can be seen as a worldwide community of faith. Neither territoriality nor size, Selznick argues, is an essential characteristic of community. "Community can be treated as a variable aspect of group experience. Groups can be more or less full-blown communities, and they can approximate community in different ways."[14] Thus, the question is not what type of social group may be designated a community, but rather what are the characteristics of group behavior that are essential to the formation of community? Selznick offers this definition of community: "A group is a community *insofar as* it embraces a wide range of interests and activities; *insofar as* it takes account of whole persons, not just specialized contributions or roles; and *insofar as* bonds of commitment and culture are shared." Understanding these characteristics of community, Selznick states, enables us both to recognize the good of being a community wherever these conditions are fulfilled and to make stronger the communities in which we presently participate.[15]

Although the distinction between nonmoral and moral good provides two distinct ways of viewing the good of community, these perspectives are related in that the one implies the other: the objective characteristics of community described by the sociologist intend their realization; human flourishing, which is the realization of community, presupposes these characteristics of being a community. The idea of community is both descriptive and prescriptive. In order to comprehend community both in terms of its nonmoral and moral good, let us consider each of the conditions for being a community in turn.

First, the social interaction that characterizes a community is comprehensive in that a structure of shared beliefs and interests binds together a wide range of activities of persons and groups that form the community.[16] The shared beliefs and interests of the community form the basis of its common life. Yet, Selznick emphasizes, "a common life is not a *fused* life." Indeed, the notion of a common life implies diversity. In a community the self-regarding behavior of individuals persists. The diverse purposes of the community's varied groups remain. The comprehensive interaction of a community requires both the independence and the interdependence of the parts that make it up. "The distinctive function of community, then, is the reconciliation of partial with general perspectives." A community is "a unity of unities" insofar as it "preserves the integrity of persons, groups, and institutions" while binding these special interests with the shared interests of the whole.[17] In this sense the good achieved by being a community is a common good, that is, a good that can be realized only in and through the social interaction of the diverse parts that make up the community.

14. Selznick, *Moral Commonwealth*, 358–59.

15. Selznick, *Communitarian Persuasion*, 20–21.

16. Selznick, *Moral Commonwealth*, 358–59.

17. Selznick, *Moral Commonwealth*, 369.

Secondly, a community involves the participation of persons as wholes, not simply of segments of a person's life. Selznick observes that we participate in society in two different ways: the one he describes as core participation, which concerns the whole of a person's life; the other is segmental participation, which concerns only a part of a person's life.[18] The difference between being a customer and being a citizen illustrates the point. Being a customer involves a social transaction that is specific and that carries obligations that are limited to the transaction, such as buying a car. Accordingly, being a customer concerns only a segment of a person's life. Being a citizen, on the other hand, concerns the whole of a person's life. Citizenship constitutes a belonging that shapes our identity as a person. It carries obligations that are ongoing and diffuse. Our participation in society involves being both a customer and a citizen. Understanding the difference enables us to recognize that the good of being in a community is not limited to the specific transactions that make up parts of our lives, but concerns those elements of our lives that pertain to its core.

Thirdly, a common history and culture are bonds that tie a community together. These bonds are sustained through the commitment of persons and groups within the community to realize the good of the community. Commitment to the good of the community does not abnegate self-interest. Community is born in the human need to cooperate with one another. Whether we strive to meet the most basic requirements of survival or to achieve the heights of human accomplishment, we need each other. "Community begins with, and is largely supported by, the experience of interdependence and reciprocity," says Selznick. But, to realize the good of being in community, self-interest must reach beyond limited goals and specific exchanges. A community is made up of continuing relationships and ongoing goals, and thus obligations to the community require a shared commitment that is open-ended and diffuse, not limited simply to contractual arrangements. Furthermore, given the diversity of human needs and abilities within the community, obligations to the community will require unequal contributions from those within the community to sustain the good of the whole. The reciprocity that makes up a community can never be fully carried out on strictly equal terms.[19] The assurance that those within the community can rely on one another in these ways fosters an atmosphere of communication and trust. "Trust is the indispensable cement of group life," Selznick states.[20] For the sake of flourishing, then, a group moves from association to community, thus creating "more enduring bonds of interdependence, caring, and commitment. There is a transition, we may say, from reciprocity to solidarity, and from there to fellowship."[21] Herein lies the moral good of being a community.

18. Selznick, *Moral Commonwealth*, 184.

19. Selznick, *Moral Commonwealth*, 362.

20. Selznick, *Communitarian Persuasion*, 25.

21. Selznick, *Moral Commonwealth*, 362.

The Failure of Community

Communities fail, however. When they do, or when human association creates imperfect communities, one or all of these conditions have not been realized: the special interests of some dominate the shared interests of all within the society; the incentives that drive specific exchanges within the society overshadow the overall good of the society to such an extent that participation within the society is reduced only to partial concerns; reciprocity within the society takes place solely in zero-sum terms, that is, exchanges that produce a gain for some result in a loss for others, thereby undermining the commitment of all within the society to the good of the whole.

The economist Joseph Stiglitz provides a graphic example of the failure of community. While visiting the country of Kazakhstan, formerly a part of the Soviet Union, he observed that greenhouses, interspersed throughout the landscape, were missing their glass. Following the collapse of the Soviet Union, during a time of transition that bred uncertainty and mistrust, individuals took for themselves what they could. The missing glass was not the act of a few miscreants, but "an almost anarchic theft by all from all."[22] For Stiglitz the greenhouses stood as a metaphor of the current state of the society. Without the glass the greenhouses could no longer serve their purpose. Private gains were made but at the loss of a functional good for the whole of the society. The myopia that was caused by fear, mistrust, and hopelessness within the society hid from sight this tragic irony: individual good that is acquired at the expense of the larger social good endangers not only the common good of the society but the individual good as well.

The Moral Good of Being a Community

We flourish as individuals only in and through society. The philosopher Aristotle, living in Athens during the fourth century BCE, established this point as a fundamental axiom in the Western philosophical tradition. In his words, the human person is "by nature a political animal." The term "political" (*politikē*) here refers to the *polis*, which is the Greek word for a city-state such as Athens. The *polis* was not merely the government, but more broadly the society—the community. The political animal is a social animal. But, unlike other social animals (here Aristotle refers to bees as an example), the human animal possesses the gift of language (*logos*). Through this gift, human beings not only give voice to pleasure and pain, as do other animals, but they also articulate "the expedient and inexpedient, and therefore likewise the just and unjust." *Logos*, in other words, indicates reason, that is, the ability to discriminate between what is advantageous and what is not, but also between moral outcomes, such as what is good and evil, what is just and unjust. The human animal is a rational animal. *Logos* gives voice to moral purpose and thus articulates the good of the *polis*. One who exists

22. Stiglitz, *Globalization and Its Discontents*, 161.

in self-sufficiency outside of the context of the *polis*, Aristotle states, "must be either a beast or a god." Such a one is not human. To be human is to be social and thus political.[23] The good that all human beings strive to realize can only occur within human communities, whether they are small, such as the family, or large, such as the state. But, of all the communities that aim at the good, says Aristotle, "the state or political community, which is the highest of all, and which embraces all the rest, aims at a good in a greater degree than any other, and at the highest good."[24]

If we restate Aristotle's axiom in a context different from his, the truth of the axiom stands, but the terms of the axiom will draw attention to themselves in different ways. Restating this axiom in the twenty-first century, in the context of a nation-state such as the United States, the term "individual" draws far greater attention and therefore stands out in sharper contrast to the term "society" than it did in Aristotle's Athens. Concerning the relation of the individual to society, Aristotle states: "the state is by nature clearly prior to the family and to the individual, since the whole is of necessity prior to the part."[25] Aristotle's words, read in the present day, elicit the specter of totalitarianism or other forms of state control in which the good of the individual is reduced to the interests of the state. Reading Aristotle's words in light of this fear, however, is an anachronism.

The priority to which Aristotle refers concerns the good that is realized in and through the *polis*, which he declares to be the highest good. "Every art and every inquiry, and similarly every action and pursuit, is thought to aim at some good," Aristotle states at the beginning of his *Nicomachean Ethics*.[26] Every form of human association, accordingly, aims at a good, which defines its nature, but not all forms of human association can realize the human good fully. Thus, Aristotle sees a natural progression from the most elemental form of human association, the household, to the uniting of households into a village, to the joining of several villages into "a single complete community, large enough to be nearly or quite self-sufficing," which is the *polis*. Self-sufficiency—not simply meeting the basic needs of life, but realizing the fullness of human capabilities—is the purpose of this natural progression from simple to increasingly complex forms of human cooperation. Thus, the self-sufficiency that is realized only in and through the *polis* is the final or highest good that every form of human association seeks to realize.[27] In this sense, the *polis* exists and has a priority to each of its component parts by nature, not by convention, because the good that the *polis* attains is a good greater than any individual or household good, which is the common good that is realized only in and through the collective decision-making (*logos*) and cooperative acts of its citizens. As the good of the whole is necessarily prior

---

23. Aristotle, *Politics* 1.2.1253a.

24. Aristotle, *Politics* 1.1.1252a.

25. Aristotle, *Politics* 1.2.1253a.

26. Aristotle, *Nicomachean Ethics* 1.1.1094a.

27 Aristotle, *Politics* 1.2.1252b.

to the good of one of its parts, so the good of the *polis* is by nature prior to the good of each one of its components, such as the family or the individual citizen.[28]

To illustrate the priority of the political good over the individual or household good, Aristotle uses the example of the human body: "if the whole body be destroyed, there will be no foot or hand except in an equivocal sense, as we might speak of a stone hand; for when destroyed the hand will be no better than that."[29] A dead hand, like the stone hand of a sculpture of the human form, is not truly a hand, but a hand in name only. The word "hand" is being used in an equivocal sense, meaning that the word, although the same word as that used to refer to one part of the human body, is referring to a different reality. So, as a hand, which is properly named a hand, achieves its nature (its good) by being a functioning part of the human body, so a human being is truly human only as a functioning part of society. Richard Kraut comments that Aristotle does not intend to say through this comparison that a human being, isolated from society, ceases to exist as a human being. Aristotle's concern here is not with the conditions of human survival, but with human flourishing. Aside from the body, the hand cannot be a hand. It is what it is only in relation to the whole. Without society, a human being suffers a twofold loss: such a one neither receives the aid of others, nor exercises the human excellences that while perfecting one's own nature contribute at the same time either indirectly or directly to the good of others and thus to the good of the society. (Aristotle names these excellences, such as being courageous and being just, virtues.) Human flourishing consists both in giving and receiving, and such reciprocity can take place only within a society. The good of being human, therefore, necessarily requires a social matrix: the prior good of society.[30]

A modern sensibility, however, with its heightened awareness of the worth of the individual in relation to society, alters Aristotle's axiom in this significant way: as the good of the individual requires the good of the society as a whole, so the good of the whole requires the good of each one of its parts, meaning the good of all within the society. For Aristotle, component parts of the *polis*—families, circles of friends, other small groups—provide distinctive goods that the political community as a whole cannot provide. The good of the whole, then, requires and must preserve the good of its parts. But, when Aristotle envisions the ideal *polis*, he denies citizenship, not only to slaves but to women and manual workers as well, allowing an elite group of wealthy citizens to live well at the expense of noncitizens, who nevertheless make up the whole.[31] In the light of a modern sensibility, the common good of society must refer both to the good of the society and to the good of the individual—that is, both to the solidarity of the whole and to the respect that each individual or each component part

28. See Kraut, *Aristotle*, 264–67.

29. Aristotle, *Politics* 1.2.1253a.

30. Kraut, *Aristotle*, 267–69.

31. Kraut, *Aristotle*, 208–9, 214–18.

of the whole merits. In this light, Aristotle's error was not that he articulated an incipient totalitarianism, but rather that he envisioned an ideal community that lacked inclusiveness. In Philip Selznick's words, the good of community is attained when a society develops "the right recipe for achieving a union of solidarity and respect."[32]

In Specific, Empirical Terms

What is the good of being a community? The question as stated is abstract, unrelated to a specific community, and thus lacking a direction that orients us toward a specific social good, a specific union of solidarity and respect. Selznick notes that the definition of community that he proposes is intentionally "weak, inclusive, and relatively uncontroversial." His purpose for defining community in this way "is not to eliminate controversy but to transfer it to a more appropriate place—a place where empirical investigation is relevant and helpful."[33] His definition of community thus serves as "a guiding ideal"[34] to the empirical considerations of particular communities concerning what constitutes the good of community.

To render the question concerning the good of community specific and empirical, we must first ask who is asking the question and what particular type of community is being considered. In light of Aristotle's notion that the good of the whole is constituted by and gives purpose to the good of its component parts, what social whole in the present age can meaningfully serve as the community in question? The conventional answer given by the sociologist is a society. Like other groups, a society is "a number of individuals who interact recurrently according to some pattern of social organization," but insofar as a society provides the most comprehensive pattern of social organization, it is "the largest group with which most people can feel a sense of personal identity, and in some ways it is the most important in its effects on the life of the individual." Like local communities, such as villages, towns, and cities, a society is "an integrative system that coordinates and binds together the great many smaller groups of which it is composed."[35] But, in comparison to local communities, the good of a society lies precisely in the comprehensiveness of its social integration. The institutional form of this social integration under the rule of law is the nation-state. Thus, given its scope, the good of being a society, in comparison to the good of each of its component parts, is the greater good. In the context of a nation-state, such as the United States, the one who properly asks about the good of community is the citizen of this national society. Here the question becomes specific, empirical, and controversial.

32. Selznick, *Communitarian Persuasion*, 21.
33. Selznick, *Moral Commonwealth*, 358.
34. Selznick, *Communitarian Persuasion*, 17.
35. DeFleur et al., *Sociology*, 83.

Such a question concerns the common good of the nation-state in which the citizen lives. But, given the increasing interdependence of nation-states in the present age concerning matters as wide-ranging as trade and finance, immigration, and the well-being of the earth's environment, the question of the common good of one nation-state inevitably broadens to being a question concerning the good that all nation-states seek in common, which is a universal common good. Issues concerning the environment or international trade and finance transcend the interests of any one nation to involve the common concerns of all. In which case, regarding such issues, the social whole being considered is worldwide in dimension.

The sociologist Saskia Sassen points out, however, that this new global reality does not occur only in and through the interactions between nation-states or through the agency of the global institutions that coordinate these interactions, such as the United Nations or the World Trade Organization. Viewing the dynamics of globalization in this way sees the nation-state in terms of its sovereignty as a closed unit, the global thereby referring to what takes place between sovereign nations. But, in fact, this new global reality takes form deep within a nation's sovereign territory and often outside of its control. A prime example of this phenomenon, where globalization takes place in and through localized practices, is what Sassen terms "the global city." New York, Los Angeles, London, Frankfurt, Tokyo, Hong Kong, Taipei, and Mexico City serve as representative instances. Cities such as these, rather than being social spaces located in a nested hierarchy of scale that runs from the local to the regional to the national, are more accurately seen as localized spaces of the global. As centers of international finance and as magnets of immigrant labor, the localized practices of these cities involve global networks and thus engage the new global reality directly.[36] In a setting such as this, the question concerning the good of being a community takes on a perspective that incorporates this new global reality. The community in question—the city—is spatially located, but the good of the community implicates a worldwide community and its good. The global city thus provides a unique site for asking the question concerning the good of being a community because, given the specific nature of the setting, although the question concerns the good of a localized community, the question at the same time pulls into view the wider global good.

But who is asking the question? As in the context of the nation-state, so also in the setting of the global city, the one who properly asks the question concerning the good of being a community is the citizen. In the present age the term "citizen," according to its precise meaning, refers to the legal relation that exists between the individual and the state. With citizenship comes national membership and identity. But, insofar as the sovereignty of the nation-state is increasingly eclipsed by the dynamics of the new global reality, do the meaning and the practices of citizenship change as well? Sassen observes in the present day a growing distance between the citizen as political subject or political actor and the state. The frontier zone of this change in the practices

36. Sassen, *Sociology of Globalization*, 3–9, 97–100.

and the project of citizenship is the global city. Here membership and identity are not subsumed wholly under the sovereignty of the nation, but include global networks of subnational spaces, whether these are centers of international finance or transnational households of immigrant workers. This unique urban setting engenders a new form of politics, which engages both the very wealthy (the financiers) and the disadvantaged (immigrant labor), one that is transnational in scope but localized in this specific space.[37]

This changing view of citizenship highlights a distinct moral meaning to the question concerning the good of being a community. As a moral question, its concern begins with human well-being in a localized setting but widens to include the well-being of the human community. The philosophers Kwame Anthony Appiah and Martha Nussbaum term this moral viewpoint "cosmopolitanism."[38] The origin of the term and its meaning lie in ancient Greece, the term first coined by the Cynic philosopher Diogenes in the fourth century BCE but then given a philosophical articulation by the Stoic philosophers of Athens and Rome from the late fourth century BCE to the second century CE. The term is composed of two Greek words: *kosmou* (world) and *polites* (citizen). For the Stoics the citizen is first and foremost a citizen of the world. This is so because, as human beings who possess the gift of reason (*logos*), we discern in and through our particular communities a common humanity, one that is united by shared moral purposes, such as creating a just society and realizing human well-being. Having the viewpoint of a citizen of the world does not abrogate local commitments, nor does it lessen the appreciation and celebration of the local, but the moral idea of the oneness of humanity does restrict and regulate all particular political arrangements, both local and national.[39] Asking the question concerning the good of being a community from the moral perspective of the world citizen locates the question in the political arrangements that seek a union of solidarity and respect in a particular community, whether local or national, but understands the terms of this union—solidarity and respect—as being universal in scope. The question concerning the good of being a community from this moral point of view ultimately requires an account of the universal common good.

THE CONTEXT OF THE QUESTION:
THE FINANCIAL CRISIS OF 2008

We further render the question concerning the good of being a community specific and empirical by considering why the question is being asked. Although the question is speculative in nature, its urgency and its specificity will lie in the social conditions that beckon the question, usually conditions of crisis. Such conditions form the

37. Sassen, *Territory, Authority, Rights*, 277–81, 314–19.

38. Appiah, *Cosmopolitanism*, xiii; Nussbaum, "Patriotism and Cosmopolitanism," 3–6.

39. Nussbaum, *Cultivating Humanity*, 56–67.

context of the question. The first text in the philosophical tradition of the West to explore in a systematic way the question concerning the good of being a community—Plato's *Republic*, written in Athens in the fourth century BCE—illustrates this point. Plato presents this philosophical inquiry in the form of a dialogue that takes place between the philosopher Socrates and a group of interlocutors. As presented in the text, this philosophical conversation takes place in 422 BCE during a time of peace, which was actually a lull in the Peloponnesian Wars between Athens and Sparta and their allies. But, in fact, Plato was constructing this dialogue concerning the good society about fifty years later in the aftermath of the defeat of Athens by Sparta.[40] This setting of defeat frames the central question that occupies this philosophical dialogue: what is justice? Seeing the dialogue in its actual setting highlights the persistence of Socrates to come to a definition of justice. It also makes the strident opposition of Thrasymachus, a teacher of rhetoric, to the inquiry by Socrates all the more striking and forceful. Confronting the search by Socrates for a definition of justice, Thrasymachus states: "What I say is that 'just' or 'right' means nothing but what is to the interest of the stronger party."[41] The search for the idea of justice as the foundation of the good society, in other words, is illusory according to Thrasymachus because the articulation of justice in the end will only reflect the self-interests of those who hold greater power.

A social crisis is fertile ground for asking social questions such as, what is the good to be achieved by being a community? The crisis not only provokes thought but also presents society with a moment of decision to act in regard to its good. Fundamental to the question concerning the good of being a community is the question first asked by Plato: what is justice? The idea of justice defines the union of solidarity and respect that is required for a community to realize its good. Aristotle, Plato's student, observed that justice holds the *polis* together. Without justice, the community disintegrates.[42] A social crisis, therefore, offers the opportunity to ask again the question of justice and by doing so to undertake a present-day discussion of the integration of solidarity and respect, the very basis of community. When we ask the question, however, we are faced with the dilemma that Plato acknowledges in his pursuit of the question: Is the idea of justice a truth that is ascertainable through discourse (logos), or is the idea of justice a mask that hides the self-interests of those with greater power? In other words, whose approach to the question of justice, and thus to the good of being a community, is the more realistic—that of Socrates or that of Thrasymachus?

The Financial Crisis of 2008: The Failure of Community, A Failure of Justice

The social crisis that forms the context of our question concerning the good of being a community is the financial crisis of 2008 that began in the financial sector of the

40. Pappas, *Routledge Philosophy Guidebook*, 4, 15.

41. Plato, *Republic* 1.338c.

42. Aristotle, *Nicomachean Ethics* 5.5.1132b. See Maguire, *Ethics*, 52.

United States but then immediately affected the whole of the US economy and eventually the world economy.[43] Although the problem was centered in the US housing market, the crisis was not simply the result of one sector of the US economy failing to function properly. The crisis reflected more broadly the failure of myriad sectors of US society to realize jointly the good that we share in common as a society. In the sequence of events that made up the crisis we see a failure of justice and thus the failure of community: first, the special interests of some were pursued at the expense of the shared interests of all; secondly, the financial incentives that fueled the crisis overshadowed the overall good of the society to such an extent that reciprocity within the society was reduced to partial (segmental) concerns alone; thirdly, that gains for some resulted in extensive loss for others undermined trust within the society—the glue that binds a society together—thereby weakening the commitment of all to the good of the whole. In short, the basic characteristics that make a society to be a community were undermined. The financial crisis then provides an unsettling example of the failure of community, which at the same time presents us with a way to consider the abstract question concerning the good of being a community and the idea of justice that is fundamental to its good in terms that are specific, empirical, and urgent.

The Crisis

A crisis usually has a turning point that demarcates the period preceding it from the period that follows it. During the course of a serious illness, for example, a decisive point will be reached, following a period of illness, when either the hope of recovery dawns (the fever breaks), or the grim realization that death is imminent occurs (medical tests reveal that the illness is terminal). This latter period remains as part of the crisis but as its aftermath. The term "crisis" may refer to the turning point, or it may refer to the sequence of events as a whole.

Social crises manifest a similar pattern, although what precisely the turning point is, when it occurred, and what actions should be pursued in its aftermath can be a matter of debate. Still, entering into the debate is crucial because by determining and understanding the turning point, we see more clearly what has been taking place, and at the same time we also gain insight into what ought to occur in the aftermath. Our understanding of the turning point, then, indicates possible futures. That we use phrases such as "a time of decision" and "a call for action" in our consideration of a social crisis points to the urgency and the importance of the actions that we take during the aftermath. How we understand the crisis, particularly its turning point, is significant because our view of the crisis will determine what actions we think ought to be taken. For example, in the consideration of the financial crisis of 2008, if we limit our discussion of the crisis to problems that occurred in the financial markets alone, recovery in the aftermath of the crisis will too readily be seen in terms of fixing

43. Tooze, *Crashed*, 5–7.

those problems and returning to what was normal before 2008, that is, a return to "business as usual." But, if we view the financial crisis with a wider focus, one that sees the crisis not only as a financial problem but also as a social problem, then recovery in the aftermath will be considered more broadly in terms of social transformation. The basic elements of the crisis remain the same, but they are now viewed from a wider perspective. The good of the financial sector, accordingly, will be viewed in light of the good of society as a whole.[44]

The financial crisis of 2008 is not over; we presently live in its aftermath. Can we determine its turning point? The economist Alan Blinder emphatically states that we can: the turning point of the financial crisis took place on Monday, September 15, 2008, when the venerable Wall Street investment bank Lehman Brothers (founded in 1850) declared bankruptcy. "There is close to universal agreement that the demise of Lehman Brothers was the watershed event of the entire financial crisis and that the decision to allow it to fail was the watershed decision. Virtually every discussion of the financial crisis divides history into two epochs: 'before Lehman' and 'after Lehman,'" says Blinder. The decision to allow Lehman Brothers to fail was made by the chairman of the Federal Reserve, Ben Bernanke, and supported by Henry Paulson, the United States Secretary of the Treasury. Their decision produced a shock wave that reverberated throughout the financial markets in the United States and then outward into global financial markets. The reason for the extreme reaction within the financial markets to their decision, according to Blinder, was this: "The Lehman decision abruptly and surprisingly tore the perceived rulebook into pieces and tossed it out the window. Market participants were thus cut adrift, no longer knowing what game they were playing. That's a formula for panic, for the replacement of greed by fear—which is exactly what happened on Lehman Day, September 15, 2008."[45] The key words in this statement, though, are "perceived rulebook." There was in fact no actual rulebook in play, only strong expectations, particularly on the part of financial markets. These expectations were the result of prior decisions that had been made by the Federal Reserve and the US Treasury.

During the six months prior to September 2008, other financial institutions had come close to failure (more accurately, insolvency), but in these instances the Federal Reserve and the Treasury had intervened to prevent the failures from occurring. In the first instance, in March 2008 the Federal Reserve was instrumental in getting the large commercial bank JPMorgan Chase to acquire the Wall Street investment bank Bear Stearns, which was failing due to its risk-taking in the mortgage market, but only by agreeing to cover twenty-nine billion dollars in questionable mortgage-related assets held by Bear Stearns, a risk that JPMorgan and its shareholders did not want to assume. In the second instance, the Treasury rescued the two government-sponsored enterprises that had been created by the federal government to facilitate home ownership

44. Calhoun, "Series Introduction," 9–12, 18–19.
45. Blinder, *After the Music Stopped*, 128.

in the United States: Fannie Mae (the Federal National Mortgage Association—its official name—was founded in 1938 and then turned into a publicly traded company in 1968) and Freddie Mac (the Federal Home Loan Mortgage Corporation—its official name—was founded in 1971 to be a competitor to Fannie Mae). Although Fannie Mae and Freddie Mac are both private corporations (that is, owned by shareholders), because the federal government had established them and had granted to them distinct benefits (such as having a line of credit with the Treasury), both shareholders and creditors assumed that the federal government guaranteed the debt of these large mortgage corporations. This was not a legal guarantee, but to the markets it seemed to be an implicit guarantee. When Fannie Mae and Freddie Mac suffered devastating mortgage-related losses in 2008, putting their solvency into question, the Treasury intervened, rendering the implicit guarantee a reality. On September 7, one week before the collapse of Lehman Brothers, the Treasury took control of both corporations, placing them into conservatorship, thereby guaranteeing the repayment of debt that was owed to their creditors.[46] In both these instances, the federal government sought to avert panic in the financial markets. But, particularly in regard to Fannie and Freddie, in the view of the economist Nouriel Roubini and historian Stephen Mihm, more was involved than just quieting markets and soothing foreign and domestic creditors: "the creditworthiness of the United States was at stake." The developing financial crisis, in other words, was more than just a problem within financial markets; it had become a grave problem for the US government as well as a threat to US society as a whole.[47]

The remedy that the government had used to stabilize the financial markets, however, had crossed a long-established line. In 1933, in the aftermath of the Great Depression, the US Congress passed into law the Glass-Steagall Act, which created the Federal Deposit Insurance Corporation (FDIC) for the purpose of insuring deposits made to commercial banks against loss if the bank should fail. During the Depression banks had failed in part due to "bank runs"—a loss of confidence on the part of depositors who would as a group attempt to withdraw their money at the same time. By providing this guarantee against loss, the government removed the fear of loss, thereby putting stability back into the banking sector. But, with the security of government insurance came government regulation, particularly with regard to the amount of risk that banks could assume and prohibitions against the speculative use of depositors' money. The FDIC continues to provide this assurance for the depositors at commercial banks to this day.[48]

Bear Stearns, however, was not such a bank; neither were Fannie Mae and Freddie Mac. For the sake of higher returns on their investments, the creditors of these institutions accepted the risk of their investments not being insured by the government. For the sake of higher profits, these institutions operated outside of the regulatory

46. Blinder, *After the Music Stopped*, 100–119.

47. Roubini and Mihm, *Crisis Economics*, 108.

48. Krugman, *End This Depression Now!*, 58–60.

supervision and protection of government entities, such as the Federal Reserve and the FDIC. But, when the Federal Reserve agreed to back twenty-nine billion dollars of risky assets held by Bear Stearns to facilitate its acquisition by JPMorgan, it in effect was insuring these assets against default. With this government guarantee in place, risk was transferred from JPMorgan and its shareholders to the US taxpayer. Because Fannie Mae and Freddie Mac are government-sponsored enterprises (hence a hybrid of public mission and private profit), the creditors of these mortgage corporations considered their investments to be secure. Only US Treasury bonds provided greater security, they thought, but Treasury bonds did not have as high a yield. With the government takeover of Fannie Mae and Freddie Mac, the creditors of these mortgage corporations did in fact retain the value of their investments, but as with Bear Stearns this rescue was made at the expense of the US taxpayer. Although due to the failure of these institutions the shareholders (the stockholders) of Bear Stearns lost almost all of their investment, and although those of the Fannies were completely wiped out, the creditors of these institutions were not.[49] But, by protecting the creditors of these financial institutions, the government had crossed a line. Private investment had been secured at public cost. The comment of one fund manager at this time was prescient: "We have crossed the Rubicon into a new financial era."[50]

The government's interventions sought to avert panic in the financial markets and, more broadly, a breakdown of the US economy. The concern was not over the impending failure of three prominent financial institutions as such, but rather that these institutions were "too big to fail," meaning that the collateral harm to other institutions and to the economy as a whole resulting from their failures would be too great and must be avoided. In the case of Bear Stearns, however, Blinder thinks that the concern of the Federal Reserve and the Treasury was, to be more precise, that Bear Stearns was "too interconnected to fail." Given the nature of the financial industry, the failure of Bear Stearns to honor its contracts would have created a domino effect throughout an industry that is interconnected and global in scope. In 1998 the problem of being "too interconnected to fail" presented itself for the first time when the impending failure of the US-based hedge fund Long-Term Capital Management (LTCM) threatened a worldwide crisis. Its failure would have been the push that would have sent other dominos falling, not only within US financial markets but in global markets as well. LTCM's failure, in other words, posed a systemic risk to the entire global financial system, as would the failure of Bear Stearns ten years later. As with Bear Stearns, the Federal Reserve intervened in the crisis of LTCM, but with one important difference: the Fed rescued LTCM by calling upon the private-sector resources of Wall Street to bail out LTCM (ironically, only Bear Stearns did not participate), but not in the

49. Blinder, *After the Music Stopped*, 105–7, 115–16.
50. Lowenstein, *End of Wall Street*, 132.

case of Bear Stearns. Its rescue relied upon the resources of the public sector.[51] A new financial era had indeed dawned.

Accompanying the government's interventions in the matters of Bear Stearns and the Fannies, however, was an additional but different kind of concern: by bailing out the creditors of financial institutions that had failed due to having made high-risk bets that did not pay off, was the government in effect enabling or indirectly encouraging even greater risk-taking by "too big to fail" financial firms in the future by letting the losses from such risk-taking in the present be passed on to others? Had the government's decisions, in other words, created "moral hazard"? The term, widely used throughout the financial crisis, comes from the insurance industry. A fundamental task of an insurer is to price risk accurately. If a homeowner intends to build a house in a fire-prone area, the price of insurance on the house must reflect that risk. If it does not, the homeowner has an incentive not only to build in the area but also to skip adding more costly fire-retardant precautions into the building of the house, knowing that should a fire occur, the cost of the loss would be passed along to the insurer.[52] The problem of moral hazard—passing the losses from excessive risk-taking on to others—had an important role to play throughout the financial crisis: from the way home and commercial mortgages were being sold and insured to the way those working in the financial industry were being compensated to policy decisions made by the government during the crisis.[53] On the weekend prior to the collapse of Lehman Brothers, Henry Paulson called together the leaders of Wall Street for the purpose of rescuing the failing investment bank. He urged them to provide the financial resources to save Lehman in order to protect their own interests (requiring billions of dollars from each investment bank) but at the same time emphasized that the government would provide no financial support. His model for this rescue was LTCM, not Bear Stearns. A primary reason for Paulson's refusal to provide government support for the bailout of Lehman was his growing concern regarding moral hazard.[54]

No agreement to save Lehman Brothers through the means of the private sector was reached that weekend. By Sunday evening Lehman's board of directors had made their decision: Lehman would file for bankruptcy online that night, which it did at 1:45 a.m. on Monday. The markets opened on Monday facing the reality of Lehman's demise, the largest bankruptcy in US history. Its creditors worldwide would lose six hundred billion dollars. The journalist Roger Lowenstein comments: "The comforting precedent set by Bear Stearns and reinforced by Fannie and Freddie—that creditors would be protected—was demolished in a stroke. If Paulson had wanted to demonstrate that investors bore a hazard, he succeeded beyond his wildest dreams."[55]

51. Blinder, *After the Music Stopped*, 62–63, 109–13.

52. Blinder, *After the Music Stopped*, 108–9.

53. Roubini and Mihm, *Crisis Economics*, 68–69.

54. For a narrative portrayal of this dramatic weekend, see Lowenstein, *End of Wall Street*, 179–201.

55. Lowenstein, *End of Wall Street*, 202.

The markets reacted that day immediately and appropriately with panic. Creditors, fearing the total loss of their investments, started a run on financial institutions in the United States and globally. The flow of credit between financial institutions slowed or stopped to the point that the constriction of credit threatened the breakdown of the entire financial system. The US government responded in turn by injecting massive amounts of capital into the financial system. On the day following Lehman's collapse, for example, the Fed extended to the failing insurance giant American International Group (AIG) an eighty-five billion dollar-line of credit to keep it from defaulting on insurance contracts that it had written on one-half trillion dollars of risky mortgage-related securities, the government's intervention hoping to forestall a cascade of losses amongst those whom AIG had insured. On that same day, the Reserve Primary Fund, the oldest and one of the biggest money market mutual funds in the United States, declared that, due to losses that it had suffered from its investments in Lehman, it would "break the buck," meaning that it could no longer return one dollar for one dollar invested in the fund. This announcement caused a run not only on the Primary Fund but on other money market funds as well. To stop the runs, the Treasury set up a program to insure money market deposits much like the FDIC's guarantee of bank deposits. Then, on Thursday of that same week, Henry Paulson and Ben Bernanke appeared before the US Congress to request seven hundred billion dollars to buy up the "troubled assets" of failing banks, which resulted in the Troubled Asset Relief Program (TARP) that Congress eventually passed on October 3, 2008. These unprecedented interventions by the government and the interventions that followed succeeded in the end. By the spring of 2009 the financial markets in the United States had stabilized, but at the price of transferring the consequences of risk-taking in the mortgage markets from the financial industry to the American people and leaving in place the problem of moral hazard. The economists Simon Johnson and James Kwak offer this observation: "Never before has so much taxpayer money been dedicated to save an industry from the consequences of its own mistakes. In the ultimate irony, it went to an industry that had insisted for decades that it had no use for the government and would be better off regulating itself—and it was overseen by a group of policymakers who *agreed* that government should play little role in the financial sector."[56]

The Failure of Community, A Failure of Justice

If the government had bailed out Lehman Brothers, would the ensuing crisis have been averted? The economist Joseph Stiglitz answers this question with a resounding no. Portraying the bankruptcy of Lehman as a stand-alone event that brought down the financial industry distorts what took place at this crucial juncture in the financial crisis. "Lehman Brothers was a consequence, not a cause: it was the consequence of flawed lending practices and inadequate oversight by regulators." Lehman's collapse

56. Johnson and Kwak, *13 Bankers*, 163–64.

"brought out into the open the long-festering problems" that existed within the financial industry as well as the consequences of lax regulation of the industry by the government, Stiglitz points out.[57] Roubini and Mihm agree: the Lehman affair "was less a cause of the crisis than a symptom of its severity." By the time Henry Paulson called together the bankers of Wall Street to negotiate a rescue of Lehman, the dominoes were already lined up waiting to fall. "On the eve of Lehman's failure, much of the damage had already been done," Roubini and Mihm emphasize. "All the financial system needed to plunge into a state of utter panic was a little push."[58]

Lehman's collapse represents more than just a failure on the part of the financial industry. Like Stiglitz's example of the greenhouses in Kazakhstan with their missing glass, the bankruptcy of Lehman Brothers stands as a representative example of the failure of community. At the heart of this failure lies this injustice: the private gains of the financial industry were made at the expense of the good of the whole of the society. By viewing the collapse of Lehman in terms of the basic characteristics that constitute a community, we see the financial crisis of 2008, not simply as the malfunction of one sector of the US economy, but more deeply as a failure of justice and thus the failure of community.

The good of being a community, first of all, is realized through the ability of the community to reconcile the particular interests of its diverse parts with the shared interests of the whole (the first condition of being a community in Selznick's definition of community stated above). The good of being a community is therefore a common good. What occurred during the years leading up to the failure of Lehman Brothers, by contrast, was the gradual consolidation of power on the part of the financial industry in the United States that enabled it to shape in decisive ways both the US economy and the policy decisions of the US government in accordance with its own special interests, but to the detriment of the whole.

The story of this consolidation of power begins in the 1970s. In 1973 the sociologist Daniel Bell foresaw a fundamental shift taking place in the social structure of the United States and other advanced industrial countries: "in the next thirty to fifty years we will see the emergence of what I have called 'the post-industrial society.'" What Bell meant by the postindustrial society was a society in which "the majority of the labor force is no longer engaged in agriculture or manufacturing but in services, which are defined, residually, as trade, finance, transport, health, recreation, research, education, and government."[59] His forecast was correct, but imprecise. The service sector as a whole did indeed surpass agriculture and manufacturing as the predominant sector. But, of the various industries that make up the service sector, the one in particular that has come to dominate the US economy, thereby altering in fundamental ways the social structure of the United States, is the financial industry. Looking back over the four

57. Stiglitz, *Freefall*, 119.
58. Roubini and Mihm, *Crisis Economics*, 106–7, 109.
59. Bell, *Coming of Post-Industrial Society*, x, 15.

decades that have ensued since Bell's forecast, sociologist Greta Krippner describes what has occurred during these years as the "financialization" of the US economy, a term that she finds more specific and thus more accurate than Bell's reference to the postindustrial society.[60]

The dramatic ascent of finance, however, cannot be seen in the standard ways that economists use to measure structural shifts in the economy. One such measure uses employment data to view change, but finance as an industry is not employment intensive, and thus in this view (relative to manufacturing and the other industries in the service sector), its place in the economy appears small and remains so even as employment in all the other service industries rises. Another standard way to view structural change in the economy is to measure each sector's contribution to the gross domestic product (GDP). In this view the industries that make up the service sector taken as a whole, including finance, surpassed manufacturing in the mid-1980s. But, in this view, the rise of finance appears to be similar to the other service industries. The contribution of the financial industry to GDP is roughly equivalent to the other industries in the service sector because its "products" are not readily apparent in the statistics of the national economy. By 2001 the share of GDP for the service sector as a whole exceeded 20 percent, while manufacturing in its decline dropped below 20 percent. Accordingly, if we use GDP as a measure, Bell's depiction of the structural change in the U.S. economy as a transition from an industrial to a postindustrial society is appropriate because by this measure the contribution of finance to GDP is commensurate with and is viewed along with the rise of the other industries in the service sector.[61]

Krippner, however, presents a very different picture of the place of finance in the US economy by examining the profits of the financial industry relative to the manufacturing sector and the other service industries taken as a whole. Profit data provide a clear view of the dramatic rise of finance in the United States: whereas in the 1950s and 1960s the profits of the financial industry were only 10 to 15 percent of all profits made in the US economy, from the mid-1980s onwards the financial industry's portion of the total soared to 30 percent and more, and by 2001 its profits exceeded 40 percent of total profits. These numbers, moreover, are conservative, Krippner emphasizes, because of what is not included in the data. The profit data come only from the cluster of business enterprises that make up the financial industry—finance, insurance, and real estate (designated with the acronym FIRE)—but the data do not include the profits of the financial service units of nonfinancial corporations. Large corporations such as the Ford Motor Company, General Motors, Sears, and General Electric developed financial service units which came to overshadow the manufacturing and retail units of the parent company in terms of profitability. In the present-day economy of the United States selling car loans has become a more profitable enterprise than selling

60. Krippner, *Capitalizing on Crisis*, 1–4.
61. Krippner, *Capitalizing on Crisis*, 30–32.

cars. Thus, the financial industry's percentage of total profits would be even higher if the profits derived through the financial channels of nonfinancial firms were included in the data as well.[62]

As the profits of FIRE and the financial units of nonfinancial corporations have increased over the past forty years, so also has the importance of finance for the US economy. The rise of finance in particular, not the ascent of the service sector in general, is the defining event of the US economy in the past four decades. This is Krippner's empirical claim, which she portrays as the financialization of the US economy.[63] That the greater source of profit in the US marketplace now comes from finance, not from the products of manufacturing or the commodities of agriculture, nor from the other industries in the service sector, points to a structural change in the US economy that significantly affects households and businesses alike. The assertion that finance has become increasingly important to the US economy can refer to the value that finance has for the economy, but this claim of importance also indicates the magnitude of the consequences that finance's dealings in the marketplace can have on the US economy and thus on US society as a whole.

One such consequence concerns debt. Apace with the growth of the financial industry has been the growth of financial debt. From 1969 to 2006 the financial sector's share of the total debt of all the sectors in the US economy increased from 7.5 percent to 31.7 percent. In the purview of the four decades preceding the financial crisis of 2008, political commentator Kevin Phillips observes: "Debt and finance, we can now see, pretty much grew together—the profits of the former helped to fuel the triumph of the latter."[64] As debt increases, however, so does risk. In the years preceding the financial crisis, the major investment banks had taken on dangerously high levels of debt. By doing so they increased their profits dramatically. Wall Street firms such as Bear Stearns, Lehman Brothers, and others at that time had debt ratios (liabilities to assets) of 30-to-1, in extreme cases 40-to-1. But, at 40-to-1, only a 2.5 percent drop in the value of the bank's assets would render the bank insolvent.[65] When rising house values stalled and then dropped, this was the fate of investment banks such as Bear Stearns and Lehman Brothers—insolvency.

Yet, despite the precarious state of the banks at this time, in the negotiations between the bankers of Wall Street and the US government during the crisis, a disparity of power existed between the negotiating parties. Johnson and Kwak comment: "When the banks faced off with the government, they held all the cards." Indeed, in their negotiations with the government, the banks engaged the government having this conviction: "In the end, the government had more to lose from major bank failures

62. Krippner, *Capitalizing on Crisis*, 3–4, 27–30, 32–33.

63. Krippner, *Capitalizing on Crisis*, 50–51.

64. Phillips, *Bad Money*, 45–46.

65. Blinder, *After the Music Stopped*, 52–53.

than did the bankers themselves, who had already made their money."[66] Excessive risk-taking had produced vast profits for the bankers, but ultimately these profits were made at the expense of the American people. The pursuit of private gain on the part of the financial industry did not contribute to but rather undermined the common good of the US society. The role of the US government in the crisis was limited to mitigating the disastrous consequences of decisions made by the financial industry.

Debt itself, however, was not the problem. In fact, debt performs an essential function in a market economy. Those with surplus capital who want to put their money to work to make a profit need to connect with those who need capital for undertaking productive endeavors, such as buying a house, paying for a college education, or building skyscrapers and interstate highways. Connecting lenders with borrowers is the work of finance. Such work concerns the technicalities of financing specific activities, such as buying a house, but these activities seek to realize a goal, such as owning a home that is affordable in which to raise a family. The economist Robert Shiller notes that finance is usually thought of, more narrowly, in terms of its technicalities, "yet financing an activity really is creating the architecture for reaching a goal—and providing stewardship to protect and preserve the assets needed for achievement and maintenance of that goal." For this reason, finance should be thought of as "a 'functional' science in that it exists to support other goals—those of society. The better aligned a society's financial institutions are with its goals and ideals, the stronger and more successful the society will be," Shiller emphasizes.[67] The concerns of finance may be segmental relative to the whole of society; still its participation in the society ultimately concerns the core, that is, the well-being of society as a whole. Herein lies the second condition for realizing the good of community—core participation.

What in fact occurred in the years leading up to the financial crisis of 2008 were decisions and actions on the part of the financial industry and the US government that produced instability and then crisis in the US economy, thus decisions and actions that adversely affected the US society at its core. The epicenter of the crisis was the US housing market, specifically home mortgages. Prior to the 1980s the home mortgage was a relatively risk-free form of financial intermediation. A commercial bank that took in deposits at one interest rate would lend that money to homebuyers at a higher interest rate and then hold the loans on its balance sheet as assets. The risk to the bank was either early prepayment of the loan or the homeowner defaulting on the loan. But, since the bank had an incentive to ensure the creditworthiness of the borrower, and homeowners consistently made paying their mortgage a priority, these risks were low. This model of "originate and hold" mortgages, however, began to give way to a new model in the 1980s: "originate, securitize, and distribute" home mortgages. This transition was facilitated by the loosening of the regulations that the US government imposed on commercial banks, resulting in the repeal of the Glass-Steagall Act in

66. Johnson and Kwak, *13 Bankers*, 184.
67. Shiller, *Finance and the Good Society*, 7.

1999 by the US Congress, which removed the barriers between commercial banking and investment banking. Mortgage loans that were once kept on the bank's books were now bundled together and sold to investors as a security. This was a far more profitable arrangement for the banks since they received full payment of the loan in the present, not at a future date, which enabled them to make more loans. Furthermore, because the risk associated with the loan was passed along to the investor, the mortgage originator had less need but also less incentive to scrutinize the creditworthiness of the borrower, which eventually resulted in a high volume of subprime loans being issued to borrowers with insufficient income and low credit scores in the years preceding the crisis. These loans were bundled into increasingly complex securities by Wall Street investment banks and sold to institutional investors who were unaware of the increased risk at the heart of these securities. This process of securitization was driven by the lure of high profits and sanctioned by the belief that house values would continue to rise. When house values stopped rising, the fragility of this market came to light. In the estimation of Gerald Davis, a professor of management at the University of Michigan, a lack of adequate government regulation coupled with innovations in finance can produce "malign incentives" in the financial industry, which have disastrous consequences for the wider society. In fact, this is what occurred. Davis comments: "Through the mortgage market, Wall Street came to Main Street like a tornado in a trailer park."[68]

A third condition for realizing the good of community concerns the bond that holds a community together. A community is based on and is realized through reciprocity. We need each other. Reciprocity flourishes when relationships in a society are built on trust. This is the glue that holds the society together. Such is the case regarding the work of finance. The financial markets are built on trust. Creditors rely on borrowers to make payments fully and on time. Borrowers rely on creditors to provide clear and complete information regarding a loan. When either side of this relationship causes doubt in the other, the relationship of trust weakens or dissolves. The panic that ensued upon the collapse of Lehman Brothers was such an instance. As home values began to drop and as the borrowers of subprime loans began to default on their loans, the securities that were derived from these high-risk mortgages as well as the solvency of the investment banks that had issued them, which were operating with perilously high debt ratios, came into question. The extreme complexity of the securities that the investment banks had created made estimating their value or calculating their risk difficult or impossible to know. Thus, when the value of the underlying assets of these securities (home values) began to fall, the investors in these securities questioned their worth. The collapse of Lehman was the push that turned these doubts into a full-fledged loss of trust that stopped the financial markets and brought the US economy to a near standstill. Joseph Stiglitz notes that in the aftermath of a financial crisis "the

---

68. Davis, *Managed by the Markets*, 146, 153. See ch. 4: "From Banks to Markets: How Securitization Ended the 'Wonderful Life.'"

real assets are much as they were before—the same buildings, factories, and people; the same human, physical, and natural capital." What has been lost is the social trust that holds all this together.[69]

That the disastrous consequences of the financial crisis of 2008 were borne not only by those whose decisions and actions brought this crisis about, but by the US society as a whole as well as the global economy, points to the failure of community that is rooted in the failure of justice. Due to the crisis in the financial markets, the United States suffered the worst recession since the Great Depression. Millions of jobs were lost as a result of the economic downturn; millions of homes were lost to foreclosure; all homes throughout the United States lost a significant portion of their value; the total loss of household wealth in the US, according to Alan Blinder, amounted to about eighteen trillion dollars, an amount that exceeds one year of GDP in the United States.[70]

The disastrous consequences of the financial crisis, however, were not shared proportionally by all, the historian Adam Tooze points out: "Those at the top of the tree on Wall Street were bouncing back apparently without shame or second thought. The bonus season in 2009 was better than ever, netting $145 billion for the executives at the top investment banks, asset managers and hedge funds, as compared with $117 billion in 2008." The disparity between Wall Street's recovery in the aftermath of the financial crisis (the government had come to the aid of the banks) and the suffering of American households did not go unnoticed by the American people. Indeed, the impetus that in the end moved Congress to enact legislation that would regulate the financial industry came primarily, neither from the US Treasury nor from the White House, Tooze emphasizes, but from the fury of the American people over the disparity in outcomes for Main Street and Wall Street in the aftermath of the financial crisis.[71] The result, on the part of Congress, was the passage of the Dodd-Frank Wall Street Reform and Consumer Protection Act, the legislative bill named after the two congressmen who were its sponsors: Senator Chris Dodd of Connecticut and Representative Barney Frank of Massachusetts.

In light of Augustine's depiction of evil as the privation of good, we see the widespread losses caused by the financial crisis—from the loss of material wealth to the loss of social trust—as an evil brought about through acts of thoughtlessness and recklessness. The judgment of evil, however, beckons a consideration of the good, one that engenders thoughtfulness and responsibility. Thus, in its aftermath the financial crisis provokes this question: What is the good of being a community? But, essential to this question is another: What is justice? Without justice, a community cannot stand.

---

69. Stiglitz, *Freefall*, 58.

70. Blinder, *After the Music Stopped*, 354–55.

71. Tooze, *Crashed*, 306–7.

The Next Step

In 2010 the US Congress passed the Dodd-Frank Wall Street Reform and Consumer Protection Act that was signed into law by President Obama on July 21, 2010. Its regulatory statutes, however, had to be translated into specific, detailed regulations. This is the work of the governmental agencies most involved in implementing the statutes, such as the Federal Reserve, US Treasury, Securities and Exchange Commission, and others. This work of "writing the regs" is a contentious process in which various interested parties seek to influence the outcome of the process. No group exhibited a greater interest in or exerted a greater pressure on this process than the financial industry, represented by its army of lobbyists and by its money in the form of political contributions.[72]

During this process of formulating and implementing the specific rules that regulate the workings of finance, the government invites public input, but given the arcane nature of the matter at hand and the overwhelming presence of the financial industry at work to influence the outcome of the process, and this in contrast to a public that was disinterested and disorganized, this process was threatened by what economists term "regulatory capture"—the threat that regulators in the end will succumb to pressure from the industry and put in place rules that represent the interests of finance, but that do not address the dangers that the workings of finance pose for society as a whole.[73] These dangers, moreover, that became evident in the aftermath of the collapse of Lehman Brothers remain so today. Indeed, in the estimation of the Stanford economist Anat Admati and the German economist Martin Hellwig, the financial system today "is as dangerous and fragile as the system that brought us the recent crisis."[74]

In the process of negotiating, implementing, and then adjusting the regulatory framework of the Dodd-Frank Act, the stakes were high. Although all interested parties involved in the process seek an outcome that is favorable to their ends, they share a common purpose, which concerns most proximately the stability of US and global markets, but then more broadly the good of the society as a whole. As political battles are waged over the implementation of financial regulation, however, this broader purpose—the common good—can readily be obscured. Can this broader purpose be brought back into focus by introducing voices other than those of finance and government into the discussion?

Rowan Williams, the former archbishop of Canterbury, argues that it can and we must. Writing in response to the financial crisis of 2008, he claims that the voice of religion, that is, theology, brings a needed perspective to the discussion of the financial crisis: "Theology does not solve specific economic questions (any more than it solves specific political or scientific ones); but what it offers is a robust definition of

---

72. Blinder, *After the Music Stopped*, 303–19.

73. Johnson and Kwak, *13 Bankers*, 93, 207; Admati and Hellwig, *Bankers' New Clothes*, 194, 203–7.

74. Admati and Hellwig, *Bankers' New Clothes*, xii.

what human wellbeing looks like and what the rationale is for human life well lived in common."[75] Including this perspective in the discussion does not alter the terms of the discussion (say, the regulatory statutes of Dodd-Frank), nor does it offer a ready solution to the practical matters of implementing the law, but it does keep the discussion from being reduced simply to the terms of finance or governmental regulation by bringing a light to bear on the broader purpose of the work of finance and government, namely, realizing the good that we as a society share in common. In the context of the financial crisis, then, we ask again the question concerning the good that being a community realizes and the justice that this good requires, but now we ask this question from the viewpoint of religion, specifically from the viewpoint of Catholic social teaching. This is the next step.

75. Williams, "Knowing Our Limits," 25.

Chapter 2

From the Viewpoint of Catholic Social Teaching

THE VIEWPOINT

The financial crisis of 2008 was the result of two institutions central to the order and stability of the United States not fulfilling their functions, these two being the economy, particularly the financial sector, and the government. In the aftermath of the crisis, blame has been placed on the one or the other of these institutions or on both.

Some economists see the cause of the crisis lying in decisions made by the government: Thomas Sowell attributes the crisis primarily to the US government's distorting intervention in the housing market for the purpose of making houses more affordable to those who could otherwise not afford them;[1] Stanford economist John B. Taylor likewise sees government as the cause of the crisis, but in his view the failure lies specifically with the Federal Reserve's monetary policy during the years leading up to the crisis, which kept interest rates unusually low, thus fueling speculative activity in the housing market.[2]

Others focus blame on the rapacious culture of Wall Street. The writer Michael Lewis in his narrative of this culture locates the cause of the financial crisis not simply in the greed of Wall Street investors and bankers: "I thought it was more complicated. Greed on Wall Street was a given—almost an obligation. The problem was the system of incentives that channeled the greed."[3] The columnist Jeff Madrick agrees. That bankers could acquire vast personal wealth while avoiding the harmful consequences of their decisions during the housing boom and bust provided "strong incentives to take maximum risk and little incentive to be concerned about losses." For this reason, in Madrick's view, "the crash of 2008 was not a systemic failure. It was a function of the

---

1. Sowell, *Housing Boom and Bust*, 29–95, 121–35.
2. Taylor, *Getting Off Track*, 1–30.
3. Lewis, *Big Short*, 256.

unchecked greed of a handful of individuals, the culmination of forty years of growing power and weakened government. And the same individuals were essentially still in charge. The age of greed continued."[4]

The Princeton economist Alan Blinder widens the spectrum of causes to include villains from the worlds of both finance and government. "It is hard to imagine how something as sweeping and multifaceted as the financial crisis could have stemmed from a single cause or had a single villain."[5] In his view, there was not one cause, but rather multiple causative factors and actors contributing to the onset of the crisis: from inflated home and bond prices to excessive borrowing on the part of financial institutions as well as homeowners to questionable subprime lending and outsized compensation that incited the recklessness of bankers to the lax or nonexistent regulation of financial markets by the government, which spawned a vast industry of shadowy trading in securities and derivatives, to finally the failure of rating agencies to provide accurate appraisals of mortgage-related securities.[6]

The Financial Crisis Inquiry Commission that was established by the US Congress in 2009 to investigate the causes of the financial crisis similarly determined that the crisis resulted from multiple causes, rooted in the actions and inactions of the many in the financial industry, the economy more broadly, and the government. The Commission's examination of the various causes led it to make this sobering point: "We conclude this financial crisis was avoidable . . . To paraphrase Shakespeare, the fault lies not in the stars, but in us."[7] The Commission likens its investigation to those of the National Transportation Safety Board that seek to determine the causes of aviation disasters so that they might be avoided in the future.[8] Here the disaster involved the US economy that implicated the global economy, a disaster that was caused not by unavoidable and unforeseeable technical mishaps, but by human decisions that had foreseeable consequences. By understanding the causes of this disaster, we as a nation and as a global community might avoid such a disaster in the future.

That during this period of recovery following the crisis the voice of religion should seek to be heard on matters regarding the crisis appears at first glance to be quaintly out of place. The financial crisis is a matter of the world, not the church. The institutions of finance and government that played such a central role in the crisis function as secular institutions, wholly outside the domain of the church. Their concerns are "this-worldly," not the "otherworldly" concerns of religion. The words of Rowan Williams, the former archbishop of Canterbury, that were quoted at the end of Chapter 1, acknowledge the demarcation that exists between the church and the secular world: theology, the voice of religion, "does not solve economic questions (any

---

4. Madrick, *Age of Greed*, 395–97.

5. Blinder, *After the Music Stopped*, 27.

6. For an account of these causes, see Blinder, *After the Music Stopped*, 27–86.

7. Financial Crisis Inquiry Commission, *Financial Crisis Inquiry Report*, xvii.

8. Financial Crisis Inquiry Commission, *Financial Crisis Inquiry Report*, xii.

more than it solves specific political or scientific ones)." Here the archbishop clearly distinguishes the transcendent concerns of religion from the internal affairs of secular institutions, such as the economy, government, and science. Yet, he adds this: in the context of the recovery what the voice of religion has to offer "is a robust definition of what human wellbeing looks like and what the rationale is for human life well lived in common."[9]

By bringing a vision of human well-being to bear on the discussion of the financial recovery, religion forces the question "what for?" to be asked regarding the recovery, not only from the point of view of religion, but from the point of view of all institutions that have a role to play in the recovery. The question implies purpose: What is the recovery for? What do the actions undertaken to repair the damage of the crisis and to protect against future financial crises intend? What does the human well-being that we seek in the aftermath of the crisis look like? Each institution will respond to the question "what for?" in a different way, according to its own distinct purpose. But ultimately the question concerns the whole—the common well-being that is achieved through the coordinated efforts of the many acting in and through these distinct institutions. The question both relativizes each institution's contribution (including religion's) and at the same time, given the distinctiveness of each contribution, highlights the need for a mutual response. No one institution can provide a full answer to the question "what for?"; a full answer requires the participation of all, including religion. An analogy can be made, Archbishop Rowen Williams asserts, between the functioning of a household and the workings of a society. Indeed, the word "economy," he points out, comes from the Greek word *oikonomos*, which means household management. A good household achieves a common well-being by ensuring the personal well-being of all who live in its domain. A good society does likewise. But a good society, like a good household, can achieve this common well-being only through the active participation of all within it. To graphically make this point, Rowan Williams calls forth the metaphor used by Jonathan Sacks, the emeritus Chief Rabbi of the United Hebrew Congregations of the United Kingdom: the good society is "the home we build together."[10]

But, religion's effort to address the financial crisis and its recovery by entering the public debate that primarily concerns two secular institutions—the financial industry and the government—implies a significant assumption on religion's part: that in the context of a pluralistic society religion can speak to this social crisis legitimately and meaningfully with a public voice. By speaking in the public forum, religion positions itself in the society as essentially a public religion, not simply a private affair, and expects all within the society to hear its voice in this manner. Yet, to many within a diverse society such as the United States, that religion would undertake to speak on matters of public concern, not just to its adherents but to all within the society, will

9. Williams, "Knowing Our Limits," 25.

10. Williams, "Knowing Our Limits," 23–24. See Sacks, *Home We Build Together*.

seem out of place, indeed an anachronism. The church in the modern world no longer stands at the center of society, speaking to all within the society with an authoritative voice as it did in the premodern period of Western history, but now speaks as one voice among many. Moreover, that religion is faced with the challenge of demonstrating the legitimacy of its voice and the relevance of what it has to say, if it chooses to speak on matters of public concern to a diverse society, simply underscores this point.

To appreciate this challenge, we must bring clearly into focus this changed relationship between the church and the modern world. Understanding this relationship will highlight the significance of the viewpoint that the church brings to matters of public concern and will show how this viewpoint can be expressed in ways that have legitimacy and meaning for believers and unbelievers alike. A viewpoint is a standpoint. If not at the center, then where is the church standing in the context of the wider society when it gives voice to the political and economic concerns of the present day?

In the Context of the Immanent Frame

The economist Albert O. Hirschman observed that in times of economic decline, or more broadly social decline, market economies and political institutions tend to respond to decline in very different ways. He caught this difference with two terms: "exit" and "voice." Exit is the response of the consumer to dissatisfaction with the market. Voice is the response of the citizen to dissatisfaction with the governance of society. As a mechanism of recovery, exit is neat (one simply switches brands or leaves the market completely), impersonal (exit avoids confrontation between buyer and seller), and indirect (the consumer's exit leaves the market to adjust). Voice functions very differently. It is messy (many voices expressed in various ways and in varying registers), public (in the many forms that political voice and action can take), and direct (voice elicits confrontation).[11] The panic that ensued from the bankruptcy of Lehman Brothers was a dramatic form of exit. The Occupy Wall Street movement that took place in Zuccotti Park in New York City in response to the financial crisis was a dramatic form of voice. But the legislative deliberations that took place in the US Congress that resulted in the Dodd-Frank Act were the expression of voice as well.

Although exit and voice provide very different mechanisms for recovery (for the former the remedy is escape, for the latter the remedy is change), Hirschman recognized the importance of the interplay between the two. Yet, he points to a significant obstacle to this coming together of market and nonmarket forces in response to social decline: the bias on the part of economists against voice and for exit. This bias is based on a model of the economy that understands markets as inherently rational, efficient, and self-stabilizing. Here voice has no place; markets are self-regulating.[12]

11. Hirschman, *Exit, Voice, and Loyalty*, 15–16.
12. Hirschman, *Exit, Voice, and Loyalty*, 16–20, 30–31.

In the years preceding the financial crisis, this model of the economy held sway. During these years, voice in regard to the financial markets was mostly absent, and if the voice of concern was expressed regarding growing risk in the financial markets, it was ignored—with one notable exception. In the spring of 1998, Brooksley Born, the chair of the Commodity Futures Trading Commission (CFTC), issued the draft of an exploratory document calling for increased market supervision of derivatives (a key source of the financial crisis), which she later published. This document immediately elicited a hostile reaction from many sides, but most significantly from Alan Greenspan, chair of the Federal Reserve, Robert Rubin, Secretary of the Treasury, Arthur Levitt, chair of the Securities and Exchange Commission, and Larry Summers, Rubin's top deputy at Treasury—all powerful regulators, all opposed to any supervision of the derivative markets. Given the force and breadth of the opposition, Born resigned as chair of the CFTC in mid-1999.[13] Her cautionary exploration was prescient but, due to the opposition that she encountered, ineffectual. Basic assumptions regarding how markets work remained unexamined and were left firmly in place.

Writing in the aftermath of the crisis, Martin Wolf, chief economics commentator at the *Financial Times* of London, acknowledges that the reigning model of economics had dulled his attention to instability in the markets as well. Then he adds this:

> For the dominant school of neoclassical economics, depressions are a result of some external (or, as economists say, 'exogenous') shock, not of forces generated within the system. The opposite and, in my view, vastly more plausible possibility is that the crisis happened partly *because* the economic models of the mainstream rendered that outcome ostensibly so unlikely in theory that they ended up making it far more likely in practice. The insouciance encouraged by the rational-expectations and efficient-market hypotheses made regulators and investors careless.[14]

In Wolf's view, the cause of the financial crisis lies not primarily in the rapacious culture of Wall Street, nor primarily in the actions or inactions of government in the markets, but more fundamentally in an idea—the understanding of markets as rational, efficient, and self-regulating.

> Yet perhaps the biggest way in which the crises have changed the world is—or at least should be—intellectual. They have shown that established views of how (and how well) the world's most sophisticated economies and financial systems work were nonsense. This poses an uncomfortable challenge for economics and a parallel challenge for economic policymakers—central bankers, financial regulators, officials of finance ministries and ministers. It is, in the last resort, ideas that matter . . . Both economists and policymakers need to

13. Lowenstein, *End of Wall Street*, 58–60.
14. Wolf, *Shifts and the Shocks*, xvi–xvii.

> rethink their understanding of the world in important respects. The pre-crisis
> conventional wisdom . . . stands revealed as complacent, indeed vainglorious.[15]

These are strong words, supported by other economists.[16] The challenge that Wolf presents to both economists and policymakers requires rethinking how markets work best for the good of all. His challenge is the expression of voice addressed to government regulators as well as to economists. In his view, voice does indeed have a role to play in the workings of the markets. The term "liberal democracy," Wolf points out, corresponds roughly with Hirschman's use of exit and voice and his emphasis on the importance of their interplay. Exit bespeaks the freedom of the individual in society; voice bespeaks the right but also the need of the individual to participate actively in the public life of the society, both in matters of government as well as in matters of the economy. "The ideal of a liberal democracy derives from the marriage of these two ideas—freedom and citizenship. It is based on the belief that we are not only individuals with rights to choose for ourselves, subject to the law; we are also, as Aristotle put it, 'political animals.'" Wolf celebrates the value and the accomplishments of free markets but underscores the point that the good of society is realized only through the choices that we make together. Our collective deliberations and decisions do not violate our personal freedom; they are to the contrary "an expression and a facilitator of that fundamental value."[17]

Wolf's depiction of liberal democracy leaves an opening for religion to enter this discussion, but at the same time there is no invitation on his part for religion to do so. His challenge is directed specifically to economists and governmental policymakers. For the voice of religion to engage this challenge to rethink how markets work best, the impetus must come from religion itself. But, if religion does enter this discussion, given the nature of liberal democracy, where does religion stand in relation to the secular institutions of government and the economy when it speaks? For its voice to be heard as legitimate and meaningful regarding matters of public concern, where must religion position itself in the society as a whole, and how must it speak within a diverse society? The one question (where?) is empirical; the other (how?) is normative. Each question implies the other. How religion must speak with a public voice in a diverse society presupposes where it stands in the society, and where it stands will shape how it speaks to be understood. Both questions imply that religion, despite its transcendent perspective, resides and speaks in a social context of meanings and interpretations that it shares with secular institutions, such as government and the economy, a context that the philosopher Charles Taylor depicts as "the immanent frame."[18] Both questions, in short, concern the relationship between the church and

---

15. Wolf, *Shifts and the Shocks*, 12.

16. See Krugman, "Why Weren't Alarm Bells Ringing?"

17. Wolf, *Shifts and the Shocks*, xxi–xxii.

18. See Taylor, *Secular Age*, 539–93.

the modern world, a relationship that is highlighted when it is viewed in contrast to the place of the church in medieval society.

The Question of Where: From Medieval to Modern Civil Society

During the Middle Ages the church stood at the center of society. This period in Western European history began in 590 CE with the consecration of Pope Gregory I and ended in 1517 CE with the dawn of the Protestant Reformation and the splintering of Western Christianity. The pontificate of Gregory, which initiated this historical period, was emblematic of the entire period. Prior to his election as pope, he had been the abbot of the monastery that he founded in Rome, but prior to taking on the life of a monk he had been the prefect of Rome, appointed by Emperor Justin, a position that entailed the governance of the city, which he carried out with exceptional ability. These two traits—monastic spirituality and political acumen—Pope Gregory conjoined in a defining way during his pontificate to provide leadership to western Europe at a time when such leadership was lacking in the aftermath of the fall of the Roman Empire (476 CE). Following Gregory's papacy, the church continued in this role of governance, not only in matters of the spirit, but in worldly matters as well. The church was the unifying factor holding these two realms together, the spiritual and the worldly.[19]

In this unifying role, the medieval church was mediating heterogeneous but related realms: first of all, in its sacramental life, the church mediated between "the other world" and "this world," bringing together the eternal and the temporal; but, secondly, in the context of "this world," the church mediated between its strictly religious affairs and the affairs of the world, bringing together the sacred and the secular. In each of these dualities—the eternal and the temporal, the sacred and the secular—the Latin word *saeculum* was used to depict the second term of the duality: the temporal and the secular. *Saeculum*, having both temporal and spatial meaning, is variously translated as century, age, or world. God's eternal time (the doxology "Glory be to the Father" ends with *per saecula saeculorum*, translated as "world without end") contrasts with secular time (*saeculum*); the office of priesthood divides between "religious" priests (those who live apart from the world in cloisters) and "secular" priests, who live in the world and minister to those living in the world (*saeculum*). Although the terms that make up each of the dualities are distinct in meaning, they imply each other, and thus each is indispensable to the meaning of the other. The secular, although distinct from the sacred, requires the sacred for its meaning, and the sacred requires the secular. The church mediated between both realms, standing in the middle, belonging to both worlds, and holding both worlds together in its sacramental life.[20]

---

19. Shelley, *Church History in Plain Language*, 161–71.

20. Casanova, *Public Religions in the Modern World*, 12–15; Taylor, "Western Secularity," 34.

With the dawn of the modern age the meaning of "secular" (*saeculum*) changed in a fundamental way. The classification of reality into two realms, the eternal and the temporal, and then the temporal realm into the sacred and the secular, had been made at the hands of the medieval church, and thus this classification reflected the viewpoint of the church. From this viewpoint the secular world (*saeculum*) was treated as an undifferentiated whole—as that which was "the other" in distinction to the sacred. For this view of the secular to change, the viewpoint from which the secular world was seen had to change. This change occurs in the sixteenth century in Western Europe with the emergence of the modern nation-state, the beginnings of the capitalist economy, the rise of the new science, and the decentering effects of the Protestant Reformation on the medieval church. As a consequence of these historical developments, the dichotomy that the medieval church had set in place between its religious affairs and the world dissolves as the world (*saeculum*) began to differentiate itself into distinct institutional spheres (the state, the economy, science). As a result, in light of this changed perspective, the church came to be viewed in the *saeculum* as one institution among other autonomous institutional spheres. The secular world was now no longer the realm distinct from the religious affairs of the church; rather the secular world was the whole of social reality, in which the church was located as a part. This change enabled the church to focus its efforts on that which was strictly religious and to relinquish nonreligious matters to other institutions, but this change also meant that the church no longer stood at the center of society. Social reality would no longer be structured around one main axis, but would be multiaxial with two axes dominating and structuring the whole—the state and the economy.[21]

This historical process of "secularization" that began in the West the sociologist José Casanova defines as the "process of functional differentiation and emancipation of the secular spheres—primarily the state, the economy, and science—from the religious sphere and the concomitant differentiation and specialization of religion within its own newly found religious sphere." The thesis of societal differentiation constitutes the core of the sociological theory of secularization but, Casanova warns, throughout the period of modernization this core thesis has been clouded with the addition of two other theses that have been woven together with this core thesis and then presented as the theory of secularization—this by both apologists of secularization as well as its critics.[22]

The one thesis postulates that with secularization will come the inevitable decline of religion, even to the point of its extinction. The second thesis postulates that the outcome of secularization will be the privatization of religion, the relegation of religion to the margins of society as a private affair outside of the public sphere. The core thesis and the two attendant theses, when combined to form one theory, produce an incoherent whole, Casanova argues. The differentiation of religion from secular

21. Casanova, *Public Religions in the Modern World*, 15, 19–25.
22. Casanova, *Public Religions in the Modern World*, 19–20.

institutions does not necessarily imply the decline of religion; nor does this institutional differentiation imply the privatization of religion. When he disaggregates the theory into its parts, he shows that whereas the core thesis of secularization is based on the historical process of institutional differentiation that occurred in the sixteenth century, the other two theses are assumptions regarding the consequences of this historical process, neither of which can be supported with empirical evidence. Whereas the decline of religion is notable in present-day Western Europe, this is not the case in the United States, where the practice of religion flourishes. Yet both the United States and the nations of Western Europe are thoroughly secularized societies in terms of the functional differentiation of religion from the secular institutions of these societies. Furthermore, although secularization made the privatization of religion possible as an option, that privatization is the necessary and universal outcome of secularization is an assumption that lacks empirical verification. Given the modern differentiation of social spheres, religion as a worldview no longer serves as the basis for the social integration of society. But from this observation the theory of secularization cannot legitimately draw the conclusion that religion as belief must now be seen as belonging wholly within the subjective realm, and that religion as an institution must now be seen as invariably standing outside the public sphere as a private practice and therefore as necessarily apolitical.[23]

Indeed, what in fact has occurred, beginning in the 1980s in the United States and elsewhere in the world, are striking instances of religion "going public": That is, religious traditions that had previously taken on, whether by intention or due to the force of social expectation, a marginal societal role devoted solely to the personal spiritual concerns of adherents are now decisively moving outside these private concerns to address from a religious perspective the political and economic concerns facing the society as a whole. The Solidarity movement in Poland, the labor movement that drew support and vision from the Catholic Church in opposing Poland's Communist regime, and the Catholic Church's involvement in the political and economic struggles in El Salvador, which led to the assassination of Archbishop Oscar Romero in 1980, serve as examples worldwide. In the United States one notable example of this change of focus was the rise of political activism within Protestant fundamentalism in the 1980s, this particularly through the agency of the Moral Majority that was founded in 1979 by Jerry Falwell, a minister in the Baptist Church. A second example comes from the intervention on the part of the US Catholic bishops into the political and economic life of the United States in the form of two pastoral letters: The first, published in 1983, was a pastoral letter addressing matters of war and peace confronting the United States, particularly with regard to the buildup of nuclear weapons; the second, published in 1986, concerned the issue of economic justice in the US economy. Neither the Moral Majority nor the US bishops speak to the issues of public concern from an antimodernist viewpoint. Rather, they both accept the autonomy of

23. Casanova, *Public Religions in the Modern World*, 20, 25–39.

the differentiated spheres of government and the economy that marks the modern era, but at the same time they intend to bring normative judgments to bear on these secular institutional spheres. In the opening paragraph of the pastoral letter on the US economy, the Catholic bishops say this: "Our faith calls us to measure this economy, not only by what it produces, but also by how it touches human life and whether it protects or undermines the dignity of the human person."[24] The bishops accept and respect the inherent workings of the economy, but they also view and judge this secular institution through the wider lens of human flourishing that requires upholding the dignity of each human person in the society. These instances of public intervention on the part of religion Casanova terms the "deprivatization" of religion.[25]

The deprivatization of religion does not end or reverse the trend of secularization in the modern world: Religion by "going public" does not threaten the individual freedoms and differentiated structures of the modern world. Rather, deprivatization presupposes the privatization of religion that resulted from the modern differentiation of institutional spheres, and thus deprivatization, like the privatization of religion, is an option available for religion in the modern world due to secularization. But, unlike the privatization of religion that locates the practice of religion in the quest for personal salvation and thus outside of the public sphere, public religion seeks a voice in the public sphere.[26] When it does so, where is religion standing in the secular society?

In the United States the answer to this question begins with the First Amendment to the US Constitution, specifically with its first two clauses, the disestablishment clause and the free exercise clause: "Congress shall make no law respecting an establishment of religion, or prohibiting the free exercise thereof." In contrast to the establishment of state churches in Western Europe (one church, although differentiated from the state, was sanctioned by the state as representing the religion of the state), the Founders of the nation undertook the novel experiment to separate constitutionally the church and the state as two distinct, independent sectors. This constitutional arrangement allowed the religious pluralism that in fact existed at that time among the people of this new nation to flourish independently of governmental control. Catholic theologian and lawyer Christopher Mooney, SJ, comments: "Americans were the first people in history to realize that religious solidarity was not needed to stabilize the social order." The separation of church and state, however, did not imply in the Founders' minds that the state would be indifferent toward religion. Rather, the majority of the Founders saw in the churches the ability to inculcate the truths necessary to establish national stability. But the state would not privilege one church over the others, nor would it intervene to settle religious differences. Thus, in this constitutional separation between the governmental sector and the religious sector of

---

24. National Conference of Catholic Bishops, *Economic Justice for All*, no. 1. Citations from the pastoral letters and other ecclesial documents are referenced according to their numbered paragraphs.

25. Casanova, *Public Religions in the Modern World*, 3–6, 220–22.

26. Casanova, *Public Religions in the Modern World*, 38–39, 215, 221.

American society, "disestablishment became a legal synonym for secularization, and religious pluralism became its cognitive and cultural corollary."[27]

This constitutional arrangement between church and state, however, took on varying interpretations in the years that followed. In a letter to the Baptist Association of Danbury, Connecticut, in 1802, President Thomas Jefferson referred to the religion clauses of the First Amendment as "thus building a wall of separation between Church & State." Jefferson's metaphor of "the wall" of separation seems to imply an absolute separation between church and state. The absoluteness of the separation implied by the metaphor, moreover, is reinforced by Jefferson's depiction of religion and government to his Baptist readers in these words: "Believing with you that religion is a matter which lies solely between Man & his God, that he owes account to none other for his faith or his worship, that the legitimate powers of government reach actions only, & not opinions."[28] In his letter President Jefferson expresses a view of religion as being a strictly private matter, standing wholly apart from the sphere of government, with no concern to intrude into its affairs, and of government, respecting the fundamental right of the freedom of conscience, as being resolved to not overstep this sacred boundary and intrude into the affairs of the church. These two institutional spheres, religion and government, are separated by a constitutional wall.[29]

Thirty years later, James Madison offered a different metaphor for interpreting the relationship between church and state. In a letter written to the Reverend Jasper Adams in response to the copy of a sermon that Adams had given and had sent to Madison, titled "The Relation of Christianity to Civil Government in the United States," Madison in his concluding remarks says this: "I must admit, moreover, that it may not be easy, in every possible case, to trace the line of separation, between the rights of Religion & the Civil authority, with such distinctness, as to avoid collisions & doubts on unessential points."[30] Madison's metaphor—"the line of separation"—evokes a very different understanding of the separation of church and state from Jefferson's wall of separation. Unlike a wall that is unmovable and impregnable, a line can be thought of as delimiting, but also flexible and movable. Indeed, given the flexible nature of the line of separation, collisions and doubts will at times occur in regard to the relation between religion and civil authority, Madison thought. The boundary between religion and government is ever changing. Where the line will be drawn at any time in the nation's history will be determined by the circumstances of the time.[31]

Both metaphors—the wall and the line of separation—have found their way into the deliberations and decisions of the US Supreme Court in the nineteenth and twentieth centuries in regard to cases that concern the relationship between religion

---

27. Mooney, SJ, *Boundaries Dimly Perceived*, 11–12. See also Mooney, SJ, *Public Virtue*, 21–28.

28. Jefferson, "Letter of January 1, 1802, to the Danbury Baptist Association," 258.

29. McBrien, *Caesar's Coin*, 64.

30. Madison, "Letter of September 1833 to the Reverend Jasper Adams," 120.

31. Mooney, SJ, *Public Virtue*, 30.

and government. Mooney comments: "It is indeed quite surprising that two figures of speech, nowhere in the Constitution, could so color its interpretation."[32] But, although both metaphors have been used by the Supreme Court, Catholic theologian Richard McBrien points out that an overview of these cases reveals no one doctrinal principle being consistently applied in the Court's decisions: "Its several theoretical appeals to the 'wall of separation' notwithstanding, the Court has adopted, *in practice*, the Madisonian rather than the Jeffersonian metaphor."[33] Moreover, given the view of the Founders that the political and social stability of the nation is established, not through governmental coercion, but through the willing consent of the people, the majority of the Founders saw that the moral and religious beliefs inculcated in the churches were an indispensable aid in fostering the consent that holds the people together. Persuasion, not coercion, must be the means by which this consent is accomplished, and here the churches play an essential role. Thus, the issue of religion and government, then and now, does not concern primarily the matter of their separation, but the nature of their relationship. "And to understand the nature of that relationship, Madison offered the more serviceable metaphor: a line rather than a wall," states McBrien.[34]

The church-state relationship as established by the First Amendment, however, is specific to the juridical relationship that exists between these two institutional spheres. Beyond this legal relationship, the church (more broadly, religion in all of its plural forms) in the United States finds its home in the society as a whole. Accordingly, the binaries "church and state" and "church and society" are not equivalent because each binary refers to a different set of relationships. The pastoral letters of the US Catholic bishops regarding nuclear war and the US economy, for example, intended to influence policy decisions of the US government, but their words were addressed to Catholics first and then to the citizens of the United States as a whole about matters of national concern.[35] In the pastoral letter on war and peace, the bishops say this: "While this letter is addressed principally to the Catholic community, we want it to make a contribution to the wider public debate in our country on the dangers and dilemmas of the nuclear age."[36] By entering into the wider public debate, the bishops speak with a public voice. What they bring to this debate comes neither in technical nor in political terms, but in the conviction that "there is no satisfactory answer to the human problems of the nuclear age which fails to consider the moral and religious dimensions of the questions that we face." The bishops bring to this public debate a distinctive voice, yet they speak "as Americans, citizens of the nation" to the people of the nation faced with the moral and political responsibility to make a conscious choice regarding the use of nuclear weapons. "This letter is therefore both an invitation and a challenge to

32. Mooney, SJ, *Public Virtue*, 30.

33. McBrien, *Caesar's Coin*, 66.

34. McBrien, *Caesar's Coin*, 55–56. See also Mooney, SJ, *Public Virtue*, 24–25.

35. McBrien, *Caesar's Coin*, 42–43.

36. National Conference of Catholic Bishops, *Challenge of Peace*, ii.

Catholics in the United States to join with others in shaping the conscious choices and deliberate policies required in this 'moment of supreme crisis.'"[37] The social space where people of faith join with others to deliberate moral and political choices such as this, the social scientist terms "civil society." This social space—civil society—is where the church stands in a secular society when it speaks from its distinctive viewpoint to matters of public concern. Our question, then, is this: What precisely is civil society? What is its importance for the society as a whole when the society addresses matters of public concern?

Our associational life takes place in a diffuse variety of social forms—in families and between families, in neighborhoods and their attendant associations, in schools and universities, in voluntary associations ranging from sports clubs to community organizations, in hospitals, in workplaces, in places of religious worship, in social movements, and in the many ways that we formally communicate with one another in society, particularly through the public media. These and the myriad other forms of social gathering that stand outside of the regulatory reach of government and apart from the contractual agreements of the market constitute civil society. What these diverse forms of social togetherness share in common is that they combine privateness, in that they are freely formed through personal choices, and publicness, in that these social relationships have an external presence and an outward expressiveness in society. These freely chosen social relationships and activities make up an independent third sector of society that mediates between the privateness (freedom) of the market and the publicness (authority) of the state. Political scientist Benjamin Barber refers to this mediating third sector as "a theater of democracy." Here we live together with others, wedding our private commitments with our public engagements. Here we join with others to deliberate and act upon our moral and political choices. Here, in the mediating third sector that is civil society, we meet as citizens. "We gain a far more flexible frame for political and civic debate when we imagine social space as having at least three distinct sectors, and think of ourselves as having plural identities and multiple purposes rather than singular destinies defined exclusively by blood or by economics." For Barber, the civil sphere, in which political and civic debate and action take place, is the social space where "strong democracy" is realized.[38]

But in the heat of debate over matters of public concern, the vital input of voices from civil society can easily be eclipsed. Why? Insofar as the government and the economy of liberal democracies stand at the center of the society as its two dominant institutions, when matters of national concern present themselves as critical issues to the society (for example, the financial crisis), the solution to such issues will be seen predominantly in terms of the one or the other of these institutions. Moreover, as the sociologist Alan Wolfe points out, the solution offered by the one institution will be envisioned in terms of the failings of the other, and vice versa. "When obsessed with

37. National Conference of Catholic Bishops, *Challenge of Peace*, no. 4.
38. Barber, *Place for Us*, 33–34.

efficiency and cost, modern liberal democracies look for market solutions to their problems; when precisely those concerns with efficiency and cost lead to problems of inequality and injustice, they turn to the state. One course offers a solution to the problems the other creates, yet simultaneously creates problems that the other offers to solve." Neither institutional solution alone, however, whether economic efficiency or public policy, adequately addresses the moral dimension of the problem or envisions fully the moral obligation that we share as citizens of a nation toward one another, the shared obligation that binds us together for the purpose of realizing the good that we seek in common. Seeing the solution to social moral issues in terms of individual freedom alone (the market) or collective obligation alone (the state) limits how we think about these issues to the choice between private interests or public obligations. We need in addition a way to think about such issues that will allow us to see beyond the dichotomy between the purely private and the purely public, one that will enable us to balance our individual needs with collective restraints, according to Wolfe: "Such an approach—to the degree that it calls on individuals to rely on self-restraint, ties of solidarity with others, community norms, and voluntary altruism—finds its roots in a historic concern with civil society."[39]

The financial crisis of 2008 is a case in point. The passage of the Dodd-Frank Wall Street Reform and Consumer Protection Act in 2010 by the US Congress was the determined response on the part of the US government to regulate an industry that had caused widespread harm to the American people and worldwide. The government's resolve is manifest in the breadth and complexity of the Dodd-Frank Act itself and in the subsequent regulations that have been formulated by specific governmental agencies to implement the statutes of the act. (Whereas the Glass-Steagall Act of 1933—the government's regulatory response to the Great Depression—was stated in thirty-seven pages, the Dodd-Frank Act amounts to 848 pages, with the detailed rule-making that implements the Act adding thousands more pages.) Yet, the economist Martin Wolf asks: "will this complex regulatory effort deliver a financial system that is both robust and dynamic?" He answers: "In a word, no. The sheer complexity of the regulatory structure makes it virtually inconceivable that it will work." The Dodd-Frank Act was born out of the breakdown of trust between the government and the financial industry. Its complexity reflects this lack of trust, Wolf thinks, but also the desire on the part of the government to preserve a financial system that it mistrusts.[40]

The response on the part of the financial industry to the Dodd-Frank Act, on the other hand, has been one of widespread resistance. A survey of more than 1,200 junior and senior professionals working in the financial services industry in the United States and the United Kingdom between December 2014 and January 2015 presents a picture of ongoing noncompliance within the industry. For example, 47 percent of all those responding to the survey stated that they thought that their competitors most

39. Wolfe, *Whose Keeper?*, 12–13; see also 187–90.
40. Wolf, *Shifts and the Shocks*, 232–34.

likely engaged in wrongful practices (both illegal and unethical); if the respondents to this question earned more than $500,000, the percentage jumped to 51 percent. (The assumption underlying the question was that a more truthful assessment of the industry as a whole would be gained if the question concerned the respondent's competitors rather than his or her own behavior or company.) The authors of the survey—Ann Tenbrunsel of The Mendoza College of Business at the University of Notre Dame and Jordan Thomas of the New York City law firm Labaton Sucharow LLP—conclude that despite the regulatory actions of government, a pervasive state of ethical decline prevails within the financial industry, posing enormous dangers to the US and global economy.[41]

To repair the wrong that the financial crisis of 2008 has brought about, more is required of the nation than reestablishing efficient markets and legislating public policy that will provide effective oversight of the financial markets. Both are necessary, but neither is sufficient, alone or in tandem. The Founders of the nation understood this fundamental truth—the order and stability of the nation will be achieved, not by the force of government alone, but through the willing consent of the people. Persuasion, not coercion, is the discourse of consent. The voices of persuasion speak in the social space that is civil society. To repair the social fabric, justice is required. Justice depends on orderly, fair markets; justice also depends on governmental regulations that determine the good of the whole; but further, in the words of the sociologist Jeffrey Alexander:

> Justice depends on solidarity, on the feeling of being connected to others, of being part of something larger than ourselves, a whole that imposes obligations and allows us to share convictions, feelings, and cognitions, gives us a chance for meaningful participation, and respects our individual personalities even while giving us the feeling that we are all in the same boat.[42]

Achieving this sense of solidarity, "in which individual rights and collective obligations are tensely intertwined," Alexander maintains, is the work of civil society. In this social space "the sphere of fellow feeling, the we-ness that makes society into society" is realized.[43]

Whether as discursive argument, exhortation, expostulation, or disputation, the voices of persuasion in the civil sphere speak to the whole of society with the intent to influence the whole. Social agreement, not social control, is the aim of this discourse. Establishing shared understandings and inspiring common actions, based on a sense of connectedness among the members of the society, are the means to this end. Neither the regulations of the government nor the incentives of the market can accomplish this goal. This can only be accomplished in the civil sphere.

41. Tenbrunsel and Thomas, *Street*.

42. Alexander, *Civil Sphere*, 13.

43. Alexander, *Civil Sphere*, 53.

In the aftermath of the financial crisis, the 2010 documentary film *Inside Job*, directed by Charles Ferguson, presented a narrative of the crisis, examining its causes and its consequences, through interviews with individuals in the financial industry, government, as well as with academic economists.[44] The intent of the documentary was both to enlighten and to incite the viewer. An attentive viewing yields both a clearer understanding of why and how the financial crisis took place and moral outrage that it did take place. The documentary ends with a soaring, panoramic view of the Statue of Liberty, symbol of freedom and democracy, and this voice-over:

> For decades the American financial system was stable and safe. But then something changed. The financial industry turned its back on society, corrupted our political system, and plunged the world economy into crisis. At enormous cost we've avoided disaster and are recovering. But the men and institutions that caused the crisis are still in power and that needs to change. They will tell us that we need them and that what they do is too complicated for us to understand. They will tell us it won't happen again. They will spend billions fighting reform. It won't be easy. But some things are worth fighting for.

Whereas the concluding words of the documentary highlight the polarity between "them" (the financial industry, government regulators, accommodating economists) and "us" (the people of the United States and worldwide), the visual image with which it ends—the symbol of liberal democracy in the United States—expresses the fundamental value that binds "us" and "them" together as a society of free people. Although the viewer may leave the documentary, in the words of one film critic, "dispirited as well as enraged,"[45] given the enormity of the crisis, the clear intent of the documentary is to elicit a spirited response on the part of the viewer by concluding with the view of the symbol that represents the good that we as a society can only realize in common.

The documentary serves as an example of discourse that is public and civil—public in that it speaks to the whole of society regarding a matter of common concern; civil in that it speaks not in the language of law nor in the language of private interest but in the language of value, the good that is shared by the society as a whole and that calls for a response on the part of the whole. Such discourse is the work of civil society. This example, however, raises the question whether the voice of religion can also participate in the work of civil society legitimately and meaningfully. The pastoral letters of the US Catholic bishops on war and the economy are certainly public insofar as they address not only Catholics but also the US society as a whole about matters of common concern. But, if the pastoral letters speak from the distinctive perspective of faith, are they civil? To this question social scientists offer differing responses.

44. Ferguson, dir., *Inside Job*.

45. Scott, "Who Maimed the Economy, and How."

Jeffrey Alexander, for one, answers no. The dispute, however, is part of a larger debate concerning the very nature of civil society itself.[46]

The most common approach among social scientists in the study of civil society is to view this sector of society through the lens of the associational life that occurs between the sectors of the economy and government.[47] But with this approach comes a twofold problem: First, are all forms of associational life to be considered part of civil society, or must we distinguish between those forms that are characteristically civil (open, inclusive, egalitarian, voluntary, public) and those that are not? A voluntary association such as the local chapter of Habitat for Humanity, whose purpose is building homes for low-income families, or the book club at a local library, whose purpose is to offer recreational, educational, and community-building resources to the local community, might be considered as representative examples of civil society. But families, having a biological not a voluntary basis, and churches, being hierarchical and doctrinally exclusive, seem not to fit into the category of civil society because they cannot fully match the defining characteristics of this sphere. Benjamin Barber acknowledges the problem, but insists that "we may wish to draw democratic civil society's perimeters generously enough to encompass groups that fall short of a pure democratic, voluntaristic ideal." To appreciate the vitality and strength of civil society for democracy, our focus must first be on that characteristic that defines the whole— the pluralism that constitutes civil society as such. Considered individually, groups may appear as uncivil (authoritarian, exclusionary), "but in combination they weave a fabric that is textured by variety and difference. It is civil society as a whole that is free, because it is a voluntary sector in which men and women can choose their own forms of association."[48] Moreover, insofar as a family provides a platform for the wider engagements of its members in civil society, and churches provide the social cohesion that binds communities together, both must be seen as necessary components of the civil sphere. "In fact, so crucial are forms of association like families and religion to the coherence and solidarity of society that strong democrats have good reason to nurture and support them even if they fail the test of democratic civility," Barber states.[49]

Secondly, how clear and firm are the boundaries that distinguish the associational life of civil society from the government and the economy? Some forms of association can readily be seen as part of civil society, but for others their place amid the sectors of society is ambiguous. For example, the American Association for Retired Persons (AARP), the voluntary association that advocates for older Americans, and the National Organization for Women (NOW), whose purpose is to promote and protect the rights of women, are large, bureaucratic associations that engage the government and the economy but belong to the civil sphere. Although each association represents the

46. For a helpful overview of the debate, see Edwards, *Civil Society*.

47. Edwards, *Civil Society*, 19–20.

48. Barber, *Place for Us*, 35–36.

49. Barber, *Place for Us*, 53–54.

interests of a particular social group, the advocacy of each ultimately intends through its voice and actions to influence government and the economy but more broadly society as a whole. But, where does the associational life of a political party or a political organization take place—in the governmental sphere or the civil sphere? Political entities such as the Democratic Party and Republican Party appear to have one foot in the civil sphere (in the work of political mobilization and in the representation of the populace) and one foot in the sphere of government (through partisan efforts to shape governmental policy). Economic entities such as labor unions likewise seem to straddle two spheres—representing the interests of workers (in the civil sphere) and taking forceful action to effect specific market outcomes (in the economy).

This ambiguity highlights a problem regarding the determination of the boundaries that separate civil society from the spheres of government and the economy, both in terms of the independence and the interdependence of the spheres: from the perspective of civil society, too firm a separation between the spheres thwarts the critical and constructive role that civil associations can play in the affairs of government and the economy; too loose a separation can result in either the market or the state exerting an undue force in civil society, thus undermining both the autonomy of civil society and social solidarity. Accordingly, with regard to the role of religion in civil society, too firm a separation between the spheres reinforces the privatization of religion, but too loose a separation, enabling the concerns of religion to be tied too closely to the interests of the state or the market, threatens to narrow religion to a faction, with its concerns representing only partisan interests.

The social scientists Jean Cohen and Andrew Arato bring insight to the problem of clarifying the boundaries that distinguish the sectors of society by emphasizing the distinctive mediating role that political parties and political organizations, as well as parliaments, play in liberal democracies between civil society and the state. These political associations, in order to distinguish them from the associations that make up civil society proper, they term "political society." A similar mediating role between civil society and markets is taken on by the firms and cooperatives that produce and distribute goods and services in the society as well as by unions and other forms of collective bargaining. These groups Cohen and Arato designate with the term "economic society." Both political society and economic society arise from civil society and share in its institutional structure, but what distinguishes these associations in their mediating role from the other associations in civil society is that "the actors of political and economic society are directly involved with state power and economic production, which they seek to control and manage." In contrast, "the political role of civil society . . . is not directly related to the control or conquest of power but to the generation of influence through the life of democratic associations and unconstrained discussion in the cultural public sphere." The voice of these civil associations is public, but as actors in the society whose purpose is to communicate as widely as possible in normative terms, the political role of these associations is "inevitably diffuse and inefficient." For this reason, "the mediating role of political society between civil society and state is indispensable, but so is the rootedness of political society in civil society." The associations that make up political society, such as political parties, represent and enact the interests of civil society but they do so, not in the language of persuasion, but through instruments of power that are employed in strategic, instrumental ways to achieve concrete political results. But, being rooted in civil society, political society (as also economic society) is exposed to and can be influenced by the open-ended, normative discourse of civil society, Cohen and Arato emphasize, and thus it is these "mediating spheres through which civil society can gain influence over political-administrative and economic processes."[50]

The documentary *Inside Job* illustrates this point. Its analysis of the financial crisis is instructive. Its call for political action is bold. But what the documentary does not present or seek to enact, in the aftermath of the crisis, is a specific program of repair. This is not its intent. The concrete work of repair lies with those associations most suited to the task, those that constitute political and economic society. Yet, the documentary speaks with a voice necessary to the repair—one that seeks to both awaken and motivate a normative response to the crisis, not only from political and economic society, but on the part of the wider society as well. To be truly effective in the concrete work of repair, political and economic society need to hear and incorporate into their response to the financial crisis this voice spoken from the sphere of civil society.

Did the pastoral letters of the US Catholic bishops in like manner speak effectively from the sphere of civil society to the governmental and economic concerns that they addressed? In terms of having the ability to bring about specific changes in governmental policies regarding nuclear armaments or the US economy, José Casanova observes, the pastoral letters were not very effective. But, judging the public relevance of these documents in these terms is misdirected, he thinks. What the bishops accomplished through the pastoral letters was twofold: first, the bishops brought a normative perspective to bear on the public debates concerning the issues of war and the economy, thereby refocusing the debates being held in technocratic terms to include moral and religious perspectives; secondly, by entering these public debates, the bishops not only demonstrated the public role of religion but also demonstrated to the wider society that all citizens have a role to play in public debates on issues that deeply concern their lives. Thus, according to Casanova, "Measured by the sheer volume of public debate which they originated, the bishops had a resounding success. Moreover, when the bishops spoke, Wall Street, the Pentagon, Congress, and the White House not only listened but felt compelled to respond."[51]

---

50. Cohen and Arato, *Civil Society and Political Theory*, ix–xi. See also Cohen, "Interpreting the Notion of Civil Society," 35–40.

51. Casanova, *Public Religions in the Modern World*, 201–3. See also Herbert, *Religion and Civil Society*, 25–27.

Most significant to their participation in these public debates, however, was the bishops' reticence to propose and promote specific policies as definitive (authoritative) answers to the issues at hand as well as their restraint in mobilizing a Catholic electorate to support such an agenda. To do either would have of necessity removed the bishops from the public debate: promoting a specific policy as the definitive answer to an issue terminates debate and begins the work of electoral mobilization. When this occurs, an association moves from being engaged in the public sphere of civil society to engaging the public sphere of political society. The universal concerns of civil discourse are replaced with the words and actions of partisan interest, thus relinquishing the broader scope of civil debate. This, in Casanova's view, the bishops did not do. Their contribution to the national debate was both public and civil.[52]

In the eyes of Jeffrey Alexander, however, the present-day involvement of religion in the civil sphere cannot properly be viewed as civil. He makes this judgment in the context of his comprehensive effort to rethink the concept of civil society as a descriptive and analytical tool for understanding this distinct social sphere in which solidarity—the basis of a vital democracy—is established and sustained. "I would like to suggest that civil society should be conceived as a solidary sphere, in which a certain kind of universalizing community comes to be culturally defined and to some degree institutionally enforced." But, given the highly complex and functionally differentiated structure of modern societies, Alexander finds that the current uses of the notion of civil society in the social sciences are too imprecise and umbrella-like in their diffuse inclusiveness to adequately represent what they intend to depict. Thus, he sets out "to understand civil society as a sphere that can be analytically independent, empirically differentiated, and morally more universalistic vis-à-vis the state and the market and from other social spheres as well."[53] Two such social spheres that he differentiates from the civil sphere are the family and religion. Although these noncivil spheres "are fundamental to the quality of life and to the vitality of a plural order," the social goods that they contribute to society are "sectoral not societal, particularistic not universalistic." The hierarchical (vertical) nature of these noncivil spheres, moreover, stands at odds with the universalizing (horizontal) community that the civil sphere seeks to create.[54] By distinguishing the civil from noncivil spheres, Alexander hopes to bring to light the universalizing intent of the civil sphere—realizing the we-ness that gives stability and cohesion to a diverse society. Thus, "to the degree that civil society gains autonomy from other spheres, its solidarity can define social relationships in a more consistently universalistic way."[55]

Solidarity that is the goal of the civil sphere, of course, is the ideal that stands in contrast to the real—civil society as marked by contradiction and fragmentation. Yet,

<hr>

52. Casanova, *Public Religions in the Modern World*, 204–7.

53. Alexander, *Civil Sphere*, 31.

54. Alexander, *Civil Sphere*, 7.

55. Alexander, *Civil Sphere*, 194.

this ideal provides real civil society with the vision of what is possible and thus offers direction to the cultural and institutional resources that civil society employs in its effort, however imperfectly, to attain this goal. This effort at building universalistic solidarity, Alexander emphasizes, is the work of civil repair.[56]

The solidary work of civil repair, however, is the proper work of associations and social movements only if they have taken on this universalizing intent. For example, Alexander differentiates groups that he terms "civil associations" from the general category of groups that sociologists refer to as "voluntary associations." Civil associations are distinctively issue-oriented, their purpose being rooted in a particular interest but broadcast to the wider public in universal terms. What distinguishes these associations as civil, then, is their communicative intent. In Alexander's eyes, there is a significant difference between a voluntary organization such as Mothers against Drunk Driving (MADD) and the Parent-Teacher Association (PTA) at a local elementary or high school. Both are voluntary groups, but the former has a communicative intent whose purview is the whole of society that the latter does not have. Moreover, civil associations such as MADD by expressing their specific concerns through the medium of public discourse become inextricably intertwined with the communicative work of other like civil associations, the collective outcome being the consort of public voices and public actions that creates the feeling of connectedness that constitutes the civil sphere.[57]

Social movements, such as the twentieth-century feminist and civil rights movements, function in civil society with a universalizing purpose similar to civil associations. Although these movements originate by addressing a particular problem, more precisely, a specific injustice such as gender or racial inequality, their effect as a movement lies in their ability to translate the problem of a particular group into being the problem of the society as a whole, this in symbolic language and civil performance that envisions the good of the whole. Thus, in response to the contradictions and fragmentation of real civil society, social movements as well as civil associations undertake the work of civil repair, guided by the solidary ideal of civil society and anchored in the communicative instruments of the civil sphere.[58]

The civil sphere is a moral sphere. A society's capacity for justice, in Alexander's view, is dependent on its ability to establish the social space that is capable of engendering a universalizing community and thus one that exists independently from social spheres with a more restricted, particularistic purpose, such as the economy, government, family, and religion. Specifically with regard to what he sees as the restricted function of religion that places it outside the moral scope of the civil sphere, he states:

56. Alexander, *Civil Sphere*, 7.

57. Alexander, *Civil Sphere*, 5, 92–93, 96–105.

58. Alexander, *Civil Sphere*, 7, 229–34.

> The religious sphere produces salvation, not worldly just deserts; it is premised upon a fundamental inequality, not only between God and merely human believers but between God's representatives, his shepherds, and those whom they guide and instruct on earth; and no matter how radically egalitarian or reformed the message, the very transcendental character of religious relationships demands mystery and deference, not reciprocity or dialogue of a transparent kind.[59]

Thus religion, while vital to the well-being of society, functions independently of the universalistic, moral purposes of civil society, Alexander thinks. For this reason, in Alexander's eyes, religion is not civil. Moreover, insofar as the moral purposes of civil society gain symbolic expression "as a generalized language that can be spoken by many different kinds of people" and are carried out by the social organizations and social movements that make up civil society, the civil sphere in his view exists as a public sphere.[60] That religion stands apart from the universalizing discourse and social institutions of the civil sphere means that religion stands outside the public sphere. In Alexander's judgment, for these reasons, religion is neither civil nor public.

To the question where does religion stand in society when it speaks to matters of public concern, the sociologists Casanova and Alexander give conflicting answers. For Alexander, religion stands outside of civil society. For Casanova, religion by going public plays a vital role in civil society. Given these opposing viewpoints, we are faced with a seeming impasse. Taking a second look at Casanova's depiction of religion as public, however, provides a way to go beyond this impasse. By asking further what Casanova means by the publicness of religion, a different question presents itself: if religion enters the public sphere, on what terms does it enter? Here the question is not where does religion stand in society when it speaks with a public voice, but by going public, how must religion speak in the public sphere with a voice that has legitimacy and meaning to a diverse society? Answering this second question gives clarity to the first, as the answer to the first gives direction to answering the second.

The Question of How: From Decree to Dialogue

The British sociologist David Herbert faults Jeffrey Alexander for identifying civil society with the public sphere. Alexander's concept of civil society, in Herbert's view, "conflates civil society with the public sphere, which we have argued are better kept analytically distinct: civil society organizations channel private opinion into the public sphere, they do not constitute the latter."[61] Casanova would agree. On this point, both Herbert and Casanova echo the understanding of the public sphere formulated by the German philosopher Jürgen Habermas. The public sphere, in the words of

59. Alexander, *Civil Sphere*, 203–4.

60. Alexander, *Civil Sphere*, 69.

61. Herbert, *Religion and Civil Society*, 75.

Habermas, is "the sphere of private people come together as a public." Private here refers to society, that is, to the social realm that exists outside the sphere of the state. Publicness pertains to the state and its administrative power. Privateness then pertains to all forms of human living that occur outside the public authority of the state, from the intimate relations within families to the contractual relations within markets. But publicness does not pertain exclusively to the state. The privateness of family and economic life, to be sure, assumes a social and therefore public relevance, but the publicness that Habermas finds most capable of being an alternative to and a critic of the publicness of the state is the civil discourse that occurs in the public sphere. Here the public sphere is seen as the social space where private viewpoints take on public form. Habermas traces the origin of the public sphere in modern society to the seventeenth- and eighteenth-century coffeehouses and salons of Western Europe where an educated elite acquired a public voice in the form of rational argument that had the ability to challenge the public authority of the state. "The medium of this political confrontation was peculiar and without historical precedent: people's public use of their reason," Habermas observes.[62] Although the face-to-face encounters that generated a public forum of rational argument in the early modern period have given way in the present day to a vast, extended network of anonymous viewers, readers, and listeners that are connected through the public media, these new channels of communication nevertheless remain the link between the private and the public and thus provide the social space whereby private viewpoints take on public form.[63]

In light of this view of the public sphere, the question regarding religion's place in society shifts from a focus on where religion stands in society to whether and how it participates in the public sphere of civil society. With regard to public debate in the civil sphere, Casanova points out that "without normative traditions neither rational public debate nor discourse ethics is likely to take place." Indeed, rational argument from a normative perspective fuels public debate, such that "normative traditions constitute the very condition of possibility for ethical discourse" in the public sphere. Thus, in Casanova's view, "it seems self-evident that religious normative traditions should have the same rights as any other normative tradition to enter the public sphere as long as they play by the rules of open public debate."[64] Here the question is not whether religion has a place in civil society, but whether religion can speak to matters of public concern in accordance with the rules of public discourse.

The privatization and deprivatization of religion are not terms that describe the nature of religion, but rather the options that are available to religion in a modern secular society. If religion (particularistic, hierarchical) chooses to enter the public sphere (the option of deprivatization), then, on what terms does it enter? How must

---

62. Habermas, *Structural Transformation of the Public Sphere*, 27; see also Calhoun, "Introduction: Habermas and the Public Sphere," 1–9.

63. Habermas, *Between Facts and Norms*, 360–66.

64. Casanova, *Public Religions in the Modern World*, 205.

religion speak to a diverse society in words and actions that have legitimacy and meaning? Casanova answers: "its public interventions will have to be and appear nonpartisan and nondenominational; that is, they will have to be framed in a universalistic language."[65] Whereas the medieval church, standing at the center of society, ruled by decree, the modern church (more broadly, all religions in the modern world), being one voice among many in a pluralistic society, intervenes in public affairs through rational argument, this being necessarily so. If the modern church enters the public sphere only to assert its religious convictions as the termination of debate or as a fixed position that it seeks to enact in society, its religious convictions remain private and its public intervention takes place on denominational and partisan terms. To take on public form, religious convictions must be presented in the public sphere in the form of rational argument, this in universal, moral terms that can be understood and shared by all in a pluralistic society. Still, the public face of religion does not leave behind its religious convictions when it enters the public sphere; rather, these religious convictions are brought to bear on matters of public concern but in a discourse that is inclusive, one in which the whole of society can participate.

A rational argument presupposes interlocutors. For this reason, if the church chooses to enter the public sphere to present a public argument, this engagement must be based on the church's commitment to dialogue with diverse others in the society. Genuine dialogue involves listening and speaking, a willingness both to learn from as well as to teach those in society who hold different views. In the give-and-take of rational argument, the church strives for social agreement, but accepts disagreement. The church comes to public argument aware that it is not in full possession of the truth regarding the good of society, but in search of the truth in consort with others who hold different beliefs. This engagement with society on the part of the church the Catholic theologian David Hollenbach describes as "dialogic universalism." In its engagement with a pluralistic society, however, the church does not dilute or set aside the distinctiveness of its faith. Indeed, a primary commandment of the gospel (love of neighbor) impels the church to find common ground (reason) on which to join with diverse others in the society to realize the good of the whole. Here faith and reason form an alliance; they are not adversaries. Christian love moves the church to go beyond the condition of tolerant acceptance that it hopes to find in a pluralistic society to actively engage society in the public act of dialogue for the sake of building solidarity, a solidarity based not only on fellow feeling (as Alexander puts it) but also on public argument. This achievement Hollenbach terms "intellectual solidarity."[66]

Achieving this ideal—intellectual solidarity—when undertaken in a complex modern society will inevitably encounter challenges that threaten to impede or to

---

65. Casanova, *Public Religions in the Modern World*, 223.

66. See Hollenbach, SJ, *Global Face of Public Faith*, 10–16, 112–18, 161–65. Hollenbach, SJ, *Common Good and Christian Ethics*, 137–59. Hollenbach, SJ, "Afterword: A Community of Freedom," 332–38.

undermine this effort. The more active and concrete the church's involvement in the public sphere, the greater the chance that its words and actions will be or appear to be partisan and denominational, this particularly being the case when religion (the sphere of civil society) attempts to influence politics (the sphere of political society), or when politics finds in religion an important resource for furthering its own political agenda. Catholic bishops' political activism and the emergence of Protestant fundamentalism into national politics in the 1980s provide instructive examples of the difficulties that religion encounters when it chooses to enter the public sphere to engage political society as well as insight into what building solidarity in a pluralistic society requires of religion when it participates in the public sphere.

In the presidential election of 1984, the political ambitions of Ronald Reagan and the Republican Party intersected with the religious ambitions of Protestant fundamentalism, particularly in the political activism of the Moral Majority, the political organization founded by the Baptist minister Jerry Falwell in 1979. Whereas the Republican Party saw in Protestant fundamentalism an important resource to use in its work of building a new conservative political coalition, Protestant fundamentalism saw in this political moment the opportunity to enter the public sphere to enact a Christian agenda that would restore a secular America to its Christian core. The legalization of abortion, feminism (particularly the Equal Rights Amendment), tolerance of homosexuality, the Moral Majority opposed; the return of prayer to public schools and the teaching of "creation science" in conjunction with evolutionary biology in the public schools, the Moral Majority supported. But the Moral Majority engaged these issues in the public sphere, not in the spirit of dialogue with the wider society, but in the form of electoral mobilization. The result was not public debate on these issues, but countermobilization on the part of the political opposition.[67]

Clearly, in this national election, the principle that religion and politics are interrelated was on display. Christopher Mooney comments: "Positively, this principle states that all religious convictions are politically relevant. But in American society it has a negative corollary: no religious conviction can declare itself politically normative." Both Reagan and the Moral Majority recognized and pursued the positive implications of the interrelationship between religion and politics—the political relevance of religious convictions—but at the same time they ignored the negative corollary to this interrelationship—that in a pluralistic society, religious convictions cannot be represented as politically normative. "What was disruptive," Mooney emphasizes, "in the interaction of religion and politics during the 1984 election was not the *fact* of interaction, but the *mode* of interaction; not the entry of the Moral Majority into the public forum but the intolerance which they brought with them. It was their religious values and theirs alone which were to be normative for the nation."[68] In this instance,

---

67. See Falwell, "Future-Word"; Byrnes, *Catholic Bishops in American Politics*, 89–90; Casanova, *Public Religions in the Modern World*, 164–66.

68. Mooney, SJ, *Public Virtue*, 14–15.

the religious convictions of Protestant fundamentalism, although stated in the public sphere, remained private in nature, viewed by the wider society as unacceptably partisan and denominational in form and content.

When the US Catholic bishops engaged the public sphere in the 1980s from a moral and religious standpoint, they did so explicitly in the spirit of dialogue. For example, in the 1986 pastoral letter on the US economy, the bishops state that "the pastoral letter has been a work of careful inquiry, wide consultation, and prayerful discernment," a work "enriched by this process of listening" and written with hope "for the dialogue and action it might generate."[69] This intention of theirs rested not only on their decision to engage the public sphere, but was based on and directed by the vision of the church and its role in the modern world as articulated in *Gaudium et spes* (*Pastoral Constitution on the Church in the Modern World*), a foundational document of the Second Vatican Council. Here "as witness and guide to the faith of all God's people, gathered together by Christ," the Council declared its will "to enter into dialogue" with the people of the world, this all-embracing conversation giving eloquent expression in the church's eyes to its "solidarity, respect and love for the whole human family, of which it is a part."[70] Moreover, when the US Catholic bishops established the National Conference of Catholic Bishops (NCCB) in 1966, along with the United States Catholic Conference (USCC), its administrative wing, this in accordance with the mandate of Vatican II, they gained the ability to engage in dialogue on national issues as a national body with the unity of a collective voice. With this institutional presence on the national stage came a significant opportunity for the bishops to bring a moral and religious perspective to bear on national political debates, but at the same time, because this public dialogue was taking place at the intersection of religion and politics, this opportunity presented challenges that threatened to undermine the bishops' contributions to public debate.[71]

The political scientist Timothy Byrnes points to the 1976 presidential election as the key episode that shapes the bishops' engagement with national politics both in terms of instruction and warning. The primary issue that pulled the bishops into the politics of the election was the legalization of abortion. Since the late 1960s the bishops had been vocal opponents of the growing effort in the United States to legalize abortion at the state level and from 1968 to 1972 had issued a series of documents condemning the practice of abortion. These documents were dialogical in nature: addressed not just to Catholics, but to all citizens, and expressed in inclusive language that combined religious belief with the American legal tradition, particularly its protection of human life. Because the abortion controversy during these years was taking place at the state level, however, the national voice of the bishops played little role in the public debate.

69. National Conference of Catholic Bishops, *Economic Justice for All*, no. 3.

70. Vatican Council II, *Gaudium et spes* (*Pastoral Constitution on the Church in the Modern World*), no. 3.

71. Byrnes, *Catholic Bishops in American Politics*, 49–53.

This situation changed decisively in 1973 when the US Supreme Court legalized abortion in its ruling in *Roe v. Wade*. Abortion became a national issue that elicited from the bishops a strong public response. Not only did the bishops condemn abortion as an "abominable crime" (words taken from the *Pastoral Constitution*, no. 51) but they also initiated an aggressive political campaign to criminalize abortion that included a lobbying effort in support of a constitutional amendment to prohibit abortion. Yet, the words and actions of the bishops were not intended to represent a strictly Catholic viewpoint, nor did they focus only on the Catholic faithful. Abortion for the bishops was a moral issue that concerned the whole of society.[72]

But, abortion in the United States in 1976 was also a political issue. Although the NCCB advocated on behalf of a multitude of issues (fair housing, penal reform, farm labor, world hunger), no issue had received the amount of attention and was lobbied for in such legislative detail by the NCCB as abortion. Some bishops in the NCCB expressed the concern that by making abortion their primary issue, to the neglect of other issues, the NCCB might be perceived by the wider society as having abortion as its only issue. This concern on the part of some in the NCCB did not hold sway. As a consequence, by setting aside other issues and giving primacy of attention to abortion, given the context of the election, the NCCB's voice was eclipsed by politics. In this political context, the antiabortion advocacy of the bishops was cause for the bishops being pulled into the politics of the presidential election and its partisan divide. Insofar as the Democratic Party (Jimmy Carter) supported the Supreme Court's decision regarding abortion and the Republican Party (Gerald Ford) did not, the NCCB's singular focus on and condemnation of abortion was readily seen by the national public as partisan support for the Republican candidate (this despite the fact that on almost all of the other political issues in the election, the bishops sided with the Democratic Party). Although the leadership of the bishops' conference stated publicly that the NCCB promoted issues, not candidates, given the context in which the statements were made, it was difficult to see the bishops' intent in the election in any other way than as an endorsement of the Republican candidate. The Republican Party, moreover, seized upon this perception of the bishops' position as a way to pull in Catholic votes, which they saw as crucial to the success of their campaign. Still, in the end, the bishops' involvement in the election had little direct effect in determining its outcome. The Democratic candidate, Jimmy Carter, won the election, receiving 56 percent of the Catholic vote.[73]

In the aftermath of the 1976 election, the debate within the NCCB over its priorities regarding social and political issues continued, but now there was a collective intent among the majority of bishops to broaden the agenda of issues that the NCCB would publicly address, thus avoiding being ensnared once again in partisan politics.

72. Byrnes, *Catholic Bishops in American Politics*, 54–61, 68. See also Mooney, SJ, *Public Virtue*, 154–55n32.

73. Byrnes, *Catholic Bishops in American Politics*, 59–61, 68–84.

The decisive step in this regard came in 1983 when the bishops issued *The Challenge of Peace*, the pastoral letter that addressed the morality of nuclear war and presented a critical discussion of US defense policy. Since the 1976 election, the bishops had continued to oppose abortion and advocate for a constitutional amendment to overturn the legalization of abortion. Their advocacy and organization regarding abortion had created the pro-life movement that became an important resource for the political strategists who were building the conservative political coalition that would play a significant role in the election of Ronald Reagan. In this sense, according to Timothy Byrnes, the bishops played an important but indirect role in the 1980 presidential election. But, other than the abortion issue, the NCCB by 1980 shared little else in common with the policy agenda of the Republican Party and the emerging new right that supported this agenda. The divergence between the bishops and the Republican coalition became vividly apparent in 1983 with the publication of the pastoral letter that presented the nuclear defense policy of the Reagan administration as a key moral issue facing the nation and provided a critique of the US policies regarding nuclear weapons. With this pastoral letter and the subsequent pastoral letter on the US economy in 1986, the bishops effectively distanced themselves from partisan political interests as well as the new religious right and its political agenda. By broadening the policy agenda of the NCCB, the bishops significantly altered the relation between the public voice of the NCCB and partisan politics.[74]

Not all of the bishops, however, agreed with this multi-issue approach. Some bishops feared that by broadening the public policy agenda of the NCCB, the wide array of issues would dilute their antiabortion advocacy. Father J. Bryan Hehir, a policy analyst at the USCC and the primary author of *The Challenge of Peace*, argued to the contrary that broadening the NCCB's agenda would enhance the church's pro-life position by linking protection of the unborn to other threats to human life, such as poverty and nuclear war. This view was then given theological articulation by Cardinal Joseph Bernardin in a public address at Fordham University on 6 December 1983 that was titled "The Consistent Ethic of Life: An American-Catholic Dialogue." In the address Cardinal Bernardin argued that disparate issues such as abortion, nuclear war, and capital punishment are best understood as moral issues if they are viewed in terms of the one moral principle that links them together—the sacred dignity of human life. What the nation requires to grapple adequately with moral issues as seemingly different as abortion and nuclear war is an ethic of life that is consistent and comprehensive—that is, one that provides a moral lens through which to view these disparate issues in relation to one another by highlighting the moral concern that they share in common. Bernardin's address, in the year leading up to the 1984 election, served both as a political strategy to prevent the church's voice from being usurped by partisan political interests and as a way to bring a comprehensive moral and theological vision

74. Byrnes, *Catholic Bishops in American Politics*, 84–91, 96–107.

to bear on issues facing the nation so that they might be discussed, not as separate issues, but as a coherent whole.[75]

The group of bishops that opposed the approach represented by Hehir and Bernardin argued that, in contrast to the potential threat to life posed by the possibility of nuclear war, the legalization of abortion was an actual and present threat to human life that called for an urgent response. As a way to bring the issue of abortion into the forefront of the 1984 election, a few bishops stepped outside the collective voice of the NCCB and on an individual basis inserted themselves into the electoral campaign—this for the purpose of bringing public attention to the church's position on abortion and to each candidate's position on this issue as well as to present publicly an alternative view to Cardinal Bernardin's consistent ethic of life. In particular, Cardinal John O'Connor, archbishop of New York, singled out the Democratic vice presidential candidate, Geraldine Ferraro, a Catholic, for public criticism of her political pro-choice position on abortion, a position in accordance with the platform of the Democratic Party, which affirmed the Supreme Court's decision to legalize abortion. The single-issue advocacy of Cardinal O'Connor and the other bishops during the election unavoidably aligned their religious interests with the political interests of the Reagan campaign, thus giving their involvement in the electoral campaign the appearance of a partisan endorsement. This the institutional voice of the NCCB avoided by addressing the moral issues of nuclear war and abortion as equally urgent and requiring the attention of all the candidates in the election. This standoff among the bishops in the 1984 election brought into public view the debate that had been going on within the NCCB since the 1970s. This ongoing debate, Timothy Byrnes points out, was not over the political relevance of religion, nor did it concern the substance of the bishops' policy agenda (the bishops' stances on the issues of abortion, nuclear war, poverty, and so forth). On these points and on the content of the pastoral letters there was overall consensus amongst the bishops. What divided the bishops was how they answered the question concerning which issues should be given priority and how the church must address these issues when it engages the political sphere. The divide between Bernardin and O'Connor was not a dispute between bishops regarding what the church teaches, but rather how the church's teaching was to be presented in the public sphere. On the matter of "how," they disagreed, and their disagreement reflected not only different answers to the question of how the church engages politics, but also how the church does so in the spirit of dialogue.[76]

Effective moral influence in partisan political debate comes, not from single-issue advocacy, but from a view of the moral good that encompasses the disparate issues that make up political debate and provides both the impetus and the framework

75. Gould, "Father J. Bryan Hehir," 198, 207–8, 213–14; Byrnes, *Catholic Bishops in American Politics*, 114–15; Bernardin, "Toward a Consistent Ethic of Life."

76. Byrnes, *Catholic Bishops in American Politics*, 6–8, 116–26; see also Heyer, *Prophetic & Public*, 139–42, 195–99.

for engaging these issues in a nonpartisan way. The comprehensive moral and theological vision called for by Cardinal Bernardin does just this: it enables the church to enact its social mission in a pluralistic society by providing a way for the church to address the full range of social issues confronting the society that transcends the partisan divisions within the society. "Inattention to the full range of issues," Catholic ethicist Kristin Heyer warns, "risks a reductionistic understanding of the Church's social mission and entanglement in interest group politics, given the temptation to skew the rest of an agenda to ensure allies' support on a single issue."[77] This the consistent ethic of life avoids by giving the church's social mission the breadth of moral vision that resists partisan entanglement.

By bringing its comprehensive moral and theological vision to bear on the issues that shape partisan political debate, however, the church encounters a further challenge: to be specific in its response to the issues at hand without at the same time being partisan. The moral principles that inform the church's stance on social and political issues are by nature abstract (abortion is a moral evil). To influence public debate in an effective way, a moral principle must be applied to the specifics of the issue under debate. Here moral principle intersects with empirical detail (the Supreme Court's decision in *Roe v. Wade*). For the church to be effective in its engagement with social and political issues, then, its public statements must combine teaching with specific application (a proposed constitutional amendment). Father Hehir points to the bishops' pastoral letters as distinctive examples of achieving this balance between principle and application: "To use the NCCB pastoral letters as an example, the teaching style found there is a mix of the exposition of principles . . . and an application of those principles in the concrete details of the policy debate." The combination of "using both teaching and advocacy, espousing both principles and policy positions" informs the teaching ministry of the church, which it undertakes "on the conviction that the strength of the Catholic moral tradition teaches *two* factors: a systematic body of principles *and* an ability to illustrate the meaning of the principles through casuistry"—casuistry being the technical term for the use of prudential judgment by the moral thinker when applying an abstract moral principle to a specific situation. What the pastoral letters demonstrate, in Hehir's view, is "that Catholic social teaching should be *both* systematic and specific."[78]

The goal of being both systematic and specific in its teaching ministry forces the church to acknowledge the limits that the church faces when it introduces Catholic social teaching into the public sphere. Cardinal Bernardin spoke to this point in a public address at Georgetown University on 25 October 1984, titled "Religion and Politics: the Future Agenda," just weeks before the presidential election. (Richard McBrien considers Bernardin's address to be "the most sophisticated treatment of the

77. Heyer, "Catholics in the Political Arena," 63.
78. Hehir, "Right and Competence of the Church," 67–68.

subject given during the entire campaign year."[79]) Bernardin affirms the right of the church to enter the public sphere to speak to matters of national concern, but when the church does so, he emphasizes, it must also recognize the limits that it faces. "The limits relate not to whether we enter the public debate, but how we advocate a public case." In a pluralistic society, religious speech in the public sphere to be legitimate and meaningful must meet two tests: "to respect the complexity of public issues and recognize the legitimate secularity of public debate." Regarding the complexity of public issues, the church must accept the fact that "the moral dimensions of our public life are interwoven with empirical judgments where honest disagreement exists. I do not believe that empirical complexity should silence or paralyze religious/moral analysis and advocacy of issues. But we owe the public a careful accounting of how we have come to our moral conclusions." Regarding the secular context of public debate, the church's public voice faces a different test: "religiously rooted positions must somehow be translated into language, arguments and categories which a religiously pluralistic society can agree on as the moral foundation of key policy positions."[80] Where the church encounters the limits of complexity and secularity most distinctly is not at the level of the moral principles that it teaches, but at the level of its application of moral principles to specific cases. Here is where controversy resides. Here the complexity of public issues and the secular context in which these issues are debated require that the church, if it chooses to enter into these public debates, adopt a posture of dialogue—listening and speaking, learning and teaching, seeking agreement, but accepting disagreement.

But, can the church apply moral principles to particular issues in public policy debate in specific terms and at the same time remain nonpartisan? The bishops would answer this question in the affirmative: the pastoral letters demonstrate that being specific while remaining nonpartisan is both possible and necessary. How? In the pastoral letter on the US economy, the bishops acknowledge that "the movement from principle to policy is complex and difficult and that although moral values are essential in determining public policies, they do not dictate specific solutions. They must interact with empirical data, with historical, social, and political realities, and with competing demands on limited resources." As with all moral thinking, the process of moral deliberation does not end with the affirmation of a moral principle, but with the concreteness of a moral decision. Achieving a moral decision regarding public policy in the form of a specific policy solution, which involves bringing moral principles to bear on the empirical details of the policy issue, is the work of prudential judgment. Here the bishops express this caution: "The soundness of our prudential judgments depends not only on the moral force of our principles, but also on the accuracy of our information and the validity of our assumptions." Whereas the bishops hold the moral principles that they bring to the debate with certitude, when they apply these

---

79. McBrien, *Caesar's Coin*, 161.

80. Bernardin, "Religion and Politics," 324.

principles to the empirical details of the issue at hand, they acknowledge that the degree of certitude necessarily diminishes. Regarding the specific solutions that they offer to the economic issues at hand, they conclude: "Our judgments and recommendations on specific economic issues, therefore, do not carry the same moral authority as our statements of universal moral principles and formal church teaching; the former are related to circumstances which can change or which can be interpreted differently by people of good will." By making this distinction between levels of moral authority, the bishops make clear their purpose when they propose specific solutions to social and political issues: they intend to debate these issues at the level of the specific application of moral principles (with a readiness to engage and accept disagreement regarding the application), not to make authoritative declarations or to give partisan endorsements. Thus, they state: "We expect and welcome debate on our specific policy recommendations." Moreover, they intend to conduct the debate "in a spirit of mutual respect and open dialogue."[81] Still, is this debate at the level of policy specifics necessary? To this the bishops respond: "we feel obliged to teach by example how Christians can undertake concrete analysis and make specific judgments on economic issues. The Church's teachings cannot be left at the level of appealing generalities."[82]

The pastoral letters provoked critical reactions from some Catholic theologians, these reactions being primarily concerned with the bishops' methodology of moving from principle to policy. "The fundamental question in my opinion," the Jesuit theologian Avery Dulles stated, is whether the bishops "ought to give detailed answers in controverted areas such as nuclear policy, taxation, or welfare programs." Dulles acknowledges that "the bishops gain more national attention by taking specific positions on contentious issues, but when one ponders the price of such specificity it becomes evident that there are good reasons for restraint." By engaging the specifics of policy issues, that the bishops might be diverted from their primary responsibilities in the church, that they can give the impression that in their eyes social and political concerns are more important than the matters of faith, that their teaching ministry can become involved in issues beyond their competency, or that it can unwittingly employ social and political theories that express their own partisan biases rather than the church's teaching—these are reasons that Dulles gives for restraint. In his view, the price of specificity regarding policy issues for the church is too high.[83]

In a response to Dulles, Bryan Hehir argues to the contrary that by not engaging the specifics of policy issues, the church abnegates its ability to adequately address social and political issues from a moral and religious perspective and thus weakens the effectiveness of its teaching ministry. "It is clear that one function of moral teaching is

81. National Conference of Catholic Bishops, *Economic Justice for All*, nos. 134–35. See also National Conference of Catholic Bishops, *Challenge of Peace*, i–ii, nos. 9–10.

82. National Conference of Catholic Bishops, *Economic Justice for All*, xii.

83. Dulles, SJ, *Reshaping of Catholicism*, 175–79. See also Benestad, *Church, State, and Society*, 215–20, 230–31. Weigel, *Tranquillitas Ordinis*, 257–85, 314–24.

to specify values and principles, duties and rights that the ecclesial and human community can use to assess social issues. It is equally clear, I believe, that a social ethic stated at this level of generality will fail to engage the issues it must address." Why? What is lost to the church's moral influence if it does not engage social and political issues at the level of specific policy? Hehir comments: "in social policy, principles in isolation from the intrinsic complexity of the issues provide little sense of direction, less guidance, and no capacity to cut into the density of socio-political discourse where decisions with significant moral content are made—often without explicit moral testing." For the church to effectively engage politics from a moral point of view it must do more than simply speak to politics; it must show how the moral principles and values that it teaches can be embodied in public policy. The church indeed pays a price for entering the political sphere to engage in public debate on matters of policy—it steps outside of the realm of moral certitude and ecclesiastical authority to engage in the complexity and contentiousness of public debate as one voice among many. But, Hehir insists, avoidance has a price as well. A price is paid "when the episcopal teaching role fails to engage the specific places where justice is done and peace preserved. There are high costs to silence also."[84]

In sum, the effectiveness of the church's public voice in a pluralistic society, when addressing matters of national concern, lies not in the assertion of hierarchical authority but in the strength of its public argument. Strong public argument requires clarity, persuasiveness, truthfulness, specificity, and civility. The late Catholic theologian John Courtney Murray, SJ—to whom both Hehir and Bernardin are theologically indebted—points to public argument as the bond that holds a society together: unlike the bond of love and unconditional commitment that unites a family, "the distinctive bond of the civil multitude is reason, or more exactly, that exercise of reason which is argument."[85] For public argument to be civil, Murray notes, disagreement must take place within the context of a more basic agreement. A consensus among the people of the society must exist and be acknowledged ("we hold these truths to be self-evident") for public argument to take place as civil discourse. "Argument ceases to be civil when it is dominated by passion and prejudice; when its vocabulary becomes solipsist, premised on the theory that my insight is mine alone and cannot be shared; when dialogue gives way to a series of monologues; when the parties to the conversation cease to listen to one another, or hear only what they want to hear, or see the other's argument only through the screen of their own categories." Here disagreement occurs outside of an awareness of or a concern for our common bond as a people. Where no prior consensus provides the common meeting ground for the expression of difference, dialogue cannot take place. "Civility dies," Murray states, "with the death

---

84. Hehir, "Principles and Politics," 170; see also Hehir, "Right and Competence of the Church," 66–67.

85. Murray, SJ, *We Hold These Truths*, 7.

of dialogue."[86] By addressing the public argument of the pastoral letters not only to the Catholic community but also to the wider society and this in moral terms that are inclusive, the bishops entered the public sphere to stand on common ground with diverse others in the society to speak to matters of national concern in the spirit of dialogue. In this regard, the US Catholic bishops' pastoral letters provide an instructive example of how the church engages in public argument that is civil. Indeed, the pastoral letters serve as models of the civil discourse that builds social solidarity.

Jeffrey Alexander would disagree with this conclusion. In his view, as we have seen, the voice of religion, being particularistic and hierarchical, functions apart from the universalizing discourse of the civil sphere and thus cannot have a proper role to play in the work of building social solidarity—in his terms, creating the sense of we-ness that is the feeling of being connected with all others in the society which motivates and undergirds the works of justice. Furthermore, that religion employs public argument as the means to engage the civil sphere in the work of solidarity would be for him problematical. What is missing in Jeffrey Alexander's depiction of solidarity is a role for public argument, which is intentional on his part. Thus, with Alexander's rejection of public (rational) argument as a medium of civil discourse, the church's teaching mission to bring a moral and religious perspective to bear on matters of public concern is presented with one further challenge.

For Alexander, the work of social solidarity (more specifically, civil repair) is accomplished neither through the instrumentality of social actions nor through rational argumentation but rather through symbolic representations of the universal, abstract goals that civil repair seeks to realize—this by particular actors in the society addressing a specific social issue using particular cultural forms (such as social performance or political ritual) set in the context of a narrative that portrays the issue as a struggle between the binary forces of good and evil, liberty and repression, purity and impurity. "Civil solidarity can be sustained only by a democratic language, a discourse that allows the abstract and universal commitments of the civil sphere to take concrete and imagistic forms. Justice is possible if there is civil solidarity, which itself depends on the vitality of a fluent and provocative moral discourse."[87] The success of the civil rights movement, in his view, was based not on direct acts of Black resistance carried out as a counterforce to white domination, but on dramatic acts of resistance (such as the bus boycott in Montgomery, Alabama, and the sit-in demonstrations at lunch counters throughout the South) that were portrayed by the leaders of the movement (in particular, Martin Luther King Jr.) and then by means of the national media as a struggle not simply between black and white citizens of the South, but as a symbolic struggle between the binary forces of justice and injustice, good and evil, in which all Americans played a part. By gaining influence over the discourse of civil society, King was able to present these acts of resistance in terms of a moral drama that fused

86. Murray, SJ, *We Hold These Truths*, 14; see 6–15.

87. Alexander, *Civil Sphere*, 38.

the particular aims of the movement with the universal aims of civil society.[88] This fusion of the particular with the universal, not the abstractness of rational argument (as represented by Jürgen Habermas), provides the means of civil repair. "Strange as it may seem, universalism is most often articulated in concrete rather than abstract language," Alexander maintains, "Universalism anchors itself, in other words, in the everyday lifeworlds within which ordinary people make sense of the world and pass their time."[89]

In a critical response to what Alexander considers to be essential to the discourse of the civil sphere, and as a defense of Habermas, the sociologist Bryan Turner argues that in order to accomplish the work of civil repair, public reasons are necessary. He sides with Alexander by acknowledging that Habermas's use of public argument pays too little attention to the influence of public emotion and social performance on the outcome of public debate. But he questions Alexander's primary emphasis on social performance and political ritual, expressed in the form of moral binaries, as the means to civil repair. Do the binary narratives of good and evil that fuel these performative acts bring about civil repair, or do they perpetuate civil discord? "In relation to the financial crisis," Turner notes, "the polarization of opinion (the binaries) has so far been dysfunctional in preventing the emergence of any rational and pragmatic solution to such issues as the debt ceiling, the regulation of banking, and the resolution of the mortgage and foreclosure crisis."[90] The documentary *Inside Job* (discussed above) might serve as an example. The film effectively portrayed the financial crisis as a conflict between "us" (US citizens) and "them" (the financial industry), a conflict that is at root a struggle between the binary forces of liberty and repression (liberty dramatically symbolized in the film with the view of the Statue of Liberty). The film's effectiveness is its ability to evoke moral outrage within civil society, but absent in the film is a presentation of reasons (political or economic) informing a program of repair. (This, of course, is not the film's intent.) Turner's critical point regarding Alexander's concept of solidarity is that civil feeling, whether of moral outrage or social connectedness, is an insufficient guide to civil repair. Public reasons are necessary as a means to accomplish this solidarity work. Turner asks: "What guarantees that structures of feeling stand in a positive relationship to the needs of democracy? What makes them universalistic rather than particularistic?"[91] Civil feeling alone, in Turner's view, cannot provide an adequate response to such questions. Only public argument can accomplish this task.

An assessment of the legitimacy and relevance of the US bishops' pastoral letters cannot be made in terms of either of these sociological alternatives considered separately, but taken together they present the church with this challenge: If the church

---

88. See Alexander, *Civil Sphere*, 293–95, 303–16, 323–33.

89. Alexander, *Civil Sphere*, 49.

90. Turner, "Civil Sphere and Political Performance," 72.

91. Turner, "Civil Sphere and Political Performance," 75.

chooses to enter the public sphere to speak with a public voice, how can it speak with meaning from the particularity of faith to a pluralistic society in terms that are inclusive of all in the society without diluting or abandoning the distinctiveness of its faith perspective? In short, how can the church's distinctive voice be reconciled with its public voice?

First, why can neither sociological alternative (neither Alexander's nor Turner's position) regarding the role of public argument in civil society adequately repudiate or justify the church's presence in the public sphere? Although the church speaks in the public sphere in the form of rational argument, it does not enter the public sphere for the purpose of rational argument (which is Turner's aim), but rather for the purpose of bringing its distinct perspective of faith to bear on matters of public concern. Thus, the presence of the church in the public sphere is based on and motivated by the particularity of its faith commitment. Yet, to speak and act publicly in a pluralistic society, the church can only do so if the distinctiveness of its voice is mediated in and through the cultural meanings and the social and political institutions of the society, which the church can only execute through the means of public argument. But, insofar as its public argument is motivated and informed by the particularity of its faith commitment, the rational form of its argument avoids the abstractness that lacks civil feeling and so undermines the effectiveness of public argument in the service of civil repair; this abstractness and lack of lack of civil feeling in discourse is Alexander's concern. Thus, the church's voice in the public sphere has the ability to circumvent the impasse represented by the views of Alexander and Turner regarding the role of public argument in civil society because the church's use of public argument is distinguishable from both sociological views. Neither particularity (faith), nor universality (reason) alone can adequately portray the church's public voice; both are necessary, and both are represented when the church speaks in the public sphere.[92] Nevertheless, the dispute between these sociologists over the legitimacy of public argument in civil society presents the church with the challenge, should it choose to enter the public sphere, to demonstrate how the particularity of faith can be represented meaningfully in the form of rational argument in a pluralistic society.

The Catholic moral theologian Charles Curran, commenting on the bishops' pastoral letter on the US economy, points to two presuppositions that govern the methodology of the pastoral letter, both of which guide the church in its mission to speak with a public voice in universal, moral terms, yet from the perspective of faith. The first presupposition affirms the need for faith to be mediated through the human. "The gospel does not provide a shortcut that avoids the human and supplies direct and easy answers to complex social problems. The gospel must be mediated in and through the human, human experience and the human sciences." Thus, Christian love, which is the heart of the gospel, "can and should become incarnate in the complex issues of economic structures and policies, but only in and through the human, with all the

92. See Fiorenza, "Church as a Community of Interpretation," 78–81.

limitations of the human as such."[93] The second presupposition concerns the fact that the pastoral letter on the economy, like the pastoral letter on peace, addresses two audiences: both the Catholic community of faith and the wider US society. Presupposed in the bishops' decision to speak to two audiences is an understanding of the moral order as one, not two. There are not two distinct moral orders, one specifically Christian and another that concerns all others outside the Christian community. As citizens, we are bound together by one social moral order. Thus, "that there is only one social moral order common to Christians and all others furnishes a strong theoretical basis for the fact that the pastoral letter can address two different audiences at the same time without involving itself in any inherent contradictions," states Curran.[94]

The first presupposition raises this question: If faith is mediated through the human, how precisely does Christian faith (more specifically, Christian love) "become incarnate" in the economic and political institutions and public policies of a liberal democracy? The second presupposition raises a different but related question: If public argument, whether by the church or other civil associations, presupposes one social moral order, what of significance can the church's voice, if it speaks from the distinctiveness of its faith perspective, contribute to public debate? Each question will be addressed in turn in the chapters that follow: the first question in Chapter 3 and the second in Chapter 4. Both questions imply a more basic question to be addressed now by way of conclusion: that the church enters the public sphere to speak to matters of social and political concern, to the wider society why should this matter?

Yet From the Perspective of Transcendence

The philosopher Charles Taylor opens his study of the secular age with this question: "why was it virtually impossible not to believe in God in, say, 1500 in our Western society, while in 2000 many of us find this not only easy, but even inescapable?"[95] As a way to highlight what it means to live in the secular age, Taylor's question focuses our attention, not on the functional differentiation of the secular spheres (government, the economy, and science) from the sphere of religion, which took place in the transition from the medieval to the modern world (as Casanova does), but on the change in the "conditions of belief" that occurred between these two eras. Whereas belief in God in the medieval period was accepted virtually by all in the society and therefore was unproblematic, in the modern period belief in God involves a choice—belief has become one option among other possible options as a way to give meaning to personal existence, society, and the cosmos—and consequently has become an option that is open to question. Being an option, belief in God is professed within a shared context of meanings with other options, notably the option of unbelief. Taylor's question does

93. Curran, "Relating Religious-Ethical Inquiry to Economic Policy," 44.

94. Curran, "Relating Religious-Ethical Inquiry to Economic Policy," 45–46.

95. Taylor, *Secular Age*, 25.

not focus on religious belief as such or explicitly on the distinction between belief and unbelief as competing theories, but rather on our experience of living in a world in which belief and unbelief are possible options. This lived experience provides the context or frame that forms the background of modern-day assertions of belief and unbelief, a context of understanding that is constituted of scientific, technological, and social meanings that enables Western modernity to understand and engage the world on purely immanent terms without reference to the supernatural. This background framework, shared by all in the West, believer and unbeliever alike, Taylor terms "the immanent frame."[96]

That the immanent frame provides the basis for a self-sufficient humanism that shapes the secular age, which Taylor terms "exclusive humanism," does not preclude the possibility of seeing or living within the immanent frame with a different viewpoint. Taylor proposes that the immanent frame can be understood as either "closed" or "open" to the transcendent. To maintain that self-sufficient humanism is the inevitable and exclusive outcome of this secular age is not a statement of fact, but a construal of the immanent frame as closed (this act of interpretation Taylor describes as "spin"). Here human "fullness" (human flourishing) is understood and sought after in purely immanent terms. On the other hand, seeing the immanent frame as open to the divine, that human fullness is envisioned most properly in terms of that which transcends it, Taylor finds to be equally valid, but also the result of spin (interpretation). Both readings of the immanent frame—closed and open—involve a "leap of faith," meaning that each reading presupposes an overall interpretation of human life and its place in the world that leaps ahead of whatever evidence or reasons we might give to justify our interpretation. Thus, each reading functions like a hunch, an intuitive sense of the whole. What distinguishes one reading from the other is whether the ground for our "anticipatory confidence"—the vision of human fullness that stands beyond but interprets and shapes our lived experience in the immanent frame—lies ultimately in worldly immanence or in divine transcendence.[97]

For Jeffrey Alexander, the idea of civil society stands beyond the contradictions and fragmentations within civil society and, as an ideal, guides and motivates the work of civil repair. "The idea of civil society is transcendental," he states: "Its discourse and institutions always reach beyond the here and now, ready to provide an antidote to every divisive institution, every unfair distribution, every abusive and dominating hierarchy."[98] The transcendental nature of this idea—its anticipatory confidence—functions wholly within an immanent context that Alexander sees as closed to the divine, and thus is the product of what he terms "a secular faith." The civil sphere "relies on solidarity, on feelings for others whom we do not know but whom

96. Taylor, *Secular Age*, 3–22, 542–51, 594.
97. Taylor, *Secular Age*, 4–20, 544–51.
98. Alexander, *Civil Sphere*, 9.

we respect out of principle, not experience, because of our putative commitment to a common secular faith."[99]

The US Catholic bishops through the teachings of the pastoral letters likewise engage in the work of civil repair, but, unlike Alexander, they approach this task from the perspective of transcendence. In the pastoral letter on the economy, for example, they state: "The basis for all that the Church believes about the moral dimensions of economic life is its vision of the transcendent worth—the sacredness—of human beings. *The dignity of the human person, realized in community with others, is the criterion against which all aspects of economic life must be measured.*" The belief that envisions the sacred worth of all human beings provides the bishops with the distinctive viewpoint by which they see and evaluate the economic arrangements of the day. "For that is what human beings are: we are created in the image of God (Gn 1:27)," they emphasize: "All human beings, therefore, are ends to be served by the institutions that make up the economy, not means to be exploited for more narrowly defined goals."[100]

Moreover, that the bishops see the sacred worth of the human person as "realized in community with others" points to a firmly held conviction on their part that being a person is to be in relation with other persons. Echoing Aristotle, they affirm that human beings are by nature social animals "made for friendship, community, and public life," that human fullness is realized "not in isolation, but in interaction with others." But to Aristotle's view of becoming a person in and through community, the bishops bring this distinctive light: "Indeed Christian theological reflection on the very reality of God as a trinitarian unity of persons—Father, Son, and Holy Spirit—shows that being a person means being united to other persons in mutual love." The bishops envision the triune unity of God as the model of solidarity that is the ideal of human community and judge the economic institutions that shape the life of society in the light of this vision of "social friendship and civic commitment that make human moral and economic life possible."[101] The bishops stand within the immanent frame and address matters of the economy in the context of the immanent frame, but they do so from a decidedly distinct perspective—the perspective of trinitarian faith.

Both the sociologist Alexander and the US Catholic bishops engage in a normative (moral) consideration of society from within the context of the immanent frame, yet from distinctively different viewpoints: Alexander from the perspective of closed immanence, the bishops from the perspective of openness to divine transcendence. That the bishops in their pastoral letters address both the Catholic community and the wider US society regarding issues of common concern, yet from the viewpoint of transcendence, raises this question: Why to the wider diverse society should the church's public voice, speaking from this distinctive viewpoint, matter? A viewpoint is a standpoint. Where we are standing, the place from which we view an object,

---

99. Alexander, *Civil Sphere*, 4.

100. National Conference of Catholic Bishops, *Economic Justice for All*, no. 28.

101. National Conference of Catholic Bishops, *Economic Justice for All*, nos. 64–66.

determines what we see. The significance of the church's viewpoint, not only for the Catholic faithful but also for the whole of society, lies precisely in what this viewpoint enables us as a society to see regarding matters of social and political concern that involve the whole of society—this in comparison with other viewpoints which do the same. The more distinctive the viewpoint the greater is its ability to shine a light on, and thereby let us see, what other viewpoints cannot. The goal of this study, then, is to demonstrate that the viewpoint of Catholic social teaching brings a light to bear on the social and political concerns of the whole of society that is distinctive to the faith community and at the same time illuminative of the whole for all who make up the whole, and thus able to contribute to the good of the whole.

OF CATHOLIC SOCIAL TEACHING

Where the church as an institution stands in society when it speaks to matters of social and political concern is civil society. *How* the church as teacher and pastor speaks in a pluralistic society with a public voice that has both legitimacy and meaning is in the spirit of dialogue. *What* the church says when it addresses matters of public concern is determined by the viewpoint that it brings to bear on these public matters.

What in essence is this viewpoint? The basic content of the church's viewpoint, the distinctive light that it brings to bear on present-day social concerns, is established in the modern era, first of all, in the tradition of papal encyclicals that specifically address the social questions of their day, beginning in 1891 with Pope Leo XIII's encyclical *Rerum novarum* (*The Condition of Labor*) and continuing to the present, represented by the encyclical *Laudato si'* (*On Care for our Common Home*) issued by Pope Francis in 2015. In addition to this tradition of social encyclicals, the church's viewpoint on social issues finds expression in other types of papal documents, such as Pope Paul VI's apostolic letter *Octogesima adveniens* (*A Call to Action*) and his apostolic exhortation *Evangelii nuntiandi* (*Evangelization in the Modern World*), issued in 1971 and 1975 respectively, and in the conciliar documents of Vatican II, particularly *Gaudium et spes* (*Pastoral Constitution on the Church in the Modern World*) and *Dignitatis humanae* (*Declaration on Religious Freedom*), issued in 1965. Furthermore, the church's authoritative teaching regarding the social issues of the day comes from international, regional, and national conferences of Catholic bishops: for example, from the international synod of bishops in 1971, which published *Justitia in mundo* (*Justice in the World*), from the regional conferences of Latin American bishops held in Medellin, Colombia (1968), and Puebla, Mexico (1979), which issued the documents that chart the social mission of the church in Latin America, particularly with regard to the poor, and from the NCCB in the United States, which published the pastoral letters on peace and the US economy in 1983 and 1986 respectively.

This tradition of papal, conciliar, and episcopal documents that addresses the social issues of the day—a tradition that extends over more than a century—represents the hierarchical, authoritative voice of the Roman Catholic Church. The architects as well as the interpreters of this tradition refer to it variously with the term "Catholic social teaching" or "Catholic social doctrine." The terms, while presently used interchangeably, point to different historical periods within this tradition as well as to the different purposes for which the terms are used.

"Social doctrine" is the appropriate term to describe the church's official pronouncements on social matters prior to Vatican II. Here the term points to the authoritative pronouncements made by the popes, stated in the form of an encyclical (a pastoral letter, written in Latin, addressed to all the bishops of the Catholic Church), which functions as instruction and application regarding the faith of the church concerning social issues. The methodology used by Pope Leo XIII in his social encyclical and later in the social encyclicals of Pope Pius XI and Pope John XXIII, was deductive and ahistorical—beginning with universal, timeless moral truths that are derived from "natural law" (the ability of human reason to perceive God's eternal law in the order and purposes of nature). These universal truths are then applied to specific social questions.[102] For example, with regard to the right to private property, Pope Leo states in *Rerum novarum*: "For it is a most sacred law of nature that a father must provide food and all necessaries for those whom he has begotten; and, similarly, nature dictates that a man's children, who carry on, as it were, and continue his own personality, should be provided by him with all that is needful to enable them honorably to keep themselves from want and misery in the uncertainties of this mortal life." Then, by way of inference, Leo concludes (with the intent to refute the doctrine of state socialism): "Now, in no other way can a father effect this except by the ownership of profitable property, which he can transmit to his children by inheritance."[103] Insofar as the term "Catholic social doctrine" refers to the authoritative statement of a moral truth by the papal teaching office that is presented to the worldwide Catholic Church as a universal and immutable truth to be applied to society, the term aptly pertains to the pre–Vatican II social encyclicals.

The term "Catholic social teaching," on the other hand, while being etymologically equivalent in meaning to social doctrine (the Latin word *doctrina* means teaching), presently carries a different connotation: teaching requires engagement (in contrast to authoritative pronouncement), which entails dialogue that involves both listening and speaking, as well as adaptability that demands attention to the needs of different interlocutors and to different historical situations. In the documents of Vatican II Charles Curran sees a methodology at work that is markedly different from the methodology employed in the early social encyclicals. *Gaudium et spes* begins, not with timeless truths, but with "the responsibility of reading the signs of the times and of interpreting them in the light of the Gospel" (no. 4). The methodology of *Gaudium*

102. Curran, *Catholic Social Teaching 1891–Present*, 54–58, 104–5. See also Curran, *Development of Moral Theology*, 192–94.

103. Pope Leo XIII, *Rerum novarum* (*The Condition of Labor*), no. 10.

et spes is inductive and historical—beginning with historically determined characteristics of the modern world (the signs of the times) and then responding in the light of faith. "For faith casts a new light on everything and makes known the full ideal which God has set for humanity, thus guiding the mind towards solutions that are fully human" (no. 11), states the Council. The approach that Vatican II initiates and that subsequent popes and episcopal conferences continue (the pastoral letters of the US bishops being a prime example) is an approach to the social issues of the day from the bottom up rather than from the top down, the method that marks the pre–Vatican II social encyclicals. Curran points to the apostolic letter *Octogesima adveniens* (*A Call to Action*) of Pope Paul VI, issued in 1971 following the Council, as a distinctive instance of this change of approach.[104] Acknowledging the wide diversity of situations in which Christians find themselves throughout the world, Pope Paul states: "In the face of such widely varying situations it is difficult for us to utter a unified message and to put forward a solution which has universal validity." Rather, the task of discernment begins with the particular Christian community, facing its specific situation, to which it brings the light of the gospel and the "principles of reflection, norms of judgment and directives for action from the social teaching of the Church."[105] Catholic social teaching, then, is an apt term to describe the Catholic Church's pastoral engagement with the modern world regarding matters of common social and political concern, the term that has generally been used since Vatican II, and the term that for the most part will be used in this study to refer to the Catholic Church's authoritative statements regarding the social issues of the modern day.

Pope John Paul II noticeably brought the term "social doctrine" back into use to depict the church's social teaching, this first in the opening address that he gave to the episcopal conference at Puebla in 1979, and then later in his social encyclicals *Sollicitudo rei socialis* (*On Social Concern*) and *Centesimus annus* (*On the Hundredth Anniversary of "Rerum novarum"*), which were published in 1987 and 1991 respectively. His purpose, however, was not to restore the original, pre–Vatican II meaning and use of the term. Indeed, Catholic theologian Donal Dorr observes: "John Paul's reinstatement of this term was a highly nuanced one, which effectively purged it of the overtones of monolithic dogmatism."[106] First of all, in these texts John Paul uses "social doctrine" interchangeably with "social teaching."[107] Furthermore, insofar as the term "social doctrine" carries the connotation of authority and immutability and reflects the unity of the church, use of the term provides an advantage in particular

---

104. Curran, *Catholic Social Teaching 1891–Present*, 58–61.

105. Pope Paul VI, *Octogesima adveniens (A Call to Action)*, no. 4.

106. Dorr, *Option for the Poor and for the Earth*, 460; see also 220–23.

107. See, for example, John Paul II, "Opening Address at the Puebla Conference," III, 7. John Paul II, *Sollicitudo rei socialis (On Social Concern)*, nos. 1–3. John Paul II, *Centesimus annus (On the Hundredth Anniversary of Rerum novarum)*, no. 2.

situations.[108] For example, in *Sollicitudo rei socialis* John Paul confronts the challenge of what he saw to be the competing ideologies of his day—liberal capitalism and Marxist collectivism—not with another ideology (that is, with an alternative model of society) but with a moral truth that is "the accurate formulation of the results of a careful reflection on the complex realities of human existence, in society and in the international order, in the light of faith and of the church's tradition" (no. 41). That in John Paul's hands this moral truth—the virtue of solidarity (nos. 39–40)—is presented as social doctrine enables him to offer it to the world authoritatively as a truth, affirmed by the whole of the church, that is "constant" (perennial), yet when brought to bear on a specific, historical situation, "ever new" (no. 3).

"Catholic social thought" is one other term that is used to refer to the means through which the church engages the world in its teaching mission. The term is more expansive than either social doctrine or social teaching when these terms are used to refer to the church's official statements regarding social issues. Catholic ethicist Marvin Mich points out that if we limit our discussion of the church's engagement with social issues solely to the official documents of the church, "we are only telling half of the story."[109] The other half of the story can be found in Catholic social movements that activate the awareness and concern that shape the church's official social documents as well as in the social movements that these documents spawn, which then give life in concrete ways to the church's official teaching. For example, Leo's *Rerum novarum* represents the ultramontane church: Ecclesial authority is centralized in the papacy in contrast to the collegiality established by Vatican II whereby ecclesial authority is shared by the pope and the church's bishops. So the social teaching of *Rerum novarum* was promulgated from the top down, but the encyclical was nevertheless influenced by and in its writing reflects the concerns of two social movements that emerged in the second half of the nineteenth century. The first originated in Germany, inspired by the preaching and writing of Archbishop Wilhelm Emmanuel von Ketteler of Mainz on "the social question"—the growing disparity between wealth and poverty in Germany as a result of the Industrial Revolution—which generated the social movement referred to as "social Catholicism" that spread throughout Western Europe. The second movement that influenced *Rerum novarum* took place in the United States, also in response to the rise of nineteenth-century industrial capitalism: It involved the first US labor union open to all workers—the Knights of Labor—which included a sizable portion of working-class Catholics. At first repudiated by some Catholic bishops in Canada and the United States for fear of socialism that they thought the union might represent, this labor movement gained a strong defender in Cardinal James Gibbons of Baltimore, who brought his argument in support of the union to Rome, which resulted in the union being officially "tolerated" by the Vatican, but then receiving widespread support by the church in the United States. When in 1891 Pope

108. Dorr, *Option for the Poor and for the Earth*, 221.

109. Mich, *Catholic Social Teaching and Movements*, 3.

Leo addresses "the condition of labor" in the world in *Rerum novarum*, both of these social movements are clearly present in his writing. The meaning of his words cannot be fully understood outside of this context "from below."[110]

Moreover, not only did prior social movements and their thinkers and activists shape Leo's words, but the writing of *Rerum novarum* in turn provoked subsequent social movements that embodied and gave concrete interpretation to the moral vision of the encyclical in ways that Leo neither intended nor anticipated. In the judgment of sociologist and Catholic peace activist Gordon Zahn, "This unanticipated extension of papal social thought turned out to be the major and most lasting contribution of *Rerum Novarum*."[111] By legitimizing criticism of the present social order through papal approval and offering moral justification for efforts on the part of Catholics to undertake social reform, Leo's encyclical became the seedbed for future Catholic social movements. Herein lies its place of honor as the first of the modern-day social encyclicals of the church.[112] But, precisely because the significance of Leo's encyclical cannot be understood apart from the social movements that inspired it and those that it spawned, the tradition that constitutes the church's social engagement in the world, the tradition that begins with Pope Leo and continues, not only in the papal social encyclicals that follow, but also in the social movements, the theological interpretations, and the pastoral applications that enable these papal documents to live and speak in the present—this tradition must be viewed as a whole. The Catholic theologian Johan Verstraeten underscores this point. We cannot separate papal teaching from this tradition of interpretation without distorting both: "they are both part of the same tradition of reflection and practice." By holding the official documents and their theological and pastoral interpretation together as one tradition, the church maintains the tradition of social Catholicism "as a living tradition," one that "goes beyond fidelity to the past and opens out to the future."[113] The all-encompassing nature of this tradition is aptly described with the term "Catholic social thought."

"But do the encyclical teachings of the Roman Catholic papacy form a coherent social ethic?" The Catholic theologian Michael Schuck asks this question at the conclusion of his comprehensive presentation of the papal encyclical tradition.[114] At first look, his account of the papal encyclical tradition that begins distinctively not with Pope Leo but with the encyclicals of Pope Benedict XIV, the first published in 1740, might suggest that the answer to his question is no. His overview of this tradition shows an eclectic use of sources and methods by the popes in writing the encyclicals as well as contradictions in the social teachings of the encyclicals that are substantive,

110. Mich, *Catholic Social Teaching and Movements*, 5–60.

111. Zahn, "Social Movements and Catholic Social Thought," 50.

112. Zahn, "Social Movements and Catholic Social Thought," 43–54. See also Mich, *Catholic Social Teaching and Movements*, 26–27.

113. Verstraeten, "Re-Thinking Catholic Social Thought as Tradition," 63, 65.

114. Schuck, *That They Be One*, 173.

not easily attributed to different historical contexts. But, the closer look that Schuck provides of this tradition reveals a coherent social ethic directing the encyclical tradition that is rooted both in an enduring critique of and a moral vision for the modern world, this insight being the benefit of starting his survey of papal encyclicals in the historical period prior to Leo XIII, the period that begins in the eighteenth century during the European Enlightenment.[115] Moreover, despite the significant theological differences that are represented in the wider tradition of modern Catholic social thought, Schuck maintains that the coherent social ethic that can be found in the encyclical tradition serves as the basis of unity in this wider tradition of Catholic social thought as well.[116] When the tradition of social Catholicism is viewed as a whole, what is it that enables this tradition to be seen as a coherent whole?

The first papal encyclicals, beginning in 1740, engage in a critical assessment of the Enlightenment, particularly the philosophical articulations of the seventeenth and eighteenth centuries that envision the foundation of society in terms of a social contract—this contract, in the words of the British philosopher John Locke in 1690, being the mutual consent of individuals who are "by nature, all free, equal and independent" yet willing to divest themselves of this natural freedom and put on "the bonds of civil society" through an agreement with others "to join and unite into a community, for their comfortable, safe, and peaceable living one amongst another, in a secure enjoyment of their properties, and a greater security against any that are not of it."[117] By contrast, the moral vision that guides the early papal encyclicals sees the human person not as independent but as interdependent by nature. Society, in this view, is not the product of a social agreement, but the outcome of fostering human relations of interdependence. Here, not consent, but mutuality is the basis of community. This moral vision, according to Schuck, which functions as a source of both social critique and moral guidance for social relations, runs through the whole of the papal encyclical tradition: "encyclical social teaching coheres around a theologically inspired communitarian ethic which has, since the eighteenth century, yielded an enduring cluster of shared, double-pulsed insights on human relations in society"[118]—double-pulsed in the sense that this communitarian ethic, when applied to Western democracies, both challenges the individualism that results from seeing society as a social contract and provides a moral view of society that envisions human flourishing in terms of a web of interdependent social relations. This communitarian moral vision, in Schuck's view, forms the coherent social ethic that runs through the variegated whole of social Catholicism. This communitarian vision, he asserts, "represents a 'tradition,' not simply of texts, but argument."[119]

115. Schuck, *That They Be One*, 180–88, 191–93.

116. Schuck, "Modern Catholic Social Thought," 629–31.

117. Locke, *The Second Treatise of Government* 8.95.

118. Schuck, *That They Be One*, 187.

119. Schuck, *That They Be One*, 188.

Charles Curran would agree. He states that the tradition of Catholic social teaching (his study begins with Pope Leo) "rests on two fundamental anthropological principles: the dignity or sacredness of the human person and the social nature of the person."[120] In the eyes of Christian faith, Curran emphasizes, the dignity of the human person comes not from human accomplishment but as God's free gift equally given to all. Herein lies our intrinsic worth as persons. We all are created in the image of God. This sacred image held by each person is realized not apart from human community but in and through the social relations that make up community. Being in relation with one another in society is not an addition to but rather an essential aspect of being human. We as persons are by nature social and communitarian. For the eyes of faith, being in communion with one another in society is to be the image of the one God who is the communion of three persons—Father, Son, and Holy Spirit—in mutual love. In the light of Christian faith, the triune unity of God is held as the supreme model of community. For Curran, as for Schuck, this theologically founded communitarian vision of Catholic social teaching runs through the whole of the papal encyclicals, providing both a distinctive anthropological basis for understanding the social, economic, and political institutions that constitute society as well as the means to critically engage these social institutions. Thus, in response to the culture of individualism that is fostered by capitalist markets and political partisanship, Catholic social teaching specifically brings to light the communitarian nature of the human person; in response to all forms of social and political collectivism, Catholic social teaching highlights its unconditional affirmation of the intrinsic worth of each individual person. Both principles—the intrinsic dignity of the human person and the social nature of being human—together form a coherent moral vision that gives unity to the tradition of social Catholicism. The fulfillment of the individual human person can only be achieved in and through relations of reciprocity in society. Such social reciprocity can only be maintained when each individual person in the society possesses equal respect in these social relations.[121] As a way to capture the coherence of these principles in a phrase, the Jesuit theologian John Coleman describes the anthropological core of this tradition as "communitarian liberalism."[122]

This communitarian moral vision, then, constitutes in essence the viewpoint of Catholic social teaching. As a distinct way of seeing and evaluating the social, economic, and political institutions of the modern world, this communitarian vision provides the unifying focus to the church's engagement with specific issues of public moral concern. We saw above, for example, that the criterion used by the US Catholic bishops to measure the US economy is *the dignity of the human person, realized in*

---

120. Curran, *Catholic Social Teaching 1891–Present*, 131.

121. Curran, *Catholic Social Teaching 1891–Present*, 131–36.

122. Coleman, SJ, "Future of Catholic Social Thought," 527. See also Coleman, SJ, "Retrieving or Re-Inventing Social Catholicism," 273.

community with others."[123] That this communitarian vision is the unifying focus of Catholic social thought, Schuck observes, "explains why Catholic social thinkers as a whole have retained a distinct understanding of freedom, equality, rights, and justice in the modern world."[124] Whether the object of study is a social institution such as the economy or moral concepts such as freedom, equality, human rights, and social justice—moral concepts which guide the human actions that create and sustain social institutions—from the perspective of social Catholicism these will be viewed in the distinctive light of this communitarian moral vision. To borrow a metaphor from the Jesuit theologian Roger Haight, "like the lens that draws rays of light to a center, but without blocking any of their light,"[125] this communitarian vision centers the Catholic Church's social teaching regarding disparate social issues and their moral consideration with its unifying focus. Thus, with regard to the question before us in this study as presented in Chapter 1—what is the good of being a community?—we now pursue this question in the light of Catholic social teaching, guided by the communitarian moral vision that centers the official social teaching of the church and informs Catholic social thought.

The Next Step

Pope Leo's *Rerum novarum* represented a significant change in the way that the church responds to human need in society. The church at that time was responding to the growing plight of the working poor (the result of the changing conditions of labor due to the Industrial Revolution) as it had traditionally responded—with direct acts of charity (food, clothing, and shelter). This Leo emphasizes in the encyclical is the proper work of the church (nos. 23–24). But Leo also responds to the plight of the working poor by pointing to the social cause of their poverty—the exploitation of labor by employers—thus presenting the condition of labor at that time as a social issue that is also a moral issue. Gordon Zahn comments: "*Rerum Novarum* goes beyond charity, however, in demonstrating its concern for labor (which, remember, to Leo was virtually interchangeable with 'poor') and speaks instead of *rights*. Its argument, while it certainly does not ignore charitable appeals to consider the worker and his spiritual and physical welfare, is based on a carefully elaborated development of the demands of justice and recognition of the essential equality of all in God."[126] In the section entitled "Just Wages," for example, Leo acknowledges that the relation between worker and employer—this particularly with regard to wages—is based in a capitalist economy on the free agreement that is made between them. But, then, Leo adds this: "There is a dictate of nature more imperious and more ancient than any

123. National Conference of Catholic Bishops, *Economic Justice for All*, no. 28.

124. Schuck, "Modern Catholic Social Thought," 631.

125. Haight, SJ, *Alternative Vision*, 53.

126. Zahn, "Social Movements and Catholic Social Thought," 51.

bargain between man and man, that the remuneration must be enough to support the wage earner in reasonable and frugal comfort. If through necessity or fear of a worse evil, the workman accepts harder conditions because an employer or contractor will give him no better, he is the victim of force and injustice."[127] Leo, moreover, not only points to adequate wages as the necessary requirement for justice in the workplace, but he also proposes a means for achieving justice in the workplace through the establishment of "workmen's associations" to promote the interests of workers, which he emphasizes as being a natural right of workers that must be protected by the state (nos. 36–38). What is new in *Rerum novarum* is Leo's insistence that besides attending to the immediate needs of the poor through works of charity, the church must further attend to the needs of the poor by addressing the social causes of poverty and by facilitating its eradication through social reform. What Leo initiates is a vision of the church's mission in the modern world that goes beyond the works of charity to include the works of justice, this particularly on behalf of the poor.

The tradition of social Catholicism in the modern era has carried forward what Leo began, but especially since Vatican II this tradition has presented the social mission of the church in far more decisive and bold ways than Leo had. *Justitia in mundo* (*Justice in the World*), the document published by the Synod of Bishops in 1971, provides a striking example. The introduction to *Justitia in mundo* concludes with this statement: "Action on behalf of justice and participation in the transformation of the world fully appear to us as a constitutive dimension of the preaching of the Gospel, or, in other words, of the Church's mission for the redemption of the human race and its liberation from every oppressive situation."[128] The key word in this statement, the one that is interpretive of the whole, is "constitutive." Here "action on behalf of justice" is not understood as an ethical corollary to the gospel, nor is it seen as one practical option among others (social activism rather than spiritual renewal) regarding the church's mission. Works of justice are an essential aspect of the proclamation and enactment of the gospel in the world, the bishops assert, and thus they are central to the mission of the church. Whereas Leo had based his argument for justice in the workplace on the natural law, thus giving his argument for the works of justice a rational foundation distinct from the gospel and from the works of charity that are called for by the gospel, *Justitia in mundo* maintains that the works of justice are "a constitutive dimension" of the gospel, thus making "the Church's mission for the redemption of the human race and its liberation from every oppressive situation" aspects of one and the same mission of the church—the mission to proclaim the gospel to the world that includes "participation in the transformation of the world." The bishops of the 1971 Synod took a decisive step beyond the social teachings of the pre–Vatican II documents and put in place the thesis that would shape future Catholic social teaching:

127. Leo XIII, *Rerum novarum* (*The Condition of Labor*), no. 34.
128. Synod of Bishops, *Justitia in mundo* (*Justice in the World*), no. 6.

the works of Christian charity and the works of social justice form one evangelizing mission of the church in the world.[129]

The theological justification that the Synod offers for this thesis comes in chapter 2 of the document, titled "The Gospel Message and the Mission of the Church." In the light of the gospel, we see our relations with one another in society as bound up with our relation with God, so that our response as a faith community to God's love, manifested in the redeeming acts of Jesus Christ, in order to be effectively realized by us in society, requires on our part concrete acts in which we love our neighbor. For this reason, the Synod states: "Christian love of neighbor and justice cannot be separated. For love implies an absolute demand for justice, namely a recognition of the dignity and rights of one's neighbor. Justice attains its inner fullness only in love."[130] Love and justice need each other. Love needs justice to be concretely realized in society. Justice needs love as both motivation and meaning for achieving its ultimate purpose, which is to realize genuine communion in society. A community without justice disintegrates. Justice is the foundation of community; the foundation of justice is love. But, in the context of a pluralistic society, the challenge to the Synod's assertion that Christian love and justice as realized in society are inseparable presents itself in this question: How can Christian love, given its distinctive particularity, be embodied in and expressed through the institutional forms of justice that structure the whole of society? To respond to this question, we must first give an account of justice as the moral norm both of the social institutions that make up society and of the human actions that create and sustain these institutions as just institutions. Christian love requires justice to be concrete. Thus, to adequately respond to the question concerning the relation between Christian love and justice in society, we must first determine this: what is social justice? This is the next step.

---

129. See Hamel, "*Justice in the World*," 496–97. Himes, OFM, "Commentary on *Justitia in mundo (Justice in the World)*," 341–42, 345–46, 352–55. Dorr, *Option for the Poor and for the Earth*, 190–94.

130. Synod of Bishops, *Justitia in mundo (Justice in the World)*, no. 34.

Chapter 3

What Is Social Justice?

The Object of Study: Social Institutions and Moral Actions

SOCIAL INSTITUTIONS

When Love Is Insufficient

At the heart of the gospel resides love—both as the revelation of God's love for us, manifested in the words and actions of Jesus the Christ, and as the call to us, the faith community, to respond to this divine love in joy and gratitude by loving God and loving one another in return. The Greek word that the New Testament uses to name this divine and human love is *agapē*. The moral life of the Christian derives its meaning and motivation from this love. *Agapē* provides both the light by which the Christian sees and interprets the moral demands of daily living and the strength to respond to these demands. But the moral demands of life require specific responses that aim at bringing about specific outcomes, and thus *agapē*, in order to be effective, must become concrete, which means that *agapē* must actively engage the world in all its complexity and on its own terms. The parable of the good Samaritan in the Gospel of Luke (10:25–37) well illustrates the meaning and motivation that *agapē* brings to moral encounters as well as demonstrates the need for concreteness if *agapē* is to be effectively realized.

The parable is introduced with a dialogue that takes place between a learned interpreter of the Jewish law and Jesus (Luke 10:25–28). The lawyer asks Jesus: "what shall I do to inherit eternal life?" Jesus asks him in return: "What is written in the law?" The lawyer responds: "You shall love the Lord your God with all your heart, and with all your soul, and with all your strength, and with all your mind; and your neighbor as yourself." In response to the lawyer's answer, Jesus concludes: "You have answered right; do this, and you shall live."[1]

But then the lawyer presents Jesus with a second question: "And who is my neighbor?" This question elicits from Jesus a reply that includes the telling of the parable (Luke 10:29–37). The lawyer's second question most likely had a legal intent. The book of Leviticus enjoins the people of Israel to love their neighbor (19:18): "You shall not take vengeance or bear any grudge against the sons of your own people, but you shall love your neighbor as yourself: I am the LORD"; then further on, Leviticus adds this stipulation (19:34): "The stranger who sojourns with you shall be to you as the native among you, and you shall love him as yourself; for you were strangers in the land of Egypt: I am the LORD your God." The lawyer was not seeking from Jesus a definition of neighbor but rather a determination of the extent of the duty to love others in the society, particularly non-Jews.[2] In the telling of the parable, Jesus does not respond to the lawyer's question regarding who is to be included in the command to love your neighbor; instead Jesus presents a striking illustration of what being a neighbor entails, which is loving the other through acts of charity, regardless of their identity and in spite of the lack of any social bond such as nationality or religion. Through acts of love the stranger (here the Samaritan) becomes a neighbor. The parable is not about determining who is our neighbor, but about the love that makes us a neighbor. Thus, the question that Jesus answers by means of the parable is not the lawyer's second question, but the first: "What shall I do to inherit eternal life?" Jesus' reply and the lawyer's acquiescent response to Jesus' question to him at the end of the parable present us with the answer to this first question—a paradigmatic portrait of what *agapē* requires:[3]

> A man was going down from Jerusalem to Jericho, and he fell among robbers, who stripped him and beat him, and departed, leaving him half dead. Now by chance a priest was going down that road; and when he saw him he passed by on the other side. So likewise a Levite, when he came to the place and saw him, passed by on the other side. But a Samaritan, as he journeyed, came to where he was; and when he saw him, he had compassion, and went to him and bound up his wounds, pouring on oil and wine; then he set him on his own beast and brought him to an inn, and took care of him. And the next day he took two denarii and gave them to the innkeeper, saying, "Take care of him; and whatever more you spend, I will repay you when I come back." Which of these three, do you think, proved neighbor to the man who fell among robbers? He said, "The one who showed mercy on him." And Jesus said to him, "Go and do likewise." (Luke 10:30–37)

1. All biblical quotations are from *The New Oxford Annotated Bible: Revised Standard Version*.

2. Jeremias, *Parables of Jesus*, 202–3.

3. Spicq, OP, *Agape in the Synoptic Gospels*, 110–12.

The Samaritan stands at the center of the parable as a disrupter to the flow of the narrative. That a traveler would be robbed and beaten on the road between Jerusalem and Jericho was not unusual. Travel on that road at that time was dangerous. That a priest (a religious leader of the Jews) and a Levite (one who assists in the temple) would be traveling on that road would not be unusual—Jerusalem was the site of the temple and Jericho was a priestly city. That both the priest and the Levite would pass by the victim, moving to the other side of the road, would not have been unusual, if their reason for doing so was to avoid coming in contact with what appeared to be a dead body, which would render them ritually unclean. The flow of the narrative would have continued uninterrupted if the third passerby had been, say, an Israelite (a Jewish layperson), thus rounding out the sectors of Jewish society. But, the third traveler to come upon the victim is a Samaritan, one who was despised by the Jews in much the same way that the Samaritans despised the Jews. The Samaritan's response to the victim disrupts the flow of the narrative: a priest sees and passes by; a Levite sees and passes by; the Samaritan sees and has compassion for the victim. Thus he stops. What did the Samaritan see? The victim had been robbed and beaten, and also stripped of his clothing. The victim's clothing would have indicated something of his identity—his social status, his nationality, his religion. But his clothing too had been taken. What the Samaritan sees is a person in need, only this. In his response to the sight of this human need lies his compassion.[4]

But, the Samaritan's compassion requires tangible steps to be taken to have an effect. The Samaritan dresses the victim's wounds and then brings him to an inn and there stays with him and cares for him. On the following day, the Samaritan pays the innkeeper to care for the victim and negotiates with him further payment if necessary, giving the innkeeper the assurance that he will return. The Jesuit New Testament scholar John Donahue emphasizes that this final action on the part of the Samaritan—bringing the victim to an inn, paying for his care, negotiating with the innkeeper—should not be seen as simply an epilogue to the narrative or as an expression of supererogation (an excess of charity). The final action taken by the Samaritan is an indispensable step to realizing concretely the meaning and the outcome of the narrative. To leave the victim who had lost everything with a debt that he could not pay would have resulted in his enslavement until he was able to pay off the debt. The Samaritan's payment and promise to pay further ensures the victim's freedom when he recovers. Donahue observes: "It is not enough simply to enter the world of the neighbor with care and compassion; one must enter and leave it in such a way that the neighbor is given freedom along with the very help that is offered."[5] The full recovery of the victim requires physical healing but also the ability of the victim to reestablish his place in society. The Samaritan's compassion leads him to care for the victim, but also to take into account and to meet the conditions necessary for the victim's full

4. Donahue, SJ, *Gospel in Parable*, 129–32.
5. Donahue, SJ, *Gospel in Parable*, 133.

return to society. The parable of the good Samaritan is a narrative of love but also of justice.[6] How so?

The Samaritan's actions on behalf of the victim are spontaneous, immediate, and personal. He is moved to act by his compassion at the sight of the victim, not by external obligation or by self-interest. The well-being of the victim is for him primary. As portrayed in the parable, his actions demonstrate a love that is purely a gift, and thus his actions depict God's love for us as gift. His actions, moreover, show a love that can be described as kindness or tenderness. The lawyer acknowledges this. To Jesus' question regarding which of the three was neighbor to the victim, the lawyer responds: "The one who showed mercy on him" (10:37).[7] But to be effective, the Samaritan's love for the victim must become concrete, which means that this love—intensely personal, wholly spontaneous and immediate to the moment—must also address the social conditions to be met if the victim is to be made whole. Here love encounters the impersonal, public structures of the society. The spontaneous gift of love is offset by the obligation to give to another what is their due. Acts of mercy meet deliberations of fairness. Here the language of love must take on the language of justice, so that the structures of justice might embody the enactments of love. To face adequately the moral challenges that society presents to us, love and justice need each other. In this task they become inseparable allies.

The parable of the good Samaritan is a teaching on discipleship. Jesus' final words to the lawyer are these: "Go and do likewise" (10:37). This parable along with the others that are told by Jesus in what is the central section of Luke's Gospel—the "travel narrative" (9:51—19:27) that recounts Jesus' journey from Galilee to Jerusalem—share this common theme: as Jesus and his disciples make their way to Jerusalem, he instructs them in the way of discipleship.[8] Accordingly, the parable centers on doing: the lawyer asks, "Teacher, what shall I do" (10:25); Jesus responds, "do this, and you will live" (10:28); then, "Go and do likewise" (10:37). Doing, however, implies seeing: what the Samaritan does for the victim is the result of seeing the victim in a distinct light that differs from how the priest and the Levite saw him. The Samaritan sees the victim in the light of his compassion. Donahue notes: "Compassion is the bridge between simply looking on injured and half-dead fellow human beings and entering their world with saving care."[9] How the Samaritan sees the victim gives meaning to his actions; his actions derive their motivation and strength from the light by which he sees.

For Luke, instruction in the way of discipleship involves both learning to see and to act with love, a love modeled on Jesus' love, which is the embodiment of God's love for us. Through the parable we come to see that for Luke what is prescribed in the law—"You shall love the Lord your God . . . and your neighbor as yourself"

---

6. Schubeck, SJ, *Love That Does Justice*, 48.

7. Spicq, OP, *Agape in the Synoptic Gospels*, 115–17.

8. Donahue, SJ, *Gospel in Parable*, 126–28.

9. Donahue, SJ, *Gospel in Parable*, 132.

(10:27)—is one commandment, not two. The one love is not commanded apart from the other; nor can the one love exist separately from the other. Loving God with all your heart takes place in loving your neighbor; loving your neighbor as yourself is the primary act by which you love God. The two loves are one and the same reality.[10] Thus, what Luke teaches us by means of the parable of the good Samaritan is that the way of Christian discipleship is the way of love—*agapē*. But, such love in order to be active and effective in the world requires the work of justice as well, which means that the way of discipleship must also be the way of justice.

In moral encounters in which the call to love our neighbor is immediate and direct, the demands of justice can easily be eclipsed, either because we see the response of love to human need exclusively as gift (charity) and thus as given apart from the obligation to give to another what is their due, or because we see our response wholly in terms of individual responsibility and thus as a moral response taking place outside of social and institutional structures.[11] For example, in a chance face-to-face encounter with a person who is homeless and who is asking for help, our attention is drawn to the immediate need of the person before us and to the specific request being made of us. Not readily apparent to us in the immediacy of this encounter are the social and institutional conditions that are also at work shaping the encounter. Some homelessness is the result of personal failure (such as drug addiction or alcoholism); some homelessness is the result of personal tragedy (such as the loss of employment or mental illness); but all homelessness is the effect of market prices. When rents increase, this particularly in urban areas and as one outcome of the millions of home foreclosures leading up to and following the financial crisis, there are winners and losers: for investors and landlords, profits increase; for low-wage workers and the otherwise poor, an increasingly larger portion of their monthly income goes to pay for rent until this is no longer sustainable. The appropriate word to describe transactions in the housing market, in which some profit largely at the expense of others, in the mind of sociologist Matthew Desmond, is exploitation. "It is a word that speaks to the fact that poverty is not just a product of low incomes. It is also a product of extractive markets."[12] This underlying cause of homelessness, when we are caught face-to-face with its effects, we most likely do not see.

In the moment of the encounter with a person who is homeless, the human need before us calls for a response that is immediate and direct. The gift of love that we freely give in such a moment is necessary, but limited, because in our response to the person in need the market conditions that are shaping the encounter remain unchanged. If we view this face-to-face encounter from a wider perspective, that is, from the perspective of the housing market that rewards some but inflicts harm on

---

10. Rahner, SJ, "Reflections on the Unity of the Love of Neighbor and the Love of God," 231–36, 247–48.

11. See the case studies in Elsbernd, OSF, and Bieringer, *When Love Is Not Enough*, 1–16.

12. Desmond, *Evicted*, 305.

others, we then see the homeless person in a new light—not only as one who is needy but also as one who is the victim of an exploitative market and thus the victim of injustice. In which case, we see our response to the homeless person in a new light as well—as a response not only of love, but also of justice. In this encounter we give to the one who is our neighbor and homeless what is their due, but still we do so in a limited way. In such a moment, as with the good Samaritan, we realize that our act of care and compassion alone is not sufficient. Justice requires more. The wider demands of justice require from us a response that addresses, not only the individual needs of those who suffer injustice, but also the underlying, structural causes of the injustice. Homelessness is not only a personal problem for the one who suffers this; homelessness is also a social problem: one that negatively affects all within the society in some way; one that is rooted in the social institutions that make up the society and in the moral actions that create and sustain these institutions. Because social injustice affects us all, it must be the concern of all within the society. For the Christian to respond effectively to social injustice, that which is most distinctive to the Christian response—*agapē*—must go beyond immediate acts of care and compassion to act on the structural causes of social injustice, this in and through the social institutions of the society. To undertake this task *agapē* requires justice as its ally if *agapē* is to become both concrete and effective.

Social Justice as Just Institutions

Fairness is a norm by which we all live. We may not always treat others fairly and others may act towards us in unfair ways, but whenever unfair acts take place, they evoke from us a response of indignation. "That's not fair," we have uttered on more than a few occasions when we are aware that a wrong has been committed. We expect others to deal fairly with us; we expect from ourselves fair treatment of them.

We have been conducting our lives according to the norm of fairness since we were about seven or eight years old. This was the observation of the child psychologist Jean Piaget. Studying children as they played the game of marbles, he observed that prior to the age of seven the play of children is at first simply psychomotor activity and then the slavish imitation of older children's play. But by the age of seven, a child's cognitive development is such that he or she begins to understand the rules of the game. When this occurs, children's play becomes cooperative, because each child in the game understands the need for all to abide by the rules. With cooperative play comes a sense of fairness—abiding by the rules—and for the first time the games of children become truly social.[13]

Since childhood our sense of fairness has broadened from the games that we played with other children to include all aspects of our relationships with others. These

13. Piaget, *Moral Judgment of the Child*, 42–47; see also 313–25.

relationships range from the most intimate to the societal and global. On a daily basis we interact with others first and foremost in the context of small, intimate groups, namely, our family and circle of close friends, groups that sociologists term primary groups. We also live our daily lives within larger, less intimate groups, referred to by sociologists as associations or secondary groups. These might be the school that one attends, one's place of business, or organizations in which one has membership, such as a club, sports team, church, or civic group. We have a relationship with others, moreover, in contexts much larger than these two spheres: Our local community and our society and its social institutions, such as the economy and the government, are social spheres in which we interact with others in very real ways. The words "We the People" that begin the Constitution of the United States point both to the fact of the relationship that we as citizens have with one another and to the scope of the relationship. The act of buying and selling, whether in a local market or the global market, involve the cooperative effort that constitutes a distinct relationship between those involved.

Questions of fairness pose themselves in each of these spheres. The issues that arise within our primary groups or in the associations to which we belong no doubt seem more urgent and appear to have a greater impact on our lives. Yet the wider social spheres that shape our lives have as great an impact, in certain ways a greater impact, on our lives. We need only think of the effect that changes in our nation's tax laws or alterations in international trade can have on us all. Thus, the questions of fairness that arise within these wider spheres, while seemingly remote, have great significance for our lives.

Because questions of fairness concern our relationship with others, they are essentially social questions. The meaning of the term "social," however, differs from one sphere of relationship to another. The term may describe the face-to-face relationships that we have with family members or with friends, or it may describe the economic relations that take place within a nation or between nations. The term "social," in other words, covers a wide spectrum of human relationships. What is distinctive about questions of fairness that concern the economy or the government is that these questions concern the society as a whole, and thus they are social questions in the broadest sense of the term. The significance of such questions lies not only in their scope but also in the basic ways in which these questions concern the lives of all involved.

The Fairness of Social Institutions as the Object of Study

Being fair in our relationship with others describes simply but aptly the object of justice. What then is the object of study of social justice? Does adding "social" to the term justice indicate that a distinct type of social relationship is being considered? The Catholic theologian David Hollenbach, SJ, notes: "Social justice is a much used but rarely defined term."[14] As a way to bring the object of social justice to light, Hollenbach refers to the philosopher John Rawls, a formative voice in the present-day discussion of justice. Rawls states that the primary concern of social justice is "the basic structure of society, or more exactly, the way in which the major social institutions distribute fundamental rights and duties and determine the division of advantages from social cooperation. By major institutions I understand the political constitution and the principal economic and social arrangements."[15]

A society is made up of the social interaction of its members. The well-being of a society depends on the organization and the stability of this social interaction, which a society attains through its institutions. The major institutions of society, in the view of sociology, are the economy, government, the family, education, medicine, and religion. These institutions form the basic structure of society.

The philosopher Rawls and the theologian Hollenbach are primarily concerned not with these social institutions as such—this is the concern of the sociologist—but with "the way in which the major social institutions distribute fundamental rights and duties and determine the division of advantages from social cooperation," as Rawls states above. In other words, the philosopher and the theologian are concerned with questions of fairness that pertain to the social interaction that is being regulated by society's major institutions, thus with questions of fairness that pertain to the society as a whole. The study of social justice, then, has as its object of study the institutions that constitute the basic structure of society, but this study views these institutions from a distinct viewpoint, namely, the idea of justice.

The significance of this study lies in the recognition that the major institutions of society shape our lives in profound ways. Rawls points out that the influence of social institutions on the members of society are "present from the start," thereby affecting "their life-prospects, what they can expect to be and how well they can hope to do." That these "institutions favor certain starting places over others," which create and sustain "deep inequalities" in the basic structure of society, is the reason for undertaking the discussion of social justice.[16] These deep inequalities affect the society as a whole; they must be the concern of all involved.

The Family Institution as an Example

In order to understand the object of the study of social justice more clearly, that is, the fairness of the major social institutions that shape our lives, let us consider experiences readily available to us all that are shaped by one social institution—the American family. As a way to focus our attention on these experiences, let us consider three ordinary questions. When a man and woman go out on a first date, who pays? When a husband

14. Hollenbach, SJ, *Common Good and Christian Ethics*, 201.

15. Rawls, *Theory of Justice*, 7.

16. Rawls, *Theory of Justice*, 7.

and wife return home after a day of work, who cooks? When the six-month-old baby of the husband and wife wakes up crying at three o'clock in the morning from a painful ear infection, who cares for the baby? At first glance the answers to these questions are obviously matters of personal choice, made by the individuals themselves wholly outside of the public sphere. But if we take a second look using the eyes of the sociologist, what do we see?

Firstly, we see that each of the three questions is asked in the context of one of three interrelated social institutions, namely, the courtship institution, the marriage institution, and the family institution respectively, which make up what the sociologist Ira Reiss has termed "the family system."[17] Secondly, we see that while the response to each question will be the result of the couple's personal decision, that decision as well as their social interaction as a whole is being shaped by the social institution that is the context of the question. A social expectation is already in place before the question is asked. An indication of this might be that an answer reverberates in the asking of the question. Thirdly, despite its influence in shaping their decision, the social institution will not be readily visible to them. What will be visible is the matter at hand. If there should be disagreement regarding who pays, who cooks, or who cares for the baby, the couple will consider the disagreement a personal problem, certainly not a social problem. The focus of their attention will be their face-to-face encounter, not the social institution that is mediating the encounter.

By viewing these three questions in their institutional context, what do we learn about social institutions themselves? Why are social institutions a primary concern of social justice? In *The Good Society* the sociologist Robert Bellah and his associates describe social institutions as a "set of mutual expectations" that mediate our relationships with others in society. "Meeting another person with no institutional context is a situation of anxiety and, possibly, fear. We don't know what to expect. We don't know how to act."[18] Social institutions prescribe what we are to expect and how we are to act in a social situation. In doing so, institutions facilitate social interaction. The couple going out on a first date is relieved of the need to negotiate who pays. Both know what to expect.

Other sociologists describe institutions as "the rules of the game in a society" that regulate social activities and relationships.[19] The rules may be formal (the laws of a society) or informal (social customs), both of which are enforced through social sanctions, either formally (legal sanctions) or informally (social disapproval). The rules and their enforcement provide the basis of social cooperation as well as a way to resolve social conflict. Strong institutions, whether they are marriage and family or the economy and government, ensure order and stability in a society. Without strong institutions or at times of institutional change daily life in a society is difficult or worse,

17. Reiss, *Family Systems in America*, 43.

18. Bellah et al., *Good Society*, 287.

19. Mantzavinos, *Individuals, Institutions, and Markets*, 83.

chaotic. This was demonstrated in the countries of Eastern Europe after 1989 with the fall of their communist governments and their struggle to initiate democratic reforms and establish market economies. Indeed these dramatic events inspired within the social sciences a heightened interest in the study of social institutions.[20]

Once social institutions become established, they take on permanence and an externality that belies their origin. They are social creations. We as a society create them, but they in turn, having been created by us, become an outside force shaping our lives. The couple on their first date and the married couple, while making personal decisions concerning the matter at hand, nevertheless are following a script that society has provided them. The German sociologist Arnold Gehlen explained the effect of social institutions on our lives using this analogy—as the instincts of an animal pattern its behavior, so the institutions of society pattern human behavior.[21] Of course, there is a fundamental difference between the instinct of an animal and a social institution—the former is a biological determinism while the latter is a convention.

Conventions are social agreements. The questions "who pays?," "who cooks?," and "who cares for the baby?" can be answered in a variety of ways. One knows this by looking within one's own society as well as by looking beyond one's society to observe how other societies answer these questions. The same point can be made regarding the economy and the government. To the questions "which type of economy?" and "which form of government?" multiple answers can be given. But at three o'clock in the morning that there are a variety of ways to answer the question "who cares for the baby?" is not helpful. That many different economies or forms of government are possible does not ensure the order and stability of this society. Stable institutions depend on the members of a society thinking and acting as if there is only one answer.

Thus, for a social institution to function effectively, the members of a society cannot think of it as a social agreement, that is, as one choice among many. The conventional nature of social institutions must be hidden from view. Moreover, the externality of the social institution's expectations or rules that pattern our behavior must also be hidden from view. There can be no distance between the actor and the script, meaning that the actor cannot think of the script as being simply a script. To perform well, the actor must become the script. So also the expectations or rules of a social institution, to be effective, cannot be thought of as external forces shaping our lives. Its expectations must become our expectations; its rules must become for us the way that we think people in society ought to act. When this occurs, the distance between the social institution and us is eliminated, thereby rendering the social institution and its influence on our lives invisible.

The married couple faced with the question "who cooks?" or "who cares for the baby?" is not aware of the social institutions that are shaping their response to these questions. They are aware of each other and the problem at hand. Yet, insofar as the

20. Campbell, *Institutional Change and Globalization*, 1.

21. Berger, *Invitation to Sociology*, 87.

woman responds to these questions as a wife and a mother and the man as a husband and a father, the institutions of marriage and family are mediating their response. The terms wife, mother, husband, and father do not refer to the woman and the man as individuals but rather to a set of social expectations that they as individuals have taken on. Sociologists refer to these expectations as social roles. They are the specific scripts that society has assigned to distinct social positions, such as wife and husband. We as individuals are the actors who have memorized the scripts and made them our own. The power of these social roles to regulate our relationships lies precisely in their not being visible as social roles because we have made them who we are as persons.

Social institutions are visible to us, however, in one distinctive way. If the social arrangement that has been established by the institution is challenged, the society will make explicit the legitimating reason that is presupposed in the social arrangement. Although the social arrangement is a convention, it is neither thought of nor practiced that way. Rather the social arrangement is thought of and practiced as if it were grounded in nature and reason. According to the anthropologist Mary Douglas, the mutual convenience of an institution's practices is never sufficient to ensure the stability of the institution. "For a convention to turn into a legitimate social institution it needs a parallel cognitive convention to sustain it."[22] The cognitive convention, which is the institution's legitimating idea, ensures the stability of the institution, not the practicality of the social arrangement. Its legitimating idea presents a justification of the institution—of its rules or expectations—that the society accepts as reflecting the natural order of things. This legitimation renders the social institution visible, while at the same time keeping its conventional nature and its social controls hidden from view.

In response to the question "who cares for the baby?" the prevalent expectation within American society is that the mother will care for the baby. For example, when professional women who had interrupted their careers by dropping out of the workforce were asked to state the reason for this personal choice, the top reason given (44 percent) was "family time"; in contrast, professional men who had interrupted their careers gave as their top reasons: "change careers" (29 percent) and "earn a degree, other training" (25 percent).[23] Whatever the personal decision of the wife and husband is at three o'clock in the morning regarding who will care for the baby, their decision is being made in the context of the social expectation that the primary responsibility lies with the mother. The basis of this expectation is a division of labor within the family that the society considers as natural because it is grounded in the biological differences between women and men. Insofar as women conceive and give birth to children, so society reasons, the task of nurturing the young, which includes related domestic tasks such as caring for them when they are sick and cooking, falls naturally to women. Insofar as men are stronger and more aggressive than women, the task of protecting and providing for the family falls naturally to them. That a man on

22. Douglas, *How Institutions Think*, 46.
23. Hewlett and Luce, "Off-Ramps and On-Ramps," 45.

a first date is expected to pay for the date is an expression of society's anticipation that he will eventually take on the task of being the primary breadwinner. If these social arrangements are challenged, the legitimating idea that sustains these arrangements will be made explicit: a natural connection exists between the biological differences between women and men and the division of labor within the family.

What is hidden from view is the conventional nature of this division of labor as well as the external force of this convention to pattern our behavior. This is brought to light by the distinction that sociologists make between sex and gender. One's sex (male or female) is a biological characteristic; one's gender (masculine or feminine) is a social characteristic. Gender consists of a set of mutual expectations within the society. Being feminine or masculine is not a biological determination but a social creation. Feminine behavior and masculine behavior are social scripts that we, as females and males, take on and make our own. Unlike the social roles that society assigns to specific social positions, such as wife and husband, the gender roles of being feminine and masculine are part of the basic structure of society in a more pervasive way. They are stable patterns within the society that shape our social behavior, including how we act as a wife and mother, a husband and father, and as a woman and man on a first date.

In order to function as stable patterns, however, these social arrangements cannot be thought of as being a convenient option among many possibilities. They will be considered by the society as reflecting the natural order of things. Still, Mary Douglas observes, grounding a social institution in nature and reason is not fully sufficient to ensure its stability. Finally, the social edifice of an institution—its expectations or rules, its sanctions, its social roles—must be secured in the concept of justice. "Justice is the point that seals legitimacy," Douglas states.[24] What a social institution prescribes will be considered by the society as what is just. If a society's institutional arrangements are challenged, its justification of these arrangements will ultimately concern, not the practicality or reasonableness of these arrangements, but their fairness.

When the feminist movement in the United States challenged the institutional arrangements of courtship, marriage, and family, beginning in the 1960s and 1970s, the object of the challenge was the unfairness of these arrangements, not simply the personal decisions of husbands and wives, fathers and mothers, and dating couples. Using the rubric "the personal is political" feminists disputed the assumed dichotomy in American society between domestic life and public life. Life within the family is made up of the personal decisions of its members, but these decisions are patterned by the gender roles of the society. Gender roles that sustain an unfair division of labor in the workplace do the same within the family. Justice, then, is the concern not only of the public spheres of the economy and government but of the family as well.[25]

By the mid-1970s a powerful antifeminist reaction had formed. The well-being of the family, antifeminists argued, depends upon clearly established roles that are

24. Douglas, *How Institutions Think*, 112–13.

25. Okin, *Justice, Gender, and the Family*, 124–33.

based on the differences between the sexes. Abolishing sex roles within the family would abolish the family. The answer to the question "who cares for the baby?" is not a matter of personal choice, but of nature, which is secured in the institution of the family. This antifeminist response weakened but did not eliminate the feminist challenge, thus leaving in place its question of fairness regarding society's answers to the questions "who pays?", "who cooks?", and "who cares for the baby?"[26]

The debate over gender roles that has run through the latter part of the twentieth century into the present day, although it involves the practical arrangements that have been negotiated by husbands and wives, divorced parents, and single mothers and fathers regarding the raising of their children, ultimately concerns the fairness of the gendered division of labor in the American family as well as in the wider society. Despite the gains that women have made in overcoming discrimination in the workplace since the late 1970s, both in terms of narrowing the pay gap between men and women and acquiring jobs that were once predominantly male jobs, women have failed to achieve equality in the workplace. The progress that women made in the 1970s and 1980s, moreover, has slowed significantly since the 1990s.[27] The reason, according to the sociologist Paula England, is twofold: first, because gender continues to be the "organizing principle" of family life, the daily care of children remains the primary responsibility of women, thus affecting their participation in the workplace; secondly, men resist taking on the work that society has traditionally assigned to women, both at home and in the workplace. Thus, the increase in women's paid labor has not been offset proportionally by the decrease in their unpaid labor at home, involving both childcare and housework, nor has a genuine integration in the workplace been achieved since changes have been one-way, with women taking on male jobs but not vice versa.[28] (There is one exception to this trend, however. While men generally have resisted taking on lower-status women's jobs, this has not been the case for all men, specifically those men who suffer bias in the workplace due to race or class. In the view of recent sociological research, men who are at a disadvantage in the job market are taking on the lower-paying, lower-status jobs of women, thus linking race and class with gender as determining factors of inequality in the workplace and in the wider society.)[29]

But occupational segregation—that lower-paying jobs have traditionally been the work of women—cannot fully explain the disparity in the incomes of men and women in the workplace, the sociologist Claudia Goldin emphasizes. Based on empirical data from her study of college-educated women (both college graduates and those who hold advanced degrees, such as the MBA, JD, MD, and PhD), she determines that the gender pay gap exists, not between occupations, but within most all occupations, and furthermore that "earnings gaps within occupations are larger for the more highly

26. Chafe, *Paradox of Change*, 217–20.
27. Blau and Kahn, "The Gender Pay Gap," 37–38, 40–41.
28. England, "Toward Gender Equality," 252–58.
29. Miller, "Race and Class Define Men Who Take 'Women's Jobs.'"

educated."[30] The reason for the disparity in incomes between men and women in professions that require the JD or MBA, for example, does not lie primarily in gender bias on the part of the employer, nor does it lie primarily in the lack of assertiveness or of negotiating skills on the part of the female employee. Rather, in professions such as law and finance, the reason for the gender pay gap lies in the structural nature of the work: these professions entail work that makes unpredictable and inflexible demands on the worker, work that Goldin describes as greedy work. Although at the start of their professional careers the wages of women and men are close to parity, the wages of women relative to men begin to decrease shortly thereafter, and the gender wage gap continues to grow in the years that follow. The statistic that is usually cited to indicate the gender pay gap is one that presents the ratio of the wages of women relative to the wages of men overall in the present-day economy, which is now approximately 80 cents to the dollar, but this statistic fails to capture the gender pay gap as it increases in the lives of women over time, particularly for women in specific professions. "At thirteen years after the MBA, the gender earnings ratio is 64 cents on the male dollar," Goldin points out.[31] The cause for the growing pay disparity throughout women's working life is rooted not in social bias but in individual choice. For the sake of greater flexibility and predictability in their work schedules, women MBAs choose less demanding work assignments (as do women in other professions, such as law), this to attend to the caregiving responsibilities of family, especially after the birth of a child. The choice, Goldin notes, although an individual decision, is shaped by the gender norms of the society. That women choose to forgo career advancement for the sake of their families while men choose to pursue careers with rigorous demands at the expense of their families, reinforces both gender inequality in the society and couple inequity in the family. (For women, the consequences of putting family ahead of employment in the workforce have been accentuated during the COVID-19 pandemic, to their detriment.) So, "due in part to the entrenched gender norms" of the society, both men and women are deprived, Goldin stresses: "men forgo time with family; women forgo career."[32]

The consequences of the gendered division of labor in the family and in the wider society, brought to light by the feminist challenge, provide an example of what Rawls means by a "deep inequality," that is, an injustice that pertains to the basic structure of society.[33] The object of discussion is not the face-to-face relationships that take place within the family as a primary group. These relationships and their personal decisions are a private matter, taking place outside the purview of the public sphere. The object of discussion concerns the social expectations that are mediating these personal relationships, which in this case are the gender roles of the society that regulate the family

30. Goldin, *Career and Family*, 156–57.
31. Goldin, *Career and Family*, 164.
32. Goldin, *Career and Family*, 14; see 1–17, 151–87.
33. Rawls, *Collected Papers*, 595–601.

institution. But in this mediating role, these social expectations are present within the family, shaping the most intimate moments of family life, as well as outside the family, influencing the institutional arrangements of the wider society. If these social expectations are unjust, then this social injustice will affect family life as well as other social spheres, such as the workplace. The injustice concerns the basic structure of society itself.

Social Institutions as Moral Institutions

That the social institution of the family as well as the other major social institutions, such as the economy and government, secure their practices in the concept of justice points to this fundamental reality—social institutions are essentially moral institutions. The social expectations or rules of the major social institutions that pattern our behavior in society are specific answers to the more basic moral question "how ought we to live together?" For this reason, the sociologist Bellah and his associates maintain, social institutions function as normative patterns for our lives. These patterns embody a conception of what is morally right or the moral good. Issues of fairness regarding the social expectations or rules of an institution ultimately invoke these moral terms. Thus, the practices of social institutions are never morally neutral arrangements to be used by us to realize our private visions of the right or the good. They themselves embody a vision of the right or the good. Controversies regarding these social arrangements will not be resolved only by means of technical fixes (the simplification of the tax code) but finally through moral argument (the reform of the tax code for the sake of greater equity). Indeed, the vitality of our social institutions, these sociologists argue, requires that they be exposed to moral debate.[34]

The study of social justice undertakes this moral debate. The object of the study concerns the fairness of the social arrangements of the major institutions that make up the basic structure of society. Although the well-being of society requires that its social arrangements create order and stability, the well-being of society first of all requires that this order and stability be just. John Rawls states: "Justice is the first virtue of social institutions, as truth is of systems of thought. A theory however elegant and economical must be rejected or revised if it is untrue; likewise laws and institutions no matter how efficient and well-arranged must be reformed or abolished if they are unjust."[35]

The importance of the study of social justice is highlighted by this observation of Mary Douglas: "The most profound decisions about justice are not made by individuals as such, but by individuals thinking within and on behalf of institutions."[36] The social arrangements of society's institutions not only regulate the day-to-day routines of our lives; they shape how we think about ourselves, about our relations with one

34. Bellah et al., *Good Society*, 4–6, 10–12, 288–90.

35. Rawls, *Theory of Justice*, 3.

36. Douglas, *How Institutions Think*, 124.

another, and ultimately about the fairness of these relationships. Not only do they constrain our choices. They also enable us to do what is right or to realize what is good. Herein lies both the power and control of social institutions over our lives as well as their moral meaning. That these social arrangements be just, that the idea of justice that legitimates these arrangements be valid, has significance for us all.

The Power of the Economy and Government to Shape Our Lives

Of the social institutions that make up the basic structure of society, the economy and the government as institutions exert "the greatest power and control over our lives."[37] Although all of the major social institutions have a similar scope—society as a whole—only the economy and the government have the power and control to shape not only individual lives but the other social institutions as well. Yet the economy and the government wield this power and control in very different ways. We can see this if we view the social institution of the family in relation to each of them.

Although relations within the family constitute a distinct social sphere, we cannot think of the family as having "an extrapolitical existence" so that in response to issues of injustice regarding the family institution, we then ask on what terms can the state intervene; the power and control of the state over the family are present from the start. The government defines what is and is not a family. The influence of the government on family life is pervasive: the act of marrying and the act of divorcing, the adoption of a child and the determination of the legitimacy of a child, the nature and extent of parental responsibility—all are regulated by the government. The defining characteristic of the social institution of government is its authority to regulate the social relations in the society, including the relations that make up the family.[38]

The defining characteristic of the social institution of the economy is exchange, that is, the mutual transactions of buying and selling that constitute a market. A child's lemonade stand in front of her house or a car dealership at the center of town is a marketplace. But the act of buying and selling that occurs in each of these places is a market. A market system exists when markets proliferate and link together in a society or globally to provide a distinct form of social coordination. Whereas the government coordinates the activities of society through the formal authority of its laws and sanctions, the economy creates social coordination through the exchanges that make up its markets. In democratic societies these market exchanges take place outside of governmental command and are therefore free exchanges. Thus, in contrast to the government, which creates order and stability in a society through coercion, the economy does so through voluntary exchange.[39]

37. Bellah et al., *Good Society*, 144.
38. Nussbaum, "Rawls and Feminism," 504–6.
39. Lindblom, *Market System*, 4.

Still, because a voluntary exchange—say, the buying and selling of a car—is a market transaction, the exchange is being controlled by the innumerable voluntary exchanges of others that make up the market. For this reason, economist and Catholic theologian Albino Barrera states: "Economic decisions are by nature constrained choices."[40] The buyer would prefer to pay less than and the seller would prefer to charge more than the market price, but the price, established by the market, is controlling the transaction. A constrained choice, nevertheless, remains a choice. Markets do not coerce the decisions of buyers and sellers as the government coerces the actions of its citizens through laws and sanctions (for example, through taxation), but markets do control in forceful ways the economic decisions that shape our lives. The circumstances of the market can compel us to choose what we find to be undesirable because the other options facing us are even more so.[41] Thus, although decisions pertaining to family life are made privately within the family sphere, the economy is influencing those decisions at the same time in decisive ways. Consider this one example.

As women entered the salaried workforce in greater numbers in the latter part of the twentieth century, families were faced with difficult decisions regarding the allocation of a finite resource—time. Prior to this, women's full-time unpaid labor in the home provided necessary support for men's full-time paid labor in the workplace. Given this social arrangement, home and workplace existed as separate but complementary spheres. These spheres conflict once women enter the workforce. Because the demands of the workplace, requiring the full attention and time of its workers, remain unchanged, less time is available for the needs of family life when both parents work or when a family is headed by a single parent, usually a woman. Although some workplaces provide family-friendly arrangements (for example, flexible work hours), these provisions soften but do not alleviate the conflict between work and family.[42] The workplace, accordingly, controls in significant ways how families spend their time. Sociologists Jerry Jacobs and Kathleen Gerson note: "The lack of time for family life is not simply a matter of questionable choices made by some individuals, but instead reflects the way choices are shaped by our economy and the structure of our work organizations."[43]

Economists describe this lack of time to attend fully to family needs, due to the increased participation of women in the workplace, as an opportunity cost. All economic decisions entail costs. Given the limitless nature of our desires and the limited nature of the resources that are available to us, our economic decisions always involve trade-offs. Each day has only twenty-four hours. The parents of a young child each may want to attend fully to the needs of the child as well as to each other and to participate fully in the workplace, but this is not possible. Decisions by the parents

40. Barrera, *Economic Compulsion and Christian Ethics*, 16.

41. Barrera, *Economic Compulsion and Christian Ethics*, 12–19.

42. Jacobs and Gerson, *Time Divide*, 96–97, 105–14.

43. Jacobs and Gerson, *Time Divide*, 14.

regarding the allocation of time between family and work must be made. Their decisions, because they are being influenced by the circumstances of the market, will be constrained choices, involving the weighing of costs and benefits. For some families, the circumstances of the market will compel them to make choices that they would not otherwise make. Economic compulsion, Barrera emphasizes, is proportional to the nature and severity of opportunity costs. A single mother, for example, may not want to leave her young child in the care of another or to pay for childcare, but the cost of fulfilling this desire may be too high for her, if potential unemployment or part-time employment would entail forgoing adequate health care or shelter for herself and her child. The market compels choices, not when our decisions concern trivial desires, but when they concern fulfilling or foregoing basic human needs.[44]

But the choices that wives/mothers and husbands/fathers, or single mothers, make regarding how they will allocate time to attend to the concerns and responsibilities of both work and family—are these decisions only theirs to make? Are these choices of time allocation private in nature, that is, simply a family matter? No, the economist Heather Boushey answers. The choice is certainly a family matter, but one that intersects with two other institutional spheres—the business world and the government. When women entered the workforce in great numbers beginning in the 1960s and 1970s, Boushey points out, American businesses lost a key asset—the silent partner who had been contributing to their profitability while making no demands for remuneration on the businesses themselves. The silent partner was "the American Wife," whose unpaid labor at home enabled "the American Worker" (the male in the family) to give full attention to the demands of his job. This work-life balance was lost as women entered the workforce. Although the conflict between the demands and responsibilities of work and family is a problem that takes place inside families, it is a problem inside businesses as well, particularly with regard to worker productivity and worker retention. That businesses have treated the problem as simply a family matter places the problem outside of the market, this to the detriment of the economy overall, Boushey argues. The problem of allocating time in families in fact exists both inside families and inside markets, and thus it is a problem for the economy as a whole. Moreover, that the government has failed to fully address the problem reinforces the view that the work-life conflict in families is in the end their problem alone. In 1971 Congress passed a bill that would have put in place a federally funded child-care program, but the bill was vetoed by President Nixon for the reason that the bill would be harmful to the American family, this by encouraging women's entrance into the workplace to the detriment of the family. Nixon's veto, Boushey emphasizes, expressed a value judgment, but one devoid of economic analysis. The government changed course in 1993 when President Clinton signed the Family and Medical Leave Act (FMLA) into law. The bill provides workers with a maximum of twelve weeks of job-protected, unpaid leave for family caregiving. The job-protected leave time can be claimed by

---

44. Barrera, *Economic Compulsion and Christian Ethics*, 16–17.

both male and female employees; thus, if both a wife and a husband are employed, family caregiving can be extended to twenty-four weeks. But the leave time is unpaid (making this an unaffordable option for many) and intended for special caregiving needs, not ongoing work-life accommodations. Here, on the part of the government, more is required. Central to the work-life conflict in families is caregiving, whether for children, for an elderly parent, or for one who is sick. But, while caregiving involves choices made within the family sphere, family caregiving also involves choices made within two other institutional spheres—the economy and the government. Here in the interplay between these three social institutions, Boushey points out, the question of fairness presents itself: "Fairness undergirds our vision of what governments, firms, and families owe one another."[45]

Due to the power and control of the economy and the government over our lives individually and over the other social institutions that shape our lives, such as the social institution of the family, the fairness of the social arrangements of these two institutions is a primary concern for us all. As citizens, we acknowledge the formal authority of the government to regulate our lives; as participants in a free market economy, we accept the outcomes of our market exchanges. But, insofar as the government has the power to coerce us through its laws and sanctions, we expect that these mechanisms of control will be fair. Even though the market choices of some can compel the market choices of others in a free market, we nevertheless expect that the outcome of these voluntary exchanges will be fair. Our expectation of fairness regarding these social institutions presupposes an idea of justice. If we judge a social arrangement to be unfair, implicit in our judgment is an expectation of how the matter ought to be. Moral debate over issues concerning the economy and the government, then, ultimately must center on what justice is and how justice is to be realized concretely in and through these social institutions. Effective moral response within the society to the unfairness of its social institutions must address directly the injustice of these social arrangements. Responding to social injustice only on individual terms will fail to fully address the issue of injustice. For example, as we saw above, when widespread homelessness in urban areas such as New York, Los Angeles, or San Francisco is the result of exploitative housing markets as well as inadequate governmental oversight of these markets,[46] acts of charity by individuals and groups, such as churches, on behalf of homeless persons are necessary, but not sufficient. As did the good Samaritan, whose compassion led him to address the external conditions necessary for the recovery of the victim, we realize that from us more is required, individually and as a society. Social justice requires just institutions. This is the object of our study.

45. Boushey, *Finding Time*, 242; see 1–22, 162–73, 226–48.

46. For the case of New York City, see Barker, "When 'Renovations' Lead to Relocation"; Barker et al., "How Courts Became Landlords' Crowbar"; Kleinfield, "Pleading for Their Homes, in Sea of Chaos and Grime."

MORAL ACTIONS

Social Justice as a Virtue

Just institutions, however, are created and maintained only through human actions, that is, by individuals acting in and through the institutions that make up the society. Given the power of the economy and the government, as well as the other major social institutions, to shape our daily lives, that these institutions originate in and exist through human agency, which is at root moral agency, can readily be obscured. Yet, as we saw in Chapter 1, social groups, whether small, such as a family, or large, such as a nation-state, demonstrate moral agency. We see this when we take into account what is distinctive to social behavior that distinguishes it from strictly individual behavior. Social behavior (group behavior) is not something wholly other than the behavior of the individuals that make up the group, but it also is not simply the aggregate of individual actions that take place within the group. Human interaction within a social group is shaped by the distinctive pattern of social organization that constitutes the group: This social organization at the same time originates in and is sustained by the decisions and actions of individuals that make up the group. (Recall the example of the decision-making process within a corporation, discussed in Chapter 1.) Social behavior, then, is the behavior of individuals acting in and through the social organization that enables the group to function as a group. For a nation-state its major social institutions constitute this pattern of social organization. Insofar as a nation-state's social organization is the product of human decisions and actions, and as long as this human agency has as its purpose concrete outcomes that can be judged, not only as being efficient and effective, but also as good and right, the human agency that creates and maintains this pattern of social organization is moral agency. Social institutions, as we saw above, are essentially moral institutions in that they are specific answers to the fundamental moral question that underlies society: how ought we to live together? But, as normative patterns for social living, society's institutions are the product of the moral actions of those who make up the society. Accordingly, regarding the matter of social justice, the object of study, in addition to just institutions, must be the moral actions that create and maintain social institutions that are just. What are these moral actions? More precisely, what is their moral purpose, and what is the normative guide for realizing this purpose?

The question indicates a distinct approach to the matter of social justice that sets it apart from the approach that John Rawls initiates. The intent of the question is to focus our attention on the moral actions that create and maintain just institutions (rather than on the abstract principles of justice that order social institutions, which is Rawls's focus) and, by doing so, to bring into view persons in society as the moral agents of these actions. From this perspective, moral actions are viewed not as discrete acts considered in themselves apart from the intention of the one who performs them, but rather, specifically in the matter of social justice, as the acts of justice of persons who are just. Here primacy of attention is given to the moral disposition of persons in society to act justly in a persistent and predictable way, having as the moral purpose of their actions the overall good of the society and having as the normative guide to this end the criterion of justice. Thus, in this view, the moral character of persons, specifically the character traits that render persons morally praiseworthy in society, not abstract principles of obligation (Rawls), must be the first concern of those who seek to bring about a society that is just. Herein lies the object of study regarding the matter of social justice—justice as a trait of character, that is, justice as a moral virtue. This approach to social justice originates in the classical Greek tradition, most notably in the philosophy of Aristotle, achieves a fundamental articulation in the medieval theology of Thomas Aquinas, and is carried into the modern age and represented in the official social teaching and more broadly in the social thought of Roman Catholicism. To this tradition, in both its classical and contemporary forms, which portrays social justice as a moral virtue, we now turn.

From Aristotle to Thomas Aquinas: Justice as a Virtue

At the opening of book 5 of the *Nicomachean Ethics*, which is devoted to the topic of justice, Aristotle observes: "We see that all men mean by justice that kind of state of character which makes people disposed to do what is just and makes them act justly and wish for what is just; and similarly by injustice that state which makes them act unjustly and wish for what is unjust."[47] Here "all men" in fact refers to a specific group, namely, the educated male citizens of Athens in the fourth century BCE, and indicates that Aristotle considers his view of justice to be not uniquely his own, but the articulation of the idea of justice that is implied in the discourse (*logos*) and actions (*praxis*) of the citizens of the Athenian city-state (*polis*).[48] What is commonly agreed upon by the citizens of the Athenian *polis* is that justice is first and foremost a virtue (*aretē*)—an excellence or strength of character that disposes one to act justly in particular situations in a ready and steadfast way and to have the desire to do so ("wish for what is just"). In his account of moral virtue in book 2 of the *Nicomachean Ethics*, Aristotle asserts: "states of character arise out of like activities."[49] One is a courageous person (a kind of state of character) due to readily and repeatedly performing courageous acts; likewise, one becomes a just person as the result of intentional, repeated just actions. Accordingly, that the virtue of justice is a "kind of state of character" (injustice—a vice—being a contradictory kind of state of character) means for Aristotle that justice, like the other moral virtues of character (such as courage and temperance), is an acquired state—that is, one that is gained only through personal effort, educational training, and the ongoing repetition of just actions. For Aristotle, the outcome of the

47. Aristotle, *Nicomachean Ethics* 5.1.1129a.

48. See MacIntyre, *After Virtue*, 147–48.

49. Aristotle, *Nicomachean Ethics* 2.1.1103b.

practice of the virtues is this: "We may remark, then, that every virtue or excellence both brings into good condition the thing of which it is the excellence and makes the work of that thing be done well; e.g. the excellence of the eye makes both the eye and its work good; for it is by the excellence of the eye that we see well."[50] So it is with the virtue of justice—this specific excellence or strength of character both renders the person as a person good and disposes the person to act well in society (to do good). In the view of Aristotle and his contemporaries, the good of society requires just actions but, more fundamentally, just persons who are thereby disposed to act justly.

Thomas Aquinas, writing in the thirteenth century, mirrors Aristotle's depiction of justice as a kind of state of character in his presentation of justice as a moral virtue. Drawing from the standard theological textbook of his day—the *Sentences* of Peter Lombard, written in the twelfth century—Aquinas offers this general definition of virtue that begins his discussion of the virtues in his *Summa* (comprehensive synthesis) of theology: "Virtue is a good quality of the mind, by which we live righteously, of which no one can make bad use, which God works in us without us."[51] That virtue is noted as a "quality" of the mind establishes the category (the genus) that formally defines virtue; that this characteristic of the mind is described as "good" refers to the distinguishing character that renders this kind of quality of the mind virtuous and thus praiseworthy; that this good quality is "of the mind" points to the source (subject) of virtue, which is our rational nature; that through the exercise of virtue "we live righteously," and due to the nature of virtue "no one can make bad use" of it, reflects the end or purpose of virtue; finally, that the definition of virtue ends by referring to the good quality of the mind that "God works in us without us" extends the definition of virtue to include the virtues whose direct cause is the grace of God, these being the infused virtues of faith, hope, and charity. Aquinas notes that if this final phrase is removed, the definition as thus stated describes what is common to both the virtues acquired through human effort and the divinely infused virtues: "a good quality of the mind, by which we live righteously, of which no one can make bad use." To Peter Lombard's definition of virtue, however, Aquinas makes one alteration. He proposes that in the definition of virtue a more suitable term to describe the formal category of virtue would be "habit" (*habitus*) of the mind, rather than "quality," because habit is the more specific term (the proximate genus). For Aquinas, then, virtue is a good habit of the mind—habit being the intentional, learned, stable disposition to act and feel in certain ways that enable us both to do good and to be good as persons.[52] Accordingly, when Aquinas specifically considers justice as a moral virtue, he presents justice as a good habit of the mind. The term *habitus* as used by Aquinas translates into Latin

---

50. Aristotle, *Nicomachean Ethics* 2.6.1106a.

51. Thomas Aquinas, *Summa Theologica* I–II.55.4.

52. For Thomas Aquinas's presentation of the essential nature of habits, see Thomas Aquinas, *Summa Theologica* I–II.49.1–4.

Aristotle's Greek term *hexis* (a state of character). For both Aristotle and Aquinas, justice is a specific state of character, that is, a distinct virtue of the mind.

But in his presentation of justice as a virtue of the mind, Aquinas moves beyond Aristotle in one significant way. The definition of justice that Aquinas states at the beginning of his treatise on the moral virtue of justice is this: "*Justice is a habit whereby a man renders to each one his due by a constant and perpetual will.*"[53] As Aquinas does with each of the virtues that he considers, he establishes in the definition of justice both the subject (the source) of the virtue and its formal object (the end toward which the virtue is properly directed). Justice is a habit, Aquinas states, and thus a virtue of the mind. This is the subject (the source) of the virtue of justice—the mind. But what precisely of the mind provides justice with its source? How Aquinas answers this question enables him to expand Aristotle's conception of justice in a more determinate way.

We as human beings have the capability both to know and to desire. Knowing and desiring are both powers of the mind—the intellective and appetitive (desiring) powers of the soul, to use Aquinas's terms. Is justice a virtue of both these powers or a virtue of only one of them? Aquinas notes that justice primarily concerns doing. One who has acquired the virtue of justice acts justly. If acting justly has become a habit, such actions are performed in a ready and repeated manner and with intention. Acting justly then requires the intention, and thus the desire, to do justice. Aquinas writes:

> Now justice does not aim at directing an act of the cognitive power, for we are not said to be just through knowing something aright. Hence the subject of justice is not the intellect or reason which is a cognitive power. But since we are said to be just through doing something aright, and because the proximate principle of action is the appetitive power, justice must needs be in some appetitive power as its subject.[54]

Knowing something theoretically does not directly cause us to act. Desiring something does. The desiring that does justice involves a movement within the self, a movement that impels the self either toward (through attraction) or away from (through aversion) something other than the self. Aquinas's term for this movement of attraction or aversion within the self in regard to something outside the self is appetite (*appetitus*).[55] One kind of movement of desire within the self occurs by means of our senses (the smell of food cooking elicits from us a response), but Aquinas is clear that sensate desiring cannot be the kind of desire that moves us to be just. The desire that moves a person to act justly must be an intentional desire and therefore a rational desire. Acting justly embodies a purpose—the desire to realize the good in society, a good that can only be apprehended through reason. Accordingly, the subject (source)

---

53. Thomas Aquinas, *Summa Theologica* II–II.58.1.

54. Thomas Aquinas, *Summa Theologica* II–II.58.4.

55. See Harack, SJ, *Virtuous Passions*, 60–61.

of justice is an *appetitus*—not the appetitive power of the senses but rather the appetitive power of the mind, the act of rational desire that Aquinas specifies as the power of the human will. Justice, according to Aquinas, is enacted only "by a constant and perpetual will."[56]

By determining that the will is the subject of justice, Aquinas advances beyond Aristotle's conception of justice by providing a more determinate understanding of the source of justice. In *The Nicomachean Ethics*, Aristotle observes: "The origin of action—its efficient, not its final cause—is choice, and that of choice is desire and reasoning with a view to an end." Choice for Aristotle is the direct cause of human action (its efficient cause). That the origin of choice lies in desire and reason enables human choice to be purposeful and thus a choice made with an end in view (its final cause), which is the good of the action to be realized by means of the choice. "Hence choice is either desiderative reason or ratiocinative desire," Aristotle states—that is, the source of choice is either reason that desires or desire that reasons. "Intellect itself"—speculative reason—"however, moves nothing," says Aristotle, "but only the intellect which aims at an end and is practical," that is, intellect in the mode of practical reason. The origin of choice and thus the source that moves us to act, according to Aristotle, lies in practical reason, the rational desire of the mind that deliberates with an end in view.[57] Justice, then, as a virtue of character acquired through repeated, intentional actions, in Aristotle's view, is built on choice—choices that are the result of practical reasoning that intends to realize an end through acting justly. That justice requires choice we see in Aristotle's definition of justice: "And justice is that in virtue of which the just man is said to be a doer, by choice, of that which is just."[58]

Aquinas, in proposing his definition of justice as a habit of the mind "*whereby a man renders to each one his due by a constant and perpetual will*," notes: "this is about the same definition as that given by the Philosopher" (this being Aristotle).[59] Present-day commentators qualify this observation by Aquinas, however. Aristotle, they point out, had not developed a concept of the will as a distinct capacity or power of the mind, as had Aquinas.[60] Both Aristotle and Aquinas understood justice to be based on choice made with an end in view, the origin of choice being the rational desire of the mind to attain that end (the good). But Aquinas, going beyond Aristotle, saw the rational desire that moves us to realize the good that is justice distinctively as the operation of the human will. That Aquinas had formulated a concept of the will as a distinct appetitive (desiring) power of the mind,[61] then, enables him to designate the

---

56. Thomas Aquinas, *Summa Theologica* II–II.58.1, 4, 9.

57. Aristotle, *Nicomachean Ethics* 6.2.1139a–39b.

58. Aristotle, *Nicomachean Ethics* 5.5.1134a.

59. Thomas Aquinas, *Summa Theologica* II–II.58.1.

60. See Copleston, SJ, *Greece and Rome*, 81; Kent, "Habits and Virtues," 117–19; Kent, "Losable Virtue"; Porter, "Virtue of Justice," 275. Porter, *Justice as a Virtue*, 119.

61. Thomas Aquinas, *Summa Theologica* I.82.1–5.

human will as the subject (source) of justice. Moreover, insofar as Aquinas conceives of justice as a good habit of the will, he sees the virtue of justice as a perfecting quality of the person who wills to be just. Justice is a perfection of the will and thus of the person who wills to act justly.[62]

The will as subject (the source of action) is necessarily directed toward that which lies outside it—the object of its desire. As a rational appetite, the will both moves and is moved with regard to that which lies outside the will. Aquinas observes: "For the appetitive power is a passive power, which is naturally moved by the thing apprehended: wherefore the apprehended appetible is a mover which is not moved, while the appetite is a mover moved."[63] The movement of the appetite, which Aquinas describes as a "mover moved," pertains to both the appetitive power of the senses and the appetitive power of the will. Consider again the smell of food cooking ("the apprehended appetible") that elicits from us a response. The cooking food moves us to respond, without the food in any way being affected ("moved"), and in our response we become a "mover moved." What distinguishes the sensate appetite from the rational appetite of the will is not the pattern of the movement, but rather the object that elicits the movement. The object apprehended by the will, moreover, need not be materially different from the object apprehended by the senses—that is, it can be the same material object but apprehended under different formal aspects. So the smell of cooking food that awakens in us the desire to eat thereby becomes the object of our sensate desire. But if the cooking food evokes in us the thought that this food might be detrimental to our health (too much fat or too much salt) and therefore not good for us, we rationally apprehend the food cooking under the formal aspect of its goodness or badness for our health, and this apprehension then elicits from us a response of attraction or aversion. In this case, the object that moves us is not the sensate object as such, but the apprehension of the sensate object under the formal aspect of being good or bad for us. The apprehension of the good, says Aquinas, is attained through the judgment of the intellect. Not directly by the senses, but by the good as apprehended by the intellect is the will moved; in turn, desire (*appetitus*) for the good as apprehended by the intellect impels the will as mover to act. Aquinas explains:

> A thing is said to move in two ways: First, as an end; for instance, when we say that the end moves the agent. In this way the intellect moves the will, because the good understood is the object of the will, and moves it as an end. Secondly, a thing is said to move as an agent, as what alters moves what is altered, and what impels moves what is impelled. In this way the will moves the intellect, and all the powers of the soul.[64]

The good as the object of desire and the will as the source of action both move the self to act, but in distinctly different ways. The object of desire moves the self as

62. See Porter, *Justice as a Virtue*, 104–13.

63. Thomas Aquinas, *Summa Theologica* I.80.2.

64. Thomas Aquinas, *Summa Theologica* I.82.4.

the end or purpose of the action and thus as a final cause. The will, as the source of action, moves the self as the efficient (direct) cause of the self's actions. The self, then, as a "mover moved," is impelled to act in two different but mutually contributory ways, according to Aquinas: indirectly, by means of the self's apprehension of the good to be attained through one's action (this as presented by the intellect as the end or purpose of the action); directly, through the agency of the will.[65] By means of the will's agency "the will moves the intellect, and all the powers of the soul," Aquinas states, thus establishing the will as the unifying power of the self and its actions.[66] Yet, the will moves the self to act only in response to that which it apprehends as good, this being the work of the intellect. For Aquinas, then, the moral act requires will and intellect, each power of the mind having a different role to play. Neither the will as the subject of moral action, nor the good apprehended by the intellect as the object of the rational desire of the will, considered independently from each other, provides a sufficient basis for understanding moral action. To explain moral action adequately both the subject and the object of the moral action must be taken into account.

Accordingly, when Aquinas offers his definition of the moral virtue of justice, he determines not only the subject of the virtue (the will), but the formal object of the virtue as well: justice is a good habit of the mind, Aquinas states, "*whereby a man renders to each one his due.*"[67] Rendering what is due to a person, what one is owed, that which is one's right—this is the formal object of justice. The Latin term that Aquinas uses to designate the object of justice is *ius* (right), a concept derived from Roman law but having its origin in classical Greek thought. That Aquinas treats the formal object of justice (in II–II, q. 57 of the *Summa*) prior to and independently of his full treatise on justice in the *Summa*, which begins with the definition of justice as a virtue (in II–II, q. 58), highlights the distinctiveness and significance that the formal object of justice has for him vis-à-vis the formal objects of the other moral virtues.

The formal object of justice concerns our relations with other persons in society, more specifically the end or purpose of the moral actions that make up these external relations—this in contrast to the moral virtues that perfect the self, exclusive of the self's relation with others, such as the virtues of temperance and fortitude (courage). In the context of social relations, rendering to each person in the relationship that which is their due—their right—constitutes the proper matter, and thus the specific good, that the moral act of justice intends to realize. Right (*ius*) stands outside the act of justice as the mover not moved, while the act of justice responds to right as the mover moved. The act of justice does not establish what is the right; rather, the right calls forth and determines the act of justice. Right, in this sense, is first; the act of justice comes next. What determines the act of justice in its specificity (its matter) is not the virtuous habit of the one who is just, but the right apprehended by the intellect

65. See Perkams, "Aquinas on Choice," 85–86.

66. See Porter, *Justice as a Virtue*, 104–5; Kent, "Losable Virtue," 109.

67. Thomas Aquinas, *Summa Theologica* II–II.58.1.

as the obligation to be met. Here the focus of attention lies not primarily with the self and its perfection, as it does with the other moral virtues, but with the other—the person or persons in society whose right makes a claim on us. Moreover, that the right of one imposes an obligation on another in society indicates a fundamental equality between the two, Aquinas maintains. For a social relationship to be just, some specific form of equality between those who make up the relationship must be established, this based on the mutual recognition of the right to be realized through actions that are just. Justice is the perfection of the will, but justice is this kind of excellence precisely insofar as the virtue of justice directs the will to that which lies outside it—the good (right) of the other that moves the will. Aquinas concludes:

> And so a thing is said to be just, as having the rectitude of justice, when it is the term of an act of justice, without taking into account the way in which it is done by the agent: whereas in the other virtues nothing is declared to be right unless it is done in a certain way by the agent. For this reason justice has its own special proper object over and above the other virtues, and this object is called the just, which is the same as *right*. Hence it is evident that right is the object of justice.[68]

That the right (*ius*) as "the term of an act of justice" guides the just act as its end or purpose "without taking into account the way in which it is done by the agent" underscores for Aquinas the difference between justice as a moral virtue and the other moral virtues. Whereas all of the moral virtues build the strength of character, that is the basis for the kind of person that we are and for the way in which we conduct our lives in the world, the virtue of justice does so with a decidedly different focus than the other moral virtues. In the exercise of the virtue of justice the focus of the virtue lies primarily with the other as other, not with the self. Whether a person fulfills the obligation of justice (the right) with compassionate concern or not is secondary to the determination of the obligation and its fulfillment. For the other moral virtues, whose purpose is the guidance of our sense appetites to their proper ends (such as the virtue of temperance), the rectitude of the self is primary. Thus, for all moral virtues other than justice "nothing is declared to be right unless it is done in a certain way by the agent."

Fortitude and temperance are the principal moral virtues that guide our sense appetites, movements within the self that are generated by a person, an object, an event outside of the self that moves the self as an object of desire (the smell of food cooking), movements that Aquinas refers to as our passions (in contemporary expression, our emotions or feelings). Unlike bodily actions in direct response to a mental command (for example, the precision and timing of the bodily movements of an accomplished athlete or of fingers typing on a keyboard), the bodily movements of

---

68. Thomas Aquinas, *Summa Theologica* II–II.57.1; see Pieper, *Four Cardinal Virtues*, 45–46; Porter, *Justice as a Virtue*, 44–45, 104–13.

the passions exhibit a certain independence from the mind—the rapturous feeling of love, the hot rush of anger, tears of sorrow, trembling with fear, sexual arousal—all are passions awakened by that which is other than the mind, but as passions (bodily movements) they reside within the self as sensate desires that move the self to act. The virtues of temperance and fortitude (courage) both guide our sense appetites to their proper ends, but in that our sense appetites move us to act in different ways (due to a distinct difference in the object of desire that moves us), different forms of moral guidance are needed. Herein lies the difference between the moral virtues of temperance and fortitude.

One kind of sense appetites (passions) moves us to act in direct response to the perceived good of a sensible object (such as food cooking). Such desires have as their proper end the attainment of pleasure and the avoidance of pain—having the joy of eating a good meal and avoiding the sadness of having no food to eat. A second kind of sense appetites moves the self to act in response to a sensible good—but in this case either it is a good and an object of desire that is difficult to obtain, or its lack as an evil that is difficult to avoid. Such difficulty awakens in the self a different set of passions. One who is homeless and poor, for example, is moved by the smell of food cooking—but, given the difficulty of obtaining food, is moved to act by passions other than and beyond the sensate desires of one who has ready access to food: passions such as fear (in this case the fear of going hungry) that provokes the counter feeling of daring (this in the pursuit of food) and hope (in this case the hope that fuels efforts to obtain food through persistent pleas for help), thus countering the obverse feeling of despair, and finally anger (in response to the evil of hunger itself). The kind of sense appetites that have as their object simply the attainment of sensate pleasure and the avoidance of pain Aquinas terms the concupiscible passions (love or hatred, desire or aversion, joy or sadness); the kind of sense appetites that can be satisfied only by means of effort or struggle he terms the irascible passions (hope or despair, daring or fear, and anger). Insofar as the concupiscible passions have as their proper end the sensible good itself, the movement of the concupiscible passions begins with the love of and desire for a sensate good (the smell of food cooking) and ends in the joy of attainment (eating the meal). The irascible passions, says Aquinas, "stand between" the concupiscible passions of love and desire (as the beginning of movement) and joy (as the end): "the irascible passions both arise from and terminate in the passions of the concupiscible faculty."[69] The irascible passions do not function independently of the concupiscible passions but rather come to the aid of the concupiscible passions, providing the emotional strength necessary to attain the sensible good. Although a homeless person's desire to eat awakens passions such as fear or daring, despair or hope, as well as anger—this in the face of want—these passions likewise intend as their end the joy of eating and avoiding the evil of being hungry. That the passions, both concupiscible and irascible, move the self to act in response to a perceived sensible good or to avoid

69. Thomas Aquinas, *Summa Theologica* I–II.25.1; see also I.81.2 and I–II.23.1–4.

what is perceived as an evil and must do so "in a certain way" (the right way) requires the guidance of the moral virtues: temperance for the sake of the concupiscible passions, and fortitude for the irascible passions.[70] Why?

Although our passions move us in a way that occurs outside of and at times at odds with the agency of the mind, the human passions are nevertheless disposed toward reason. As feelings or emotions, the passions are in one sense simply bodily movements, and as such they are neither praiseworthy nor blameworthy. Aquinas describes human passion as a "bodily transmutation," meaning a bodily change that occurs within us as a response to that which lies outside us.[71] In response to danger we tremble with fear. This spontaneous bodily change moves us to act—we may flee from the danger (due to the overwhelming feeling of fear), or we may stay to confront the danger (due to the overwhelming feeling of daring). But the right action requires that our emotional response to the danger be felt in the right way, which means that how we feel about the danger (the way in which we are moved) must conform to the reality of the danger. Thus, a good outcome to our response to danger depends not only on right action but also on right passion—that is, passion felt in the right way. To use the observation made by Aristotle, human passions, such as fear or daring, "may be felt both too much and too little, and in both cases not well; but to feel them at the right times, with reference to the right objects, towards the right people, with the right motive, and in the right way, is what is both intermediate and best, and this is characteristic of virtue."[72] A good outcome to our response to danger requires achieving the proper balance—what Aristotle terms the "mean" (*mesotēs*) or the "intermediate" (*mesos*)—between countervailing feelings of fear and daring in regard to the danger: too little fear and too much daring leads to a foolhardy response, but too much fear and too little daring results in a cowardly response. Finding the proper balance in this case, as with the movement of all the passions, is the work of virtue, specifically the work of practical reason, whose perfection is realized through the virtue of prudence. How we respond emotionally to a specific danger as well as the choice that we make in its regard must be in accordance with the nature of the threat. Properly assessing the reality of the danger and determining the steps necessary to deal adequately with the danger require the proper exercise of practical reason, which is the function of the virtue of prudence, also termed by Aristotle practical wisdom. Aristotle states: "Virtue, then, is a state of character concerned with choice, lying in a mean, i.e. the mean relative to us, this being determined by a rational principle, and by that principle by which the man of practical wisdom would determine it."[73] The passions, both concupiscible and irascible, in order to realize their end or purpose (attaining the sensible good) need reason as their guide. Practical reason determines the mean for the

---

70. Thomas Aquinas, *Summa Theologica* I–II.60.4.

71. Thomas Aquinas, *Summa Theologica* I–II.22.1.

72. Aristotle, *Nicomachean Ethics* 2.6.1106b.

73. Aristotle, *Nicomachean Ethics* 2.6.1107a.

passions ("the mean relative to us"), the intermediate state that avoids the extremes of passion—the vice of too much (excessive passion) or the vice of too little (deficient passion)—both of which frustrate the attainment of the sensible good, which is the end or purpose of the passions.

So, despite the fact that our passions move us in a way that occurs independently of our minds, in order for our passions to move us to act "in the right way," we require the guidance of practical reason, the intellective faculty that is perfected by the virtue of prudence. The subject (source) of the virtue of prudence, then, is the practical intellect. By means of the virtue of prudence, the passions acquire the rational guidance necessary for them to attain their proper ends. But, can the passions themselves, both the concupiscible and the irascible powers of the sense appetites, be the subject of virtue as well? To this question both Aristotle and Aquinas answer yes.

Aquinas draws upon metaphors used by Aristotle to demonstrate how the passions, despite having the capacity to act independently of the mind, are nevertheless the subject (source) of virtue, virtue being a habit of the mind. To the objection that the passions cannot be the subject of virtue because the mind (for Aquinas, the soul) rules the body, Aquinas responds by employing Aristotle's metaphors as a way to make a crucial distinction:

> The body is ruled by the soul, and the irascible and concupiscible powers by the reason, but in different ways. For the body obeys the soul blindly without any contradiction, in those things in which it has a natural aptitude to be moved by the soul: whence the Philosopher says . . . that the *soul rules the body with a despotic command* as the master rules his slave: wherefore the entire movement of the body is referred to the soul. For this reason virtue is not in the body, but in the soul. But the irascible and concupiscible powers do not obey the reason blindly; on the contrary, they have their own proper movements, by which, at times, they go against reason, whence the Philosopher says . . . that the *reason rules the irascible and concupiscible powers by a political command* such as that by which free men are ruled, who have in some respects a will of their own. And for this reason also must there be some virtues in the irascible and concupiscible powers, by which these powers are well disposed to act.[74]

The difference between bodily movements that are the result of the "despotic command" of the mind (the bodily movements of an athlete performing or fingers typing on a keyboard) and those that result from the "political command" of the mind (the emotive responses of fear and daring that are felt in the right way according to right reason) is that the bodily movements of the passions have the capacity to participate in reason by following the directives of reason while retaining their integrity as bodily passions, Aquinas observes, and thus they have the capability to move us to act in the right way. Right action requires right passion. But, for the passions to be felt

---

74. Thomas Aquinas, *Summa Theologica* I–II.56.4 *ad* 3.

in the right way and thus to move us to act in the right way, what is required of the passions is not only that they move us in conformity with right reason, but that this conformity becomes a habit of the sense appetites to feel and to act in the right way. Precisely because the irascible and concupiscible passions are capable of moving us to feel and to act in accordance with reason, and this in a habitual manner, Aquinas sees the passions as the subject of virtue—the irascible passions as the subject of the virtue of fortitude, the concupiscible passions as the subject of the virtue of temperance. Aquinas concludes:

> Therefore in the matter of the operations of the irascible and concupiscible powers, according as they are moved by reason, there must needs be some habit perfecting in respect of acting well, not only the reason, but also the irascible and concupiscible powers . . . therefore the virtue which is in the irascible and concupiscible powers is nothing else but a certain habitual conformity of these powers to reason.[75]

Temperance, then, is the virtuous habit of the mind that guides our sense appetites to their proper end, which is desiring and attaining the sensible good in the right way; fortitude is the virtuous habit of the mind that guides our sense appetites in regard to the sensible good that is difficult to attain and thus guides our desire for the arduous good in the right way. Both temperance and fortitude—insofar as they are habits of the mind (intentional, learned, stable dispositions to feel and to act in the right way) by which we achieve and maintain a proper balance (the rational mean) in the movements of our sense appetites toward the sensible good and away from that which is evil—are perfections of the self: specifically perfections of the passions of the self. The focus of the exercise of these moral virtues is the self, the rational mean determined by the virtue of prudence being the guide to realizing the rectitude of the self. In this regard, as Aquinas stated above, "nothing is declared to be right unless it is done in a certain way by the agent."

The focus of the moral virtue of justice, in contrast, is not on the rectitude of the self, but on fulfilling the right (*ius*) of the other "without taking into account the way it is done by the agent." Like the virtues of temperance and fortitude, the virtue of justice depends on the virtue of prudence as its guide to act in accordance with reason, but unlike the other moral virtues, the rational guide for justice given by prudence—the rational mean—is the "real mean," Aquinas points out, that is, the mean determined not in regard to matters relative to us but in regard to matters that are external to us.[76] To fulfill the obligation of justice (the right), one must give to the other what is their due, "neither more nor less,"[77] this determination of the real mean being the work of prudence. The focus of the virtue of prudence in regard to matters of justice does not

75. Thomas Aquinas, *Summa Theologica* I–II.56.4.

76. Thomas Aquinas, *Summa Theologica* II–II.58.10.

77. Thomas Aquinas, *Summa Theologica* I–II.64.2.

concern the inner passions of the self, but rather the specific external social relations that constitute the obligation of justice. A realistic assessment of the nature of the social relations and of the means necessary to meet the obligation of justice in terms of these social relations is the work of practical reason and thus the proper work of the virtue of prudence. The actual fulfillment of the obligation to render to another what is their due through concrete action, however, has its source in the human will, not the practical intellect, and thus is the work of the virtue of justice, this being the perfection of the will. Justice presupposes prudence but, at the same time, for the directives of prudence to be effectively realized in the form of concrete actions, prudence requires justice. Prudence without justice becomes mere cunning in the service of self-interest. Justice without prudence loses its grounding in reality and becomes ineffectual in its effort to bring about the good in society. What unites prudence and justice as virtues is that they share a common purpose, which is to realize the good in society, but they accomplish this purpose in different but contributory ways. Prudence, as the virtue of the practical intellect, determines the way to the good by disclosing the truth (the reality) of the good; justice, as the virtue of the rational appetite of the will that desires the good, makes the reality of the good concrete. But, besides justice, do the other moral virtues, specifically fortitude and temperance, have a role to play as well in realizing the good in society? In other words, for Aquinas, is there a functional relationship between the rectitude of the self and the rectitude of society? Although the object of justice is to render to the other what is their due "without taking into account the way it is done by the agent," do the other moral virtues as virtues of character, nevertheless, play a role in the work of justice?

The intellectual virtue of prudence and the moral virtues of justice, fortitude, and temperance, Aquinas designates as the cardinal virtues (from the Latin *cardinalis*, the adjectival form of the noun *cardo*, which means hinge) because on the strength of these four virtues depends the whole of the moral life. Each virtue plays a foundational role in our pursuit of the human good, but not in the same way and not with equal primacy.[78] Since the moral virtues, in order to realize the human good, must do so in accordance with reason, the intellectual virtue of prudence, the perfection of practical reason, necessarily has primacy in all moral endeavors in the form of guidance. "Prudence," as Aquinas defines it, "is *right reason applied to action.*" What the right reason of prudence brings to moral choice and thus to action is counsel and judgment regarding what is to be done, but finally and chiefly prudence brings to action the act of command, "which act consists in applying to action the things counselled and judged."[79] That the command of prudence intends the human good, which is the good of reason realized concretely, and that the concrete action taken to realize the good in accordance with reason is the work of justice, places the moral virtue of justice then as second to prudence in the order of primacy. Aquinas states: "prudence,

78. See Thomas Aquinas, *Summa Theologica* I–II.61.2.

79. Thomas Aquinas, *Summa Theologica* II–II.47.8.

since it is a perfection of reason, has the good essentially: while justice effects this good, since it belongs to justice to establish the order of reason in all human affairs."[80] What prudence commands, justice, as the act of the will, realizes.

The moral virtues of fortitude and temperance come next in the order of primacy, fortitude being primary to temperance. Neither fortitude nor temperance contributes directly to the actual realization of the good, as do prudence and justice, but rather indirectly insofar as these moral virtues "safeguard this good, inasmuch as they moderate the passions, lest they lead man away from reason's good," says Aquinas. Because the passions occur outside of the agency of the mind and yet have the capability to follow the directives of reason and thus to participate in what reason intends and what the rational appetite of the will desires, the passions have the ability to contribute, albeit indirectly, to the realization of reason's good. The good that reason knows and the will desires, the passions feel, this when the passions move us to act in accordance with reason. But, given their independence from the mind, the passions, both irascible and concupiscible, also have the ability to cloud reason and to distract the will from enacting reason's good. Being paralyzed by fear or swayed by immoderate sensate pleasures can readily thwart our pursuit of the good. Thus, according to Aquinas, in undertaking to make the good real, prudence and justice need the virtues of fortitude and temperance as strengths of character that safeguard the realization of the good "by removing obstacles thereto." In this regard, "fortitude holds first place, because fear of dangers of death has the greatest power to make man recede from the good of reason: and after fortitude comes temperance, since also pleasures of touch excel all others in hindering the good of reason." Yet, the moderation of our passions, while essential to the realization of the human good, is ancillary to making the human good concrete, this end or purpose being the work of justice. Of the ends of the moral virtues, then, the end or purpose of the moral virtue of justice holds primacy of place, second only to that of the intellectual virtue of prudence, given the primacy of reason over the rational and sensate appetites. Aquinas concludes: "Wherefore among the cardinal virtues, prudence ranks first, justice second, fortitude third, temperance fourth, and after these the other virtues."[81]

The Virtue of Justice in Relation to the Moral Act

The hierarchical ranking that Aquinas gives to the virtues presents a portrait of the moral life in terms of its main components—the virtues—and offers an account of the relation of the virtues to one another. The ranking of the virtues as well as the depiction of their mutual relationship is based on the nature of each virtue, this being determined by considering the end or purpose that each virtue intends to realize (the object of the virtue). But such an account of the virtues and their relationship is necessarily abstract,

---

80. Thomas Aquinas, *Summa Theologica* II–II.123.12.

81. Thomas Aquinas, *Summa Theologica* II–II.123.12; see also I–II.66.4.

meaning that the virtues being considered are viewed in terms of the specific nature of each virtue but apart from the actual living of the moral life. Aquinas is aware of this. In his response to the question "Whether the Moral Virtues Are Better Than the Intellectual Virtues?" Aquinas makes this distinction: "A thing may be said to be greater or less in two ways: first, simply; secondly, relatively . . . Now to consider a thing simply is to consider it in its proper specific nature." In which case, to consider something simply (*simpliciter*) is to understand it on its own terms and not in terms of, that is to say, relative to, something else (*secundum quid*). Thus, simply considered, "the intellectual virtues, which perfect the reason, are more excellent than the moral virtues, which perfect the appetite," because "the object of the reason is more excellent than the object of the appetite: since the reason apprehends things in the universal, while the appetite tends to things themselves, whose being is restricted to the particular."[82] Insofar as the excellence of a virtue is determined by its object, according to Aquinas, the virtues that perfect the intellect, which has as its object universal truth, excel the moral virtues of the appetites, which have as their object the particular good. Simply considered, the intellectual virtues are primary to the moral virtues.

"But if we consider virtue in its relation to act, then moral virtue, which perfects the appetite, whose function it is to move the other powers to act . . . is more excellent,"[83] Aquinas maintains. In which case, by changing the focus of attention to the actual living of the moral life, we are led to consider, first of all, moral action and the good that human acts seek to realize. From this perspective, primacy is given to the will rather than the intellect and to that virtue that perfects the will, which is the moral virtue of justice. The source of moral action lies not in the intellect but in the will. The speculative intellect understands, the practical intellect judges and commands, but only by means of the will does the moral agent act. Herein lies the moral perfection of the human person—doing good—the will being the power that moves the intellect and the passions to act, that is, to realize the good concretely. But, doing the good presupposes desiring the good. This the will does. As rational desire (*appetitus*), the will is both mover and moved: The will is moved by the good as apprehended by the intellect, and the will is mover insofar as the will moves the self to act for the purpose of realizing the good, the object of desire. The source of moral action, then, lies in desire, either desire toward that which is good (attraction) or away from that which is evil (aversion). The habit of the will that perfects the will's desire to realize the good is the moral virtue of justice. While the object of justice is the good that moves the self to act, the good apprehended by the intellect being the right (*ius*) of the other that stands apart from the self and that is determined independently of the self, the subject (source) of justice lies in the self—the will's desire to realize the good that is justice. Thus, relative to the moral act, the virtue of justice, seen as the rectitude of the will both to do good and to desire the good that one does, holds primacy among the

---

82. Thomas Aquinas, *Summa Theologica* I–II.66.3.

83. Thomas Aquinas, *Summa Theologica* I–II.66.3.

virtues for Aquinas. Not only does the virtue of justice dispose us to act justly; the virtue of justice perfects in us the desire to do so as well. Desire entails movement within the self, both as moved and mover, this with the intention of realizing the good concretely. Here the focus is not on the relation of the virtues considered in terms of their specific natures, but on the interaction of the virtues seen in terms of the genesis, execution, and completion of the moral act. From this perspective, a distinct portrait of the active moral life emerges, one that holds the virtue of justice at its center. How so?

The good of justice is the end or purpose that moves the self to act justly. Aquinas observes: "Now good has the aspect of an end, and the end is indeed first in the order of intention, but last in the order of execution."[84] By acting justly, we intend to realize the good of justice. As intention, the good that moves us to act comes first, but in the order of execution the concrete realization of the good, the act as executed, comes last. What, then, comes first in the order of execution? Love, Aquinas responds. Moral action begins in love. Whether the movement within the self toward that which is good begins in the sense appetite that is the concupiscible passion or in the intellectual appetite that is the will, the initiating principle of movement within the appetite, in response to the good as apprehended, is love (*amor*). Given the difference between the sense appetite and the intellectual appetite, the form that love takes in each differs: that which moves the sense appetite—the concupiscible passion—is a sensate love, whereas the love that moves the intellectual appetite—the will—is a rational love.[85] But, the pattern of movement in each is the same. This pattern Aquinas describes as circular:

> The appetible object gives the appetite, first, a certain adaptation to itself, which consists in complacency in that object; and from this follows movement towards the appetible object. For *the appetitve movement is circular . . .* because the appetible object moves the appetite, introducing itself, as it were, into its intention; while the appetite moves towards the realization of the appetible object, so that the movement ends where it began. Accordingly, the first change wrought in the appetite by the appetible object is called *love*, and is nothing else than complacency in that object; and from this complacency results a movement towards that same object, and this movement is *desire*; and lastly, there is rest which is *joy*.[86]

Being moved by the good—the appetible object (the object of desire)—the self undergoes a change within itself, this change occurring in the form of the self's love of the good. Aquinas describes this change in the self as an "adaptation" (*coaptatio*) to the object of desire and as a "complacency" (*complacentia*) in the object. The Latin word *coaptatio* means aptitude, inclination, or kinship; *complacentia* means satisfaction or

84. Thomas Aquinas, *Summa Theologica* I–II.25.2.

85. Thomas Aquinas, *Summa Theologica* I–II.26.1; see Wadell, CP, *Primacy of Love*, 79–93, 145–47. Gallagher, "Will and Its Acts," 84–85; Pasnau, *Thomas Aquinas on Human Nature*, 242.

86. Thomas Aquinas, *Summa Theologica* I–II.26.2.

delight. The terms indicate that a relationship is established between the self and the good when the self is moved by the good. As the object of desire, the good does not stand apart from the self solely as an end to be attained, but in moving the self, the good becomes a part of the self in the form of love, thus creating in the self an inclination toward and a delight in the good as the object of desire. For one who is hungry, being moved by the smell of food cooking (a sensate love) or by the judgment that this cooking food is nutritious and thus healthful (a rational love) creates in the person who is hungry an inclination toward and a delight in the object of desire—the cooking food. From the love that is awakened in the hungry person for the cooking food ("I would love to have some of the food") proceeds the movement of desire for the food that culminates in the joy of attainment—eating the food. Thus, the movement of love, followed by the movement of desire, leading to the joy of attainment, ends where the movement began, that is, with the good, the object of desire.

In the execution of the moral act, Aquinas describes as an "affective union" the relation between the end or purpose of the moral act—the good that moves the self—and the love of the good awakened within the self that is the initiating principle of movement toward the good: this union takes place prior to and is distinct from the actual union that occurs when love is conjoined with that which is loved—the good as the object of desire.[87] As love and then desire, whether sensate or rational, the end or purpose of moral virtue preexists in us affectively, Aquinas states in *Disputed Questions on Truth* (*Quaestiones disputatae de veritate*)—this as an inclination toward or a complacency in that which is loved, an inclination or complacency acquired and sustained by means of the habit of moral virtue. Accordingly, through the practice of the moral virtues, we experience the good that is the end or purpose of the virtues in a direct and present, albeit incomplete way. Being temperate, courageous, and just, in this sense, is its own reward, not simply the means to attaining the reward, that is, the good. For this reason, the end of the moral virtues—what Aquinas terms "the proximate end of things to be done"—has an affective hold on us in a way that the end or purpose of the intellectual virtues does not.[88] Thus, the good that is justice preexists in the one who seeks justice as a rational desire. To depict this desire as a "hunger and thirst" for justice, much as Jesus does in the Sermon on the Mount (Matt 5:6), although figurative, nevertheless well portrays the affective human experience that grasps the good, by being moved by the good, that the act of justice intends to realize.

Yet, the good that moves us to act in a just way, as the good that moves us to act in a temperate or courageous way, is a particular good that we experience as a good for us in the present moment (thus, "the proximate end of things to be done"). What is missing in this concrete experience of the good is the understanding of why this particular good is in fact good as such and thus part of the overall good of the moral life (this being the work of the virtue of understanding) and the practicality of how this

87. Thomas Aquinas, *Summa Theologica* I–II.25.2, *ad* 2; see also I–II.26.2 *ad* 2.

88. Thomas Aquinas, *Truth* 5.1; see Hoffmann, "Prudence and Practical Principles," 175–80.

particular good might be realized concretely according to reason (this being the work of the virtue of prudence).[89] Accordingly, for this wider perspective, the intellectual virtues must come into play in the execution of the moral act, centrally through the virtue of prudence, which brings the universal principles of truth, intuitively grasped by the understanding, to bear on our effort to attain a particular good. However, unlike the virtues of the speculative intellect—wisdom, knowledge, and understanding—which concern "necessary things" (universal truths), the intellectual virtue of prudence is concerned with "contingent things," that is, "things to be done" (practical actions), which makes prudence a close and necessary ally to the moral virtues that are likewise concerned with "things to be done," according to Aquinas.[90] Indeed, in the execution of the moral act, the virtue of prudence and the moral virtues need each other. Whereas the moral virtues rightly dispose us toward the end of things to be done, the virtue of prudence provides the necessary rational guidance regarding the means for attaining the end of things to be done. What the moral virtues gain from prudence is right reason; what prudence gains from the moral virtues is right appetite. Moral choice requires both. Aquinas explains:

> No moral virtue can be without prudence; since it is proper to moral virtue to make a right choice, for it is an elective habit. Now right choice requires not only the inclination to a due end, which inclination is the direct outcome of moral virtue, but also correct choice of things conducive to the end, which choice is made by prudence, that counsels, judges, and commands in those things that are directed to the end. In like manner one cannot have prudence unless one has the moral virtues: since prudence is *right reason about things to be done*, and the starting-point of reason is the end of things to be done, to which end man is rightly disposed by moral virtue.[91]

But, although prudence and the moral virtues through their mutual interaction create the path to the end of things to be done, neither determines the end itself that the moral act seeks to realize. While prudence in its role as rational guide to the execution of the moral act provides the requisite deliberation regarding the means to the end that the moral virtues seek to realize (the proximate end of things to be done—the particular good), prudence does not appoint the end itself of moral virtue. On this point Aristotle provides a helpful analogy:

> We deliberate not about ends but about means. For a doctor does not deliberate whether he shall heal, nor an orator whether he shall persuade, nor a statesman whether he shall produce law and order, nor does any one else

---

89. See Hoffmann, "Prudence and Practical Principles," 170–75, 180–82.

90. Thomas Aquinas, *Summa Theologica* II–II.47.5; see also I–II.57.2.

91. Thomas Aquinas, *Summa Theologica* I–II.65.1; see also I–II.58.4–5.

deliberate about his end. They assume the end and consider how and by what means it is to be attained.[92]

Prudence, as right reason applied to moral action, functions in a manner analogous to the doctor who is engaged in the art of healing. As the practice of medicine assumes as its end the healing of the patient, so the virtue of prudence assumes as its end the good that is to be realized. When prudence deliberates about things to be done, the virtue of prudence, as rational guide to the moral virtues, assumes as given the end that the moral virtues intend to realize through moral action, which is the particular good: the sensible good as the end that moves the sense appetites (such as attaining food); the rational good as the end that moves the rational appetite (such as attaining nutritious food). Prudence does not deliberate as to whether the self should pursue the good, sensible or rational, but only deliberates regarding the means to be taken to attain the good in a reasonable manner. What prudence provides is the way to achieve and maintain the proper balance (the rational mean or the real mean) between too much (excess) and too little (deficiency) in the movement of the appetites toward that which is their proper end and away from that which is evil, this in accordance with reason. What prudence does not do is appoint the end that the moral virtues seek to realize. However, Aquinas points out, neither do the moral virtues themselves appoint the end—the good—that they intend to realize. For both the virtue of prudence and the moral virtues, the end of things to be done, which is the good, is assumed as given, not the result of their determination.[93] What, then, determines the end of things to be done? Aquinas answers: nature itself.

All of nature, Aquinas maintains, consists of movement (*appetitus*) toward an end. Trees growing, clouds forming, fires burning, rocks falling—all are natural movements that aim at an end or purpose. The latter two examples Aquinas specifically uses to exemplify the point that "nature is nothing other than a principle of motion and rest in that in which it is primarily and *per se* and not *per accidens*." That a fire moves upward and that a rock falls downward exhibits movement that is rooted in the nature of each, that is, movement whose source is in and through the nature of the thing itself (*per se*), and not as the result of an extrinsic or accidental cause (*per accidens*). The nature of each, moreover, is the intrinsic principle of both its motion and its rest. Aquinas states: "For those things which are naturally moved to a place, also or even more naturally rest in that place. Because of this, fire is naturally moved upward, since it is natural for it to be there. And for the same reason everything can be said to be moved naturally and to rest naturally in its place."[94] Thus, a falling rock falls to the earth, this being the place where it naturally finds rest in accordance with its nature, whereas the flames of a fire dance upwards, naturally finding rest (their place) in the

---

92. Aristotle, *Nicomachean Ethics* 3.3.1112b11–16.

93. Thomas Aquinas, *Summa Theologica* II–II.47.6.

94. Thomas Aquinas, *Commentary on Aristotle's Physics* 2.1.145.

air, this in accordance with the nature of fire. In the natural movements of rocks and fire, as in the natural movements of trees and clouds, the human mind discerns purpose or direction toward an end, this purposeful movement being determined by the nature of the thing itself. Aquinas describes such purposeful movement as the natural love (*amor naturalis*) or the natural desire (*appetitus naturalis*) in the thing toward its end, and insofar as realizing the end ("to rest naturally in its place") fulfills the natural movement of the thing in accordance with its nature, the end (that which fulfills the natural desire of the thing in motion) is the good.[95]

In using *appetitus* to depict the natural movements of things in nature, such as rocks and fire, toward their proper ends—the same term that he uses to describe the natural movements of the sense appetites and the rational appetite—Aquinas intends the term *appetitus* to be understood analogically. An analogical term provides a way to highlight differences while at the same time holding these differences together in a concept that points to what these differences share in common. What differentiates natural appetite from both sensate and rational appetite is the source of movement: whereas the movement (desire) of natural appetite toward the good is rooted in the nature of the thing itself as the inner principle of its motion, the movement (desire) of the sensate and rational appetite toward the good results from the conscious apprehension of a sensate or rational good in that which is other. "Therefore, just as the natural appetite tends to good existing in a thing; so the animal or voluntary appetite tends to a good which is apprehended," states Aquinas. Despite that which distinguishes them as movements in nature, these distinct forms of *appetitus* share something in common that is foundational to their movement—each naturally "tends" to the good which is its end, says Aquinas: this in accordance with its nature. *Appetitus*, then, whether natural, sensate, or rational, is for Aquinas a natural inclination in the thing—a tending—to the good that is the fundamental characteristic of all movements in nature. Aquinas succinctly states this point by quoting the words of Aristotle that open the *Nicomachean Ethics*: "*the good is that which all desire*."[96]

Given the primacy of the good as the end that all movements in nature desire, Aquinas, commenting on Aristotle's words, points out that the good cannot be directly perceived or understood as such, but can be known only in and through its effects, that is, only in and through the specific inclinations toward the good that nature's movements exhibit. Like being (*esse*)—the act of existence by which all concrete beings become actual—the good is a primary reality that cannot be defined, but can only be described in terms of its effects. Aquinas explains: "Now primary things cannot be understood by anything anterior to them, but by something consequent, as causes are understood through their proper effects. But since good properly is the moving

---

95. Thomas Aquinas, *Summa Theologica* I–II.26.1.

96. Thomas Aquinas, *Summa Theologica* I–II.8.1; see Aristotle, *Nicomachean Ethics* 1.1.1094a 3; see also Thomas Aquinas, *Summa Theologica* I.80.1.

principle of the appetite, good is described as movement of the appetite."[97] Thus, in order to consider the end of things to be done—the end (the good) that the virtue of prudence and the moral virtues seek to realize—Aquinas directs our attention to instantiations of the good that are perceived and understood in and through the natural inclinations toward the good (the end) in the things of nature. This he does by offering a schematic yet panoramic view of the order or levels of the natural inclinations to the good that make up the things of nature. The good is what all things in nature desire, Aquinas maintains. Thus, by describing the levels of desire (inclinations to the good) in the things of nature, beginning at the level of existence that all creaturely beings share in common (including human beings) and culminating at the level of existence that distinguishes human beings from all other forms of being, Aquinas portrays the essential movements in nature that enable us to conceive the good that nature determines as the end of things to be done.[98]

The fundamental desire (inclination) that all things in nature share in common is the desire to be. The force of a fire that resists being extinguished, the petals of a flower opening to the light of the sun, an animal stalking its prey, a human being striving to acquire the basic necessities to live a healthful life, such as having sufficient food, clean water, adequate shelter—all such movements exhibit the fundamental inclination of things in nature to realize their actuality (being), which in and of itself is desirable (good). "Goodness and being," Aquinas notes, "are really the same, and differ only in idea."[99] That the human mind recognizes in the human desire to live and, more fully, to flourish, a natural inclination to the good that human beings share with all other beings in nature, enables the mind to perceive in this inclination not only purpose in nature (the desire to be) but moral purpose in all human striving (the desire to be as a good). Moreover, the desire to be that is manifest in the movements of nature, the mind perceives as a law of nature, one that is exhibited in the natural impetus in all creaturely beings toward self-preservation and avoidance of that which threatens a being's existence. Aquinas observes: "Because in man there is first of all an inclination to good in accordance with the nature which he has in common with all substances: inasmuch as every substance seeks the preservation of its own being, according to its nature: and by reason of this inclination, whatever is a means of preserving human life, and of warding off its obstacles, belongs to the natural law." Thus, Aquinas formulates the natural inclination to self-preservation (the desire to be) that human beings share with all creatures as a precept of the natural law, a precept that he then uses as a directive and the basis for the moral life. This basic precept, however, presupposes a more fundamental precept of the natural law—the metaphysical truth that the good is what all beings desire, when brought to bear on matters of practical

---

97. Thomas Aquinas, *Commentary on the Nicomachean Ethics* 1.1.9; see Pinckaers, OP, *Sources of Christian Ethics*, 408–12.

98. Thomas Aquinas, *Summa Theologica* I–II.94.2.

99. Thomas Aquinas, *Summa Theologica* I.5.1.

reasoning and moral concern, provides the foundation and directive for all moral reasoning. Aquinas designates this foundational directive as the primary precept of the natural law and the first principle of practical reason: *"good is to be done and pursued, and evil is to be avoided."*[100] Herein lies the foundation and the end or purpose of the moral life—the end that nature determines.

The specific inclinations to the good that mark the movements of nature, then, give substance to this fundamental precept of the natural law, comprehended by the intellect, that good is to be done and evil avoided. Beyond the natural inclination to self-preservation that characterizes all things in nature, Aquinas identifies a second level of desire in nature that human beings share specifically with other animals: exceeding the natural desire simply to be, animals (including humans) are moved by the natural inclination to perpetuate the species through sexual mating and the nurture of offspring, this nurture in human life taking the form of the socialization and education of the young. At this level of existence, the desire to be manifests itself as the desire to live, a dynamism that carries within itself the natural inclination to bring forth new life and to enable this new life to thrive. Whether as a mother bird hovering over her chicks in the nest or human parents attentively caring for their infant, animals naturally exhibit an inclination to protect and nurture their young, an inclination toward the good as the end that nature itself determines (the perpetuation of life).[101]

The third level of existence that Aquinas demarcates pertains specifically to human beings. The distinguishing characteristic of this level of existence is the rationality that is proper to human existence. Human rationality, as we have seen, manifests itself in the form of knowing and desiring, these two acts of the mind being the expressions of the intellective and appetitive powers of the soul, according to Aquinas. That the human mind functions in these two ways—as knowing (the function of the intellect) and desiring (the rational desire of the will)—leads Aquinas to formulate the natural inclination to the good that is specific to human nature in two distinct ways: as "a natural inclination to know the truth about God, and to live in society."[102] Let us consider the first: our natural inclination to know the truth about God, which Aquinas sees as an essential determinant of human nature.

For both Aristotle and Aquinas, the human intellect by its very nature has an inclination (an intellectual desire) to know the real (being) and thus to know the true. Aristotle gives voice to this natural inclination in all human beings in the opening words of the *Metaphysics*:

> All men by nature desire to know. An indication of this is the delight we take in
> our senses; for even apart from their usefulness they are loved for themselves;
> and above all others the sense of sight. For not only with a view to action, but

---

100. Thomas Aquinas, *Summa Theologica* I–II.94.2.

101. Thomas Aquinas, *Summa Theologica* I–II.94.2; see Porter, *Nature as Reason*, 118–21.

102. Thomas Aquinas, *Summa Theologica* I–II.94.2.

> even when we are not going to do anything, we prefer seeing . . . to everything
> else. The reason is that this, most of all the senses, makes us know and brings
> to light many differences between things.[103]

Wonder is the source and the ongoing impetus that moves the intellect to know, say Aristotle and Aquinas, the wonder that begins in the senses which show the world to us, that then leads to rational inquiry—this being the work of the speculative intellect that seeks to discover the causes of things, both particular and universal, and ultimately to discover the first and final cause of all things, which for Aquinas is God the Creator. Such wonder awakens in all human beings the desire to know the truth—certainly in the minds of philosophers, theologians, and poets, but also in the person who suddenly sees the everydayness of life in a new light, or in the young child who looks upon the world with curious and astonished eyes. The desire that wonder inspires to know the truth is a desire to know the truth not for its usefulness, but for itself: the desire finally rests in the truth that is ultimate. The desire (inclination) in human beings to know that which is ultimate, Aristotle and Aquinas represent as the love of wisdom—a love that begins in wonder.[104] Aquinas sees in the natural inclination in human beings to know the truth, and this ultimately as the truth about God, an essential determination of human nature, and thus a precept of the natural law. But the end (to know the truth about God) that moves the intellect does so, not as a law that is imposed on the intellect from without, but as the good that moves the intellect, according to its nature, from within as intellectual desire—the good that preexists in the movement of the intellect as the love of wisdom.

The second way that human beings incline to the good that is by nature their proper end is to live in society, says Aquinas. In concert with Aristotle, Aquinas maintains that we as human beings are by nature social animals. The perfection (fulfillment) of our human nature is realized in and through the social relations that make up our lives and that constitute human society. Aristotle makes this point in the *Politics* by asserting that the human being is "by nature a political animal," the *polis* (city-state) being the community of free citizens in and through which the human good is achieved.[105] As human beings, Aristotle states in the *Nicomachean Ethics*, we are "born for citizenship."[106] The desire to live in society—to be a citizen—is not first a matter of personal choice but an expression of our nature as human beings. But unlike other social animals that bond and function together for a common end

---

103. Aristotle, *Metaphysics* 1.1.980a21–26.

104. Aristotle, *Metaphysics* 1.2.982b11–25; Thomas Aquinas, *Commentary on the Metaphysics of Aristotle* 1.3.53–57. For a luminous meditation on wonder as the beginning of wisdom, see Pieper, *Leisure the Basis of Culture*, 127–46.

105. Aristotle, *Politics* 1.2.1253a 2. See Thomas Aquinas, *Commentary on Aristotle's Politics* 1.1.20–21, 23.

106. Aristotle, *Nicomachean Ethics* 1.7.1097b11. See Thomas Aquinas, *Commentary on the Nicomachean Ethics* 1.9.112.

(Aristotle uses bees as an example), the human animal is distinctively a social animal that is rational. Thus, for human beings the natural inclination to live in society will be distinctively a rational inclination: the human good that is by nature a social good is a rational good. What this means for Aquinas is that the human animal, unlike other social animals, both comprehends and desires the good (in this case, to live in society) that is the proper end of being human. Moreover, the movements in nature that we as rational beings discern as purposeful, that is, as the inclination in things of nature toward their proper ends, Aquinas sees as having the imprint of the Divine Mind, which for Aquinas is the eternal law. He states: "Wherefore, since all things subject to Divine providence are ruled and measured by the eternal law . . . it is evident that all things partake somewhat of the eternal law, in so far as, namely, from its being imprinted on them, they derive their respective inclinations to their proper acts and ends." But precisely by being rational in nature, Aquinas adds, "the rational creature is subject to Divine providence in the most excellent way, in so far as it partakes of a share of providence, by being provident both for itself and for others."[107] Accordingly, the natural inclination that human beings have to live in society, while a determination of human nature (and thus a precept of the natural law which is an expression of the eternal law), is at the same time the rational desire that moves human beings from within to act concretely in pursuit of the good that can be realized only in and through society. Through our ability as rational creatures to comprehend and desire the ends or purposes of the movements in nature—here specifically the human inclination to live in society—we partake knowingly and willingly in the Divine plan (the eternal law). Our human nature impels us to live in society, but we perfect this natural inclination to the good by acquiring the right disposition (appetite) to realize the social good concretely, this specifically by means of the virtue of justice. To live in society is a natural inclination of human nature; to live in society justly leads to the fulfillment (perfection) of human nature.

The virtues, then, both intellectual and moral, Aquinas sees as perfecting the natural inclinations that move us distinctively as human beings to the good—in the form of both knowing and desiring.[108] In the execution of the moral act, our natural inclinations to the good determine the end of the moral act, whereas the virtues—specifically, the virtue of prudence and the moral virtues—determine the means by which the end is realized. Both prudence and the moral virtues are moved by the good—the end of things to be done—and, for this reason, Aquinas maintains that the end of things to be done, the good which moves the self to act virtuously, preexists both in the practical intellect and in the concupiscible and rational appetites, but in different ways—in the practical intellect in the form of knowledge and in the appetites in the form of desire. Aquinas describes the distinct ways in which the end moves the self to act in *Disputed Questions on Truth* as follows:

107. Thomas Aquinas, *Summa Theologica* I–II.91.2.

108. See Porter, *Nature as Reason*, 175–76; Pinckaers, OP, *Sources of Christian Ethics*, 404–5.

Now, the end of things to be done pre-exists in us in two ways: first, through the natural knowledge we have of man's end. This knowledge, of course, as the Philosopher says, belongs to the intellect, which is a principle of things to be done as well as of things to be studied; and, as the Philosopher also points out, ends are principles of things to be done. The second way that these ends pre-exist in us is through our desires. Here the ends of things to be done exist in us in our moral virtues, which influence a man to live a just, brave, or temperate life. This is, in a sense, the proximate end of things to be done.[109]

Given that the virtue of prudence counsels, judges, and commands the self to act in light of the end of things to be done but does not determine the end, what specifically is the end that determines the virtue of prudence? What moves prudence to deliberate? Aquinas states: "*synderesis* moves prudence."[110] The term *synderesis*, as used by Aquinas, denotes the "natural habit" of the intellect that is specific to practical reason—the habit of the mind that moves the self to act in the light of the primary precept of the natural law and the first principle of practical reason, which is that good is to be done and evil avoided. The habit is rooted in the intuitive grasp of the understanding that comprehends the universal truth that all created beings tend to the good, which is their proper end in accordance with their nature, and thus for the virtue of prudence this truth provides the end or purpose of its deliberations. What moves prudence to deliberate in all matters of practical, moral concern is the fundamental truth of practical reason, which is that good is to be pursued and evil avoided. This first principle of practical reason prudence assumes as its end or purpose in every act of deliberation. Thus, much like the doctor who instinctively assumes as the end of all medical interventions the healing of the patient, so the virtue of prudence intuitively assumes as its end that good is to be done and evil avoided.[111]

What is the end or purpose that moves the moral virtues? The proximate end of things to be done, says Aquinas, which is the particular good that is specific to the natural inclinations that move human beings to act concretely—the inclination to self-preservation, to propagate the species, to know the truth, to live in society—the particular good that preexists both in the natural inclination to the good as desire for the good and at the same time as the determination (obligation) of our nature that must be met (thus, a precept of the natural law) if the human good is to be realized. Satisfying our hunger by eating food both fulfills our natural desire for this sensate good and meets a basic requirement of our biological nature. So it is with our natural inclination to live in society: what we comprehend and desire as a human good (to live in society), we also perceive as a moral obligation, insofar as the natural inclination to live in society—a basic requirement (obligation) of our human nature—intends its perfection (the good). "Whatever pertains to this inclination belongs to the natural

109. Thomas Aquinas, *Truth* 5.1.
110. Thomas Aquinas, *Summa Theologica* II–II.47.6 *ad* 3.
111. Thomas Aquinas, *Summa Theologica* I.79.12.

law," states Aquinas. He observes, by way of example, that a person, to live in society, must "avoid offending those among whom one has to live."[112] The obligation to respect those with whom we live in society lies not in a source outside of human nature, but as a determination of human nature, this obligation being a specification of what living in society requires if its end or purpose (the social good) is to be realized. Meeting this obligation is the work of the virtue of justice. The natural inclination of human beings to live in society finds its perfection (fulfillment) only in this way—in and through the disposition of the moral virtue whose formal object is to render to others in society what is their due, this being the virtue of justice. At the center of the active moral life that intends the good, one that necessarily involves our relations with others, stand acts of justice.

Social Justice as a Moral Act

The right (*ius*)—what is due to another person—is realized in different ways in a society, this difference being determined by the distinct ways in which we as members of a society relate to one another in the society.[113] Because our social relations have different forms, the act of rendering to the other in society what is their due—the act of justice—will have different forms as well. For Aquinas, the consideration of the interplay of human relations that take place in a society yields three basic types of social relationship that structure a society: the relation between one individual or particular group and another, the relation between the social whole and the individual, and the relation between the individual and the social whole. These three types of social relationship are not discrete, static spheres that make up a society, but rather are distinct yet interdependent forms of social living that constitute the vitality of a society and are the distinct ways in and through which the good of the society is realized by those who make up the society. To each of these forms of social relationship, Aquinas maintains, there corresponds a distinct type of justice.[114]

The first and most evident type of justice is the act of justice that directs the interaction between one individual or particular group and another. This Aquinas terms commutative justice (*iustitia commutativa*)—the Latin noun *commutatio* refers to any type of exchange or barter that takes place between people in a society. Secondly, the type of justice that is done when the common goods of a society are distributed fairly—in contemporary society, goods such as material wealth, political power, natural resources, education, and health care—Aquinas terms distributive justice (*iustitia distributiva*). With both types of justice, in the social relationship there is a creditor (the one who is owed what is due) and a debtor (the one who has the obligation to render to the other what is due). Both types of justice envisage an individual as a

112. Thomas Aquinas, *Summa Theologica* I–II.94.2.

113. See Hollenbach, SJ, "Modern Catholic Teachings," 213, 219.

114. See Pieper, *Four Cardinal Virtues*, 70–75.

creditor in the social relationship—that is, as one to whom something is due. Commutative justice, for example, concerns the fairness of the interaction that occurs in the workplace between employee and employer or in the marketplace between buyer and seller. Each individual in the social relationship is both creditor and debtor to the other: labor in exchange for salary (and vice versa), payment in exchange for product (and vice versa). Here the act of justice, says Aquinas, "is concerned about the mutual dealings between two persons." With distributive justice, on the other hand, an individual is the creditor (the one who is owed what is due), but the debtor in this social relationship is not another individual, but rather the social whole: This whole in modern democracies is represented by the elected officials of the government and indirectly by the voters. In this social relationship, Aquinas observes, "there is the order of the whole towards the parts, to which corresponds the order of that which belongs to the community in relation to each single person." Here justice is done when the rightful claim of each individual in the society to a share of the common goods of the society is met.[115] However, Aquinas points out that unlike commutative justice which has an arithmetical preciseness to it (for example, the market price of a product in a capitalist economy), distributive justice is necessarily proportional, based on the complex relationship between persons in society and the social goods distributed by the government, both in terms of benefits and burdens. (For example, in the United States, the government uses progressive tax brackets based on the taxpayer's income.)[116] Yet, despite the authoritative source of distributive justice (the government), this authority is not unrestricted in scope, but directed to and thus limited by what is due to each person in the society. Moreover, in the relationship between the social whole and the individual, what is required is not only the fair distribution of goods on the part of the government, but the willing acceptance on the part of the individual to the distribution. For justice to be realized in this relationship, both the good of the social whole and the good of the individual must be represented and acknowledged. Aquinas observes:

> The act of distributing the goods of the community, belongs to none but those who exercise authority over those goods; and yet distributive justice is also in the subjects to whom those goods are distributed in so far as they are contented by a just distribution.[117]

The third type of justice concerns the relation between the individual and the social whole. In this form of social relationship, the individual is the debtor (the one who has the obligation to give to the other what is due). The other, the creditor in this relationship, is the society (the social whole to which something is owed by the individual in society). In this relationship, the individual and the social whole do not

---

115. Thomas Aquinas, *Summa Theologica* II–II.61.1. See Pieper, *Four Cardinal Virtues*, 81–103.

116. Thomas Aquinas, *Summa Theologica* II–II.61.2.

117. Thomas Aquinas, *Summa Theologica* II–II.61.1 *ad* 3.

stand apart from one another as separate entities, as is the case with the type of social relationship that calls for commutative justice. Here the good of the individual and the good of the social whole imply one another, as they also do with distributive justice. The good of the individual is realized only in and through the social whole, but the good of the social whole, to be realized and maintained, demands something from each individual in the society—right actions that contribute to the good of the whole. What distinguishes the good of the individual from the good of the social whole lies in the nature of the good for each: the acts of commutative justice and distributive justice intend the particular good of the individual, whereas the acts of justice on the part of the individual in relation to the social whole intend the common good of the whole. For Aquinas the proper object of this third type of justice is the common good of the society. Aquinas variously terms this type of justice general justice (*iustitia generalis*) or legal justice (*iustitia legalis*). The latter term highlights the end or purpose of law in a society: "since it belongs to the law to direct to the common good . . . it follows that the justice which is in this way styled general, is called *legal justice,* because thereby man is in harmony with the law which directs the acts of all the virtues to the common good," states Aquinas. Paying one's taxes honestly and willingly not only exhibits compliance with federal and state laws but also shows both a recognition that this act contributes to the common good of the society and a ready disposition to act in this way. The former term—general justice—highlights the directive nature of this third type of justice with regard to the other types of justice and the other moral virtues. The particular good that comes from one who is temperate or brave or from one who acts justly toward their neighbor in the end contributes to the common good of the whole. The end or purpose of general or legal justice is precisely this—to direct particular acts of virtue to the common good. Aquinas comments:

> Now it is evident that all who are included in a community, stand in relation to that community as parts to a whole; while a part, as such, belongs to a whole, so that whatever is the good of a part can be directed to the good of the whole. It follows therefore that the good of any virtue, whether such virtue direct man in relation to himself, or in relation to certain other individual persons, is referable to the common good, to which justice directs: so that all acts of virtue can pertain to justice, in so far as it directs man to the common good. It is in this sense that justice is called a general virtue.[118]

As a way to illustrate this third type of justice, let us consider again a chance face-to-face encounter on a city street with a person who is homeless and poor and who is asking for our help. Their question to us is simple and direct: "I'm hungry; can you help me get something to eat?" For our part in this encounter, we can either ignore the question and quickly move on (the request being viewed by us as intrusive and the need of the person being seen by us as a problem for which we have no responsibility);

---

118. Thomas Aquinas, *Summa Theologica* II–II.58.5; see also II–II.58.6.

or, being moved by the question and by the need of the person before us (thus, being moved by compassion for the person), we stop and give money to this person in need. Is this act of generosity on our part an act of justice?

To our query Aquinas would offer a nuanced response. Strictly speaking, the act of generosity is not a type of justice, according to Aquinas, because one who is generous—Aquinas refers to this character trait as the virtue of liberality (*liberalitas*)—gives freely to another out of what is theirs, whereas justice gives to another what is due to them out of obligation. Generosity originates in us; justice originates in the right of the other. Yet, Aquinas adds, both generosity and justice are similar in that both are "directed chiefly to another," and both are "concerned with external things . . . albeit under a different aspect."[119] In the example of a person responding to the need of another who is homeless and hungry, the "external thing" that is exchanged is money, but unlike the exchange that is directed by commutative justice, in which there is an equality of exchange between the parties (payment in exchange for product), here the exchange takes place "under a different aspect," namely, as money freely given to meet the need of another person. Accordingly, in this particular monetary exchange between the two individuals, there is neither a creditor nor a debtor in the relationship. Thus, from the perspective of this specific transaction between two people, the act of generosity on the part of one, while seen as an act of moral virtue, appears not to be an act of justice.

But this perspective is limited. If we restrict our view of this specific transaction simply to the exchange of money between the two people on a city street, we miss seeing the other forms of social relationship that are in play in this transaction. Aquinas would agree. Homelessness is a personal problem, but homelessness is at the same time a social problem that affects all in the society. In 2018 the headline of the editorial page of the *Los Angeles Times* asked: "Can a City with 58,000 Homeless Still Function?" The editorial began: "Homelessness affects the lives of all Angelenos, not just those forced to live on the streets. And it does so almost daily, in ways large and small." The editorial ends with these words: "At stake here is the quality of life for everyone in the county, not just the people without homes."[120] A year later, the magnitude of the problem was on display when Los Angeles County reported the 2019 homeless count: 58,936 homeless living throughout the county, with 36,300 of those living in the city, this increase despite 619 million dollars that were used by the county and the city to address the problem.[121] In an encounter with one who is homeless, what holds our attention in an immediate way is their plight, not the structural causes of their homelessness (for example, the lack of affordable housing). Yet, shaping this encounter in a very concrete way is the failure of distributive justice on the part of the

---

119. Thomas Aquinas, *Summa Theologica* II–II.117.5.

120. *Los Angeles Times* Editorial Board, "Can a City with 58,000 Homeless Still Function?"

121. See Oreskes and Smith, "County Homelessness Increases 12%"; Lopez, "Total Abdication of Leadership."

government as much as the personal need of the one who stands before us. The structural causes that render the person who is homeless a creditor in relation to the social whole appear remote, yet are real and present, to the specific encounter in which we find ourselves. Addressing structural injustice is primarily the work of government; still, as voters and by having a voice in civil society, this is our work as well. But, the immediacy of the need before us calls for a specific and direct response on our part. Moreover, that we perceive this need not only as the personal problem of one but as the social problem of all in the society renders our response to the one in need an act not only of generosity, but of justice. From the perspective of the common good of the society, we stand in relation to the request of the one who is homeless as a debtor. Our act of generosity, while directed to the specific need of the person before us, intends as well the common good of the whole, and thus we are moved to give freely to one in need, and at the same time, by meeting this particular need, to render to the social whole what is its due. In this way the act of general justice, whose proper object is the common good, directs the virtue of generosity, as well as the other moral virtues (such as the virtue of fortitude in the face of adversity), to its own proper end. Herein lies the work of justice as a general virtue.

When Love Informs Social Justice

To the third type of justice, which Aquinas calls legal or general justice, the modern tradition of Catholic social teaching gives the name "social justice," the term first appearing in Pope Pius XI's 1931 encyclical *Quadragesimo anno (After Forty Years)*. Later, the US Catholic bishops in the 1986 pastoral letter on the economy, while continuing to use the term social justice, also refer to this type of justice as "contributive justice."[122] Although the name for this third type of justice changes in the modern tradition of Catholic social teaching, the meaning given to the term by Aquinas in the medieval period remains essentially the same. Social justice, as general justice, concerns individuals in society acting for the common good. The concern for social justice in the modern period of Catholic social teaching, moreover, brings with it a further concern: the need on the part of the church to establish clearly the relationship between social justice and Christian love (*agapē*).

Thus, in *Quadragesimo anno*, in addition to introducing the term social justice into the modern encyclical tradition, Pius XI makes a further distinctive move: he closely aligns social justice with what he terms social charity. The encyclical commemorates the fortieth anniversary of the first modern social encyclical—Pope Leo XIII's *Rerum novarum (The Condition of Labor)*, issued in 1891. Pope Pius XI addresses the economic injustices of the day, this in the context of the worldwide depression that occurred in the 1930s. Neither the unregulated competition of free markets nor

---

122. Pius XI, *Quadragesimo anno (After Forty Years)*, no. 88; National Conference of Catholic Bishops, *Economic Justice for All*, no. 71. See Curran, *Catholic Social Teaching 1891–Present*, 188–91.

the economic supremacy of the few that has replaced free competition in the markets can provide "a true and effective guiding principle" for economic life. "More lofty and noble principles must therefore be sought in order to regulate this supremacy firmly and honestly: to wit, social justice and social charity," Pius XI asserts. "To that end all institutions of public and social life must be imbued with the spirit of justice, and this justice must above all be truly operative. It must build up a juridical and social order able to pervade all economic activity. Social charity should be, as it were, the soul of this order," states the pope.[123] Social charity here refers not to direct acts of charity that seek to moderate the consequences of injustice (the giving of alms to the poor, such as food, clothing, shelter) but to acts of Christian charity that have as their wider social intent to imbue the institutional structures of justice with something more—the spirit of love. "Charity cannot take the place of justice unfairly withheld," says Pius, "but, even though a state of things be pictured in which every man receives at last all that is his due, a wide field will nevertheless remain open to charity. For, justice alone, even though most faithfully observed, can remove indeed the cause of social strife, but can never bring about a union of hearts and minds." To attain social harmony such as this, charity is required. For Pius, in the virtue of social charity lies "the main principle of stability in all institutions."[124]

Relating social charity to social justice gains further articulation in subsequent papal encyclicals. For Pope John Paul II, in his 1987 encyclical *Sollicitudo rei socialis (On Social Concern)*, the reality of the interdependence of the peoples of the world, within nations and between nations, an interdependence that takes place in and through economic, political, cultural, and religious institutions, calls for a distinct moral response on the part of the peoples of the world, a response enabled by what John Paul terms the virtue of solidarity. This virtue "is not a feeling of vague compassion or shallow distress at the misfortunes of so many people, both near and far," the pope states; rather, "it is *a firm and persevering determination* to commit oneself to the *common good*; that is to say to the good of all and of each individual, because we are *all* really responsible *for all*."[125] But, John Paul notes, Christian charity brings to the work of solidarity something more: "In the light of faith, solidarity seeks to go beyond itself, to take on the *specifically Christian* dimension of total gratuity, forgiveness and reconciliation. One's neighbor is then not only a human being with his or her own rights and a fundamental equality with everyone else, but becomes the *living image of God*," the God who for Christians is one God in three persons—Father, Son, and Holy Spirit—the communion of the three being the "supreme *model of unity*" that enlightens and inspires "our *solidarity*."[126]

---

123. Pius XI, *Quadragesimo anno (After Forty Years)*, no. 88.

124. Pius XI, *Quadragesimo anno (After Forty Years)*, no. 137; see Mich, *Catholic Social Teaching and Movements*, 79–80.

125. John Paul II, *Sollicitudo rei socialis (On Social Concern)*, no. 38 (italics original).

126. John Paul II, *Sollicitudo rei socialis (On Social Concern)*, no. 40; see Dorr, "Solidarity and

Pope Benedict XVI likewise takes up the relationship between Christian charity and social justice in his 2009 encyclical *Caritas in veritate (Charity in Truth)*. The pope states: "On the one hand, charity demands justice: recognition and respect for the legitimate rights of individuals and peoples. It strives to build the *earthly city* according to law and justice. On the other hand, charity transcends justice and completes it in the logic of giving and forgiving." Charity requires that justice be done; but justice achieves its perfection only in charity. What animates a society is not simply respecting the rights of others in and through the institutional forms that structure the society, but more fundamentally engendering the kind of human social relationships that take place in and through the institutional structures of society to be "relationships of gratuitousness, mercy and communion," says Benedict.[127] A society flourishes when each member of the society intends the good of all in the society—the common good that is realized, not as an end that stands outside of the human relationships that constitute the society, but as an end that is embodied in these social relationships. "The more we strive to secure a common good corresponding to the real needs of our neighbors, the more effectively we love them," Benedict observes. "This is the institutional path—we might also call it the political path—of charity, no less excellent and effective than the kind of charity which encounters the neighbor directly, outside the institutional mediation of the *pólis*."[128]

For Pius, as for John Paul and Benedict, social justice and social charity are distinct yet inseparable—inseparable in that social charity, to be effective and concrete, requires that the obligations of social justice be met, whereas justice, to be fully realized in society, requires the direction of social charity (to achieve "a union of hearts and minds," according to Pius); the two are distinct one from the other in that acts of charity can never substitute for the work of justice ("charity cannot take the place of justice unfairly withheld," to use the words of Pius), nor can the universal demands of social justice limit charity simply to an auxiliary role in relation to justice, such as merely providing the inspiration needed for fulfilling the work of justice.[129] By establishing the relation between social justice and Christian love (*agapē*), however, the papal encyclicals provoke this fundamental question: In a pluralistic world, how precisely does Christian charity relate to social justice in such a way that the integrity (the essential form or nature) of each is maintained and yet the relationship of both can speak meaningfully and act effectively in a world constituted by a diversity of peoples? A theoretical question such as this is not addressed in the social encyclicals, which are primarily pastoral in intent. To pursue this question, we turn again to Aquinas.

Integral Human Development."

127. Benedict XVI, *Charity in Truth*, no. 6; see Dorr, *Option for the Poor and for the Earth*, 328–29, 331–33.

128. Benedict XVI, *Charity in Truth: Caritas in Veritate*, no. 7.

129. See Calvez, SJ, and Perrin, SJ, *Church and Social Justice*, 162–73.

For Aquinas, the virtue of Christian charity is a general virtue like the virtue of general justice, which means that the virtue of charity directs all the virtues to its own proper end, including the virtue of general justice, thus imparting its form on all the virtues, while at the same time maintaining the integrity of each virtue. Aquinas explains: "In morals the form of an act is taken chiefly from the end." So, for example, the essential form of an act of justice is derived from its end (its formal object) which is to render to another what is their due. What distinguishes an act of general justice from an act of particular justice is the universal nature of the proper end of general justice—not the specific good of a particular act of justice such as commutative justice, but the common good of society. The ends of particular justice and general justice, which form these distinct virtues, are proximate ends, this in distinction to what Aquinas terms the last or final end of human life, which is union with God. The final end—union with God, this by the grace of God, which Aquinas portrays as friendship with God—is the proper object of the virtue of charity. As final end, the divine good moves the will to act out of the will's love of the divine good, and in doing so the will's love (charity) directs all the other virtues to the final end. "It is charity which directs the acts of all other virtues to the last end, and which, consequently, also gives the form to all other acts of virtue: and it is precisely in this sense that charity is called the form of the virtues, for these are called virtues in relation to 'informed' acts," states Aquinas.[130] But the form by which charity informs the acts of the virtues is not the essential form (formal cause) of the virtue, but the form of the last end (final cause). The virtue of charity, for example, does not replace the essential form of social justice determined by its own proper end—the common good; rather charity directs or commands the acts of social justice toward its own proper end—the divine good. In this way, acting for the common good takes on a new life, guided by a new light. Indeed, Aquinas portrays the virtue of charity as the mother of all the virtues: "And since a mother is one who conceives within herself and by another, charity is called the mother of the other virtues, because, by commanding them, it conceives the acts of the other virtues, by the desire of the last end."[131] Informed by charity, social justice acts for the common good but does so out of love of God and for the end or purpose of realizing the divine good.

A second look at the parable of the good Samaritan (Luke 10:25–37) provides a way to illustrate the relationship between social justice and Christian love (*agapē*). The narrative of the parable involves movement. The man, who is beaten and robbed, was traveling down the road from Jerusalem to Jericho. Subsequently, a priest and a Levite, also traveling down the road, come upon the man, but at the sight of the victim, move away to the other side of the road (aversion). The Samaritan, also traveling down the road, sees the man and is moved by compassion, a visceral response that

---

130. Thomas Aquinas, *Summa Theologica* II–II.23.8; see also II–II.58.6; Keenan, SJ, *Goodness and Rightness*, 124–37.

131. Thomas Aquinas, *Summa Theologica* II–II.23.8 *ad* 3.

impels him to the victim (attraction). In the Greek text, the verb that is used to depict the Samaritan's compassion is *splagchnizomai*, which literally means to be moved in one's entrails. "What happened to you makes me feel sick to my stomach," we might say. The Samaritan's compassion models Jesus' compassion. The word that is used to describe Jesus' response to the widow and mother from Nain whose only son had died (Luke 7:13) and to the leper who approaches Jesus to beg Jesus that he be made clean (Mark 1:41) is the same Greek word. Being confronted and thus moved by the suffering of another, both Jesus and the Samaritan move not away from but toward the one who suffers. What is not immediately clear in these scriptural texts, however, is why being deeply moved within oneself leads to movement without (external action). We might have sympathetic feelings for another's misfortunes, but such feelings do not necessarily move us to address those misfortunes in external, concrete ways. This, of course, is a theoretical question and not the concern of the scriptural texts. Aquinas has an answer to the theoretical question, however, which at the same time offers a way to deepen our understanding of these biblical passages. The answer that Aquinas provides, in short, is this: compassion, while being a passion, is also a virtue.

Misericordia is the word that Aquinas uses to depict compassion: the term literally means having a sorrowful (*miser*) heart (*cor*), which is translated as mercy or pity. "Mercy signifies grief for another's distress," Aquinas states. (The Latin word for grief here is *dolor*, meaning a sorrow that is physically painful.) Here the suffering of one becomes the suffering of the other. Both the priest and the Levite and then the Samaritan, upon seeing the victim, respond to an evil, but in different ways—the Samaritan makes the evil his own. The Samaritan's response indicates an openness and a vulnerability on his part to the distress of the victim, a feeling that immediately creates a bond between the Samaritan and the victim. But why did the Samaritan act on this feeling to eliminate the victim's suffering? "Now this grief may denote, in one way, a movement of the sensitive appetite, in which case mercy is not a virtue but a passion; whereas, in another way, it may denote a movement of the intellective appetite, in as much as one person's evil is displeasing to another," observes Aquinas.[132] If through my compassion your suffering has become my suffering, then it follows that your good becomes my good as well. In which case, by comprehending the good that the encounter intends and then understanding that the good of each is the good common to both, "one person's evil is displeasing to another" in such a way that the one who is moved by the distress of the other not only feels the other's distress but desires its elimination. Such desire (*appetitus*), then, is a passion (a movement of the sensitive appetite), but in light of the good comprehended as end or purpose, such desire is the rational desire (a movement of the intellective appetite) that impels the will to act to realize the good. Responding to the victim's need, which entails practical reasoning (treating the victim's wounds, taking him to the inn, negotiating with the innkeeper), this for the purpose of restoring the health of the victim and enabling him to reclaim

132. Thomas Aquinas, *Summa Theologica* II–II.30.3; see also II–II.30.2.

his place in society, is the work of justice (general justice). At the same time, in this act of justice, the feeling of compassion that moves the Samaritan is neither abrogated nor mitigated. For Aquinas, a passion, when ruled by reason, becomes a right passion and thus a virtue. Right passion engenders right action. To the objection that mercy (compassion) cannot be a virtue because virtue concerns making right choices, which depend on good counsel, whereas passions such as mercy hinder counsel, Aquinas responds that this objection applies only "to the mercy which is a passion unregulated by reason: for thus it impedes the counselling of reason, by making it wander from justice."[133] Mercy as right passion, on the other hand, safeguards the work of justice (as do the moral virtues of temperance and fortitude) by providing an affective grasp of the good that justice seeks to realize. In this way, mercy (compassion) both enlivens and enlightens the work of justice. With the virtue of mercy, justice acquires a heart.

Jesus concludes his telling of the parable of the good Samaritan with this question to the lawyer: "Which of these three, do you think, proved neighbor to the man who fell among robbers?" The lawyer answered: "The one who showed mercy on him" (Luke 10:37). In his answer to Jesus' question, the lawyer acknowledges the relationship between mercy and being a neighbor. Here being a neighbor implies a relationship of mutuality, thus a relationship of friendship that is constituted by the act of mercy.[134] The Samaritan's compassion in response to the need of the victim establishes a relationship between the two in which the suffering of one becomes the suffering of the other, the good of one becomes the good of the other. The actions of the Samaritan display both gratuitous love and obligatory demand, this insofar as the victim's need makes a claim upon the Samaritan. Yet, the love freely given on the part of the Samaritan does not stand apart from or at odds with the demand that the victim's need makes on him. The interaction that takes place between the Samaritan and the victim is not one of my giving from what is mine in response to the obligation to give you what is yours, but rather the good intended in the transaction can only be mine if it is also yours.[135] What is required to realize the good of living in society, according to Aquinas, is justice, but also mercy (compassion). Both moral virtues, moreover, need each other. Mercy is the fuel that ignites justice; justice is the rational guide that directs mercy. But, in the light of the parable that Jesus presents, both virtues are directed by the virtue of charity to its own proper end: "You shall love the Lord your God . . . and your neighbor as yourself" (Luke 10:27). This commandment of the law the lawyer recites as the answer to the first question that he posed to Jesus: "what shall I do to inherit eternal life?" (Luke 10:25). The commandment intends union with God, more specifically, friendship with God. "Charity signifies not only the love of God, but also a certain friendship with Him; which implies, besides love, a certain mutual return of

---

133. Thomas Aquinas, *Summa Theologica* II–II.30.3 *ad* 1.

134. See Jeremias, *Parables of Jesus*, 205.

135. See MacIntyre, *Dependent Rational Animals*, 119–28.

love, together with mutual communion," Aquinas states.[136] Thus, for one who acts out of love of God, according to Aquinas, the final end (union with God) "is already possessed: since the beloved is, in a manner, in the lover, and, again, the lover is drawn by desire to union with the beloved."[137] Acts of mercy and justice that intend proximate ends, if enacted out of the love of God, are directed to the final end—the divine good that impels the will to act. Yet the love of God that both motivates and informs acts of virtue as final cause neither alters the essential nature of the moral act nor replaces the proximate end of the moral act with the final end. The final words of the Samaritan to the innkeeper before departing are these: "Take care of him; and whatever more you spend, I will repay you when I come back" (10:35). The parable, while being a paradigmatic portrait of *agapē*, as a portrait of justice remains unfinished.

The Next Step

As the object of study, social justice concerns both the major social institutions that structure society and the moral actions of the members of society that create and maintain these institutions—thus, both institutions that are just and the moral character of a people who are just. But, given that these are two distinct spheres of justice—social institutions and moral agents—will each as the object of study yield a conception of social justice that is distinct from the other? Moreover, that each distinct approach to the study of social justice—by way of institutions and moral virtue—originates in a different historical period, each with its own distinct view of society, simply underscores the concern. The problem becomes readily apparent when we place side-by-side two modern-day approaches to social justice, that of John Rawls and that of Catholic social teaching.

Rawls articulates his understanding of social justice as just institutions in the context of the philosophical tradition of the European Enlightenment, in particular by drawing upon the idea of society understood as a social contract, a theory that was formulated by the Enlightenment's most influential thinkers. At the beginning of *A Theory of Justice* Rawls states: "My aim is to present a conception of justice which generalizes and carries to a higher level of abstraction the familiar theory of the social contract as found, say, in Locke, Rousseau, and Kant."[138] The basis of society, according to this tradition, is the mutual consent of those who make up the society to set aside the natural freedom that each possesses as an individual in order to take on the obligations of civil society, mutually agreed upon by all in the society, for the sake of the advantages that this mutual agreement provides. The contribution that Rawls makes to this tradition is his formulation of the principles of justice that establish the fairness

136. Thomas Aquinas, *Summa Theologica* I–II.65.5.

137. Thomas Aquinas, *Summa Theologica* I–II.66.6. See also Keenan, SJ, *Goodness and Rightness*, 124–27.

138. Rawls, *Theory of Justice*, 11.

of the institutions that constitute the basic structure of society and, presented as the object of the social contract, that in theory would be freely chosen by all within the society on the basis of reason. For Rawls, then, a just society is the product of moral choice, ruled by the principles of justice that order the society's institutions.

The tradition of Catholic social teaching and more broadly Catholic social thought in both its classical and contemporary forms stand in contrast to Rawls's approach to the matter of social justice. As we saw in Chapter 2, society is envisioned in this tradition, not as a social contract, but first and foremost as a web of interdependent social relations that exist prior to choice. As human beings, we are social by nature (not social by choice), and thus our fulfillment—our good—as human beings is realized in and through the concrete decisions and actions by which we foster our interdependence with one another in society. Social reciprocity is the moral good that is the basis and the goal of a just society. The moral actions that embody this social good, in the view of the Catholic tradition, must be the object of study of social justice. In and through these moral actions the good of being a community is realized.

At first look, what Rawls considers to be the object of study of social justice differs significantly from the object of study in social Catholicism. For Rawls the matter of social justice concerns the principles of justice that order the institutions of society. "They are the principles that free and rational persons concerned to further their own interests would accept in an initial position of equality as defining the fundamental terms of their association," Rawls states.[139] The principles of justice are necessarily abstract (encompassing all particular institutional arrangements) and objective (accepted freely on the basis of reason by all within the society). Insofar as the principles of justice are objective standards of what is right and thus impartial, these principles have priority over conceptions of the good within society, which according to Rawls unavoidably exhibit partiality and thus lack universal adherence. For Rawls, given the original agreement by all within the society to live according to the principles of justice that order the institutions of society—this Rawls terms "justice as fairness"— implicit in this agreement is the will on the part of all "to conform their conceptions of their good to what the principles of justice require." Accordingly, "in justice as fairness the concept of right is prior to that of the good."[140]

The communitarian moral vision that is at the heart of social Catholicism, on the other hand, holds the social good as primary and thus foundational to determinations of the right, that is, the concrete obligations of justice. Social reciprocity—the good of being a community—constitutes the foundation and moral purpose of a just society. The social good, as the object of desire, provides normative guidance and purposeful motivation both in terms of what we do (our moral actions) and in terms of the kind of persons that we become in society through our moral actions (our moral character). At the same time, in and through our moral actions and due to our moral

139. Rawls, *Theory of Justice*, 11.
140. Rawls, *Theory of Justice*, 31.

character, we create and maintain the social good. Here the object of study regarding social justice is primarily people who are just that make up the good society and the moral actions by which they create and maintain just institutions. Thus, in the view of social Catholicism, in the conception of justice as virtue the concept of the good is prior to the concept of right.

Does this difference in priorities between the right and the good for Rawls and social Catholicism produce opposing conceptions of social justice? Catholic theologian Jean Porter thinks not, but to make this point she refers to Aquinas. "Aquinas gets justice right," she declares, not because he presents an account of social institutions that would be useful for today's discussion, but because "he lays the foundations for a comprehensive theory of morality that has a commitment to right relations at its core."[141] The foundation and purpose of right relations for Aquinas lie in our social nature—our natural inclination to live in society that intends the human good. We realize the human good only in and through right relations with others, which means just relations in society. Aquinas clearly determines the right in relation to the good, but to use Porter's words: "So far from setting the right and the good in opposition to one another, Aquinas grounds the right in the good without compromising its overriding force."[142] So it is with the tradition of social Catholicism. The concept of social justice that lies at the heart of social Catholicism does not stand in opposition to that of Rawls. The one does not exclude what the other affirms, and thus the two can be seen as complementary. Yet, at the same time, which moral concept is given priority—the good or the right—proves decisive for the way in which social justice will be considered.

That social Catholicism gives primacy to the good over the right, however, calls forth specific questions regarding the nature of the good. The good of the social whole is the common good. Herein lies the end or purpose of all social relations that make up society and the end or purpose of the social institutions that structure these relations. But as the moral norm that governs human relations in society, what precisely is the common good? How is the common good defined, and by whom is this determination made? Lastly, given the scope of the common good as the end or purpose of the social whole, Catholic theologians Jean-Yves Calvez, SJ, and Jacques Perrin, SJ, pose this question regarding the common good as the norm of social justice: "Is not the gain in extent bought at the cost of a loss of precision? Is not this very far removed from the simplicity and strictness of the standards of commutative justice, which rest, it would seem, on equality between reciprocal services?"[143] They think that this is not the case with social justice, but their question and the other questions regarding the nature of the common good as the norm of social justice must be considered. This is the next step.

141. Porter, *Justice as a Virtue*, 5.

142. Porter, *Justice as a Virtue*, 271.

143. Calvez, SJ, and Perrrin, SJ, *Church and Social Justice*, 151.

Chapter 4

What Is Social Justice?

The Norm

THE PROBLEM OF DEFINING THE COMMON GOOD

Social Institutions: Competing Moral Viewpoints

Given our social nature as human beings, how ought we to live together? The question is both a practical question and a moral question. The word "ought" indicates the normative nature of the question: "ought" connotes expectation as well as obligation by pointing to a standard or a model that must be met, which is the norm. The expectation or obligation can refer to a practical outcome or to a moral purpose. In which case, a norm can be either nonmoral (if it concerns a practical outcome) or moral (if it concerns a moral purpose). As a way to see the difference, consider these two examples.

The first example concerns etiquette: when meeting people, if they extend their hand to us, we ought to shake their hand. By doing so, we are fulfilling an expectation or rule of etiquette in our society that provides two people with a way of greeting each other. The second example concerns the law: when the government imposes taxes on our earnings, we ought to pay our taxes. By fulfilling this legal obligation, we provide the government with the necessary means to fund public services, and we avoid the punishment of the government for not doing so. Shaking hands and paying taxes—each serves a practical purpose. In both instances the word "ought" refers to expectations or obligations that are based on convention: the first on the social agreements of etiquette and the second on the social agreements of the law. Both etiquette and law provide practical answers to the question concerning how we ought to live together. But shaking hands and paying taxes also serve a moral purpose. The simple act of a handshake expresses social solidarity, in which we acknowledge the other's personhood. By paying our taxes, we contribute our fair share to the good of the society and we expect that the government's assessment of our share will be fair as well.[1] When we view these social practices in the light of their moral purpose, the word "ought" refers to expectations or obligations that are based on a conception of the right or the good, not simply on convention. A simple handshake and paying taxes are now seen in terms of their moral meaning.

The social institutions that make up our society provide normative answers to the question of how we ought to live together. These answers are first and foremost practical in that the conventional arrangements of each institution give order and stability to the society. But, insofar as these social arrangements concern human well-being, we judge them not only in terms of their social effectiveness but also in terms of their rightness or their goodness, that is, in terms of moral meanings that are anchored in the norm of justice. This moral evaluation, however, does not take place solely in the minds of autonomous individuals, but—to return to the point made by Mary Douglas in the previous chapter—the moral evaluation takes place in the minds of individuals "thinking within and on behalf of institutions." Moreover, due to the distinctly different purpose that each social institution serves, moral argument within the society that concerns the justice of the social arrangements of society is made up of competing viewpoints, not simply those of individuals themselves, but those of society's institutions. The legitimating idea of one institution challenges and, accordingly, evokes the legitimating idea of another. Douglas notes: "When individuals disagree on elementary justice, their most insoluble conflict is between institutions based on incompatible principles. The more severe the conflict, the more useful to understand the institutions that are doing most of the thinking."[2]

Thus, in posing this basic social question—how as a society ought we to live together?—to the major institutions of society, with the intention of eliciting a moral response from them, we find that these institutions, particularly the dominant institutions, do not answer collectively with one voice. Indeed, the norm of justice that rules the social arrangements of one appears incompatible with that of another. Justice viewed in terms of society's institutions is not one, but many. The competing moral viewpoints of the major social institutions, accordingly, present a fundamental challenge to the effort to understand and define the nature of the good of the social whole—the common good—this being the task undertaken by Catholic social teaching, which sees the common good as the norm of social justice. Given the diversity of viewpoints that the social institutions structuring modern-day society represent, can the norm of justice that governs society as a whole be seen as one, or must we allow

1. Bellah et al., *Good Society*, 10.
2. Douglas, *How Institutions Think*, 125.

that the norm of social justice will necessarily be manifold? To bring this problem clearly into view and to consider how the problem might be resolved, we begin the task of defining the common good by taking into account how justice is conceived in each of three major social institutions: the economy, the government, and religion. Each presupposes a concept of justice seemingly incompatible with the others.

Justice from the Viewpoint of the Economy

To understand how the economy answers the question concerning how we ought to live together, we turn to the one who can speak most suitably on behalf of this institution—the economist. In response to the question, however, the first point that the economist Thomas Sowell would make is that the question is improperly asked of the economy if the question intends to elicit a moral meaning: the word "ought" implies a normative view, but no moral norms can be discerned in the workings of the economy, especially not the norm of justice. The science of economics describes how economies function; it does not prescribe how economies ought to function in order to fulfill a moral purpose. To use the words of Thomas Sowell:

> Economics is a study of *cause-and-effect* relationships in an economy. Its purpose is to discern the consequences of various ways of allocating scarce resources which have alternative uses. It has nothing to say about social philosophy or moral values, any more than it has anything to say about music, literature, or medical science. These other things are not necessarily any less important, they are simply not what economics is about. No one expects mathematics to explain love and no one should expect economics to be something other than what it is or to do something other than what it can.[3]

Every society is faced with the fundamental problem of allocating its scarce resources. Despite the abundance of a society's resources, whether they be fertile lands, mineral deposits, or labor, these resources are scarce because they are finite. The unlimited desires of its people and the finite nature of its resources require a society to allocate these resources, which have alternative uses, and to do so in the most efficient manner possible. (For example, wood is a finite resource that provides for a society its building materials, furniture, pencils, paper, among other goods.) The purpose of the economy in any society, then, is the allocation of scarce resources and their alternative uses in the most efficient manner possible.

But how this allocation takes place can vary. In a market economy, which is based on voluntary exchange, allocating scarce resources takes place through prices. What price a buyer is willing to pay and what price a seller is willing to receive determines what resources will be used and how they will be used. "*Resources tend to flow to*

3. Sowell, *Basic Economics*, 41.

their most valued uses," Sowell emphasizes.[4] Prices, which are set by the innumerable voluntary exchanges that make up a market, indicate the value that resources have and thus allocate their use. This way of allocating resources stands in sharp contrast to command economies, in which the allocation of resources is managed by the government. Whereas the allocation of scarce resources in a market economy reflects the decisions of the many, in a command economy this allocation is determined by a few but affects the many. Sowell points to the economy of the former Soviet Union as an example of the inefficiency that such a way of allocating scarce resources breeds. In a land of natural wealth, the people of the Soviet Union suffered chronic shortages of basic goods. At the same time that warehouses were filled with an oversupply of unwanted goods, people waited in long lines to purchase an undersupply of the goods that they needed. The practical outcome of this way of allocating resources was a high degree of waste in production and of want in consumption. The practical outcome of a price-coordinated economy, on the other hand, is a society that allocates its scarce resources and their alternative uses in the most efficient manner possible.[5]

A price-coordinated economy, then, is preferable to a command economy due to the efficiency of its markets. This judgment does not rest on a moral reason; it does not express a moral value. But this judgment does imply that the conventional arrangements of a market economy have a nonmoral or premoral value. In order to understand the difference between a nonmoral value and a moral value, let us first consider what we mean when we use the word "value."

The term "value" refers to whatever we find important. Some things or activities are important to us merely because we find them to be personally satisfying (playing soccer rather than reading a book). In this case, what has value for one person may not have value for another. Other things or activities are important to us because of their utility, that is, because of what they produce or the state of affairs that they bring about. In this case, our appreciation of something's importance does not rest in our subjective preferences, but on the good that has been produced. The value of a price-coordinated economy, accordingly, lies in the efficiency of its markets. Because this good has an objective status independent of our preferences, we expect others to value as well what we find important, and so we are willing to argue for this valuation by pointing to the good that has been produced. The process of articulating and assessing the value of something finally results in a norm, which is a statement of what ought to be done.[6] The social expectations or rules that pattern the conventional arrangements of the economy are normative for the society because they articulate what the society values, which in the case of a price-coordinated economy is its utility, namely, the efficient allocation of the society's scarce resources and their alternative uses by means

---

4. Sowell, *Basic Economics*, 10.

5. Sowell, *Basic Economics*, 7–15.

6. O'Connell, *Principles for a Catholic Morality*, 118, 155–58.

of prices, not government control. In its social expectations or rules, the economy provides normative answers to the question concerning how we ought to live together.

Describing a market economy as having a nonmoral value, however, raises the question whether moral value can be ascribed to a market economy as well. What would moral value be in this case, and how does it differ from nonmoral (or premoral) value? Catholic moral theologian Timothy O'Connell describes the difference between nonmoral and moral values in this way: nonmoral values are "doing-values" whereas moral values are "being-values." Nonmoral values portray what we ought to do. The normative articulation of these values provides specific scripts for how we ought to live together. Moral values portray how we ought to be as human beings. They provide no specific script for life, but rather by defining the qualities of being human, moral values provide goals for enacting every life-script. They portray the sort of person that we ought to be. Be just, be honest, be respectful of life, these are normative articulations of the ideals for living a fully human life. Moral norms such as these are not the result of wishful thinking, but judgment concerning what constitutes the moral end or purpose of every human being. Thus, like nonmoral values, moral values have an objective status independent of our subjective preferences. They portray an objective goodness. But unlike nonmoral values, the good of which is derived from their utility, the good that moral values portray is a good in itself. Being just, being honest, being respectful of life, or in terms of society considered as a whole, being a community, these are valued by us, not simply for the good that they bring about, but because they are good in themselves.[7]

Do the conventional arrangements of a market economy express a moral value in this sense? The economist Milton Friedman offers a response to this question. In *Capitalism and Freedom* Friedman sets forth the thesis that economic freedom is necessary for political freedom. The primary threat to the freedom of the individual in society is the concentration of power that can take place in the government. This concentration of power takes place when economic power and political power are joined together under the authority of the government. Then the government's power to coerce its citizens becomes absolute. But when economic power remains separate from political power, the economy retains the ability to check the power of the government. A market economy does this, not by opposing the government with its own concentration of power, but rather by dispersing power in the market through its voluntary exchanges. Through the autonomy of the market, cooperation within the society takes place without coercion. Minimizing the ability of one to coerce another in the society creates political freedom. Economic freedom, then, is a necessary means for achieving political freedom.[8] Herein lies its utility. But more fundamentally, "economic freedom is an end in itself," Friedman states, because "freedom in economic arrangements is

---

7. O'Connell, *Principles for a Catholic Morality*, 118–19, 155–61.

8. Friedman, *Capitalism and Freedom*, 7–16.

itself a component of freedom broadly understood."[9] Presupposed in the economic arrangements of the market economy of a society is a moral value—the freedom of the individual.

This moral value functions as the legitimating idea of a market economy. When challenged, the social institution of the economy will make explicit this moral value. The primary challenge to the economy occurs when the government intervenes in the market, not only because the power of the government can limit economic arrangements, but because its power to coerce can limit the freedom of the individual. The intervention of the government in the market, then, is a practical issue, but ultimately it is a moral issue that will be resolved only through a discussion of justice.

Friedman allows that the government has a necessary role to play in relation to the economy but emphasizes that this role is limited. First of all, in order for the economy to function effectively, law and order must exist within the society, so that contracts freely made are enforceable. This the market is unable to do for itself. Government, not the economy, creates and enforces the rules of the game. Secondly, certain market imperfections require government regulation. Friedman points to two: monopolies and "neighborhood effects." Voluntary exchange in a market requires that alternatives exist for both buyers and sellers. A monopoly, which is one buyer or seller controlling a market, prevents the market from functioning efficiently. To correct this market inefficiency, the market requires government intervention. Furthermore, markets are not efficient when a third party involuntarily shares the costs of a voluntary exchange between buyer and seller (a neighborhood effect). Air pollution resulting from the manufacturing of a product is an example. The cost of the product that is borne by the buyer and the seller does not include the external cost of air pollution, which is borne by those who are not a party to the exchange. Because the price of the product does not include this neighborhood effect, the price fails to allocate resources efficiently in the market. Friedman accepts that monopolies and neighborhood effects require government intervention, but in these instances government regulations serve only the purpose of fostering more efficient markets and thus greater economic freedom.[10] Government intervention in such instances does not restrict but rather ensures the freedom of the individual in the marketplace.

Justice from the Viewpoint of the Government

The economist Rebecca Blank, however, argues that the government has two further interventionist roles to play in relation to the economy that are valid, but she acknowledges that neither of these roles can be justified in terms of the norms of the free market. In the first role, the government uses its authority to restrict the scope of markets either by prohibiting exchanges in the market (e.g., the sale of child pornography) or

9. Friedman, *Capitalism and Freedom*, 8.
10. Friedman, *Capitalism and Freedom*, 14, 25–32.

by discouraging exchanges through heavy taxation (e.g., the use of tobacco products). In the second role, the government limits markets, either by providing alternatives to the market, such as public services (e.g., public education, Social Security) that are alternatives to the private sector (e.g., private education, private pensions), or by altering market outcomes for the sake of those who are harmed by these outcomes. When it aims to mitigate harm, the government redistributes the resources of the market to aid those who have suffered changes or failures in the market, either by altering market outcomes, such as by providing unemployment insurance to workers, or by mandating certain market conditions, such as by requiring employers to pay workers at least at the minimum-wage level. In each of these ways that the government intervenes in the market, the government's decisions are based on social values other than market values, and insofar as the government is democratic, these social values reflect what the society itself considers to be important.[11]

Consider the issue of the minimum wage. The economist will point out that the government's mandate to set a level below which wages cannot fall creates an inefficient allocation of resources in the labor market. In a market economy, prices (in this case, wages) allocate resources. In all markets, when prices rise, demand falls, causing supply to increase. In the labor market, if the price of labor is artificially raised through government mandate, the demand for labor by employers falls, particularly for unskilled or low-skilled labor, producing a surplus of labor accompanied by a decline in jobs. This the economist argues. Thomas Sowell comments: "Unfortunately, the real minimum wage is always zero, regardless of the laws, and that is the wage that many workers receive in the wake of the creation or escalation of a government-mandated minimum wage, because they lose their jobs."[12]

The argument in support of the minimum wage, however, is a noneconomic argument, Rebecca Blank points out. While minimum-wage laws have a cost, which can be the increase in unemployment among unskilled and low-skilled workers, they also have a twofold benefit: by guaranteeing that wages will not fall below a certain point, the government both underscores the worth of work and also ensures that work will be worthwhile by providing adequate recompense.[13] The argument for the minimum wage is based on its utility for the society as a whole: even those who work at the lowest-paying jobs in the society ought to work with dignity and have the ability to fulfill basic economic needs. By raising the federal minimum wage, inequality (particularly gender and racial inequality) in the society decreases, the productivity and retention of workers in the workplace increases, millions of low-wage workers are lifted out of poverty, and the economy grows—points of argument that supported the Raise the Wage Act of 2019 (H.R. 582/S.150) that the US House of Representatives passed on July 18, 2019, but that was not voted on in the US Senate. The bill was reintroduced

11. Blank and McGurn, *Is the Market Moral?*, 43–49.

12. Sowell, *Basic Economics*, 163.

13. Blank and McGurn, *Is the Market Moral?*, 46–47.

both in the House of Representatives (H.R. 603) and in the Senate (S. 53) in 2021. The bill, if passed, would raise the federal minimum wage gradually from the current $7.25 an hour to $15 by 2025. To the economist's argument (such as Thomas Sowell's) that raising the minimum wage would hurt the very workers it intends to help, one recent study, by economists Anna Godøy and Michael Reich, of the effects of raising the minimum wage to $15 an hour on low-wage workers, citing strong evidence from income data taken at the county level (not solely at the state level), demonstrates that such a wage increase would not significantly imperil low-wage jobs and would greatly reduce household and child poverty.[14] Here the argument for raising the minimum wage is based on its nonmoral or premoral social value, which is the practical outcome that the society considers to be important. But insofar as the argument implies the recognition that in the market's allocation of resources a qualitative difference exists between, say, piles of discounted shirts and blouses on the remainder table of a department store and the lives of workers who are employed in low-wage jobs, the argument implies a moral value as well. What precisely is this moral value?

The political scientist Robert Dahl observes that the institution of democratic government is founded on "the logic of equality."[15] In a democracy all citizens participate in the governing of the society as political equals. To the question "why should citizens be considered political equals?" Dahl responds that democracy as a form of governance is based on the moral value that human beings possess an intrinsic equality. Accordingly, in the decisions of government, the good of one citizen ought to be given equal consideration to the good of another, because all citizens have equal worth.[16] When challenged by the economy, the government evokes this moral value as the legitimating idea that ultimately justifies its political arrangements, such as the mandate for a minimum wage. Whether a citizen enjoys or suffers the outcomes of the market, or whether a citizen is unable to participate in the market, such as one who is disabled or elderly, the good of each ought to be acknowledged equally in the decisions of the government that will affect all. In the eyes of the government, the fair allocation of the society's resources must take into account the equal worth of each of its citizens, which may entail the redistribution of resources to aid those who are at a severe disadvantage in the market economy.

Disputes between the economy and the government over issues such as the minimum wage, therefore, reflect competing viewpoints, not only regarding the value of practical outcomes, but also regarding moral values themselves. Each institution offers a normative answer to the question: how ought we to live together? Each answer presupposes a concept of justice. But, with regard to the allocation of resources, what justice is for one institution may be injustice for the other. Inasmuch as justice

14. See Godøy and Reich, "Minimum Wage Effects in Low-Wage Areas."
15. Dahl, *On Democracy*, 10.
16. Dahl, *On Democracy*, 62–66.

understood in terms of being equal stands in opposition to justice understood in terms of being free, justice is not one but many.

Justice from the Viewpoint of Religion

The social institution of religion further provides a normative answer to the question: how ought we to live together? In the case of Christianity, the norm is stated in the Acts of the Apostles in its description of the primitive church in Jerusalem, this following the descent of the Holy Spirit upon the followers of Jesus on the day of Pentecost:

> Now the company of those who believed were of one heart and soul, and no one said that any of the things which he possessed was his own, but they had everything in common. And with great power the apostles gave their testimony to the resurrection of the Lord Jesus, and great grace was upon them all. There was not a needy person among them, for as many as were possessors of lands or houses sold them, and brought the proceeds of what was sold and laid it at the apostles' feet; and distribution was made to each as any had need. (Acts 4:32–35)[17]

What is normative in this description of the primitive community, however, is not the specific way that the Jerusalem community shared its possessions, that is, by selling personal property and giving the proceeds of what was sold over to the community to be distributed by the apostles according to need. Although some Christian communities have imitated the sharing of possessions that is depicted here—most notably, monastic communities—the practice of holding possessions in common was limited in the earliest period of Christianity's history to the Jerusalem community and never widespread after that.[18]

Rather, the norm being portrayed here can be seen in the description of the primitive community as being "of one heart and soul" and as being a community in which "there was not a needy person among them." Luke, the author of Acts of the Apostles, presents the Jerusalem community as the ideal community to the Greco-Roman Christians that make up his own community.[19] In describing this community in terms of being "one heart and soul," Luke echoes two well-known Greek proverbs. The philosopher Aristotle, for example, refers to these proverbs in the *Nichomachean Ethics* in his discussion of friendship: in friendship two people are "a single soul," and "what friends have is common property."[20] But for Luke, the unity of the community, its fellowship, which is expressed in the sharing of possessions, is the gift of the Holy Spirit. Moreover, that "there was not a needy person among them" is the practical

17. All biblical quotations are from *The New Oxford Annotated Bible: Revised Standard Version.*

18. Johnson, *Sharing Possessions*, 21–23.

19. Johnson, *Sharing Possessions*, 128–29.

20. Aristotle, *Nicomachean Ethics* 9.8.1168b.

outcome of fulfilling the command that God gave to the people of Israel to give alms and care for the poor in their midst (Deut 15:4–5). Because the Jerusalem community observed this command, they overcame the barriers that divide the rich and poor in society and were blessed with the unity of friendship in the Spirit of God.[21]

Being "of one heart and soul," that is, being a community, is valued here, not for its usefulness, but rather for its intrinsic goodness. Being a community is a moral value. What precisely is valued is the solidarity of the community (being of one heart and soul) and the compassion that the members of the community have for those in their midst who are in need. In whatever way the redistribution of resources takes place within the community, all within the community value the good of each member, and so "there was not a needy person among them." Luke's description of the ideal community provides a normative answer to the question: how ought we to live together? Caring for the needy in our midst is an essential requirement for realizing the ideal of being one heart and soul and thus being a community.

Luke's vision of the ideal community presupposes a distinct notion of justice. This notion was given a modern-day articulation by Mel Reese, a political activist who represented an advocacy group in Washington, DC—the Ecumenical Alliance for Peace and Justice—that sought to bring this biblical vision to bear on the public policies of the US government. He portrayed justice in this way: "Justice means taking care of one another . . . Parents need to care for their children, and people need to work to support themselves and take care of the community. The community needs to enable people to work and care for one another, to enter in and have a voice in public. It needs to care for the poor."[22]

The viewpoint that in a society justice means "taking care of one another" stands in contrast to the notions of justice that legitimate the social arrangements of both the market economy and the government. This viewpoint envisions not only the family but also the larger society as an interdependent whole in which the good of one member is tied to the good of the others. The well-being of society in this view rests on the mutual care that its members offer to one another. A just society is one that allocates its resources in such a way that it takes into account the fulfillment of basic human needs, so that there will not be "a needy person among them."

Comparing this viewpoint with that of the market economy provides the sharpest contrast. In the eyes of the economist, society is "the collection of individuals who compose it,"[23] their relationships consisting in the private exchanges into which they freely enter based on mutual self-interest. The well-being of society in this case is based on the aggregate sum of these free exchanges. A just society is one in which the allocation of resources takes place only through the free exchanges of the market. All forms of governmental coercion that redistribute resources for purposes other than

21. Karris, *Invitation to Acts*, 63–65.

22. Bellah et al., *Good Society*, 194.

23. Friedman, *Capitalism and Freedom*, 1.

correcting imperfections in the market are therefore unjust. This view of justice does not oppose the efforts of some within the society to address the basic needs of others, but these efforts are understood as voluntary acts of charity and not as obligatory acts of justice.

Although the government considers the care of its citizens, including the poorest and weakest members of the society, to be a primary responsibility, and thus, like religion, addresses human need, the government, unlike religion, views human need through the lens of citizenship. The members of a political community, the philosopher Michael Walzer observes, provide for one another "security and welfare." Insofar as this communal provision is regulated by the government, "every political community is in principle a 'welfare state.'"[24] In the eyes of government, then, the well-being of society requires the fulfillment of certain basic needs of its citizens. A just society in this view allocates its resources in such a way that these needs are met. For democratic societies in particular, the norm by which the government regulates the allocation of resources is not human need as such, but the equal status of its citizens in regard to the fulfillment of human need. The primary reason why the government addresses some needs and not others lies not in the urgency of the need but in the perception that if the need is unmet, political equality is threatened.[25] Thus, equality, not compassion, is the moral value that rules a democracy's care of its citizens. The government, moreover, provides this care through the stipulations of legislation (such as the minimum-wage law), not through the generosity of friendship.

Is the Norm of Social Justice One or Many?

Given the competing moral viewpoints that the institutions of the economy, government, and religion bring to bear on the question concerning how we ought to live together, we are then faced with this question: Can the order and stability of society, and thus the good of society, be secured if the norm of justice that regulates the social arrangements of the society is manifold? In view of the institutional diversity of modern-day society, can the norm of social justice be many and yet provide normative (moral) guidance to the society as a whole? If so, how? Or, in order to establish and maintain the cohesiveness of a diverse society, must the norm of social justice that guides the society be one? If so, what precisely would this norm be, and how would it be determined? Hence the question before us is this: Is the norm of social justice one or many? Let us consider three answers to this question from three distinct viewpoints.

---

24. Walzer, *Spheres of Justice*, 64, 68.

25. Miller, *Principles of Social Justice*, 30–32.

One Answer from the Social Sciences

From the perspective of sociology, Robert Bellah and his associates would respond to this question in this way: in a stable but vibrant democracy, the norm of justice must be many. "We advocate taking advantage of society's institutional pluralism to escape from the logic of one kind of institution (for example, the market) by looking at it from the standpoint of another (for example, the church)," they state. Echoing the anthropologist Mary Douglas, they observe that if social institutions think (that is, provide normative patterns for our lives), "what they think about is other institutions: they translate the means and ends of other institutions into their own logic. Thus, economic institutions interpret educational institutions as a business," for example. The importance of a strong plurality of institutional viewpoints within a society is that the interplay of these viewpoints prevents any one viewpoint from fully translating the others into its own logic. "If we want a democratic society," they emphasize, "we need to maintain a plurality of institutions; we need to avoid economic as well as political totalitarianism."[26] The economist Rebecca Blank would agree. She notes that the success of the market economy in the United States influences how we as individuals think and act in other social spheres. We tend to carry the core values of the market—the values of individual freedom, self-interest, and competition—both into our personal relationships and into other institutional domains. But precisely for this reason, she states, the other-interested behavior that is fostered by religion serves as a needed "counterweight" to the self-interested behavior that is valorized by the market model of behavior. Despite the accomplishments of the market, its values cannot fully define how we ought to live together. The moral values of solidarity and compassion as well as political equality provide important alternative viewpoints to the market's values, which promote the pursuit of individual interest, and thus these alternative viewpoints provide a needed counterbalance to the moral viewpoint of the market.[27]

But social institutions in a pluralistic society do not simply coexist with each other; they come into conflict with one another. The present-day controversy regarding raising the minimum wage is a case in point. Using the metaphor of a counterweight or counterbalance as a way to describe the relationship between diverse institutions in a society implies an intended outcome of equilibrium. However, with respect to specific social issues, describing the relationship between institutions in terms of one institution translating the logic of another into its own logic highlights a relationship of competition and conflict. With conflict between social institutions comes public argument (the arguments for and against raising the minimum wage, for example), but productive public argument necessarily presupposes that among the disputants in the argument there is a consensus, some common point of agreement that they share despite their deep disagreement. Finding this point of agreement in public argument,

26. Bellah et al., *Good Society*, 292.
27. Blank and McGurn, *Is the Market Moral?*, 20–22, 51–54.

Bellah and his associates point out, is a critical step to engaging and perhaps resolving public argument about a specific social issue and thus the conflict between social institutions. To make this point, they refer to the words of the late Catholic theologian John Courtney Murray, SJ, who states: "The whole premise of the public argument, if it is to be civilized and civilizing, is that the consensus is real, that among the people everything is not in doubt, but that there is a core of agreement, accord, concurrence, acquiescence. We hold certain truths; therefore we can argue about them."[28] Yet, finding this point of agreement in the public argument between social institutions is only the first step to engaging the argument, not the final outcome. Establishing a consensus among the contending institutional viewpoints starts the conversation, but the conversation (public argument) only takes place if the normative viewpoint of each institution is fully represented. The consensus does not minimize the viewpoints of the social institutions involved in the argument, but rather the consensus, once established, enables each viewpoint to represent itself in the public argument in its full distinctiveness. Herein lies the vibrancy and stability of a democracy. In the view of the social scientist, the norm of social justice, if it is to be a guide to public argument and its outcome, must be many.[29]

One Answer from Philosophy

The philosopher John Rawls argues that in order to secure the order and stability of a society the norm of justice must be one. In democratic societies the discussion of social justice begins amid a plurality of viewpoints, which consists of "comprehensive religious, philosophical, and moral doctrines" that are incompatible with one another yet reasonable to hold. These viewpoints are comprehensive doctrines insofar as they intend to state the whole truth, but in pluralistic democracies no one of these comprehensive truths is held by all citizens within the society. Thus, the fundamental question facing liberal democracies is this: "How is it possible that there may exist over time a stable and just society of free and equal citizens profoundly divided by reasonable though incompatible religious, philosophical, and moral doctrines?" The answer to this question, according to Rawls, lies in a conception of justice that the plurality of comprehensive doctrines can endorse.[30] This conception of justice specifies "the fair terms of social cooperation between citizens regarded as free and equal, and as fully cooperating members of society over a complete life, from one generation to the next."[31] Rawls gives to this conception of justice the name "justice as fairness."

The object of social justice for Rawls, as we saw in the previous chapter, is the basic structure of society—more specifically, "the way in which the major social

28. Murray, SJ, *We Hold These Truths*, 10.

29. Bellah et al., *Good Society*, 299–301, 304–5.

30. Rawls, *Political Liberalism*, xviii, xx.

31. Rawls, *Political Liberalism*, 3.

institutions distribute fundamental rights and duties and determine the division of advantages from social cooperation."[32] What, then, is the content of the conception of justice that regulates the social arrangements of society's major institutions? Moreover, if the conception of justice establishes "the fair terms of social cooperation," how are these terms to be decided?

Rawls responds to the second question by stating that the conception of justice cannot be derived from any of the incompatible comprehensive doctrines that divide society, since fairness requires that all within the society agree to the terms of social cooperation. No comprehensive doctrine—religious, philosophical, moral—can provide the basis for such an agreement. Fairness further requires that this social agreement regarding the terms of cooperation takes place in conditions that are themselves fair. The terms of the agreement will be fair only if the conditions in which the agreement is made are fair. For example, no party to the agreement can have an unfair bargaining advantage over the others. Nor can coercion or deception enter into the agreement. But, in fact, no actual society is free of these limitations.[33]

Thus, as a way to articulate a conception of justice that is fair, Rawls devises a thought experiment that envisages a setting in which the conditions for choosing the terms of social cooperation are fully fair. The thought experiment is conducted as follows: Let us imagine a bargaining situation in which representatives of the society have come together to choose a conception of justice that will regulate the major institutions of the society. These representatives will negotiate on behalf of the citizens of the society, considered as free and equal, who inhabit different social positions and hold varying beliefs that are based on incompatible comprehensive doctrines. In order to eliminate any advantage that might come from having a particular social position or from affirming a particular comprehensive doctrine, or from other social characteristics—such as race or ethnicity, gender or inborn talents as strength and intelligence—the thought experiment places those who are determining the fair terms of social cooperation behind "a veil of ignorance." Here (in this hypothetical setting), when the representatives deliberate over the conception of justice, they do not know the place in society or the other social characteristics that define themselves or those that they represent. The veil of ignorance ensures that the parties in the deliberation are "symmetrically situated" so that none can realize an unfair advantage. Moreover, due to the veil of ignorance, the reasons that each party offers as justification for a certain conception of justice will be restricted to the fairness of the concept itself, with no other type of reason being admissible into the discussion. Rawls terms this hypothetical point of view from which the articulation of justice as fairness commences "the original position."[34]

32. Rawls, *Theory of Justice*, 7.

33. Rawls, *Political Liberalism*, 22–23.

34. Rawls, *Justice as Fairness*, 15–18.

Of the various conceptions of justice that are possible, what conception will the bargaining parties in the original position choose as the most reasonable conception for a democratic society that is made up of citizens who are free and equal? First of all, insofar as the basic structure of society profoundly shapes our lives, both in terms of its political institutions and in terms of its economic and social institutions, the conception of justice must determine the fair terms of cooperation that will regulate these social arrangements, particularly those of the government and the economy. Secondly, since in democratic societies inequalities in the basic structure are unavoidable, then the conception of justice must show how these inequalities can be justified to free and equal citizens as fair but inevitable in a unified system of social cooperation. Finally, given the reasonable pluralism of democratic societies, the conception of justice must be presented in terms that all citizens within the society will recognize and accept as being politically legitimate; in this sense, "the conception of justice must be a political conception."[35]

Owing to the makeup of the basic structure of society, Rawls proposes that the conception of justice that is chosen in the original position will consist of two principles: the one will concern the political institutions of the basic structure, particularly the "constitutional essentials" of a liberal democracy; the second will concern the economic and social institutions of the basic structure, particularly the inequalities that are created and sustained by these social arrangements. The role of the first principle is to secure the basic liberties of each citizen in the society in an equal way; the role of the second is to ensure that the inequalities of the basic structure, although inevitable, are fair. The second principle accomplishes this role, first, by requiring that fair equality of opportunity exists in the society for all, despite its inequalities; and secondly, by ensuring that the inequalities that the economic and social institutions of the basic structure engender will in fact have the greatest benefit for the worst off, not the well-off, in the society.[36] This latter part of the second principle, which Rawls names "the difference principle," accepts economic and social inequalities (differences) in society, but only if these differences contribute to a unified system of social cooperation that is fair. Thus, by requiring that economic inequalities benefit the least advantaged in the society, the difference principle ensures a fair system of cooperation. Rawls states: "The difference principle is essentially a principle of reciprocity."[37]

A liberal democracy will be a society of fair cooperation, then, if it regulates the social arrangements of its major institutions according to these two principles of justice, which Rawls sees as working in tandem.[38] He articulates these two principles as follows:

35. Rawls, *Justice as Fairness*, 39–41.
36. Rawls, *Justice as Fairness*, 47–48.
37. Rawls, *Justice as Fairness*, 64.
38. Rawls, *Justice as Fairness*, 46n10.

> (a) Each person has the same indefeasible claim to a fully adequate scheme of equal basic liberties, which scheme is compatible with the same scheme of liberties for all; and
>
> (b) Social and economic inequalities are to satisfy two conditions: first, they are to be attached to offices and positions open to all under conditions of fair equality of opportunity; and second, they are to be to the greatest benefit of the least-advantaged members of society (the difference principle).[39]

The significance of the thought experiment that results in these two principles of justice is that it enables us to see, according to Rawls, what is the basis of the validity of the conception of justice that rules a liberal democracy. The principles of justice are the outcome of the social agreement that is made by those in the original position. The validity of the principles lies in the fairness of the procedure by which the principles are chosen, that is, behind a veil of ignorance. No criterion independent of this procedure, such as a divine command or an independent order of moral values, validates this conception of justice; only the fairness of the procedure itself does this. For this reason, Rawls emphasizes that this conception of justice is strictly a political conception, that is, a conception that is the result of the social agreement which is made by free and equal citizens in fully fair conditions.[40]

But, given the reasonable pluralism of a democratic society, how does the political conception of justice provide the basis for a unified and stable society? Rawls responds: Although the citizens of a liberal democracy hold incompatible beliefs and values, in a well-ordered society (that is, an ideal society) they agree to the fair terms of cooperation that are specified by the principles of justice, and thus this conception of justice becomes the basis of social unity. Rawls describes this social unity as an "overlapping consensus" of comprehensive doctrines. Because the conception of justice is established independently of all comprehensive doctrines, and thus is "freestanding," it can serve as the focus of this overlapping consensus. Citizens who hold incompatible comprehensive doctrines are able to endorse this political conception of justice without relinquishing their comprehensive viewpoints. They assent to the principles of justice, but they do so each in their own terms and thus from their own comprehensive viewpoint. Therefore, despite the divisions in society that comprehensive doctrines create, the citizens of a pluralistic democracy find unity in the principles of justice on which they all agree.[41]

The political conception of justice further engenders social unity by providing the citizens of a pluralistic society with the "public reasons" that they require to justify to one another their political decisions and actions. The mandates of government are by nature coercive, but in a democracy the coercive power of the government is essentially "the power of the public, that is, of free and equal citizens as a collective body."

39. Rawls, *Justice as Fairness*, 42–43.

40. Rawls, *Political Liberalism*, 89–90, 97–99.

41. Rawls, *Political Liberalism*, 39–40, 133–34.

Accordingly, the political deliberations and decisions of the public that concern the basic structure of society must be expressed in terms that all citizens can reasonably understand and endorse. This obligation Rawls describes as the moral duty of civility.[42]

But not all reasons that are expressed in public are public reasons. The voluntary associations that make up civil society, such as churches, universities, and professional groups, offer reasons regarding matters of great social and political concern, but these reasons Rawls terms "nonpublic reasons." These are not the private reasons of individuals, and when these nonpublic reasons are stated in the context of a particular association, they are publicly stated with respect to the members of the association. They are nonpublic, however, with respect to the political society, that is, with respect to citizens as a collective body. Nonpublic reasons express the comprehensive religious, philosophical, and moral doctrines of the many voluntary associations that make up the "background culture" of the public political culture. "There are many nonpublic reasons," Rawls states, "and but one public reason" which is rooted in the political conception of justice. Only in the terms of public reason can citizens come together in common agreement.[43]

Given this distinction between public and nonpublic reasons, must we conclude that for Rawls nonpublic reasons—say, religious reasons—must be excluded from the political deliberations of a constitutional democracy? Rawls addressed this question late in his professional career in the essay titled "The Idea of Public Reason Revisited." Rawls allows that religious reasons can enter into and seek to influence public political deliberation *provided that* the religious argument demonstrates that public political reasons in fact support its comprehensive viewpoint and vice versa. This stipulation Rawls refers to as "the proviso." The civil rights movement of the 1960s, particularly the speeches of Martin Luther King Jr., well illustrates the proviso. Although King's speeches and actions were inspired by a biblical vision of justice, he at the same time based his argument against the injustice of segregation on the political values of the US Constitution. In which case, King's nonpublic reasons did not replace the public reasons of the Constitution but rather brought attention to and supported them. Rawls adds that when religious argument enters into political deliberation, the value of liberal democracy as an overlapping consensus is highlighted. When religion accepts the stipulation of the proviso and only then enters into political deliberation, its acknowledged inclusion accentuates the diversity of those in the deliberation, and thus "the commitment to constitutional democracy is publicly manifested." Still, the inclusion of religious argument into political deliberation, Rawls maintains, "does not change the nature and content of justification in public reason itself."[44] Religious argument can support but cannot alter the political conception of justice upon which the unity and stability of a pluralistic democratic society depends. Public reason alone,

42. Rawls, *Political Liberalism*, 216–18.

43. Rawls, *Political Liberalism*, 212–13, 220.

44. Rawls, "Idea of Public Reason Revisited," 591–93.

based on the political conception of justice, must regulate the political deliberations of a democratic society if the society is to realize a genuine social unity.

The social unity that the political conception of justice achieves in a democratic society Rawls recognizes as a moral good. Although religious and nonreligious comprehensive viewpoints hold various conceptions of the moral good, that is, "conceptions of what is of value in human life, as well as ideals of personal virtue and character," these conceptions cannot provide the end or moral purpose of a political society.[45] Indeed, if the unity of a political society is established on the basis of a comprehensive doctrine, it can be maintained only through the oppressive power of the state, not the social agreement of its citizens.[46] Thus for Rawls, in a pluralistic society the social unity of an overlapping consensus of comprehensive doctrines established through the political conception of justice has intrinsic value and, for this reason, it is a moral good.

The political conception of justice, then, includes both the idea of the right (the principles of justice seen as principles of moral obligation) and the idea of the good (the intrinsic value of a well-ordered society based on the principles of justice). The two ideas are complementary, Rawls states, and so both must be included in an adequate conception of justice. Yet, in their relation to one another, the right has priority over the good. In order to be included in the political conception of justice, ideas of the good must be strictly political. This restriction and the scope of its limits are determined by the principles of justice. Herein lies the priority of the right over the good. "This priority means that admissible ideas of the good must respect the limits of, and serve a role within, the political conception of justice."[47]

Amid the plurality of answers in a democratic society to the question concerning how we ought to live together, the political conception of justice, according to Rawls, provides a normative answer that unifies and ensures the stability of the society. It can do so because it is the result of a social agreement that is made in fully fair conditions by citizens who are free and equal. Despite the manifold conceptions of the good that divide the citizens of a liberal democracy, they find unity in the concept of the right, established in the original position, to which they all agree. Accordingly, for Rawls, the norm of social justice is one, not many.

One Answer from Religion

When the Roman Catholic Church issued *Gaudium et spes* (*Pastoral Constitution on the Church in the Modern World*) at the conclusion of the Second Vatican Council in 1965, the Council offered to the world a conception of social justice that, like Rawls, portrays justice in terms of social unity and thus articulates the norm of social justice as

45. Rawls, *Political Liberalism*, 175.

46. Rawls, *Political Liberalism*, 37, 146.

47. Rawls, *Political Liberalism*, 173–76, 201–4.

one. But, unlike Rawls, the Council's conception of justice sees the basis of social unity lying, not first of all in the social agreement that is the basis of political society, but in the very nature of being human. The scope of its conception, then, is not restricted to the political, but concerns the well-being of humanity as a whole. Its focus is not the particular, but the universal. The Latin title of the *Pastoral Constitution* which is taken from the first words of the document—*Gaudium et spes* (joy and hope)—points to the moral purposes of humanity itself, not only of the Christian community:

> The joys and hopes, the grief and anguish of the people of our time, especially of those who are poor or afflicted, are the joys and hopes, the grief and anguish of the followers of Christ as well. Nothing that is genuinely human fails to find an echo in their hearts. For theirs is a community of people united in Christ and guided by the holy Spirit in their pilgrimage towards the Father's kingdom, bearers of a message of salvation for all of humanity. That is why they cherish a feeling of deep solidarity with the human race and its history.[48]

Thus, in proposing its conception of justice, the Council addresses not only the members of the church, but "the entire human family" (no. 2). Moreover, insofar as the Council sees the basis of social unity as lying in human nature itself, it views the ideal of human solidarity as the moral purpose of humanity as a whole and thus as the moral good that rules all social arrangements. The question "how ought we to live together?" the Council answers in terms of this moral good. In this moral good the Council finds the norm of social justice. In contrast to Rawls, the Council's discussion of justice gives priority to the good over the right.

But, although the scope of the Council's vision of the moral good is universal, the basis of this vision is particular, namely, the faith of the believing community. To the issues of social justice the Council brings the light of faith in order to see clearly, to judge accurately, and to act effectively on the matters of justice that concern us all. "For faith casts a new light on everything and makes known the full ideal which God has set for humanity, thus guiding the mind towards solutions that are fully human" (no. 11). Thus, in the light of the creation stories of the book of Genesis, the Council sees the human person as created in the image of God. Herein lies the dignity of every human being. Furthermore, in creating the human being as male and female, God created human beings, not as solitary beings, but as social beings. "This partnership of man and woman constitutes the first form of communion between people. For by their innermost nature men and women are social beings" (no. 12). We are social by nature, and thus we are created by God to live in communion with one another. God's desire is "that all men and women should form one family and deal with each other as brothers and sisters. All, in fact, are destined to the very same end, namely God himself." Indeed, Jesus "when praying to the Father 'that they may all be one . . . even

---

48. Vatican Council II, *Gaudium et spes* (*Pastoral Constitution on the Church in the Modern World*), no. 1.

as we are one' (Jn 17:21–22)" indicates "that there is a certain similarity between the union existing among the divine persons and the union of God's children in truth and love" (no. 24). In the eyes of the Council, the mutual love between the persons of the Trinity serves as the model of society.

The vision of faith that the Council articulates provides a distinctive answer to the question "how ought we to live together?" The human good of solidarity and compassion, seen in the light of faith, forms the heart of the answer. Clearly the Council's statements represent what Rawls termed a comprehensive doctrine. These statements express a viewpoint that intends to articulate the whole truth; yet, this viewpoint, although reasonable, is not shared by all within a world that is made up of diverse comprehensive viewpoints. This the Council acknowledges.

At the same time, "to foster vital contact and exchange between the church and different cultures," the Council undertakes the effort to express this viewpoint "in suitable terms" that are both understandable and acceptable to the whole human family. In fact, throughout its history of evangelization, the church has sought to adapt its vision of faith "to the understanding of all and the requirements of the learned." Furthermore, by describing its encounter with the diverse cultures of the world as an "exchange," the Council intends this encounter to be one of giving and receiving, speaking and listening, on the part of the church (no. 44). Given the good that human solidarity intends, the Council understands that its consideration of the matters of justice must take place in the form of a dialogue with the diverse cultural viewpoints of the world as well as with the specific viewpoints of the social institutions that make up society. The basis of the dialogue between the church and the world is a shared humanity that concerns "the dignity of the human person, the community of men and women, and the deep significance of human activity." The hope that the church brings to this dialogue is that "it can help to make the human family and its history still more human" (no. 40).

The focus of the dialogue between the church and the world concerns "the laws of social living which the creator has inscribed in people's spiritual and moral nature" (no. 23). The laws of social living, in this view, are not the products of social convention (legal stipulations), but the articulations of the moral purposes of all human activity. In regard to the matters of social justice, the church centers its discussion on the human good that is the moral purpose of social arrangements such as the economy or the government. The mutual interdependence that is achieved in society through such social institutions as the economy or the government fails to be a genuine solidarity if this interdependence is realized outside of a dialogue on the moral purposes of these social arrangements. The church's contribution to this dialogue, in the eyes of the Council, is the light of faith that it brings to the dialogue. "Christian revelation greatly fosters the establishment of such communion and at the same time promotes deeper understanding of the laws of social living which the creator has inscribed in people's spiritual and moral nature." (no. 23). But, to take part in this dialogue, the church must articulate its vision of faith in terms that are understandable and acceptable in a pluralistic world.

The church undertakes this task by focusing on the human good, which is the end or purpose of all human striving. The starting point of its discussion lies in this observation: the good of the human person can be realized only in and through society, that is, through the basic social institutions that give order and stability to society. Accordingly, the good of the individual person is necessarily intertwined with the good of the society. "Life in society is not something accessory to humanity" (no. 25). Human beings are by nature social beings. Thus, matters of justice, whether they concern the social relations between individuals or groups within a society, will always intend the good of the society as a whole, which is the common good. The Council defines the common good as "the sum total of social conditions which allow people, either as groups or as individuals, to reach their fulfillment more fully and more easily."[49] Moreover, the Council emphasizes that insofar as human interdependence is increasingly a global interdependence, the common good must be considered in universal terms. Consequently, "the resulting rights and obligations" that come from thinking of the common good as a moral good must be "the concern of the entire human race" (no. 26).

What the Council means by "the sum total of social conditions" in its description of the common good can be stated in terms of what the West has named "human rights." Every human being ought "to have ready access to all that is necessary for living a genuinely human life" which includes:

> food, clothing, housing, the right freely to choose their state of life and set up a family, the right to education, work, to their good name, to respect, to proper knowledge, the right to act according to the dictates of conscience and to safeguard their privacy, and rightful freedom, including freedom of religion. The basis of these rights and the corresponding obligation to fulfill them lies in the sublime dignity of human persons, who stand above all things and whose rights and duties are universal and inviolable. (no. 26)

The dignity of every human being requires that human rights be seen as moral claims that are shared equally by all human beings. The Council states that "while there are just differences between people, their equal dignity as persons demands that we strive for fairer and more humane conditions. Excessive economic and social disparity between individuals and peoples of the one human race" (no. 29) violates, not simply the moral rules of fair distribution, but more fundamentally the very humanity of those who suffer from the unfair distribution of the world's goods. Unfair and thus inhumane social conditions both disregard the human rights of the individual and

---

49. This definition of the common good was first articulated by Pope John XXIII in the 1961 social encyclical *Mater et magistra (Christianity and Social Progress)*. See John XXIII, *Mater et magistra (Christianity and Social Progress)*, no. 65.

undermine the good of the society as a whole. Human dignity has a social basis. The dignity of the individual is expressed and maintained through the social institutions of the society. Unless the social conditions by which individuals achieve a genuinely human life are equally accessible to all individuals within the society, neither the good of the individual nor the good of the society is realized. The good of the individual and the common good are necessarily intertwined.

David Hollenbach, SJ, comments that the Council's understanding of human rights contrasts with that of the West in one significant way: by viewing human rights in terms of the common good, the Council bypasses the purely individualistic understanding of human rights that prevails in the West. Whereas the liberal tradition of the West views human rights as the rights of the individual vis-à-vis the coercion of the state, the Council, by viewing human rights in the context of the common good, understands human rights as the social conditions that must exist if every individual in the society is to participate fully in the life of the society. Human rights, in this view, are the basic requirements of genuine solidarity.[50] Thus, along with the civil-political rights of the individual that the West has traditionally affirmed, such as "the right to act according to the dictates of conscience and to safeguard their privacy, and rightful freedom, including freedom of religion," the Council also affirms socioeconomic rights, such as the human right to food and housing, work and education (no. 26). Living a genuinely human life in society demands not only the protection of political freedoms, but also the fulfillment of basic human needs. Ensuring that every human being has "ready access to all that is necessary for living a genuinely human life" (no. 26) requires that we think of human rights not solely as "political trumps held by individuals" against the collective goals of society, this as proposed by the American philosopher Ronald Dworkin,[51] but as the "duties of solidarity." In the eyes of the Council, the "protection of human rights and the advancement of the common good are mutually correlative, not opposed to each other."[52]

Thus, "the best way to fulfill one's obligations of justice and love is to contribute to the common good" (no. 30), states the Council. The "need to transcend an individualistic morality" is even more urgent today in an increasingly interdependent world. "All must consider it their sacred duty to count social obligations among their chief duties today and observe them as such. For the more closely the world comes together, the more widely do people's obligations transcend particular groups and extend to the whole world" (no. 30). The norm of social justice, then, in the view of the Council, is the common good, either the common good of a particular society or the universal common good. Social justice is the human act (more broadly, the human virtue) that realizes this norm in concrete ways. Contributing to the common good consists of those human actions that create and maintain the social conditions that enable

50. Hollenbach, SJ, "Commentary on *Gaudium et spes*," 279–82.

51. Dworkin, *Taking Rights Seriously*, xi.

52. Hollenbach, SJ, "Commentary on *Gaudium et spes*," 281.

human beings to achieve their full humanness. To the question "how ought we to live together?" the Council answers: by acting for the common good. That the common good as a norm provides purposeful direction to society's institutions in meeting the conditions of human fulfillment—social institutions such as religion, the economy, and government—demonstrates its unitive nature; that the common good as a norm establishes the basis of social unity in and through the normative viewpoints of society's institutions demonstrates its manifold nature. Here, in the light of Catholic social teaching, the norm of social justice is one and many.

ON DEFINING THE COMMON GOOD: THE ROLE OF THE CHURCH IN RELATION TO MARKETS AND GOVERNMENT

By making the common good the norm of social justice, the Council presents this moral good as the norm that ought to regulate the social arrangements of society's institutions. But, is this an instance of one social institution, namely religion, thinking on behalf of other institutions by translating "the means and ends of other institutions" into its own logic, this being the challenge that the sociologist presents to social institutions when they engage in public argument?[53] The Council's response to this challenge would be no for two reasons. First, by entering into a dialogue with the social institution of the economy (nos. 63–72) and the social institution of government (nos. 73–76), the Council acknowledges the "rightful autonomy" of each social institution. "If by the autonomy of earthly affairs is meant the gradual discovery, utilization and ordering of the laws and values of matter and society, then the demand for autonomy is perfectly in order" (no. 36). In the Council's eyes, the role of the church in this dialogue is not to propose alternative models of the economy or government, but to engage in a dialogue concerning the moral purpose that each social institution shares in common with the others, namely, realizing the human good.

Secondly, insofar as the common good is the human good, the dialogue between the church and the social institutions of the economy and government concerning the moral purpose of each institution takes place on common ground. In proposing the common good as the norm of social justice, the Council is not presenting to the institutions of the economy and government a competing moral viewpoint, but rather proposing a way for each social institution, including the church, to see its legitimating idea, that is, its normative viewpoint, in relation to the others. What the biblical vision of solidarity and compassion, the democratic vision of equality, and the market's vision of freedom share in common is that each moral value reflects a normative view regarding the human good. But, because the human good can be realized only in and through the plurality of the social institutions that make up the society as a whole, achieving the human good requires an understanding of the common good,

53. Bellah et al., *Good Society*, 292.

which is the final end or purpose of each of the social institutions. This understanding, however, is accomplished, not through the agency of one institution, but through the dialogue between all institutions. Defining the common good requires a common effort. Thus, regarding matters of social justice, the common good as the moral norm of justice does not stand in distinction from or apart from the normative views of religion, the economy, or government, but rather embraces the plurality of these diverse viewpoints and thereby provides the basis of social unity for the normative views of these distinct social institutions. Defining the common good brings about social unity, but does so only by taking into account the normative viewpoints of society's institutions. The common good if viewed apart from the pluralism of society's institutions is without content; social institutions without the direction of the common good lack social unity and final purpose. In the eyes of the Council, the norm of social justice (the common good) as the basis of the social unity that encompasses and directs the plurality of social institutions is for this reason both one and many.

The Council's proposal to consider the matters of social justice in terms of the common good, however, blurs the distinction between public and nonpublic reasons that is established by Rawls. The Council's effort to dialogue with the institutions of the economy and government reflects the fundamental viewpoint that the Council holds concerning the role of the church in the modern world. "One of the gravest errors of our time is the dichotomy between the faith which many profess and their day-to-day conduct." In the view of the Council, the Christian faith is not solely a private matter. A genuine expression of the Christian faith must be "more than the fulfillment of acts of worship and the observance of a few moral obligations" (no. 43). A genuine faith expresses itself in public ways. Indeed, the right to religious freedom, proclaimed by the Council, includes not only the right of religion to be free of the control of the government, but also the right and duty of religion to be involved in the shaping of public affairs.

But, how and to what extent can faith influence public affairs in a pluralistic society? According to Rawls, the church's distinctive voice concerning the matters of justice rightfully has a place in the sphere of civil society, the sphere that Rawls describes as the background culture of the political society. In this sphere the Council's view of social justice is expressed in terms that Rawls describes as nonpublic reasons. Furthermore, Rawls allows that alternative conceptions of justice have a place in the discussion of social justice, if the conception of justice is stated in the terms of public reason. "Political liberalism, then, does not try to fix public reason once and for all in the form of one favored political conception of justice," he states. Thus, in Rawls's opinion, "Catholic views of the common good and solidarity when they are expressed in terms of political values" are admissible in the public discussion of justice.[54]

Hollenbach, however, questions whether Rawls's distinction between nonpublic and public reasons must be seen exclusively as a "one-way relationship." Certainly,

---

54. Rawls, "Idea of Public Reason Revisited," 582–83.

in a liberal democracy, the reasons of religion cannot supplant the public reasons that unite the democracy. The Council does not intend to overstep the separation of church and state that exists in modern liberal democracies. "The political community and the church are autonomous and independent of each other in their own fields" (no. 76), says the Council. Nevertheless, according to Hollenbach, "in the language of the Catholic tradition, the relation between faith and reason is not all in one direction: faith should be reasonable and 'make sense,' but reason can also be informed by faith."[55] How so?

The biblical vision of solidarity and compassion that informs the Council's understanding of the common good, though it is expressed in terms that are understandable and acceptable in a pluralistic society, is nonetheless—to use Rawls's term—a comprehensive doctrine, rooted in the faith of the believing community, regarding what constitutes the good society. By bringing this biblical vision to bear on the social arrangements of the government and the economy, the church brings to light the moral purpose that the institutions of religion, government, and the economy share in common, namely, the human good realized in and through these social institutions. In this light the social arrangements of the government and the economy are seen not as morally neutral arrangements to be used by individuals in the society to realize their personal vision of the good, but rather as normative patterns by which individuals in the society realize the human good in common. By engaging in this dialogue, the church addresses the political and economic values that the citizens of the society hold in common regarding the human good. The outcome of this dialogue can affect what political society and economic society consider to be of moral value. Moreover, locating this dialogue in the context of civil society highlights the church's purpose for entering into this dialogue. Concerning matters of justice, the church's intent is not to present alternative views of government and the economy to the society, but to change minds and hearts in regard to what is of moral value to political and economic society (this we saw in Chapter 2). The Council honors the separation of church and state, but at the same time affirms that faith, economics, and politics are inextricably linked.

Still, we are left with this question: If the church enters into a dialogue with the economy and government regarding the common good from the particularity of faith, on what basis does this dialogue take place? What is the common ground (consensus) on which the major social institutions of society, including religion, meet to engage in public argument regarding the common good? In other words, in the view of Catholic social teaching, what precisely is "common" in regard to the common good? That there can and must be common ground on which social institutions meet for public argument regarding the matters of social justice is a point of agreement between Rawls and Catholic social teaching. But what constitutes the common ground is the point of disagreement that divides these two conceptions of social justice. Bringing

55. Hollenbach, SJ, *Common Good and Christian Ethics*, 167.

this disagreement into view highlights the distinctiveness of each viewpoint, but also underscores the challenge that each presents to the other.

What is "Common" in the Common Good?

As we saw at the end of Chapter 3, the difference between the view of social justice in Catholic social teaching and that of Rawls is not only the difference between two present-day viewpoints concerning social justice, but also the difference between two moral traditions. In Catholic social teaching the formulation of the norm of social justice draws upon the tradition that is the older: the origin of the idea of the common good lies in Athens in the fourth century BCE in the philosophy of Aristotle; the idea acquires a systematic formulation in the thirteenth century CE in the theology of Thomas Aquinas; and the idea is given modern-day expression in the social movements, the social thinkers, and the official teachings of Catholic social teaching. The moral tradition that Rawls draws upon begins at the dawn of the modern age in the West in the seventeenth- and eighteenth-century philosophies of John Locke, Jean-Jacques Rousseau, and Immanuel Kant.[56]

The principles of justice that Rawls formulates presuppose the understanding of society expressed by these early modern thinkers, namely, that society is the product of the implicit social agreement of persons equally situated who are rational and free, which these philosophers termed "the social contract." Justice in this moral tradition is understood in terms of the moral rules that articulate the social contract. Here the moral category of the right (moral rules or principles) has priority over the good. In the moral tradition that originates with the Greeks, on the other hand, society is understood, not as a social contract, but as the natural and necessary condition of human fulfillment. The good of human fulfillment, that is, the good of each person in the society, requires a society that is good. Justice in this moral tradition is understood in terms of the human acts that realize the good society. Here the moral category of the good (human fulfillment) has priority over the right. These two moral traditions, then, engender two different ways to consider the matters of justice. The one, by considering justice in terms of moral rules, focuses our attention on justice as an ethics of obligation. The other, by considering justice in terms of the human acts that bring about the social good, focuses our attention on justice as an ethics of virtue. The one tradition does not exclude what the other affirms, and thus the two traditions can be seen as complementary. Yet, which moral category has priority— the right or the good—determines in decisive ways how the matters of social justice will be discussed.

The concept of social justice presented by Rawls, at first look, appears to be the more suitable view for providing the basis (the common ground) for public argument

---

56. Rawls, *Theory of Justice*, 11.

among social institutions in a pluralistic society regarding the matters of social justice. The principles of justice provide the basis of social unity precisely because they are "freestanding," that is, determined on the basis of reason, outside of the partiality of the comprehensive doctrines held by those who make up the society. Thus, despite the incompatibility of comprehensive doctrines in a pluralistic society, the citizens of a liberal democracy find common ground—a space of impartiality—in the principles of justice that serve as the focus of an overlapping consensus of comprehensive doctrines. In this overlapping consensus, Rawls finds the basis of social unity for a pluralistic democracy.

This social unity, moreover, Rawls recognizes as having intrinsic value to the society and thus as being the moral good of a well-ordered society. He dismisses the view of the social contract held by some that envisions society as being solely the aggregate of the private ends of individuals and associations that make up the society (thus society as being "the collection of individuals who compose it," to use the words of the economist Milton Friedman quoted above), and society's institutions as having as their primary purpose the realization of these private ends. "It is sometimes contended that the contract doctrine entails that private society is the ideal, at least when the division of advantages satisfies a suitable standard of reciprocity. But this is not so, as the notion of a well-ordered society shows," Rawls states.[57] What a well-ordered society provides for its citizens, beyond the means to realize their private ends, is a shared final end—the good of social union. Indeed, Rawls emphasizes, a well-ordered society "is a social union of social unions,"[58] which thus exhibits "the preeminent form of human flourishing" and, accordingly, the "value of community."[59]

The good of a well-ordered society for its citizens, however, differs from the good envisioned by various religious, philosophical, or moral comprehensive doctrines held by the citizens of the society in this fundamental way: "While it is true that they do not affirm the same comprehensive doctrine, they do affirm the same political conception of justice; and this means that they share one very basic political end, and one that has high priority: namely, the end of supporting just institutions and of giving one another justice accordingly," says Rawls in *Political Liberalism*. The good of a well-ordered society and, by implication, the good of the individual citizen lies precisely in having a common conception of justice. The shared final end of the political conception of justice, Rawls proposes, "may be among citizens' most basic aims by reference to which they express the kind of person they very much want to be"—the kind of person who has developed a "sense of justice, that is, one that enables them to understand and to apply the principles of justice, and for the most part to act from them as their circumstances require."[60]

57. Rawls, *Theory of Justice*, 522.
58. Rawls, *Theory of Justice*, 527.
59. Rawls, *Theory of Justice*, 529.
60. Rawls, *Political Liberalism*, 202.

While Rawls does not exclude the notion of the good from the consideration of justice or exclude from consideration the good as envisioned by comprehensive doctrines when these doctrines endorse the good of justice from within their own distinctive perspectives, given the reasonable pluralism of liberal democracies, he nevertheless restricts the consideration of the good to the right—that is, to the political conception of justice. Rawls explains: "the priority of the right does not mean that ideas of the good must be avoided; that is impossible. Rather, it means that the ideas used must be political ideas: they must be tailored to meet the restrictions imposed by the political conception of justice and fit into the space it allows."[61] In this space, established by the principles of justice, citizens of a well-ordered society find common ground for public argument. What is to be gained, then, if we as a society give priority to the good over the right when we engage in public argument concerning matters of social justice? Furthermore, what challenges will we face if our collective discussion of justice begins, not with the principles of justice, but with the good of society?

Public argument regarding social justice that gives priority to the conception of the good immediately faces the problem that Rawls avoids: the array of views within society regarding the social good that are diverse, incompatible, and partial—this insofar as views of the good originate in and represent specific, distinct social and institutional settings and thus distinct social goods. The discussion of social justice that begins with the good of society encounters from the start what Rawls has termed the reasonable pluralism of democratic society. Accordingly, the approach to social justice that begins from the perspective of the good of society as a whole must demonstrate on what basis—on what common foundation—the good of the social whole is determined and can be discussed regarding the matters of social justice. Given the diversity of social goods that make up society, is there a fundamental good that is common to this diversity—a common good that underlies and gives purpose to the pursuit of diverse goods in the society? What precisely is common in the common good?

As a way to initiate a response to this question, let us consider the question in a simpler form, that is, as a question concerning *a* common good which is readily available to our lived experience. Consider a family celebration. Members of the family—parents, children, grandparents, aunts, uncles—have come together to celebrate something of importance (value) to the family, say, the birth of the newest family member. In celebrating this blessed event, feelings of joy and gratitude are shared mutually (in common) by all members of the family, and yet these celebratory feelings are experienced and expressed differently by the different members of the family. The family celebration involves both commonality (the participants are all members of one and the same family) and difference (the diversity of the ages of the participants brings complexity to the family celebration, thus constituting a manifold experience). Here commonality that includes difference is experienced as a *communality* (being a community). The joy of the celebration is communal in that the experience of the

61. Rawls, *Political Liberalism*, 203; see Riordan, SJ, *Politics of the Common Good*, 118–22.

celebration is more than the sum of each individual member's happiness. The celebratory joy comes about only in and through the interaction of all members of the family, but precisely for this reason the communal joy presupposes and requires the differences that make up the family to be played out. The children's joy is different from the joy of the adults and yet both constitute the family's experience. Herein lies the common good of the celebration—the mutual joy of the family. What is common in this particular common good is not a sameness of feeling and expression within the family, but rather the shared (thus diverse) feelings and expressions of joy that make up the family celebration. The foundation of what is common in this common good, therefore, lies in the relationships themselves that constitute the family as a whole and its shared celebration.[62]

But, can this notion of *a* common good be extended by way of analogy to include the notion of *the* common good of a society as a whole or the notion of *the* global common good? If so, is "the gain in extent bought at the cost of a loss of precision?"[63] This question, posed by Jean-Yves Calvez, SJ, and Jacques Perrin, SJ, was presented at the end of Chapter 3 as the challenge that must be addressed if the notion of the common good is to provide meaningful moral guidance to the social whole. By giving the moral norm of the common good a societal and global reach, does the norm become unavoidably so vague and imprecise that it is rendered ineffectual as a moral guide—being a hopeful wish, but not a determinative guide?

To respond to this challenge, we must first show on what basis the good of society as a whole or the global common good is determined. Given the diversity that exists within national societies and between nations on a global scale, is there a "one and the same" (a commonality) that nevertheless underlies and constitutes this diversity? Though the goods that we pursue as human beings are many, is there a good that is common to these diverse goods and thus fundamental to their nature?

The question echoes a philosophical problem that is anchored in classical Greek philosophy, particularly Aristotle.[64] The problem concerns the relation between the one and the many. Here the problem specifically concerns the relation between human nature (as being one and the same) and the diverse instantiations of human nature in present-day societies worldwide and throughout history, and thus by implication the problem of understanding the human good as being both one and many.[65]

Commenting on Aristotle, Thomas Aquinas points out that the many presuppose the one. Conceptually and ontologically, the one is prior to the many. At the same time, perceptually (experientially) the many are prior to the one. Consider a trip to the market to buy apples. What first meets our eye are the many different types of apple that are available to us. But our comparison of the different types of apple can only

62. See Haldane, "Natural Law and Ethical Pluralism"; Kirk-Duggan, "Rose by Any Other Name?"

63. Calvez, SJ and Perrin, SJ, *Church and Social Justice*, 151.

64. See Aristotle, *Metaphysics* 10.3.1054a20–55a2.

65. Haldane, "Natural Law and Ethical Pluralism," 129–30.

take place in light of the conceptual awareness that there is something common (one and the same) to them all—the common nature of apple. We perceive differences as such only on the basis of what is common to these differences. Yet, what is common to the differences has reality (concrete existence) only in and through the particular differences. The common nature of apple does not exist simply as a general concept of the mind apart from individual apples, but exists—takes on actual form—in the form of individual apples. The common nature of apple the mind comprehends, but does so only through our sensible perception of individual apples and their various kinds. Here the many presuppose the one (the common nature of apple). But the one manifests itself in the many (the various kinds of apple). Aquinas states: "For even though things which are divided are many, they do not have the formal note of a many until the fact of being one is attributed to each of the particular things concerned. Yet nothing prevents us from also saying that the notion of multitude depends on that of unity insofar as multitude is measured by one; and this already involves the notion of number."[66] What is immediately evident to our senses is the many, whether this be the many kinds of apple or the many kinds of human good, but what is not evident to our senses—that which is "prior and more intelligible by nature" yet "known by us only derivatively" by our intellect through our senses, says Aquinas[67]—is the one and the same nature that is comprehended by the intellect and attributed to each individual one (this particular apple or this particular human good) that makes up the many. This one and the same nature is the common foundation that underlies and constitutes the many. Our comprehension of the common nature, furthermore, enables us to evaluate the many. We know the difference between a good apple and a bad apple on the basis of our comprehension of the nature of apple. What something ought to be (its good) is perceived and evaluated by us on the basis of what it is (its nature). As this is the case with apples, so it is with the human good as well. Thus, to understand and evaluate properly the diversity of social goods (the many) that we as human beings pursue, we must determine the common foundation (what is common in the common good) that gives these diverse goods meaning and purpose.

What, then, is the common foundation (the one) that underlies and constitutes the diversity of social goods that we as human beings pursue (the many)? Furthermore, how does this foundation provide the basis (common ground) for public argument regarding the matters of social justice? Unlike Rawls, for whom the basis (common ground) for public argument lies in the political conception of justice, this being the outcome of the hypothetical agreement of free and equal citizens in the original position (Rawls's version of the social contract),[68] the tradition of Catholic social teaching envisages the foundation that provides the common ground for public

---

66. Thomas Aquinas, *Commentary on the Metaphysics of Aristotle* 10.4.1998.

67. Thomas Aquinas, *Commentary on the Metaphysics of Aristotle* 10.4.1990.

68. Freeman, *Rawls*, 142.

argument regarding social justice as being universal in scope and thus as encompassing yet transcending the sphere of the political.

How ought we to live together? The normative nature of the question (ought) concerns the matters of social justice. As the question expands—the more encompassing the "we" becomes—the more far-reaching the "ought" becomes, in order to remain proportional to the question. For Rawls, "we" refers to the citizens of a constitutional democracy. The "ought" in question refers to the political conception of justice (the right), derived in the original position, which provides "a public basis of justification for the basic structure" of the constitutional democracy. "Justice as fairness," says Rawls, "seeks common ground—or if one prefers, neutral ground—given the fact of pluralism. This common ground is the political conception itself as the focus of an overlapping consensus."[69] Here on this common ground, established by an implicit social contract, the citizens of a well-ordered society find the basis for public deliberation about the matters of social justice that concern all within the polity.

For the tradition of Catholic social teaching, by contrast, "we" refers to human beings as such. What ought to be—how we ought to live together—has its foundation in the nature that we as human beings have in common. The political scientist Mary M. Keys observes: "The higher and more expansive the building, the deeper, wider, and more secure its foundations must be."[70] In order for the concept of justice to serve as a normative guide, not only for the institutional arrangements of a specific political regime, but more widely for the universal breadth of human affairs, the concept of justice must be grounded on a foundation suitable to the scope of the task. This foundation Keys finds articulated in the writings of Aristotle and Aquinas, first and most fundamentally in the notion that the human person is by nature social and political. Aquinas, however, goes beyond Aristotle by widening, deepening, and securing this foundation through his use of the natural law as the lens through which to view human nature.[71]

Through this lens—this we considered in Chapter 3—Aquinas sees all of nature, including human nature, as movement toward a specific end or purpose, the end being determined by the nature of the thing itself (for example, an apple ripening being movement toward its end or purpose—to be an apple that is good). The purposeful movement in nature Aquinas describes as the natural inclination in nature toward the good, that is, as the movement in nature toward fulfillment or becoming actual. This purposeful movement human beings share in common with all things in nature—inanimate and animate—as the fundamental inclination to be (self-preservation), and with all animals as the fundamental inclination to propagate (the perpetuation of life). Distinctive to human beings, given human rationality in the form of both

69. Rawls, *Political Liberalism*, 192; see also Rawls, "Justice as Fairness."

70. Keys, *Aquinas, Aristotle, and the Promise*, 88.

71. See Keys, *Aquinas, Aristotle, and the Promise*, 59–110; see also Thomas Aquinas, *Summa Theologica* I–II.94.2.

knowing (the movement of the intellect) and desiring (the movement of the will), is the natural inclination in human beings to know the truth (ultimately the truth about God) and to live in society. In these fundamental ways—in the natural inclination to be, to perpetuate life, to know the truth, to live in society—human beings are inclined toward the good. That these fundamental inclinations—a tending to the good—move human beings to act in purposeful ways to realize the good leads Aquinas to see in these natural inclinations the foundation of moral purposes and thus the precepts of the natural law. But, as directives of the moral life, are these precepts of the natural law irreducibly many, or do they have a common foundation that is rooted in human nature? Aquinas asks this question in I–II.94.2: "Whether the Natural Law Contains Several Precepts, or One Only?" The intent of the question is not only to highlight the many—the precepts of the natural law that are rooted in the natural inclinations of human nature toward the good—but also to determine the one, that is, the common foundation that is the root of the many. The Latin word that Aquinas uses for this common foundation is *radix*, which means root. What is the common root?

Common to our nature as human beings are the natural inclinations that move us toward the good, but these fundamental inclinations do not realize the good. More is needed. This, as we saw in Chapter 3, is the work of the virtues, both the moral virtues and the virtue of prudence. Whereas the natural inclinations of human nature determine the specific goods to be realized by us, the virtues provide the means by which these goods are concretely realized, and in this way the virtues are the perfections of our natural inclinations. That we are inclined by nature toward the good, that the good moves us to act through the exercise of the virtues, underscores the point that for Aquinas the good not only pulls us as the end or purpose to be realized but preexists in us either in the form of desire (pushing us)—whether as sensate desire or as the rational desire of the will—or in the form of knowledge: the practical intellect's comprehension of the good, which serves as the light by which the practical intellect directs our actions. But, neither the desire for the good that moves the moral virtues, nor the practical intellect's comprehension of the good that guides the deliberations of prudence, sufficiently accounts for the moral obligation to act, that is, to realize the good concretely. The foundation (root) of moral obligation lies in the practical intellect's grasp of the universal truth "that *good is that which all things seek after*," and thus, according to human reason, it follows as the self-evident (*per se nota*) first principle of practical reason, and accordingly as the first precept of the natural law (indeed, of all law), "that *good is to be done and pursued, and evil is to be avoided. All other precepts of the natural law are based upon this*," states Aquinas.[72]

That we view a human action as a moral action that ought to be done is founded on the practical intellect's fundamental habit or disposition within every human being: through our actions the good is to be pursued and evil avoided. In this first precept of the natural law lies the foundation of all the precepts of the natural law, and thus in

72. Thomas Aquinas, *Summa Theologica* I–II.94.2.

this one common root we find the basis of the many directives of the moral life. To the objection that since the natural law follows from human nature, and human nature is one but has many parts so that the natural law will consist either of one precept or many precepts, Aquinas offers this response: "All the inclinations of any parts whatsoever of human nature, e.g., of the concupiscible and irascible parts, in so far as they are ruled by reason, belong to the natural law, and are reduced to one first precept"—that good is to be done and evil avoided—"so that the precepts of the natural law are many in themselves, but are based on one common foundation,"[73] this foundation being the first precept of the natural law.

Relevant to the present-day discussion of social justice, Aquinas's approach to justice through the lens of the natural law has two advantages over Rawls's approach. The first advantage is the universal scope given to justice when the foundation of justice is seen to lie in human nature itself, specifically in the natural inclination of human beings to live in society as the proper end (the good) of being human. Moreover, that this basic determination of our nature requires its perfection (its realization) through the exercise of the virtues of prudence and justice points to the second advantage: that the human good realized through the virtue of justice is both social and personal. For Aquinas justice is a personal virtue, not simply "the first virtue of social institutions," as Rawls asserts.[74] The good that justice realizes concretely in society preexists in us in the will's rational desire to realize the good that is justice and in the practical intellect's disposition, which assumes as the fundamental premise in all deliberations regarding justice, that good is to be done and evil avoided. Here we see, in addition to the universality and objectivity of justice, the interiority of justice. Justice in the hands of Aquinas becomes wide (exhibiting universality) but also deep (exhibiting interiority).[75]

The good of the social whole—whether societal or global in scope—that is realized through acts of justice presupposes that the persons who act justly in society have themselves acquired the moral character of one who is just, this rooted in the rational desire of the will to be just. Rawls acknowledges that a just society, one based on the principles of justice, requires good persons and thus moral virtue, specifically the moral sentiment that he describes as having a sense of justice: "it is rational for those belonging to a well-ordered society who have already acquired a sense of justice to maintain and even strengthen this moral sentiment."[76] The benefit of acquiring the virtues for Rawls, such as a sense of justice, is that the virtues "are sentiments and habitual attitudes leading us to act on certain principles of right," and thus they "support adherence to these standards." The virtues as moral sentiments, according to Rawls, provide the motivation and support to act on the principles of justice, but

---

73. Thomas Aquinas, *Summa Theologica* I–II.94.2 *ad* 2.

74. Rawls, *Theory of Justice*, 3.

75. See Keys, *Aquinas, Aristotle, and the Promise*, 124, 185, 196–99.

76. Rawls, *Theory of Justice*, 436.

it is the principles of justice (the right) that determine what justice is and what ought to be done.[77] For Aquinas, on the other hand, the justice that ought to be done has its foundation in the natural inclination of human beings to live in society and its realization (perfection) in the moral virtues of prudence and justice. Here the virtues of prudence and justice not only dispose us to act justly in society, but they embody concretely what justice is and the good that justice intends. A just society, a just global order, requires not only institutions that are just but also persons who are just. Mary Keys comments: "By incorporating natural law, its broader common good, and the will explicitly into his dialectic, indeed into the very definition of justice, Aquinas is able simultaneously to situate justice more deeply in the interiority of a person and to extend its scope more broadly toward a universal good."[78]

What Aquinas contributes to the tradition of Catholic social teaching regarding social justice is a way to conceive of the foundation of social justice—what is common in the common good—as being both universal and personal. What is common in the common good is as wide as the natural inclination in human nature itself to seek the good in and through society and as deep as the rational desire of the human will to realize the social good, this through the exercise of the virtue of justice, at the direction of the practical intellect that is moved to deliberate on all matters concerning the social good on the basis of what Aquinas saw as the first precept of the natural law—that good is to be done and evil avoided. The commonality of human nature that is the foundation of social justice and thus the common ground for dialogue on matters regarding social justice, although conceived and stated abstractly, is manifested concretely in the day-to-day strivings that constitute the lives of all human beings in their interconnectedness and interdependence. In our commonality as human beings, furthermore, lies the foundation of our compassion for others in society, this enacted through the exercise of the virtue of mercy, which enlivens and enlightens acts of justice by giving justice a heart, as we saw in Chapter 3. Despite all that makes us different, we are as human beings one and the same. That the deliberations, decisions, and acts regarding the matters of social justice ultimately "are reduced to" or "lead back to" (the Latin verb that Aquinas uses is *reducere*, which has this meaning)[79] the first precept of the natural law, however, raises this question: What precisely is the good that is to be done and pursued in common, and how is this good to be determined in relation to the plurality of goods that move human beings to act? Here again we are faced with the problem of the one and the many.

77. Rawls, *Theory of Justice*, 437.

78. Keys, *Aquinas, Aristotle, and the Promise*, 198.

79. Thomas Aquinas, *Summa Theologica* I–II.94.2 *ad* 2.

What Is "Good" in the Common Good?

To respond to this question—what is "good" in the common good?—let us take a second look at the distinction, presented above, between nonmoral and moral value. Something of value we consider as good—as a good for us that we personally find satisfying (a subjective preference), as a good due to its utility, either as a useful good for us (pursuing an education) or as a useful good for the society as a whole (a price-coordinated economy), or finally as a good that we consider as being a good in itself, an intrinsic good. The human good that is realized through the practice of the moral virtues is an intrinsic good such as this. Being just, courageous, or temperate as a way of life is a good in itself, a moral good that is valued for its own sake, not simply for its usefulness or for the personal satisfaction that such a way of life might give us. Unlike the good that for us is a personal preference, the useful good and the moral good both have an objective reality that lies outside of our subjective preferences, and thus both we consider as an objective good, not only for us, but for all people. But, the basis of our valuation of each type of good is distinctly different: A useful good refers to an objective state of affairs that we value as a good, such as the market efficiency of a price-coordinated economy, whereas the moral good has its basis in human nature itself, specifically in the ends or purposes essential to being human that we as human beings seek to realize. The useful good has a nonmoral value in that its goodness (value) lies in the objective state of affairs that our actions intend to realize. Articulated as a norm, a nonmoral value provides us with a script, that is, a plan of action that tells us what we ought to do in order to achieve the useful good. For example, to live a good life, exercise daily, eat a balanced diet, pursue an education, and treat people with respect; to achieve a good society, as a citizen vote conscientiously, as an employer pay fair wages, as a fellow human help those in need in the society. Because such norms prescribe specific actions that we ought to do in order to realize the useful good (that is, a balanced, thriving personal life; a stable, orderly society), they are termed "material norms," this in distinction to those norms that express moral values, which are termed "formal norms." A moral value provides us with an ideal for living a fully human life: being just, courageous, and temperate as a way of life. Articulated as a formal norm (be just, be courageous, be temperate), a moral value portrays the sort of person that we ought to be, but does not tell us specifically what we ought to do. In this sense, a moral value is devoid of specific content. It portrays the goal of life, but it does not provide a life-script, as do nonmoral values. Moral values give meaning and purpose, and thus direction, to nonmoral values, but nonmoral values provide specific content to moral values. The formal norm "be just" presents us with a moral ideal; an employer paying workers a fair wage provides us with a concrete instance of the ideal. As a way to highlight the necessary interdependency between the two types of value for the moral life, nonmoral values are also referred to as "premoral values." Nonmoral values (premoral values) point to the *matter* of the moral life; moral values express the *form* of the moral life. The moral life as actually lived calls into play both types of value.[80]

The common good, as a norm, articulates both nonmoral and moral value. As a moral value, the common good portrays the ideal of society, which is the good of being a community. In the words of David Hollenbach, SJ, "The common good . . . is a value to be pursued for its own sake. This suggests that a key aspect of the common good can be described as *the good of being a community at all*—the good realized in the mutual relationships in and through which human beings achieve their well-being."[81] But the common good articulated as a moral norm, which is a formal norm, is without specific content. What specific social conditions must be fulfilled if the good of being a community is to be realized? Here, with this question, our focus changes from considering the common good as a formal norm to viewing the common good in terms of material norms—that is, in terms of nonmoral or premoral values, which concern the things or activities that a society considers important and that ought to be realized due to their utility. In the *Pastoral Constitution*'s description of the common good, considered above, we see an attentiveness to the material norms of the common good. The common good, the Council states, concerns "the sum total of social conditions which allow people, either as groups or as individuals, to reach their fulfillment more fully and more easily" (no. 26). Describing what these social conditions are and observing how they are fulfilled through the basic institutions of society provides content to the common good. Being a community has intrinsic value. As a good in itself, being a community is the goal that all human acts in society ought to intend. But, stated as a goal, the common good is abstract—a formal norm without specificity. That a society ensures ready access for all within the society to such fundamental necessities as food, housing, education, and rightful freedom provides the social conditions (thus a concrete plan of action) for realizing the common good, which is the moral good, in the Council's view. Here, in terms of these social conditions and their fulfillment, the common good becomes concrete. The Council's presentation of the common good, however, is succinct; its depiction of "all that is necessary for living a genuinely human life" in society (no. 26) is presented in summary form only. This is understandable, given the purpose of the Council's document, which is pastoral in intent. But if we look again at the Council's depiction of the common good with Aristotelian-Thomistic eyes, what do we see?

---

80. O'Connell, *Principles for a Catholic Morality*, 117–19, 154–64; McBrien, *Catholicism*, 992–94; Gula, SS, *Reason Informed by Faith*, 283–99; see also Riordan, *Global Ethics*, 10–18.

81. Hollenbach, SJ, *Common Good and Christian Ethics*, 81–82.

The Good Is Primary to Desire

"The good is that which all desire," Aquinas states, quoting the words of Aristotle that appear at the beginning of the *Nicomachean Ethics*.[82] For Aquinas, "all" refers to all things in nature, the animate and the inanimate, and of the animate, all living things, which in today's terms would extend from single-celled bacteria to human beings. But, to speak of the good that all things in nature seek in universal terms, and to do so in a meaningful way, a basis of comparison must be established. Aquinas finds the basis of comparison—this we saw in Chapter 3—in the purposeful movement of all things in nature toward their proper end, which is their good. Aquinas characterizes this purposeful movement as desire (*appetitus*) for the good—this whether the desire is the natural *appetitus* (the natural movement) of a ripening apple, the sensate *appetitus* of an animal caring for its young, or the rational *appetitus* of human beings having come together to resolve a matter of social concern. In each instance of desire (movement), the good intended is the fulfillment of the purposeful movement that is determined by the nature of the thing itself. In each instance, we see manifested an inclination—a tending—toward the good which is the fulfillment or perfection of the nature of the thing, thus fulfillment or perfection as a good apple, the good of progeny, the good society. Here, in all movements of nature, primacy lies with the good, not desire. As the end or purpose of movement, the good is the cause of desire (the final cause). At the same time, as the end or purpose of movement in nature, the good as fulfillment or perfection is manifested only in and through the concrete movements of the things in nature toward their proper ends—apples ripening, animals nurturing their young, human beings engaging one another in dialogue regarding the social good. Hence, for Aquinas, the good as end or purpose is primary to desire, but the reality of the good takes on concrete form in and through the concreteness of nature's movements—in the desire for the good.[83]

Accordingly, for Aquinas, we know the good that is the common good, not in abstraction, but in concreteness, that is, in and through the specific acts of justice that seek to realize the good of society as a whole. Moved by the good that justice desires, we act to realize the good by meeting the concrete demands of justice in society, demands we see not as obligations that stand outside of the good (our good or the good of society as a whole), but demands we comprehend as necessary components (the social conditions) of the good. The good that is the common good moves us to act, but in our deliberations and actions regarding justice, our comprehension of the good also guides us. As the end or purpose of justice, the common good informs our actions, both by rendering our concrete actions for justice intelligible and by serving as the ideal (the formal norm) that gives to our acts of justice their direction and purpose. Here, in the eyes of Aquinas, primacy lies with the good that is the common good—both as the

---

82. Thomas Aquinas, *Summa Theologica* I–II.8.1. See Aristotle, *Nicomachean Ethics* 1.1.1094a3.

83. See Thomas Aquinas, *Commentary on the Nicomachean Ethics* 1.1.9.

good that is comprehended and intended, and as the good that is realized concretely. What moves us from intending the good to executing the good is our desire for the good, but it is the nature of the good itself that awakens and shapes our desire.[84]

Desire Is Primary to the Good

When in the present day the economist speaks of the common good, a very different picture of the common good from Aquinas's picture comes to light. In contemporary economics, desire is primary to the good; from this perspective, what we consider good is determined by what we desire. The French economist Jean Tirole (awarded the 2014 Nobel Prize in Economics) recognizes the importance of the common good as a guiding principle—this at a time when the world is, in his words, "marked by the financial crisis, increased unemployment and inequality, the ineptitude of our leaders in coping with climate change, the undermining of the European project, geopolitical instability and the migrant crisis resulting from it, and the rise of populism around the world." In response to this wide array of world problems, Tirole asks: "Have we lost sight of the common good? If so, how might economics help us get back on track in pursuing it?" Economics is concerned with the incentives that move markets, particularly with regard to the way people react to market incentives. The key problem for Tirole regarding people's behavior in markets is this: "These material or social incentives, combined with their personal preferences, define their behavior; and this behavior may or may not be in the general interest. The quest for the common good therefore involves constructing institutions to reconcile, as far as possible, the interests of the individual with the general interest." In order to undertake the task of establishing institutions that will facilitate the convergence of individual interests with the general interests of society, Tirole employs Rawls's thought experiment—to put oneself (and thus one's individual interests) behind a veil of ignorance, so that by not knowing one's place in society, one does not know what one's individual interests are in relation to the general interest; then Tirole has us consider this question: "in what social system would you like to live?" In our response to this question, economics can help, Tirole thinks. While economics does not intend to take from society its role in determining the common good, economics can contribute to the quest for the common good, in two ways: first, because economics sees markets not as ends in themselves, but as instruments to achieving ends, by distinguishing between means and ends, economics enables discussion to focus properly on ends, such as the common good; and, secondly, once the common good has been defined, economics provides the tools necessary to realize the common good.[85] Unlike Rawls's thought experiment, however, which has as its purpose the articulation of the principles of justice on which to base a well-ordered society, Tirole's thought experiment seeks to realize the common good

84. See Thomas Aquinas, *Summa Theologica* I–II.25.2.

85. Tirole, *Economics for the Common Good*, 1–5, 11.

through the convergence of individual and general interest, this particularly in and through the working of the market economy. What is notable in Tirole's undertaking is that the common good is seen primarily in terms of individual and general interest, that is, in terms of market incentives. In other words, for Tirole, the good that is the common good is determined by desire.

The perspective from which Tirole views the common good has its origins in the thought of formative thinkers of the early modern age. Of particular significance in this regard is how the good and its relation to human desire or feeling is conceived in the thought of the seventeenth-century English philosopher Thomas Hobbes and the eighteenth-century Scottish philosopher David Hume. Both see the good, not as pertaining to the things of nature as such, but as an expression of desire or feeling within us toward the things of nature. This view is shaped by the predominance of the secular worldview that defines the age—a period marked by the emergence of nation-states, the development of the capitalist economy, the rise of the new science, and the decentering of religion (as we saw in Chapter 2). What the new science gave to Hobbes and Hume was a method, that is, a way to see the world empirically on its own terms, thus a view of the world stripped of the metaphysical and religious viewpoints that had defined the medieval period. For both philosophers the scientific method that had been employed so successfully in the natural sciences offered the hope that it could do the same for philosophy. Hume, for example, observes: As the science of human nature (philosophy) "is the only solid foundation for the other sciences, so the only solid foundation we can give to this science itself must be laid on experience and observation."[86]

Accordingly, when Hobbes views nature through this empirical lens, what he sees is bodies in motion, this whether the body is a physical body (such as a rock falling), the human body, or the body politic—the state, which Hobbes names Leviathan. Regarding the human body, as with all animal bodies, Hobbes sees two types of motion: vital motion (such as blood coursing through the body) and voluntary motion (such as going from one place to another, speaking, and moving our limbs). The latter motion in human bodies begins in our minds (specifically in our imagination), then in "small beginnings" of motion within our bodies, which Hobbes calls endeavor. "This Endeavor, when it is toward something which causes it, is called Appetite, or Desire," he states. The contrary motion he names "Aversion." Hobbes acknowledges that these terms—appetite and aversion—have roots in the Latin and Greek philosophical traditions, but for him the meanings of these terms change in fundamental ways when they are applied to human bodies in motion viewed through the empirical lens of science. Because the human body is in a continual state of change, our appetites and aversions will be in a continual state of change as well. For this reason, Hobbes states, "it is impossible" that the same object would always cause in human bodies "the same Appetites, and Aversions: much lesse can all men consent, in the Desire of almost any one and the same Object." Furthermore, insofar as the object of desire is what we call

---

86. Hume, *Treatise of Human Nature,* xx.

good and the object of hate is what we call evil, then the words of good and evil that we use, Hobbes observes, "are ever used with relation to the person that useth them: There being nothing simply and absolutely so; nor any common Rule of Good and Evill, to be taken from the nature of the objects themselves." For Hobbes, the basis of what we call good and evil lies in us—in our desires—not in the object of our desires. Neither good nor evil are absolute terms, says Hobbes; rather good and evil are terms whose meaning or use is determined relative to us, or if the terms of good and evil are used in the context of the state, then their meaning or use is determined relative to the one who represents the state, which is the sovereign.[87]

When David Hume comes to the third and final part of his treatise on the science of human nature, which is entitled "Of Morals," he declares: "Morality is a subject that interests us above all others: We fancy the peace of society to be at stake in every decision concerning it."[88] Given the importance of the moral decisions that we make, particularly the decisions on which the peace of society depends, Hume is led to undertake an inquiry into the nature of morality, employing the empirical method of science. His inquiry begins not with divine authority seen as the basis of morality nor with a consideration of the end or purpose of human nature, but with our perceptions. "It has been observ'd, that nothing is ever present to the mind but its perceptions; and that all the actions of seeing, hearing, judging, loving, hating, and thinking, fall under this denomination," Hume states.[89] But, if morality is based on our perceptions, we must ask: perceptions of what? On what basis do we make moral judgments? If in making a moral judgment, we distinguish between good and evil, between virtue and vice, what is the foundation upon which we make these distinctions? Not on the basis of reason, Hume maintains. As a way to illustrate this point, Hume has us consider an instance of vice—an act of willful murder. "Examine it in all lights, and see if you can find that matter of fact, or real existence, which you call *vice*," Hume instructs. We can observe the facts of the incident—the victim, the weapon—and we can reason about the circumstances of the incident and the motive of the killer. But, can we point to the evil or vice of the act as a matter of fact as well? Hume continues: "In which-ever way you take it, you find only certain passions, motives, volitions and thoughts. There is no other matter of fact in the case. The vice entirely escapes you, as long as you consider the object." Yet, as we consider the incident, Hume observes, an imperceptible change occurs in our discussion: we move from "is" statements (discussing the facts of the incident) to "ought" statements (making the moral judgment that this act was evil). For Hume the problem is this: the conclusion (moral judgment) that this act was evil, an act of vice, cannot validly be drawn from the statements of fact regarding the incident, as if the moral judgment is a rational deduction from the statements of fact, because the moral judgment is of an "entirely different" nature than the statements of

87. Hobbes, *Leviathan* 1.6, 30–32.

88. Hume, *Treatise of Human Nature* 3.1.1, 455.

89. Hume, *Treatise of Human Nature* 3.1.1, 456.

fact. Where then in our observation of the willful murder can we find the basis of our moral judgment? Hume states: "You never can find it, till you turn your reflexion into your own breast, and find a sentiment of disapprobation, which arises in you, towards this action. Here is a matter of fact; but 'tis the object of feeling, not of reason. It lies in yourself, not in the object."[90]

The feeling (perception) of moral approbation or disapprobation that is the basis of our moral judgments, the feeling to which we give the name of virtue or vice, however, is a feeling of a particular kind, according to Hume. Virtue causes in us a feeling of pleasure; vice causes in us a feeling of pain. But, unlike the pleasure that comes from good music and good wine (Hume's examples), a goodness that is enjoyed precisely for the pleasure that it gives us, the pleasure of virtue and the pain of vice is distinctive in that this pleasure or pain is derived from actions or character that awaken in us a moral sentiment of approbation or disapprobation that pertains, not to a particular interest on our part, but to a general interest that lies beyond our self-interest. "'Tis only when a character is considered in general, without reference to our particular interest, that it causes such a feeling or sentiment, as denominates it morally good or evil," Hume maintains.[91] In this case, is justice to be considered a moral virtue? No, says Hume. The basis of justice is self-interest. Human beings enter into society for the purpose of satisfying basic human needs, this through the possession and use of external goods. "This can be done after no other manner, than by a convention enter'd into by all the members of the society to bestow stability on the possession of those external goods, and leave every one in the peaceable enjoyment of what he may acquire by his fortune and industry," Hume states. "This convention is not of the nature of a *promise*," he points out (and thus not of the nature of a social contract), but rather this convention expresses "only a general sense of common interest" among all members of the society and a willingness on their part "to regulate their conduct by certain rules," much like two people rowing a boat together—their coordinated effort does not come from a prior promise or agreement, but rather from the common interest that they have in achieving a successful outcome to their mutual effort. This example that Hume offers points to the utility of self-interest on the part of all members of a society when their self-interest is exercised in and through the convention of society. Accordingly, on the basis of this convention, Hume states, "there immediately arise the ideas of justice and injustice."[92]

With justice and its laws, then, comes a sense of natural obligation. But with justice can there also come a sense of moral obligation? Yes, says Hume. But, the basis of such a moral sentiment lies outside the common interests that are served by the convention on which justice is based. An injustice that takes place outside the sphere of our particular interests can nevertheless be observed by us as an injustice injurious

90. Hume, *Treatise of Human Nature* 3.1.1, 468–69.
91. Hume, *Treatise of Human Nature* 3.1.2, 471–72.
92. Hume, *Treatise of Human Nature* 3.2.2, 489–90 (italics original).

to the society as such, and thus the pain that unjustly afflicts others in society becomes our pain as well, just as justice enacted on behalf of the public interest can be observed by us as a good for others in society that is a source of pleasure not only for those others but, given their good, a source of pleasure for us. What renders justice a moral virtue and injustice a moral vice, according to Hume, is the moral sentiment of sympathy, the feeling for others in society that enables us to gain pleasure from justice served to others and to suffer pain from injustice inflicted on others in the society. Hume concludes: "*Thus self-interest is the original motive to the* establishment *of justice: but a* sympathy *with public interest is the source of the* moral approbation *which attends that virtue.*"[93] For Hume, the moral good that is justice in society has its basis in fellow feeling.

If what we consider good is determined by what we desire or on the basis of feeling, can the social good be perceived and realized by us on this basis as well? Given the singularity of human desire or feeling, can the foundation of social cohesion be found here? Only if the many desires that move human bodies become one desire and the many bodies become one body, this being the artificial body of the state or commonwealth, Hobbes answers. For the sake of their self-preservation as individuals and to be rid of the perpetual conflict of warring desires between individuals, this accompanied by the realization on the part of human beings that unless they enter into a covenant with one another in which they mutually agree to lay down the right of their individual desires and to place themselves under the authority and force of "a Common Power" ("Covenants, without the Sword, are but Words," says Hobbes), they will never achieve the peace and security of social unity—it is for these reasons that human beings will willingly enter into such a covenant with one another. By doing so, Hobbes states, they "conferre all their power and strength upon one Man, or upon one Assembly of men, that may reduce all their Wills, by plurality of voices, unto one Will." This one, whether one person or one assembly of persons, represents the unified whole and is called sovereign; the many are called subjects. (Hobbes allows for various forms of government, such as monarchy or democracy.) Hobbes continues: "This done, the Multitude so united in one Person, is called a Common-wealth, in latine Civitas. This is the Generation of that great Leviathan."[94]

Hume, to the contrary, finds the principle of social cohesion, not in the authority and power of government, but in the social virtues, such as "meekness, beneficence, charity, generosity, clemency, moderation, equity," and this primarily in the social virtue of sympathy, "which takes us so far out of ourselves, as to give us the same pleasure or uneasiness in the characters of others, as if they had a tendency to our own advantage or loss." Moreover, while justice for Hume, unlike the social virtues which are natural virtues (natural passions) that lead directly to the good of others in society,

---

93. Hume, *Treatise of Human Nature* 3.2.2, 498–500 (italics original).

94. Hobbes, *Leviathan* 2.17, 93–96; see 2.19, 102–9 for the forms of government that Hobbes considers.

is an artificial virtue, based in self-interest and established through convention, when taken as "a general scheme or system of action" agreed to by all in the society, the self-interest of justice is "advantageous to the society" and in this way contributes to the public good as a useful good that, when attended by "our sympathy with the interests of society," becomes a moral good.[95]

Hume's close friend Adam Smith amplified Hume's views, first, by giving primacy of place to the virtue of sympathy in the opening sections of his presentation of moral philosophy—*The Theory of Moral Sentiments*—thus underscoring the social nature of morality;[96] and, secondly, by employing Hume's notion of the utility of self-interest as an interpretive key to understanding the modern science of economics, which originates with Smith and is formulated by him in *The Wealth of Nations*. Whereas a society flourishes by means of the social virtues, such as sympathy and beneficence, a society functions in a cohesive manner at a most basic, day-to-day level through the division of labor in which the members of society meet one another's needs through the workings of their self-interest, observed in "the propensity to truck, barter, and exchange one thing for another," says Smith. To expect cooperative behavior from one another to come from beneficence only is a vain hope, Smith thinks. We are far more likely to succeed in our practical dealings with each other by appealing to the self-interest that binds us together (recall Hume's example of two people rowing a boat together). Indeed, according to Smith, "It is not from the benevolence of the butcher, the brewer, or the baker that we expect our dinner, but from their regard to their own interest. We address ourselves, not to their humanity but to their self-love, and never talk to them of our own necessities but of their advantages."[97] But, self-interest played out in the marketplace, where buyer and seller act only in their self-interest, intending only their own security and their own gain, never intending in their transaction to promote the public interest, nor having knowledge of how they might do so, this self-interest nevertheless leads to an unintended consequence in that the transaction between buyer and seller is "led by an invisible hand to promote an end" which plays no role in either of their intentions, Smith states—this end being the public benefit and thus the social harmony that the market creates through their transaction.[98]

To the question whether the social good can be perceived and realized on the basis of the singularity of human desire or feeling, Hume and Smith offer a very different answer from that of Hobbes. For Hobbes social cohesion, and thus the social good, can be gained only through the coercion of government, whereas Hume and Smith find such cohesion in the social cooperation engendered by the self-interest of individuals being carried out in society. Here we are faced with a stark choice:

95. Hume, *Treatise of Human Nature* 3.3.1, 578–80.

96. Smith, *Theory of Moral Sentiments* 1.1.1–4, 3–25. See Copleston, SJ, *Modern Philosophy*, 159–62.

97. Smith, *Wealth of Nations* 1.2, 6–7.

98. Smith, *Wealth of Nations* 4.2, 194.

both views presuppose the primacy of individual desire in relation to the good, but for Hobbes this means that the good of social cohesion (the peace and security of social unity), to be attained, must be imposed on the diversity of individual desires through the power and authority of the sovereign (one will), this for the individual's own good and with the individual's willing acceptance; for Hume and Smith, the good of social cohesion is attained only in and through the exercise of individual freedom in society (many wills), this at the service of the individual's self-interest and outside of governmental control. Yet, despite the difference between these two views, they share a fundamental point in common: that the social good is determined by human desire means that all efforts at social harmony begin with singularity but also end with singularity. Both views see the social good as determined by the self-interest of the individual in society; the difference between these two views lies in the way in which each envisions the realization of individual self-interest. In which case, for both views, despite their differences, the social good, seen in terms of the utility of self-interest, is necessarily the aggregate of individual goods, and thus the social good is reducible to the good of individuals in society.

This early modern viewpoint, which the philosopher Charles Taylor terms "philosophical atomism," is carried forward into the present day and embodied in the modern social sciences as a presupposition that they hold as self-evident. In the eyes of the social scientist, according to Taylor: "The events and states which are the subject of study in society are ultimately made up of the events and states of component individuals. In the end, only individuals choose and act. To think that society consists of something else, over and above these individual choices and actions, is to invoke some strange, mystical entity, a ghostly spirit of the collectivity, which no sober or respectable science can have any truck with." This approach to the study of social phenomena the social sciences refer to as "methodological individualism," Taylor notes. In this view, social phenomena, and thus public and social goods, are "decomposable" (Taylor's term) in that they are reducible to the component goods of the individuals that make them up.[99]

This methodological approach we see exemplified in the economist Jean Tirole's description of the common good considered above, which concerns the quest to establish institutions that will facilitate the convergence of individual interests with the general interest. Indeed, Tirole states: "The economist's approach is that of 'methodological individualism,' according to which collective phenomena are the result of individual behavior and in their turn affect individuals' behavior."[100] For Tirole, the quest for the common good begins with individual self-interest and ends there as well. In the economist's eyes, the common good, considered in terms of the general interest, is a social good that is necessarily decomposable, reducible to individual interest and thus reducible to the desires of the individual. This methodological approach to social

99. Taylor, "Irreducibly Social Goods," 129–30.

100. Tirole, *Economics for the Common Good*, 87.

phenomena that begins and ends with the singularity of human desire is likewise that of the sociologist Jeffrey Alexander. As we saw in Chapter 2, Alexander states (echoing Hume) that justice is based on solidarity, which for him is the feeling of being connected with others in society, and so the work of justice—building solidarity—involves evoking in others in the society feelings of social connectedness or moral outrage—this through the symbolic representations that social movements employ to portray the work of civil repair as the struggle between good and evil, justice and injustice. Here the fellow feeling of solidarity—the feeling of we-ness—is necessarily decomposable, that is, reducible to the civil feelings of the individuals that make up society. But, does this account of the social good by the economist and the sociologist—whether as the common good that is the collectivity of individual interest or as the solidarity of fellow feeling—fully account for what is social in the social good? Taylor thinks that it does not. Thus, to bring to light what is missing in the approach of methodological individualism, he asks this question: "Are there any irreducibly social goods?"[101]

The Common Good as the Social Good

When two people are faced with an exigent situation that requires a mutually agreed upon response on their part, is there more at play in their response to the situation than simply the concrete action that is decided upon and taken? Is there a social dimension to their response that is not reducible to the particularity of their decision and action? Yes, Taylor answers. The deliberation that takes place between the two people requires thoughts that occur in the minds of the two individuals, but this obvious fact does not warrant reducing this situation simply to the particularity of their thoughts and their decision. To do so is to miss the social dimension of their interaction. "Thoughts exist as it were in the dimension of meaning and require a background of available meanings in order to be the thoughts that they are," Taylor states.[102]

To illustrate Taylor's point, let us consider again the dilemma taken from family life that was presented in Chapter 3: When the six-month old baby of a married couple wakes up crying at three o'clock in the morning from a painful ear infection, who cares for the baby? The response on the part of the husband and wife is a personal decision, yet at the same time, as we saw, the social institutions of marriage and family are mediating their response, this in and through the social expectations of the roles of wife and mother, husband and father, that they inhabit. These social roles provide a background of meaning to the couple's decision; they do not take the place of their decision, and given that the decision is the focal point of attention, these social expectations remain mostly invisible and unexamined. Still, the particularity of the couple's decision cannot be fully understood outside of this background of meaning.

101. Taylor, "Irreducibly Social Goods," 127.
102. Taylor, "Irreducibly Social Goods," 131.

Moreover, the deliberation between the wife and the husband presupposes a "common understanding" (Taylor's term) that underlies their deliberation—an understanding not reducible to the wife's understanding or the husband's understanding individually, but rather is a common understanding shared by them that is rooted in the social institutions shaping their response to their crying baby. (This common understanding Mary Douglas terms the legitimating idea of an institution, as we saw in Chapter 3.)

Thus, the social roles that give meaning to our individual decisions and actions and the common understanding that justifies (legitimates) these decisions and actions, in that they provide cohesion and stability to society, are social goods. That such meaning and justification, while shaping our individual decisions and actions, are societal in extent, embedded in the institutional structures of the society, renders these social goods undecomposable—that is, they are not reducible simply to the good of the individual. The designations of wife and mother, husband and father, are not simply the predicates of an individual, but rather terms designating the social roles, and thus the social expectations, that these individuals have taken on as their own. The social goods of shared meaning and common understanding are, in Taylor's words, "irreducibly social goods."[103]

Accordingly, Taylor would see the deliberation that occurs between the wife and husband regarding who will care for the baby as having two dimensions—the one being the practical decision that the couple makes, the other being the background of meaning that serves as an ideal or norm against which their decision is being made. Taylor sees the two dimensions as having a circular relation—the individual decision of the couple presupposes the reality of the social roles that shape their behavior, yet their behavior gives concrete existence to the social roles. This circular relation, moreover, is dynamic in character in that while social roles shape individual behavior, individual behavior over time modifies social roles. The change or evolution of social roles due to changes in individual behavior and its circumstances, however, does not render social roles decomposable to individual behavior, Taylor emphasizes, but rather indicates the dynamic relation that exists between the two dimensions. "The two dimensions can't be collapsed into one," Taylor insists. "But methodological individualism involves attempting just such a collapse. It is based on the belief that the background can either be ignored . . . or can somehow be reduced and decomposed" into the particular acts of individuals. "On either variant, it's a fundamental mistake."[104]

These are strong words from Charles Taylor. His concern is that methodological individualism privileges instrumental reasoning that has as its purpose satisfying individual desires, but does so at the expense of losing sight of the wider social dimension of shared meaning and common understanding. To either ignore this wider social dimension or simply reduce it to individual decisions and actions has a serious consequence, Taylor thinks. "As long as you think that all goods must be individual,

103. Taylor, "Irreducibly Social Goods," 131–40.
104. Taylor, "Irreducibly Social Goods," 134.

and that any other construal is incoherent, you can't see that there is a *moral* argument here."[105] His words are directed at "welfarism," an extreme version of welfare economics that uses the utility of individual happiness as the only basis for social evaluation and as a guide for public policy.[106] But his words can readily be applied to the situation of the wife and husband who are deciding who will care for the baby in the middle of the night. If we view their deliberation only through the lens of instrumental reasoning, we might see the expression of personal preferences, practical concerns regarding work schedules, personal attributes such as generosity or commitment, and the intention on their part to realize a good outcome both for their own benefit and that of their baby—but not until we widen our view of the good by considering the social dimension at play in their deliberation will we see the moral argument that is at the root of their deliberation: an argument that concerns the fairness (justice) of the gendered division of labor in the American family and in the society as a whole. This wider view of the good both welfarism and more broadly methodological individualism either do not see or reject in principle, but precisely for this reason this methodological approach, in Taylor's view, loses the ability to engage in moral argument. As long as the human good is seen only in terms of the individual good (individual desire), the human good as the moral good will remain unseen, undiscussed, and therefore unattainable in the society. For Taylor what is wrong with this methodological approach taken by the social sciences is this: "It prevents this argument from happening."[107] Why is this so?

Bargaining and arguing as speech acts are fundamentally different in form and intention. Bargaining with another person begins and ends with self-interest. That through the bargaining process both parties satisfy their self-interest means that they will judge the outcome of the process to be a success. What holds the two parties together throughout the process of bargaining is the desire on the part of each to realize their self-interest (recall Hume's example of the two people rowing a boat together). Argument, on the other hand, begins with disagreement between two parties, but for the argument to proceed beyond their disagreement toward a resolution, some point of agreement must be held in common and acknowledged by those who disagree (as we saw above). There must be something outside of their individual interest that they are arguing about, something that stands outside of the contention that each party brings to the argument, something about which they agree and for this reason they can argue about it. Finding this point of agreement begins the argument and allows it to move forward, but then the question is this: What holds the two parties together throughout the argument, this especially if the argument is public argument? The argument itself, Catholic theologian John Courtney Murray, SJ, would respond.

105. Taylor, "Irreducibly Social Goods," 145.

106. For a discussion of the limitations of welfarism from the perspective of an economist, see Sen, *Idea of Justice*, 272–82.

107. Taylor, "Irreducibly Social Goods," 145.

Argument, that which he describes as reasoned conversation in society, means "living together and talking together."[108] Engaging in argument with the other in society binds us to the other. Achieving a resolution to the argument solidifies this bond. Argument does not diminish or destroy community but rather builds community. But, argument in this sense is fundamentally different from the discourse of present-day American politics and from the bargaining that takes place in the marketplace, both of which are driven by self-interest (desire)—political self-interest and economic self-interest. Whereas political interest and economic interest begin and end in individual desire, argument (particularly public argument) begins and ends in the social space of shared meaning and common understanding. Only here in this social space will the point of agreement or consensus that argument requires be found. Argument that is moral argument further underscores this point. Moral argument is necessarily social argument. Discussing the human good from the moral point of view requires a view wider than the individual good. Thus, to limit discussion of the human good to the individual good, this in terms of political interest or economic interest, not only distorts our view of the human good, but also prevents the moral argument regarding the human good from taking place. To see this point concretely, let us look again at the social issue of raising the minimum wage in the American workplace, discussed above.

Raising the Minimum Wage as an Example

Jean Tirole emphasizes that, despite market failures and the need for public policy to correct them, "the overwhelming majority of economists are . . . in favor of the market. But they see it simply as an instrument, never as an end in itself."[109] Accordingly, with regard to the issue of raising the minimum wage, this as one step toward rectifying economic and social inequality in the United States, the economist brings a needed set of tools to the issue: the ability to measure inequality empirically, understand its multiple causes, and propose and evaluate possible solutions such as redistributing wealth by means of public policy (such as raising the minimum wage).[110]

But, according to Tirole, "When we understand the extent of inequality and have analyzed the effects of redistributive policies, we can begin to make choices about the kind of society we want. On this an economist has little to say, except as an ordinary citizen." In other words, according to Tirole, what the economist brings to a social issue such as raising the minimum wage is instrumental reasoning, but offers no substantive view regarding the end or purpose of the economic analysis and its proposed solutions, this end or purpose being "the kind of society we want" (Tirole's words). Here "we" refers to the collective interest of those who make up the society. With

108. Murray, SJ, *We Hold These Truths*, 13.

109. Tirole, *Economics for the Common Good*, 34.

110. Tirole, *Economics for the Common Good*, 50–61.

regard to a market issue such as the minimum wage, the choice facing the society as a whole—policymakers as well as citizens—concerns unavoidable trade-offs between redistribution and economic growth and with regard to redistribution itself choices between raising the minimum wage or using the tax system, such as relying on a tax credit to workers with low or moderate incomes (for example, the Earned Income Tax Credit). Tirole points to the undesirable consequences that can come from governmental policy that raises the minimum wage (such as a rise in unemployment for low-wage workers) and acknowledges the need for more information (empirical data), but on these matters of public policy that require compromise (hence bargaining), the difficult choice between alternative options that "we" make will not be the result of public argument: rather "the choice depends on attitudes toward redistribution, a personal value judgment," says Tirole.[111] This is the way markets work. In the end, through the eyes of the economist, the social good (the public good) is reducible to and thus limited to the individual good. From the perspective of market efficiency, public choice regarding the minimum wage will be made in terms of the utility of self-interest. But on the moral value of this public choice the economist will be silent. From this perspective there is no moral argument.

When political self-interest controls governmental decision-making, we likewise see the absence of public argument and thus the absence of moral argument as well. As discussed above, the Raise the Wage Act of 2019 that would have increased the minimum wage to $15 an hour was passed in July 2019 by the Democratic-controlled House of Representatives and sent to the Republican-controlled Senate, but it was never brought to a vote by the Senate. Due to the Senate's inaction (no public argument, no vote), the federal minimum wage remained at $7.25 an hour, the wage level initially set by the US Congress in 2009.

An argument requires expressed disagreement in order to take place. Regarding the minimum wage, how would this argument unfold? At the institutional level, when the federal government intervenes in the market by mandating a minimum-wage level to ensure that low-wage workers earn a livable wage, an argument with the economy ensues, this primarily because the reasons that the government offers for its intervention in the market are noneconomic reasons. From the viewpoint of the economy, government intervention in the labor market undermines the efficiency of the market by determining the price of labor on a nonmarket basis. From the perspective of the government, by mandating the level below which the wages of workers cannot fall, the government protects the dignity of workers and their ability to meet basic human needs. The argument, as we have seen, has an empirical dimension: Does the federal mandate raising the minimum wage in fact harm workers by reducing the number of low-wage jobs, for example, by creating a market condition that motivates employers to devise ways to move away from hiring low-skilled workers in favor of hiring more highly skilled workers at the higher pay rate? A study cited by the economist Andrew

111. Tirole, *Economics for the Common Good*, 57; see also 255–56.

Yuengert comes to this conclusion.[112] Or does a mandated increase in wages, on the one hand, lead to the greater productivity and worker retention in low-wage jobs and, on the other hand, reduce wealth inequality across the society—all without hurting employer profits? The study by the economists Anna Godøy and Michael Reich, discussed above, shows that raising the minimum wage to $15 an hour does little harm to the low-wage job market but has great benefit to those who suffer poverty. The economist Seema Jayachandran points to two recent studies—one of nursing homes, the other of department stores—that demonstrate the benefits of raising the minimum wage: the wage increase (referred to as an "efficiency wage") improved worker productivity and service quality, which led to greater consumer satisfaction, which was then instrumental in not reducing employer profits.[113]

Here, in terms of these empirical studies, the argument against and for raising the minimum wage focuses our attention on the practical outcomes of government intervention in the labor market that are observable, measurable, and describable, thus practical outcomes that are seen as establishing an objective state of affairs. In which case, the valuation of the objective state of affairs that results from raising the minimum wage—whether the valuation comes from the viewpoints of government or the economy, or the valuation is based on the differing empirical studies by economists—concerns the material good that governmental intervention does or does not bring about. Despite their differences, the disputants in the argument share this point of agreement: The argument is about the utility of raising the minimum wage, which—whether for or against—concerns its status as a social good that is objective and thus independent of personal preferences. Here the argument concerns a social good that is not reducible to the individual good.

Bringing the concept of value to bear on the results of these empirical studies widens the policy discussion regarding the minimum wage to include the social dimension of shared meaning and common understanding, thus giving the policy discussion the form of a public argument that is at root a moral argument. That the state of affairs the empirical studies describe is portrayed as a good that has an objective status outside of subjective preferences implies that all in the society ought to value this good as well, this whether the good is seen as maintaining efficient labor markets or as ensuring that work will be worthwhile to all workers in the society. But, the public policy scholar Mary Jo Bane notes, public policy analysts themselves avoid applying the concept of value (the good) to the findings of their studies. Policy outcomes are judged by the analysts "empirically according to how effectively they promote aggregate well-being and how efficiently they use scarce resources."[114] She acknowledges that these empirical studies are often inconclusive, notably studies on the effects of raising the minimum wage that offer conflicting conclusions or present

112. Yuengert, "What Can Economists Contribute," 43, 59n17.
113. Jayachandran, "Raise for Workers."
114. Bane, "Public Policy and the Common Good," 65–66.

policy options that involve trade-offs that affect specific groups differently. Moreover, she points out, given the quantitative approach of these policy studies, the outcomes of policy choices that are not easily quantifiable, such as the effect that these choices have on social cohesion or fairness in the society, are not given a place of importance in the policy discussion.

To address these limitations in public policy analysis regarding a social issue such as raising the minimum wage, Bane turns to the tradition of Catholic social teaching, specifically to the US Catholic bishops' 1986 pastoral letter on the economy. On the imagined premise that the bishops are planning to issue a pastoral letter on the common good in the twenty-first century, this modeled on the 1986 pastoral letter that included specific public policy recommendations, she advises the bishops that with regard to the present-day public policy debate on the minimum wage, the bishops can make two important contributions. The first concerns establishing priorities regarding difficult policy choices: "You can emphasize that some groups and some effects have priority over others, based on your commitments to the poor, to the equal human dignity of all, and to the achievement of human flourishing in community," she tells the bishops. No policy decision on a complex issue will be entirely free of pain for all those who will be affected by it, she observes: "While acknowledging, for example, that a minimum wage increase might bring about a small increase in both unemployment and consumer prices, you could argue that the positive effects on poor families are likely to be great enough to outweigh these potential negative effects." The second contribution has to do with the argument itself regarding the minimum wage: "You can also make a contribution by recognizing that men and women of good will can legitimately disagree about how to interpret the relevant empirical evidence and about how to balance competing values," Bane advises the bishops.[115] Legitimate disagreement is precisely what moves the argument forward and what holds the disputants together. To actively engage in the argument, not only sustains the argument, but also builds community. Thus, according to Bane, on a disputed policy issue such as raising the minimum wage, the church has a distinct contribution to make, in terms of both the values that it brings to the argument and the commitment that it makes to engage in the argument in the spirit of dialogue. But, insofar as the argument over raising the minimum wage appears to be primarily an argument between the government and the economy, what place does the church have in this argument? What is the role of the church in relation to markets and the government in a public argument such as this?

The public argument regarding the minimum wage centers on disagreement "about how to interpret the relevant empirical evidence and about how to balance competing values," according to Bane's assessment. The empirical evidence grounds the argument in objective (concrete) reality, this being the work of social scientists. The competing values in the argument indicate what is of importance to the

115. Bane, "Public Policy and the Common Good," 82–83.

argument's interlocutors, an importance that has an objective reality independent of personal preference. The argument's interlocutors, Bane emphasizes, should be seen by the bishops as "men and women of good will" who legitimately disagree regarding the empirical evidence and the competing values at play in the argument. But, as we have seen, when individuals disagree over a social issue such as raising the minimum wage, the disagreement expressed is not simply that of the individuals themselves, but a disagreement between the viewpoints of the social institutions that are shaping the argument, viewpoints that are being expressed through the individuals who disagree. Here the argument involves the disagreement between the economy and the government regarding the utility (material good) of mandating a minimum-wage level, this either from the perspective of the efficient allocation of resources in the labor market or from the perspective of governmental legislation (such as the Raise the Wage Act of 2019) that secures the dignity and material well-being of low-wage workers. Each perspective envisions an objective state of affairs that it sees as a useful good for the whole of society. These differing perspectives, then, represent competing nonmoral values. The church, by entering the argument, changes the focus of the argument in one significant way: the argument between the economy and the government becomes a moral argument. By bringing the biblical vision of solidarity and compassion to bear on the issue of raising the minimum wage, this through the church's commitment "to the poor, to the equal human dignity of all, and to the achievement of human flourishing in community," in Bane's view, the church provokes an argument with the economy and the government regarding the minimum wage primarily on moral terms.

In the face of the church's moral challenge, the economy and the government will each respond to the church and to each other on the basis of the institutional justification that is the legitimating idea of each institution: The economy will justify economic freedom on the basis of the intrinsic freedom of the individual as a moral good; the government will justify its legislative decisions, not simply on their utility, but on the moral value that all citizens possess equal worth. The legitimating idea of the economy and of the government each provides a common understanding (justification) of the conventional arrangements of that institution, but neither legitimating idea alone provides the basis for a normative discussion with the other institutions in the argument. Thus, we are left with this question: Is there a basis or common ground on which the church, the economy, and the government can come together to engage in argument regarding a social issue such as the minimum wage?

We find this common ground only if we widen our view beyond the specific nonmoral and moral good that each institution seeks to realize, to consider first the shared meaning that underlies the specific meanings of solidarity and compassion, individual freedom, and democratic equality—meanings that render the specific purpose of each institution intelligible. The shared meaning that underlies these specific meanings is the human good itself. Herein lies the point of agreement that is the basis of the argument. What the church, the economy, and the government are arguing about regarding the minimum wage is the human good. But, for the argument to move forward, the normative discussion between these institutions regarding the human good requires a common understanding of the human good that is shared by these social institutions, an understanding that is wider than the specific nonmoral and moral good that each institution seeks to realize. Here the normative discussion of the human good between these institutions takes place only on the basis of the common understanding of the human good as the common good. Accordingly, regarding the public policy issue of raising the minimum wage, the church's commitment to the working poor, the economy's affirmation of individual freedom in the market, and the government's upholding of democratic equality—all are moral viewpoints that must be fully represented in the argument, but represented in such a way that each viewpoint demonstrates its contribution to the common good. Here the common good provides the norm for balancing the competing values of the economy, the government, and the church, and thus provides a way for each social institution to see its legitimating idea in relation to the others. But, then, in terms of the argument regarding the minimum wage, how precisely does the common good serve as the basis for argument between the economy, government, and the church?

To respond to this question, let us return to the Second Vatican Council's definition of the common good in the *Pastoral Constitution*, again looking at the Council's words with Aristotelean-Thomistic eyes: the common good is presented as "the sum total of social conditions which allow people, either as groups or as individuals, to reach their fulfillment more fully and more easily" (no. 26). The term "fulfillment" here is dynamic in meaning in that the term indicates movement or striving toward an end or purpose; thus, human fulfillment is seen not as the termination of striving, but as the coming to fruition of what human beings are by nature. To describe the fullness of being human, the Aristotelean philosopher Richard Kraut employs the biological metaphor of flourishing: "flourishing is primarily a biological phenomenon: 'flower' and 'flourish' are cognates. Above all, it is plants, animals, and human beings that flourish when conditions are favorable. They do so by developing properly and fully."[116] The Thomistic philosopher John Haldane would add that by using biological life as a way to understand human fulfillment, we see human fulfillment, and thus the human good, as a process that consists of a plurality of functions with a unifying purpose: "life involves the integrated operation of vital functions. Not every human good must be an expression of *the* human good, but every such good must be intelligible as part of human life." A healthful diet is essential to human flourishing, but human flourishing is not defined wholly in these terms. Accordingly, Haldane observes: "Just as one and the same plant has roots, stem, branches, leaves and flowers and functions associated with each, all subserving the well-being of the whole, so human nature has many parts and functions, each subject to particular norms, yet each integrated within

---

116. Kraut, *What Is Good and Why*, 131.

a whole."[117] The good of the whole is perceived and understood only in and through its parts and functions, just as the good of each part and function is perceived and understood fully only in relation to the other parts and functions and in relation to the good of the whole. Thus, in light of this way of seeing human fulfillment, the "social conditions" that enable human beings who make up the society to realize their fulfillment (both as groups and as individuals) are not, as conditions, simply the means to this end, but rather the necessary components that constitute this end. In which case, the "sum total" of these social conditions is not an aggregate, decomposable sum (reducible to distinct, autonomous parts), but rather the unity of vital functions and parts that constitute the human good, which is the social good. Here the common good is this social good.

To argue effectively for or against raising the minimum wage, this from the moral viewpoints of the economy, the government, and the church, then, requires that the common good, both as the nonmoral and moral social good, be the common understanding that serves as the basis for normative discussion between these social institutions. Meeting this challenge is precisely the point at which the economy's response in the argument falters.

The economist Milton Friedman, as we saw above, posits the freedom of the individual as the basic moral value that justifies free markets. Friedman acknowledges that the government has a coercive but limited role to play in relation to markets, such as maintaining the rule of law (for example, by enforcing legal contracts) and mitigating certain market imperfections (for example, by countering the market power of monopolies), but other than these instances, markets to be efficient must function independently of governmental control. Minimum-wage laws, then, are the unwarranted intervention of government in the labor market, in Friedman's view, because they do not allow labor markets to function efficiently. "Minimum wage laws are about as clear a case as one can find of a measure the effects of which are precisely the opposite of those intended . . . insofar as minimum wage laws have any effect at all, their effect is clearly to increase poverty," declares Friedman.[118]

The economist and Catholic theologian Daniel K. Finn, however, points out that Friedman's argument, while asserting the moral value of the freedom of the individual, fails to engage the other competing values in the argument, the consequence being that for Friedman there is no moral argument here. Neither does he address the empirical studies by economists that present a different picture of the effects of raising the minimum wage. In which case, there is no nonmoral argument here either. (The economist Thomas Sowell, as we saw above, also flatly asserts the harmful effects of minimum wage laws, making no attempt to weigh opposing evidence regarding the empirical effects of raising the minimum wage.) Finn observes: "Because Friedman believes moral values are adjudicated only by an internal process of subjective

117. Haldane, "Natural Law and Ethical Pluralism," 135.
118. Friedman, *Capitalism and Freedom*, 180.

preference and because no rational progress can be made in interpersonal conversation about values, freedom plays the role of the only feasible value on which to rely in the face of the inevitable conflicts among people in democratic societies."[119] Accordingly, for Friedman (and for Sowell) the discussion regarding the minimum wage can take place in a meaningful way only in terms of price theory (the law of supply and demand), this in regard to the labor market, with individual freedom being the only moral value at play in the argument, this whether individual freedom pertains to the actions taken by employers, workers, or consumers in the market. What controls this discussion then is the paradigm of efficient markets.[120] But, is this a sufficient basis for engaging in a normative discussion regarding the minimum wage? If we view markets through a lens wider than the efficient-markets paradigm (that is, if we view markets in light of the common good), what effect will this have both on how we understand markets and on how we engage the argument regarding the minimum wage?

To the question "Are markets just?" Milton Friedman (and Thomas Sowell) would respond that this is a mistaken question. Daniel Finn would agree. The wage that a worker is paid by an employer, if it is above the minimum-wage level set by the government, is the result of current supply and demand in the free market. To ask if the wage is a just wage is the wrong question to ask because the norm of justice does not apply here, that is, to the mechanics of a price-coordinated economy. To bring to light the moral dimension of the market, according to Finn, we must ask a different question—the right question: "Under what conditions are the outcomes of markets just?"[121] What distinguishes this latter question from the former is that the latter question has a context that is wider than the question that asks simply whether the current market price of labor is just. To ask about the conditions that must be met if a market outcome is to be considered just, such as paying a just wage, widens our view of the market, thus enabling us to evaluate the market outcome from a moral point of view. A just wage is a living wage, that is, a wage that enables a full-time worker to satisfy basic human needs. That a full-time wage meets the basic conditions of human living renders the wage just. Here we are concerned, not with a market transaction viewed only in terms of supply and demand, but with the market transaction viewed in light of the conditions that must be satisfied to realize the human good which is the moral good. Finn's point is this: "It is impossible to evaluate the justice of markets by looking at markets alone."[122]

Markets are part of and function within wider institutional contexts—contexts that are political, social, and cultural. To view markets outside of their institutional contexts, and to consider the justice of markets outside of the moral purposes of these institutions is akin to studying a plant or animal outside of its natural environment.

119. Finn, *Moral Ecology of Markets*, 14; see 13–15.

120. See Dembinski, "Toward a Financial Education," 36–39.

121. Finn, *Moral Ecology of Markets*, 103, 108.

122. Finn, *Moral Ecology of Markets*, 104.

Finn offers this analogy: as the biologist studies a particular species of plant or animal in the context of the organism's environment, that is, its ecology, so the consideration of the justice of markets requires that we view markets in their moral context, that is, their moral ecology.[123] Finn's analogy encourages us to see the social institutions of the economy (and thus markets), the government, and the church as vital functions of the social whole that has a unifying moral purpose, which is the common good. In which case, we see these social institutions, not as autonomous sectors acting independently from one another in the society, but as social institutions that imply one another, while maintaining their distinctness, in the moral ecology of the common good.

Viewing market choices in light of the interplay in society between the institutions of the economy, government, and the church effectively changes how we engage the moral argument regarding the minimum wage. What underlies Friedman's argument regarding the minimum wage is his notion of freedom, which he defines as "the absence of coercion," this whether freedom pertains to economic freedom or political freedom. Here economic freedom is viewed strictly in terms of the voluntary choice that is made between seller and buyer, employer and employee, in a market exchange. Coercion takes place when one party to the exchange is presented with limited choices or no choice at all. For Friedman the value of the free market is evident in its ability to check the power of coercion and thus protect the pursuit of self-interest in all market exchanges.[124] But this view of economic freedom clouds the wider institutional contexts, and thus the moral ecology, in which moral choices and thus the moral argument regarding the minimum wage take place.

Can the economist propose a view of economic freedom that is at home in this moral environment and so contribute to this moral argument? Yes, says the economist Andrew Yuengert: "the economist's commitment to a worldview in which individual interest is paramount still has something important to offer the common good tradition."[125] The economist's contribution to the discussion of the common good lies precisely in the primacy of attention that the economist gives to human agency in society, specifically to the economic agency that drives markets. Even though the economist views market transactions through the lens of methodological individualism, Yuengert notes, the economist's attention to market choices cannot be blind to the wider social dimension of market transactions insofar as individual market choices necessarily involve other market participants, the result being the coordination of decisions and actions that has as its aim the mutual benefit of all involved in the market exchange (recall Hume's example of the two people rowing the boat). Market coordination such as this, seen more broadly, results in what economists describe as the undirected (spontaneous) order of the market. Seen in this light, according to

123. Finn, *Moral Ecology of Markets*, 104–5. For a view of markets as embedded in society from a sociological perspective, see Carruthers and Babb, *Economy/Society*, 7–9.

124. Friedman, *Capitalism and Freedom*, 14–15.

125. Yuengert, "What Can Economists Contribute," 37.

Yuengert, "the economy and the social order are in dynamic equilibrium, driven in part by individual human agency."[126] Here economic freedom is viewed, not simply as freedom from coercion, but as a socially engaged freedom that is responsive to the restrictions of governmental policy.

Meeder's Restaurant, located in the southwest corner of the state of New York on the shore of Lake Erie, very close to the border of Pennsylvania, is a case in point. Since 2013 the State of New York has been gradually increasing the state-mandated minimum wage. By 2019 the state minimum wage had been raised to $11.10, then raised to $12.50 in 2020 and to $13.20 in 2022. Pennsylvania by contrast has kept its mandated minimum wage at the federal level of $7.25 an hour. Given the disparity between these minimum-wage levels and the fact that this disparity exists in the close proximity of bordering counties, Meeder's Restaurant for one served as an optimal test case for researchers at the Federal Reserve Bank of New York analyzing the outcomes of raising the minimum wage and thus provides a glimpse at the interplay between economic agency and the policy effects of raising the minimum wage. To maintain profitability, the owners of the restaurant raised menu prices (although customers barely noticed) and invested in new equipment that would make food production more efficient (the restaurant offers twenty-six different kinds of pie), this without losing their customer base to restaurants in neighboring Pennsylvania and without firing workers or reducing their hours of work. The low-wage workers at Meeder's, for their part, benefited from their wages being significantly higher than the wages of their counterparts in nearby Pennsylvania. Moreover, what the researchers found overall was that, despite the higher New York minimum-wage level, low-wage employment in the southern border counties of New York adjacent to Pennsylvania for the most part did not suffer a significant decline.[127]

Meeder's Restaurant offers a granular view of the common good from an economic perspective: the social good in this case is the economic good shared by the workers, the customers, and the owners of the restaurant. To employ a distinction made by John Haldane, the good here is "a *good-for-many,* taken collectively, rather than *a good to many,* taken distributively." Although the good—being a profitable restaurant—is the good of individual workers, customers, and owners, this good is not simply the aggregate good of the individuals involved and thus decomposable (a good to many), but rather the good is a shared good, which is the good of the whole (a good-for-many). Here the common good is perceived in terms of "the *communicability* of the integrated sum of social and personal elements" (the willed interaction of the restaurant's customers, workers, and owners), which "contrasts with a notion of commonality as a mere function of convergent interests. The common good is essentially shared," Haldane emphasizes.[128] A shared good such as this requires not only

---

126. Yuengert, "What Can Economists Contribute," 43; see 40–47.

127. Smialek, "As Push for Higher Wages Grows."

128. Haldane, *Practical Philosophy,* 227 (italics original).

the market coordination of participants (the law of supply and demand), but also their willed cooperation and a shared trust in one another. Indeed, mutual trust and mutual goodwill, especially in markets where compromises must be made by the market participants, are essential ingredients to realizing efficient markets, according to the economist Joseph Stiglitz.[129] Still, from the economist's viewpoint, is there a moral argument to be made here with regard to raising the minimum wage? Yes, but the moral argument becomes evident only when the economy enters into dialogue with the government and the church.

From the perspective of the economist, a couple having dinner at Meeder's Restaurant participates in a voluntary market exchange between the couple as customers of the restaurant and the owners and workers of the restaurant. However, given the increase in the minimum wage, this voluntary exchange requires an adaptation on the part of the customers (to higher prices) and the owners (to a decrease in profits)—an adaptation that is nevertheless freely made by all parties to the exchange. This voluntary exchange thus has a wider social dimension that is not reducible to the particularity of the voluntary exchange, this social dimension being the background of meaning (involving a shared meaning and a common understanding) in which the voluntary exchange takes place. The dinner being enjoyed by the couple at Meeder's is the focus of their attention, not the background of meaning to the voluntary exchange, yet the particularity of this market transaction can be perceived and understood fully only in light of the wider dimension of the shared meaning and common understanding that shapes the market transaction. If we view the market transaction outside of its wider social context, we see only a personal choice (an expression of individual freedom) on the part of the couple. However, if we view their choice to have dinner at Meeder's in its wider social context (which includes New York's raising the minimum wage), we see an expression of economic freedom that is not simply freedom from coercion, but rather a shared freedom, that is, "a kind of freedom that can exist only in a community linked together by bonds of reciprocal solidarity," according to David Hollenbach.[130] In this case, the meaning of economic freedom expressed in the couple's market choice, when viewed in its wider social context, is a freedom shared with the economic freedom of the owners and workers of the restaurant. Here economic freedom is seen as a good-for-many, and thus *a* common good.

The wider social dimension that is the background of a particular market transaction such as this, however, remains out of sight and unexamined until the economic arrangements that structure the market transaction (such as raising the minimum wage) are challenged, particularly by economic self-interests or political self-interests. The challenge to raising the minimum wage elicits a response on the part of the social institutions mediating the market transaction, a response that gives voice to the legitimating idea (justification) of each institution. In response to the challenge, the

129. Stiglitz, *Price of Inequality*, 121–26; see Finn, *Moral Ecology of Markets*, 136–37.

130. Hollenbach, SJ, *Common Good and Christian Ethics*, 83; see 82–85.

moral argument (dialogue) begins, this among the institutional voices answering the challenge, but for the moral argument to proceed, the argument must be based on a common understanding shared by the participants, this being the norm of the common good. For the economist Yuengert, the undirected order of the market that is the result of economic agency (the efficient allocation of resources) is a component of the common good, but at the same time Yuengert acknowledges that market order does not necessarily benefit all within the society, and thus undirected market order requires direction (regulation) as well. Yuengert elaborates:

> Since the order is itself common to an economy, not being the intention of the individual participants, its maintenance and its boundaries are a joint responsibility and a component of the common good. The recognition of this order does not negate a community's responsibility for regulating the market. Markets are, after all, a means and not an end to human fulfillment.[131]

Like the economist Jean Tirole, Yuengert sees the market as a means to an end, not as an end in itself; unlike Tirole, however, Yuengert sees the end or purpose of market activity in terms of human fulfillment (an objective good), not simply in terms of the fulfillment of individual desire (a subjective preference). That the economist sees the end or purpose of market order in terms of human fulfillment (the common good) provides a basis for dialogue between the economy and other institutional voices. That the economist acknowledges that the economic good of market order offers only "an incomplete account of human fulfillment" (Yuengert's words)[132] provides motivation to the economist to engage other institutional voices in dialogue regarding human fulfillment. With regard to raising the minimum wage as a moral argument, the institutional voices that have the most to contribute to the argument, besides the economy, are the government and the church. These two institutional voices add breadth and depth to the moral argument, thus enabling the economy to see its moral viewpoint (the economic freedom of the individual) in a wider moral context. For the economist, then, in light of the common good, the maintenance and setting the boundaries of market order are to be seen as the joint responsibility of all three institutions.

The government through legislation provides direction to the undirected order of the market by setting boundaries (limits) to the free market. To situate the free market in its proper context, Robert Reich, public policy analyst and former government official, emphasizes that the government "*creates* the market," this by means of the laws and rules of public policy.[133] For this reason, governmental legislation regarding the minimum wage is rightly seen, not as the government's intrusion into the autonomous sphere of the free market, but rather as mandating a limit that the government

131. Yuengert, "What Can Economists Contribute," 47.

132. Yuengert, "What Can Economists Contribute," 39.

133. Reich, *Common Good*, 23–24 (italics original). Daniel Finn also makes this point. See Finn, *Moral Ecology of Markets*, 118–19.

places on the free market. Here, in terms of the legislation that raises the minimum wage, we see on the part of government the expression of a moral ideal and a political concern. The moral ideal concerns political equality—the citizens of a democracy must all participate in the governance of the democracy as political equals, this based on the moral ideal that all human beings are intrinsically equal. The political concern pertains to the present and growing economic inequality in the United States, a concern that raises "the question of whether substantial economic inequality is compatible with democracy," this question posed by the political scientist Larry Bartels.[134] In a democracy can political equality coexist with extreme economic inequality without undermining the democracy? If we answer this question in the negative, we see the Raise the Wage Act of 2019, passed by the US House of Representatives, not simply as governmental legislation with the purpose of improving the lives of low-wage workers (a good to many), but as an act of Congress to strengthen the democracy overall by ensuring that the wages of the working poor are livable wages and thus wages that are just (a good-for-many). The good of the social whole requires this—that all citizens of the democracy have the ability to participate fully in the life of the society with dignity and the means to meet basic human needs. In which case, we see the act of Congress, not as the government's attempt to usurp the function of the economy (economic agency), but as legislation to guide the economy in light of the common good.

In the eyes of the church, a public policy issue such as raising the minimum wage, while economic and political in nature, is at root a moral issue, and it is from this perspective that the church would enter the argument. At the same time the moral issue concerns the workings of both the economy and government, and so the church engages this moral argument effectively only in dialogue with the moral (institutional) viewpoints of the economy and government. From the perspective of the church's moral viewpoint—here we draw upon the teaching of the US Catholic bishops in their 1986 pastoral letter on the US economy, imagining (as does Mary Jo Bane above) the bishops addressing this present-day policy issue—the church widens and deepens the moral context of the public policy issue of raising the minimum wage by perceiving and acting on the issue in light of the biblical vision of solidarity and compassion. Here we find expressed a normative view of being a community. The biblical vision of solidarity and compassion is rooted in the experience of the primitive church (as we saw above)—being a community "of one heart and soul" in which "there was not a needy person among them" (see Acts 4:32–35). The biblical vision, at first glance, appears incompatible with a discussion of public policy and unsuitable as a moral guide to enacting public policy. The bishops, however, find in the language of human rights the common basis for dialogue between the faith of the church and a public policy issue such as raising the minimum wage. In the light of the biblical view of solidarity, the bishops describe human rights as "the minimum conditions for life in community." Here the right to a livable wage would be seen, not simply as

134. Bartels, *Unequal Democracy*, 2.

a person's individual right vis-à-vis the government or the economy, but as a human right that ensures the worker's dignity and ability to participate fully as a member of the society, the denial of this right resulting in the marginalization and powerlessness of the worker, thus rendering the worker a nonmember of the society.[135] Ensuring that the wages of the working poor are just by raising the minimum wage, however, should not be seen as a matter of equal treatment of the poor on the part of government, but rather as preferential treatment of the poor, the bishops would emphasize. The biblical basis for giving priority to the poor lies in the Christian sense of compassion: "The obligation to evaluate social and economic activity from the viewpoint of the poor and the powerless arises from the radical command to love one's neighbor as one's self," the bishops state.[136] But, for the bishops, the wider basis for bringing this priority—the preferential treatment of the poor—to bear on a public policy issue such as the minimum wage, this as a moral norm, lies in the understanding, shared with the economy and government, of the common good: "The prime purpose of this special commitment to the poor is to enable them to become active participants in the life of society. It is to enable *all* persons to share in and contribute to the common good."[137]

The moral argument for raising the minimum wage, therefore, is a shared argument between three institutional viewpoints, an argument that has a common point of agreement (one that concerns the human good) and an argument that takes place on the basis of a common understanding (that as a human good raising the minimum wage contributes to the common good). That the church brings its distinct moral viewpoint into the argument allows each of the other institutions to see its viewpoint in a new light, while retaining its own distinctiveness: here economic agency is seen as rooted in the "call to community"; citizenship is seen in terms of the virtue of civic commitment. "Solidarity," the bishops state, "is another name for this social friendship and civic commitment that make human moral and economic life possible."[138]

The moral argument regarding raising the minimum wage, however, did not take place in the US Congress in 2019. Indeed, there was no argument there of any kind. The Raise the Wage Act of 2019, voted on and passed by the Democratic-controlled House of Representatives and then sent to the Republican-controlled Senate, was not voted on by the Senate. Accordingly, without a vote in the Senate, there was no opportunity to challenge the Act publicly and thus no possibility to engage in public argument regarding the Act. The political scientists Jacob Hacker and Paul Pierson pose this question: "Can the absence of a government response to rising inequality really be treated as a form of policy? Absolutely—when it takes the form of 'drift', the deliberate failure to adapt public policies to the shifting realities of a dynamic economy." Drift is

---

135. National Conference of Catholic Bishops, *Economic Justice for All*, nos. 77–84; see also Hollenbach, SJ, "A Communitarian Reconstruction of Human Rights, 138–42.

136. National Conference of Catholic Bishops, *Economic Justice for All*, no. 87.

137. National Conference of Catholic Bishops, *Economic Justice for All*, no. 88.

138. National Conference of Catholic Bishops, *Economic Justice for All*, nos. 63, 66.

"the passive-aggressive form of politics," they explain, in which public policy is managed, not through deliberation and action, but through the inaction of government leaders (no public argument, no vote). "Our point is that nothing happening to key policies while the economy shifts rapidly can add up to something very big happening to Americans who rely on these policies," they state. The failure of the government to update minimum-wage legislation to meet the changing social and economic conditions of the present day, in their view, is a case in point.[139]

But, then, the question is this: Why did the federal government not act to update the minimum wage in 2019? Why has Congress left the matter to state legislatures to deal with in a piecemeal fashion? That there is a need to raise the federal minimum wage is clear: The minimum wage, because it is not indexed to inflation, has fallen in terms of real value steadily from its high point in 1968 until 2009 when the minimum-wage rate was set at $7.25 per hour (a 26 percent drop in its real value), and this decline in the real value of the minimum wage has continued to the present day. Moreover, that the federal minimum-wage law has had widespread public support since its inception in 1938 (the Fair Labor Standards Act of 1938), and that periodic increases to the minimum wage have had the support of the public as well, makes the present government inaction even more problematical, according to the political scientist Larry Bartels. Based on the empirical evidence of research conducted by contemporary political science, he draws this conclusion: "the politics of the minimum wage seem to be driven much more by partisanship and ideology than by public opinion or, for that matter, economics."[140] Furthermore, Bartels points out: "The substantial erosion of the minimum wage over the past 50 years stands as a dramatic example of the American political system's unresponsiveness to public sentiment."[141]

What this means for low-wage workers is that with regard to a matter as significant to their working lives as earning a livable wage, low-wage workers have no political voice, either individually or, given the present-day decline of labor unions both in terms of political influence and union membership, collectively. The unresponsiveness on the part of leaders in government to public sentiment regarding the minimum wage, however, is partial. The political and economic interests that stand to benefit most from governmental inaction regarding updating the minimum wage, this being the interests of the affluent constituents of the democracy, do have a political voice that enables their policy preferences to be represented in Congress. Bartels notes this disparity with concern:

> These disparities in representation are especially troubling because they suggest the potential for a debilitating feedback cycle linking the economic and

139. Hacker and Pierson, *Winner-Take-All Politics*, 52–53.

140. Bartels, *Unequal Democracy*, 199; see 198–232.

141. Bartels, *Unequal Democracy*, 231. For a recent account of public support for raising the minimum wage and legislative action at the state, county, and city level, see Friedman, "Base Wage of $15 Gains in Popularity across U.S."

political realms: increasing economic inequality may produce increasing inequality in political responsiveness, which in turn produces public policies that are increasingly detrimental to the interests of poor citizens, which in turn produces even greater economic inequality, and so on.

The concern over the disparity in representation in Congress regarding a policy issue such as the minimum wage, and thus a way to explain the government's inaction, is not that one group (the working poor) suffers harm and that another group benefits (the political and economic elite). Rather, the concern for Bartels is that the democracy as a whole suffers harm. The outcome of the disparity in representation in Congress, according to Bartels, is "a starkly *unequal* democracy," the concern then being this: "effective political equality is unlikely in the face of substantial economic inequality." Thus, genuine democracy (political equality) is undermined in a society marked by extreme economic inequality.[142] Here, with regard to the government's inaction on raising the minimum wage, we see an example of the interplay between the economy and government that is driven by economic and political self-interest. Here there is no moral argument, one that is based on the common good as its norm, and because of this absence there is no vision of the good of being a community—the social good that is the foundation and moral purpose of a just society.

The Next Step

Outside of the limits that government places on the free market, the market is driven by the individual desires, and thus the individual decisions and actions, of all who participate in the marketplace. The result is a spontaneous (undirected) order, made up of market participants acting independently of one another and making individual decisions based on their particular needs and circumstances. From this undirected market activity comes an unintended order. Markets work. But, if the individual decisions and actions of market participants, although motivated by what the participants see as a desired good for themselves, nevertheless produce a collective harm (for example, deep economic inequality in the society), will the awareness of this overall harm be a sufficient incentive to the market participants to alter their behavior—their decisions and actions—in the marketplace? More importantly, insofar as the collective harm requires a collective response on the part of society for the harm to be mitigated or eradicated, will this awareness of harm be sufficient to motivate market participants, as well as others in the society, to cooperate with one another to address this harm mutually, particularly if the social good that such cooperation intends stands at odds with individual self-interest? In short, does having an understanding of the common good motivate us sufficiently to act for the common good, particularly if acting for the common good requires collaborating with others in the society to realize the common good?

142. Bartels, *Unequal Democracy*, 344–45.

The question presents a fundamental challenge to the use of the common good as the norm of social justice. We met this challenge in one form at the conclusion of Chapter 3 in terms of the question that the Catholic theologians Calvez and Perrin raise regarding the understanding of the common good. Given the universal scope of the common good as the end or purpose of the social whole, will the understanding of the common good be necessarily so vague, its determination necessarily so imprecise, that the norm while aspirational will be ineffectual as a moral and nonmoral guide? The task of Chapter 4 has been to address this challenge in light of the Aristotelian-Thomistic tradition by demonstrating the logical and ontological relationship between the one and the many, and thus the relationship between the common good as the end or purpose of the social whole (whether as the good of a society as a whole or the global common good) and the instantiations—the many—that give reality to the common good as the ideal—the one.

But, if we broaden our consideration of the common good from understanding the common good as a norm to include a consideration of acting for the common good, we are then faced with this question: Will our perceiving and understanding the common good in and through its instantiations (the social conditions of human fulfillment) lead us necessarily to act for the common good? No, both Aristotle and Aquinas would answer. What is missing in the question as stated, they would emphasize, is the role of desire, both sensate and rational desire, in acting for the common good. For Aquinas, as we saw in Chapter 3, a moral action—such as acting for the common good—has its source, not in the speculative intellect (understanding), nor in the practical intellect (practical reasoning), but in the will. As rational desire, the will, being moved by the good that is apprehended by the intellect, moves the self to act in order to realize the good (the object of desire) concretely. The good that first moves the will to act is a particular good—a good for us, either a sensate good or a rational good—but to desire this particular good not only as a good for us but for its goodness as such, this is the work of the intellect (understanding). Accordingly, acting for the common good presupposes our first being moved either by a concrete sensate desire (the feeling of compassion for one who is homeless) or by a concrete rational desire (the desire—for the good of the workers and the local community as well as for the good food—to patronize a restaurant that has raised its prices to pay its workers a just wage); but in each instance the singularity of the desire that moves the will to act for the good, in order to be realized not simply as a good for us but as a social good, requires that the will be moved to act by the wider perspective of the common good—the perspective that the understanding provides to the will as a normative guide. Still, what moves us to act concretely for the common good is not the clarity of our understanding of the common good, but the rational desire of the will to realize the common good. But, then, herein lies the challenge: Insofar as acting for the common good has its source in the singularity of the will's desire, but realizing the common good requires collaborating with others (with the singularity of many wills) on a societal or global basis in light of the common good, does the need for the cooperation of many wills ultimately render acting for the common good futile—utopian in expectation but unrealistic in practical implementation?

Neither the market nor the government alone can provide an adequate response to this challenge. The undirected activity of the market (the cooperation of many wills) brings about an unintended order. But market order might not be beneficial to all in the market. As we have seen, the labor market efficiently allocates resources in terms of supply and demand, but the outcome of this market allocation presently leaves millions of low-wage workers in the society without a livable income. This fact of economic inequality, furthermore, is accentuated by the fact that a disproportionate number of workers in low-wage jobs are people of color—Black, Hispanic, and Native American workers in particular—thus making the issue of economic inequality in the workplace also an issue of racial inequality in the society.[143] Is the remedy to this social harm that comes from free market choices to be found only in the correction of the market that comes from governmental coercion? Yes, Thomas Hobbes would answer. In his view, as we saw above, the many wills that constitute a society can attain social cohesion and thus the social good only through the authority and power of one will, which is the sovereign (the government). No, the Aristotelian-Thomistic tradition would respond. Acting for the common good has its source in the singularity of the will's desire, but in all moral action the will is both mover and moved—moved by the good that lies outside it, yet mover insofar as the will in its desire for the good moves the self to act to realize the good. Here the good—the object of the will's desire—both stands apart from the self as the object of desire and resides in the self in the form of love. From this perspective, a societal response through the cooperation of many wills to a collective harm, such as economic and racial inequality in the labor market, is theoretically possible and thus, in this view, not limited to the choice between the self-interested behavior (individual desire) of market participants and governmental correction of the market through legislation. Here the basis for social cooperation lies in the recognition of the good that the participants who collaborate seek in common and thus the good, desired by the participants, that moves them to act.

But, is the cooperation of many wills to realize the good in common in fact possible, particularly on a societal and global scale? What is the challenge that must be met if societal and global cooperation are to take place? What is the basis of the hope that in acting for the common good justice will be realized, this as a social good and a global good? These are the questions that must be answered if acting for the common good is to be seen as a realistic and effective response to social and global injustice. This is the next step.

---

143. For a consideration of the relation between economic and racial inequality in the context of the history of minimum wage legislation by two economists, see Derenoncourt and Montialoux, "Raise the Minimum Wage."

Chapter 5

Acting for the Common Good

THE CHALLENGE

What You See Depends on Where You Stand

Experiential knowledge is necessarily perspectival and thus partial. Standing before a large oak tree, we see only one side of the tree; to see the other side of the tree, we must change our perspective—our viewpoint. What we see of the oak tree depends on where we stand. This spatial observation can be extended metaphorically to theoretical knowledge. Two natural scientists—say, a physicist and a botanist—standing before the oak tree see the same object but they each see it from the distinct perspective of their particular science and thus each is seeing the tree in a different way. A comparable point can be made with regard to evaluative knowledge—what we see depends on what we value—but with this difference: whereas theoretical knowledge results in understanding, evaluative knowledge leads to doing. What we value (where we stand) shapes what we see, and on the basis of what we see, we are moved to act. A householder might value the oak tree for its shade and thus sees the tree as a useful good. An artist, on the other hand, values the tree for its beauty and thus sees the tree in terms of its intrinsic goodness. Despite the difference in their evaluative viewpoints, because they each value the tree as a good, both the householder and the artist will be moved to care for the tree and to care about the tree. How we act is determined by what we see, and what we see is shaped by what is important to us, that is, what we value. In our engagement with the world a necessary relationship exists between values, seeing, and doing.

We saw this relationship between values, seeing, and doing in our consideration of the parable of the good Samaritan (Luke 10:29–37) in Chapter 3. The priest and the Levite and then the Samaritan encounter the victim of robbers left by the side of the road. That the priest and the Levite move away from the victim and that the Samaritan goes to the victim is determined by what they see, and what they see is shaped by what they value—for the priest and the Levite the value of maintaining ritual purity by not touching what could be a dead body moves them to pass by the victim that they see; for the Samaritan the value of compassion for a human being in need moves him to stop and attend to the victim that he sees. The parable illustrates what being a neighbor entails by highlighting the value of love (*agapē*) for the other that makes us a neighbor. What the Samaritan sees and how the Samaritan acts toward the victim are shaped by what is of fundamental value to him.

The political scientist Jennifer Hochschild underscores the importance of establishing the relationship between values, seeing, and doing in the social-scientific analysis of public opinion and its relation to public policy, a relationship which she describes in terms of the "connections among values, perceptions of fact, and political prescriptions." She affirms the introduction of values as an essential component in the empirical study of public opinion by social scientists, but at the same time she stresses the importance of connecting values to facts, especially the misperception of facts on the part of citizens and the effect that this has on the formulation of public policy. Hence the title of her essay is this: "Where You Stand Depends on What You See."[1] Our perception of facts (what you see), in her view, shapes our values (where you stand) and vice versa. Thus, she asks: "To what degree are citizens' political attitudes and policy preferences based on, or at least supported by, mistaken perceptions of fact?" She points out, for example, that the white population in the United States greatly overestimates the percentage of the population that is made up of Black and Hispanic Americans: "at least twice the actual number in the American population," she states. Such a misperception of fact affects how whites evaluate affirmative action policies in employment and education, leading them to judge such programs not as a necessary policy response to address racial and ethnic inequality and bias, but as granting special preference to some in the society at the expense of others, this in a competitive environment. If the white population was presented with accurate data—currently, that Blacks make up 12.1 percent and Hispanics 21.1 percent of the population while the white population makes up 55.8 percent of the total US population—would these facts make the white population more accepting of affirmative action programs? "Probably not," says Hochschild. "None of us are that logical, and opposition to affirmative action has many more causes than an arithmetic calculation of its threat to one's position."[2] Facts alone, even if presented clearly and accurately, cannot bear the weight of responsibility for altering what we see or directing how we act. Values are needed. But values need facts if values are to be grounded in the objective world and if they are to serve as reliable guides for the political judgments that lead to political prescriptions. Therefore, Hochschild states: "I hypothesize that perceptions of fact help to shape values, help to transform general values into particular views, and perhaps are

1. Hochschild, "Where You Stand," 313.
2. Hochschild, "Where You Stand," 318.

shaped in turn by values or policy preferences and political attitudes," this in regard to "the polity as a whole, as well as for individuals' political stances."[3]

But, if facts can shape values, can facts in some instances also change values? Can facts that are clearly and accurately presented but that contradict what we value (where we stand) cause us as individuals or as a society as a whole to change what we hold to be of value? Yes, Hochschild would respond, but with this qualification: how such change occurs depends on how we understand and hold values. A value held by us as a principle (for example, that political and economic equality requires equal opportunity) is more likely to allow for dialogue with other, even contradictory principles and to be open and responsive to change when confronted with contradictory perceptions of fact regarding an issue such as affirmative action. However, a value rooted in "deep-seated predispositions or fundamental constructs that stem from childhood socialization, community ties, or searing personal experiences," Hochschild observes, is more likely to be unresponsive and inattentive to facts that contradict what the value intends while being responsive and attentive to perceptions of fact that confirm the value and its political and policy implications. Here countervailing facts brought forth for the purpose of changing such deep-seated values face a daunting challenge. Unlike facts that serve as examples to support or to refute a principle, such as the principle of equal opportunity, facts stated against a deep-seated attitude, such as the attitude in the white population regarding racial inequality in the workplace and in educational opportunities, are more likely to be presented not so much as examples but as evidence and thus have more work to do to change the attitudes (values) of the white population regarding affirmative action. Here facts contribute effectively to changing such values (deep-seated attitudes) only when the facts are combined with values that provide an alternative viewpoint that is relevant to the political prescriptions that will bring about change.[4] In this case, the alternative viewpoint enlarges our view by offering a different perspective and thus enables facts to be perceived in this wider context. The percentage of Black and Hispanic Americans in the US population is presented then as a fact in the wider context of social concern that is rooted in a value that changes our perspective—the value of equal opportunity. It is from the perspective of this value (where we stand) that the fact takes on meaning (what we see) for the issue at hand.

All knowledge—experiential, theoretical, evaluative—is determined by where we stand, understood either literally or metaphorically. "We always stand somewhere, and the place where we stand determines what we see," says Catholic moralist Timothy O'Connell. "Human knowledge, then, is never totally objective. It is always partial, always limited." But, for this reason, to go beyond this limitation, we must move, that is, change our perspective or engage other perspectives. "Reality is bigger than our understanding. True, the knower can move from one placement to another. We can

3. Hochschild, "Where You Stand," 321.
4. Hochschild, "Where You Stand," 321–24.

educate ourselves to other ways of understanding; we can move from one location to another. The one thing we cannot do, however, is see reality from all points of view at once."[5] In order to see the other side of the oak tree, we must move from where we are standing. Theoretical development in the sciences takes place when collaboration between different scientific viewpoints occurs. A deeper and encompassing appreciation of the oak tree, which leads to more attentive care of the tree, results from seeing the good of the tree as both useful and beautiful. The telling of the parable of the good Samaritan focuses our attention on two viewpoints—that of the priest and the Levite, and that of the Samaritan. But there is a third viewpoint represented in the parable— that of the victim lying by the side of the road. If we change our viewpoint to that of the victim, what do we see? From the perspective of the victim, we more readily see in the compassionate acts of the Samaritan God's compassion for all those in society who are left by the side of the road (the marginalized) and all those who have been victimized by the forces of injustice in society. Thus, from the viewpont of the victim in the parable, we realize that loving our neighbor means not only responding to the need of one, but also being in solidarity with those in our society who are the victims of injustice. From this viewpoint, we enlarge the meaning of the parable and broaden our understanding of what loving our neighbor entails.[6] Going beyond the partiality of our viewpoint by changing our viewpoint or by engaging other viewpoints (values) enables us to expand our knowledge of reality, this in experiential, theoretical, and evaluative ways.

But, our viewpoint—the value or values that we hold—can also inhibit our achieving a larger view of reality by leading us to ignore, minimize, or restrict other viewpoints. A deep-seated predisposition or a fundamental mindset based on childhood socialization or community expectations, Hochschild points out, can be the basis of values that we hold firmly but that restrict our perception of reality, and thus our perception of facts, and that are resistant to change. If we broaden Hochschild's observation to include values embodied in the institutional and cultural norms and practices of a society, we see that society as a whole can be shaped by values that are firmly held but that restrict our understanding and skew our evaluation of society's larger purposes, and that are resistant to change. This, however, we cannot see until these social values are challenged by an alternative viewpoint. Why?

How we as a society act will be determined by what we see through the lens of the society's institutional and cultural expectations, and what we see will be shaped by the institutional and cultural norms (values) of the society. As we saw in Chapter 3, institutional and cultural norms and practices are conventions (that is, social agreements), but for social norms to function effectively as the basis of order and stability in the society, they are perceived by the society as necessary, grounded in nature and reason, not as social creations that are one possibility among many. To

5. O'Connell, *Principles for a Catholic Morality*, 179.
6. See Donahue, SJ, *Gospel in Parable*, 133–34.

such questions as "which type of economy?" and "which form of government?" as well as "who cares for the baby?" a variety of answers can be given, but in a stable, orderly society its members think and act as if there is only one answer to these questions. Thus, institutional and cultural norms (values) and practices, once established, take on a permanence and a necessity that hides their origin as social creations. Moreover, that we as a society think of institutional and cultural values, not as external forces shaping our lives, but as our values individually held, this both hides the conventional nature of these social norms and makes them resistant to change. Indeed, the power of social norms to shape our lives comes precisely from their not being seen by us as social conventions (for example, gender roles) but rather thought of as norms (values) that we have personally chosen as our own. Institutional and cultural norms and practices become visible—draw our attention—if they are challenged, which elicits an institutional justification in the form of a legitimating idea (gender roles are rooted in the biological differences between men and women). Expressing the legitimating idea of institutional and cultural norms and practices, nevertheless, leaves hidden their conventional nature and the social controls that they exert on society. Only when the challenge comes from an alternative viewpoint will the conventional nature of social norms and their power to shape our lives in society come to light (such as the alternative viewpoint of the feminist movement, the basis of its critical evaluation of gender roles).

But the alternative viewpoint is a partial viewpoint, like the viewpoint that it challenges, and it is seen as such by the society. Thus, to effectively challenge the dominant viewpoint of the society's institutions and culture, the alternative viewpoint must draw the eyes of society to see what it sees through the lens of its viewpoint (for example, the unfairness of the gendered division of labor in society, both in the family and the workplace, this viewed from the perspective of the feminist movement). That the alternative viewpoint is an evaluative viewpoint means that its challenge to the dominant viewpoint will be based on its vision of what is the right or the good regarding the institutional and cultural norms and practices of the society (thus in its critique of gender roles the feminist movement brings the concept of justice as equal respect to bear on the institution of the family as well as on the economy and government). In its challenge to the dominant viewpoint, however, the alternative viewpoint will be faced with its own challenge: to establish through its partial viewpoint the basis for the willed cooperation of all in the society to realize a common purpose, while at the same time avoiding the charge of relativism (being a partial truth with no valid claim to a wider objective reality) and the charge of ideology (being a partial truth that is used to mask self-interest). To accomplish this task, the alternative viewpoint must bring into society's view the right or the good that it sees in terms of the institutional and cultural norms and practices of the society in such a way that other partial viewpoints come to see what it sees but through their own partial viewpoints, much like the householder and the artist who both see the good of the oak tree and thus act to care for the tree, but do so from their distinct perspectives (likewise, the feminist movement, although it was created by women, for women, has as its fundamental purpose not simply improving the lives of women but achieving mutuality in human relationships in society based on respect, caring, and equality, this to the benefit of men, to be seen as such by men, as well as to the benefit of women).

Here then is the question that we must first address if we are to understand and to realize collectively through our actions the right or the good that we as a society pursue in common: Is there presently in American society a dominant viewpoint that is rooted in social values that shape what we as a society see, this through the institutional and cultural norms and practices of the society—a viewpoint that determines how we as a society act? If this is the case, then we are compelled to ask: What is the dominant viewpoint? In what ways does the dominant viewpoint shape how we as a society act? Does the dominant viewpoint enable or inhibit our efforts as a society to realize society's larger purposes and to respond effectively to dangers that the society faces as a whole? Is the dominant viewpoint open to dialogue with other viewpoints, or is it resistant to change when challenged by alternative viewpoints?

Where We Stand as a Society: The Dominant Viewpoint

A fundamental threat to our well-being as a society, the Catholic ethicist Simon Harak thinks, is "how we fall victim to the temptation *not* to be moved in our culture," particularly regarding matters of injustice.[7] The problem lies not in the markets as such, nor in the government as such, but in us—we who make up the society. The problem pertains to us as individuals, but more significantly the problem pertains to us collectively as a society. The problem is rooted in the values that shape what we as a society see and, in this light, determine how we as a society act. Thus, the problem is rooted in our culture—the ideas and valuations that shape our collective lives together. That we as members of the society are not moved or resist being moved to act on matters of grave concern that threaten the society, or on matters that call to us to be realized for the sake of the greater good that will benefit the lives of all in the society, raises this question: Is there a discernible cause that keeps us as a society from being moved to act, either to avoid a social evil or to realize a social good? Yes, says the historian and the sociologist, each addressing the question from the distinct perspective of their discipline. The cause lies in the dominant viewpoint that shapes what we see and how we act as a society. In the historical and sociological analyses that they present, they describe the viewpoint that dominates late twentieth-century and early twenty-first-century American culture.

7. Harack, SJ, *Virtuous Passions*, 122–23.

The Dominant Viewpoint in the Light of Historical Analysis

Daniel T. Rodgers trains his historian's eye on late twentieth-century American society, specifically its last three decades, in order to describe, not the significant political and social events of these years, but the words that gave rise to the prominent ideas and metaphors of the age—words that shaped the culture of this period in American history and gave it coherence. What Rodgers finds striking in the emergence of this historical period is its decisive break from the preceding period that originates in the aftermath of World War II, a period marked by the intense, ongoing rivalry between the Soviet Union and the Western Bloc of nations, a geopolitical confrontation that was labeled the Cold War. Evidence of the break can be found in the words that were now being employed, words expressing the ideas and metaphors of the age: "from the speeches of presidents to books of social and cultural theory, conceptions of human nature that in the post–World War II era had been thick with context, social circumstance, institutions, and history gave way to conceptions of human nature that stressed choice, agency, performance, and desire," observes Rodgers. "Viewed by its acts of mind, the last quarter of the century was an era of disaggregation, a great age of fracture."[8]

Of the ideas and metaphors that define the age and provide a way for the members of society to think about society and their place in it, the metaphor that dominates the culture of the age is the word "market." Rodgers notes: "In an age when words took on magical properties, no word flew higher or assumed a greater aura of enchantment than 'market.'" Here the word "market" is an abstract concept, used in a decontextualized manner to describe the individual transactions of voluntary exchange in society. Although the word is a term of economics, its meaning as a metaphor serves as the model for the optimization of individual desires, decisions and actions that take place in the society as a whole.[9] The significance of the term "market" as a dominant metaphor of the age can be seen when viewed in the context of a fundamental change of view that took place within the science of economics in the twentieth century.

The primary focus of the science of economics from its origins through most of the twentieth century had been on the production of wealth, considered in terms of the three factors requisite for the production of wealth—land, capital, and labor. (Adam Smith begins *The Wealth of Nations* observing the productive benefits of the division of labor in a pin factory.) But the focus of economics changed in the last quarter of the century, made evident with the ascendancy of the term "market," here understood in terms of individualized transactions. This change redirected the study of economics from a focus on wealth production to a focus on wealth exchange, and the exchange of wealth became abstracted from specifiable conditions of time, place, and institutional norms, taking place instead in an idealized realm of individual preferences,

8. Rodgers, *Age of Fracture*, 3.
9. Rodgers, *Age of Fracture*, 41–42.

free choice and instrumental reason. The change in focus was the difference between viewing the economy through a wide lens (the view of macroeconomics) and viewing the economy through a narrow lens (the view of microeconomics). The change in focus, moreover, meant that markets were seen in different ways, either as powerful but inevitably imperfect (macroeconomics) or as perfect, at least in an idealized form (microeconomics). Through the wide lens of macroeconomics, the economy is viewed in terms of the complexity and difficulty of coordinating the diverse factors of production—land, capital investment, and labor—and doing this under the regulations of government, the outcome being the total output of these factors working together, which is termed the gross domestic product (GDP). In this view, the goal of macroeconomics is the stabilization of the fluctuations that occur in the overall flow of production and thus the stabilization of imperfect markets. Through the narrow lens of microeconomics, the economy is viewed very differently. Here the focus is on the individual transactions between buyers and sellers, consumers and producers. Orchestrating these transactions are prices—the price that the seller is demanding and the price that the buyer is willing to pay. A perfect market transaction is one in which the price that is set is the price that both the seller and the buyer desire. Here the ideal market price creates an equilibrium between supply and demand, and thus an equality between the desires of the seller and the desires of the buyer. Through the competitive interchange between buyer and seller in the marketplace, it is possible then that an ideal price (the equilibrium price) can be reached, and in this way, markets can be self-stabilizing. Accordingly, through the free interchange between individuals in the marketplace, perfect markets are achievable. Although microeconomics and macroeconomics are very different viewpoints, they are nevertheless viewpoints on one and the same economy. Thus, both viewpoints are represented in the modern study of economics. Yet, economics textbooks that once began with chapters on macroeconomics to present the science of economics in complex, real-world terms, and only in their final chapters considered the ideal markets of microeconomics, now begin with chapters on prices and markets—the basic themes of microeconomics—to introduce the science of economics. This change in the ordering of textbook chapters has entailed a change in focus, a change inspired in part by the failure of the macroeconomic viewpoint to predict and to provide an effective remedy for the economic turbulence that occurred in the 1970s due to the devastating combination of high inflation and high unemployment in the national economy: This change in focus from macro- to microeconomics as the proper starting point for thinking about economics pushed the idea of the market as the ideal realm of economic transaction (and more broadly as the ideal realm of individualized freedom) to the forefront. As a model for economic activity, the market became for the study of economics the dominant viewpoint.[10]

10. Rodgers, *Age of Fracture*, 41–47, 63–68, 74–76; Smith, *Wealth of Nations*, 1.1, 3–6. For an instructive account of the difference between the viewpoints of macroeconomics and microconomics by two leading economists, see Heilbroner and Thurow, *Economics Explained*, 71–80, 143–52. For

But, since the 1970s, the market has become more than just the dominant viewpoint in the field of economics. The market has become, in Rodgers's words, "the dominant social metaphor of the age."[11] Words that are central to our collective understanding of society and to the values that we hold as a society, and particularly as a democracy, have had their meanings change in significant ways during the last quarter of the twentieth century—this due to the influence that the metaphor of the market has had on American culture. Two such words, noteworthy in the defining role that they play in American life, that have undergone a dramatic change in terms of how they are understood and held as values by the American populace are the words "freedom" and "justice."

During the period of the Cold War, freedom was a word that held a place of prominence in the speeches of the post-1945 American presidents. Use of the term in presidential speeches brought into view the sharp contrast between freedom as the fundamental value of American democracy and the totalitarian rule of the Soviet Union. Here freedom—its meaning and value—was situated in a thick context of social and political relationships and the obligations attendant to these relationships. Rodgers comments: "Freedom was at the center of Cold War political rhetoric, but within these urgent contexts, freedom was inescapably social and public." Given the rivalrous confrontation of the Cold War, the practices of American freedom made urgent demands on the American people as a whole. Being a free people brought with it the obligations of civic responsibility and mutual sacrifice. Thus, Rodgers adds: "To act freely within these terms was to act not alone but within a larger fabric of relationships, purposes, obligations, and responsibilities."[12] This thick (wide) view of freedom gave way to a thin (narrow) view of freedom in the 1980s in the presidential speeches of Ronald Reagan. Here freedom was situated in the mind's ability to dream, to imagine a future without limits, a future not tied to the past. Here the enemy of freedom was no longer a hostile political regime, but now the enemy was envisioned as residing within the mind itself. "By the time Reagan entered the White House, freedom's nemesis had migrated into the psyche. Freedom's deepest enemy was pessimism: the mental undertow of doubt, the paralyzing specter of limits," Rodgers notes. In Reagan's presidential speeches, "the face of the nation's enemies was reconstructed. They were no longer the masters of the Kremlin; now they were the doubters, the qualifiers, the realists without vision." Here the rhetoric of freedom was grounded, not in a political vision, but in the psychology of self-actualization. In Reagan's speeches, freedom became privatized and individualized, fragmented into the acts of self-realization.[13] But, this view of freedom, given voice by Reagan, was not Reagan's or his speechwriters'

______

an example of an introduction to the science of economics that begins with the study of prices and markets, see Sowell, *Basic Economics*, 7–60.

11. Rodgers, *Age of Fracture*, 44.

12. Rodgers, *Age of Fracture*, 16.

13. Rodgers, *Age of Fracture*, 25, 30; see 22–40.

creation. Rather Reagan's speeches gave voice to the ideas that were shaping the age. Indeed, says Rodgers, "in the enchanted, disembedded, psychically involuted sense of freedom that slipped into Reagan's speeches . . . there were more parallels with the intellectual dynamics of the age than many observers recognized at the time. The realm of free, spontaneous action that Reagan celebrated mirrored the way in which the economists began to reimagine the spheres of exchange as self-acting, naturally regulating markets."[14] Shaping Reagan's words was the dominant viewpoint of the market.

The vision of society that the metaphor of the market evokes is one of disaggregation—one in which the individual desires, decisions, and actions of buyers and sellers, and by extension the individual desires, decisions, and actions of citizens overall, make up the whole. The problem that this disaggregated view of society presented to the political theorists and philosophers of the last quarter of the twentieth century was how to articulate a basis for society that would provide cohesion to the whole, that is, an understanding of mutual obligation within the citizenry, particularly with regard to matters of justice. In an age in which the market had become the dominant metaphor of society, what would make a society just?

While the question concerning the justice that each citizen owes to all others in the society was not new, Rodgers observes, the answers to the question that emerged at this time in political theory, revitalized by the problem that the ascendency of the market had created, were new. Rodgers points to John Rawls's *A Theory of Justice*, published in 1971, as the first and most celebrated academic response to this problem. Rawls established the basis for social cooperation in society on two principles of justice (this we considered in Chapter 4): The first ensures the basic liberties of each person in the society in a way that is equal for all; the second addresses the inevitable inequalities that exist in a society by ensuring fair, equal opportunity for all in the society, despite these inequalities, and by ensuring that the social and economic inequalities that do exist are nevertheless to the benefit of the least advantaged in the society. What especially interests Rodgers here is the thought experiment that Rawls employs to come to these two principles of justice, this because the hypothetical situation that Rawls creates in which representatives of the society deliberate and choose the principles of justice starts "with the conditions of market choice (individual, self-interested actors, in an arena of unfettered rationality)." The reasoning of those who construct the principles of justice, Rodgers emphasizes, is "precisely the reasoning of classic market actors endeavoring to maximize their advantage in the context of uncertainty." Yet, because those who deliberate and choose in this hypothetical situation do not know their identity (their place in society), the self-interest that motivates their choice of principles will not be reducible to their particular self-interest but will reflect the general interests of society. In this bargaining situation, because the participants do not know if they are rich or poor, well educated or poorly educated, the principles of justice that they construct will favor the least advantaged in the society

14. Rodgers, *Age of Fracture*, 39.

and, accordingly, will support the redistribution of wealth and advantage in a society where inequalities prevail. Thus, in Rawls's thought experiment, although it begins with the self-interest of the individual (a beginning that resembles the conditions of market choice), given the "veil of ignorance" behind which the participants deliberate, "reasonable people would not choose markets as the standard of justice. In their own self-interest, they would choose something like the welfare state instead," Rodgers comments. In the end Rawls's thought experiment arrives at a conception of justice, with its attendant notion of equality, that is as wide as the society that it guides. But, Rodgers notes, by the end of the 1980s, Rawls's thought experiment had been offset by views of justice that had narrowed in scope. Absent from the political debate at this time were the expansive notions of equality and inclusivity that were central to Rawls's concept of justice. Rodgers states: "From both left and right critics of Rawls's great so-cial contract, forged in a sense of mutual obligation of each to all, came smaller, more intimate, but also more partial understandings of society. Rawls's vision of justice as a contract in each other's welfare that was as broad as the nation itself came to be seen, in this context, more and more unreal."[15] At work shaping these developments in political theory was the dominance of the view of society as a disaggregated whole.

In this era, Rodgers points out, two noteworthy critical responses to Rawls's concept of justice were based on visions of justice that differed not only from Rawls's but also one from the other—the one being a libertarian vision and the other being a communitarian vision; yet both responses to Rawls shared the same point: that his large view of justice was unrealistic in the present age of disaggregation and had to be replaced with a view of justice that was smaller and more fitting to the concerns of the society in an age of fracture. But the conception of justice of the one was markedly different from that of the other.

The libertarian view of justice, developed by the philosopher Robert Nozick in *Anarchy, State, and Utopia*, published in 1974, which was a pointed refutation of Raw-ls's *A Theory of Justice*, placed the freedom of the individual at the very center of justice. All forms of coercion, whether political, social, or cultural, that limit the freedom of the self are acts of injustice. Justice is enacted only in the concrete exchanges between individuals, a just exchange being one that is fair and one that is freely consented to by the parties involved. Because the ideal of justice that Rawls fashioned was based on a hypothetical rational choice that takes place outside the concrete exchanges in society, bringing this ideal to bear on these exchanges can only be seen as coercion—that is, as the imposition of the ideal of justice on the private exchanges between individuals in society, which restricts their freedom of choice. Nozick's view of justice, moreover, assumes a view of society that is granular (as had the economist Milton Friedman). Society is made up of individuals and their interactions with one another, this only. To look for something more in society—say, equality—is to seek what is illusory, and when the state aims for equality as the goal for wealth redistribution (for example,

15. Rodgers, *Age of Fracture*, 182–85.

through taxing earnings) and thus for justice as a goal, the result is not justice but oppression: through the power of the state, benefits for some in the society are acquired at the expense of others. Justice for Nozick is found only in the contracts freely entered into by individuals in the society, nothing more. Rodgers comments: "Though Nozick did not put it quite this way, justice was whatever free markets made with the inputs given to them."[16]

But, whether justice is based on the freedom of the individual (Nozick) or on the principles of justice that can be applied uniformly to all spheres of social living (Rawls), both concepts of justice are similarly abstract, universally applied norms that guide the self-interested individual,[17] and thus neither concept of justice is able to provide sufficient normative guidance on the particular matters of justice embedded in the varied, distinct spheres of life that make up a particular community and that shape the lives of the people who inhabit these spheres. This was the counterargument that the political philosopher Michael Walzer presented in debate with Nozick in a lecture course that the two taught jointly at Harvard University in 1971 and that Walzer subsequently articulated in *Spheres of Justice*, published in 1983. For Walzer, Rodgers notes, "the principles of justice were contextual not universal, rooted in the social understandings already at work in actual lives," social understandings that were specific to the distinct spheres that make up the life of a community.[18] Justice, according to Walzer, concerns the distribution of social goods (such as wealth, health care, education, and political power, to name a few), but this not according to a criterion of "simple equality" that would govern the distribution of social goods to individuals in society in an equal, uniform way, but rather according to the criterion of "complex equality" that first takes into account the different meanings of social goods (for example, the difference in meaning between wealth and health care as social goods), which then requires that different social goods be distributed according to different criteria—that is, each according to its own meaning. Injustice in a society occurs, not when inequality takes place in one distinct sphere (for example, the unequal distribution of wealth in a market economy), but when the criterion of distribution in one sphere influences the distribution of social goods in other spheres (thus, when the criterion of wealth distribution, due to its dominance in the society, influences the distribution of the social goods in other spheres, such as health care, education, and political power). Complex equality, then, describes the nature of the social relations in a society in which citizens recognize and respect the boundaries between the social spheres that make up the society and the distinct criterion of justice that stands at the center of each of the spheres. "There is no single standard," Walzer states, "a single

16. Rodgers, *Age of Fracture*, 187–91; see Nozick, *Anarchy, State, and Utopia*, 32–33.

17. Alasdair MacIntyre supports this point in his comparison of Rawls and Nozick in light of the bonds of community. See MacIntyre, *After Virtue*, 244–55.

18. Rodgers, *Age of Fracture*, 193–94.

standard against which all distributions are to be measured."[19] Accordingly, that the members of a political community provide security and welfare for one another, this regulated by the government, underscores the necessity of the welfare state in Walzer's view, yet the communal provision of the welfare state cannot stand as the sole criterion of justice for the society overall. Justice in Walzer's eyes is fundamentally pluralistic in nature, falling into distinct forms of normative guidance for the many forms of communal life that make up society. The result, Rodgers points out, is that in the radical pluralism of Walzer's vision of justice, "the little became . . . the tacit substitution for the whole."[20] What is missing in Walzer's vision of justice, and also in Nozick's vision, is an expansiveness wide enough to provide a basis for the cohesion of the whole.

The sense of the nation as a cohesive whole that was pervasive in American society during the period of the Cold War, but was lost during the age of fracture, was awakened on September 11, 2001. Rodgers comments: "Talk of choice gave way, for a moment, to talk of collective will, obligations, and connections. A new and strenuous nationalism sprang into being. The demands of the whole suddenly became imaginatively and insistently real." Yet, the danger and urgency of the moment that the terrorist attacks of 9/11 created could not undo the culture of disaggregation, shaped by the metaphor of the market, that had come to dominate American life over the past three decades, leaving Americans with a lack of cultural and institutional resources to respond to this national crisis and to the national crises that were to follow, such as the financial crisis of 2008 (discussed in Chapter 1). Rodgers concludes: "The age of fracture had permanently altered the play of argument and ideas. The pieces would have to be reassembled on different frames, the tensions between self and society resolved anew. But how that would be done, amid the anger and the confusion, the liberations and the anxieties, still hung in the balance."[21]

The Dominant Viewpoint in the Light of Sociological Analysis

The question before us is this: Why are we as a society inclined not to be moved to act collectively in response to matters of grave concern that affect us all in the society or regarding matters that promise a greater good for all if realized through our collective action in the society? The sociologist provides an answer to this question not unlike that of the historian, but the sociologist's response differs in this way: Here the focus of attention is on the cultural mores (the ideas and habitual practices) of the American people, particularly the culture of individualism that shapes American lives. From the words spoken by American citizens themselves about their day-to-day lives and about the matters that were of most importance to them, the sociologist Robert Bellah and four collaborators fashioned a portrait of American individualism which they saw

19. Walzer, *Spheres of Justice*, 10; see 3–30, 64–69; see also Miller, "Complex Equality."
20. Rodgers, *Age of Fracture*, 197.
21. Rodgers, *Age of Fracture*, 256, 271.

as the dominant viewpoint through which Americans gave meaning and purpose to their lives individually and collectively. The research for the study was conducted primarily through active interviews (a dialogue between the person doing the research and the person being interviewed with the intent to clarify assumptions or ideas left implicit in the interviewee's responses) and through participant observation (the researcher observes group behavior by actively engaging in the group experience), and only secondarily through survey questionnaires. The research methods employed were determined by the purpose of the study. Whereas data from surveys present a summation of the private views of the public, the active interview has the form of a public conversation which Bellah and his associates intended to be the first step toward a public conversation on a national scale. The researchers chose to concentrate on white, middle-class Americans in their interviews, this because in their estimation individualism as a cultural trait that pertains to Americans overall could be observed and its effects on society could be evaluated more clearly and efficiently here. The interviews, along with participant observation, took place between 1979 and 1984 (note: the same period of time that is the focus of the study undertaken by the historian Rodgers) and included people working in various occupations and living in different parts of the country. What came to light in these interviews both for the researchers and those being interviewed was a question that is ultimately a moral question: What qualities of character are necessary for creating and maintaining a free republic? Must there be a coherence between the kind of people that we are—our character—and the kind of society that we build? In which case, must there be a meaningful relationship between our private lives and public life? Does the culture of individualism as the dominant viewpoint of the American people support or undermine our collective lives together?[22]

The term "individualism," Bellah and his associates point out, was used early on by the nineteenth-century French political philosopher and social observer Alexis de Tocqueville to describe what he saw as a distinctive characteristic of the American people. Tocqueville had come to the United States from France in the 1830s to observe firsthand the developmental beginnings of a modern democracy, one in which the freedom of the people was a foundational value. He recognized in the mores of the American people—what he at times referred to as "habits of the heart"—ideas and habitual practices that bound the individual citizen to the wider public sphere, thus providing the necessary basis for maintaining a free republic, practices such as family life, civic involvement, and carrying on religious traditions. At the same time, Tocqueville pointed to a set of ideas and practices also at work shaping the lives of the American people that he labeled with the term that had recently come into use—individualism. "Individualism is a calm and considered feeling which disposes each citizen to isolate himself from the mass of his fellows and withdraw into the circle of family and friends; with this little society formed to his taste, he gladly leaves the greater society to look

22. Bellah et al., *Habits of the Heart* (1985 ed.), vii–xii, 297–307.

after itself," Tocqueville wrote in *Democracy in America*. Individualism is not the same as egoism, he stressed; yet, in terms of the effect that individualism has on the citizen's relation to the public sphere, the result is the same, which is isolation—here the individual citizen's concerns are not those of "the greater society" but only those of the "little society formed to his taste."[23]

While Tocqueville admired the spirit of economic enterprise in the American people, he warned that its individualistic focus, if not checked by the wider views of society that the practices of political participation and religion inspired, would undermine the very foundations of freedom on which the democracy was based. The fear, according to Tocqueville, was that individualism, if it were to become the dominate trait of the American people, would be fertile soil for the rise of despotism, not the hard despotism of tyranny, but a "soft despotism" in which the form of a free democracy would stand, but its substance would be lost, this loss not clearly perceived or acknowledged by the American populace. Tocqueville's warning is the leitmotif of the study of American individualism undertaken by Bellah and his associates. More than twenty years after its original publication in 1985, they emphasized that for the American people Tocqueville's warning has only grown more insistent. That the life opportunities of the nation's citizens have become increasingly unequal (in such spheres as work, health care, education), that the profits from economic growth in the nation have disproportionately enriched mainly those few (the 1 percent) who stand at the top of the income ladder, that the growing inequality in the United States stands in sharp contrast to that of other developed countries, this challenges the very notions of freedom and equality that are the foundational values of the American republic. Bellah and his associates ask: "Why, then, have Americans been unwilling or unable to halt the growth of inequality or to use our increasing wealth for the common welfare?"[24] Indeed, why are we as a society not moved to act collectively in response to a harm that threatens us all, a harm that portends the undoing of our democracy? The answer to this question the researchers found in the words of the Americans whom they had interviewed.

What the researchers discovered in these conversations was that the cause of our inaction as a people regarding a threat to our democracy, such as the growth of inequality in our society, lies first and foremost not in personal attributes that inhibit our response but in the limitations of our cultural resources. "If there are vast numbers of a selfish, narcissistic 'me generation' in America, we did not find them, but we certainly did find that the language of individualism, the primary American language of self-understanding, limits the ways in which people think," they stated.[25]

23. Quoted in Bellah et al., *Habits of the Heart* (1985 ed.), 37; see viii, 36–39.

24. Bellah et al., "Preface to the 2008 Edition," ix–x. See Stiglitz, *The Price of Inequality*, particularly 1–27: "America's 1 Percent Problem."

25. Bellah et al., *Habits of the Heart* (1985 ed.), 290. Based on recent empirical research, psychologist and neuroscientist Abigail Marsh underscores the point that individualism does not necessarily

The problem of inaction regarding matters of collective concern, the researchers came to see, was not selfishness as a dominant trait in the people that they interviewed, but rather the problem was observed in the words that those being interviewed drew upon to explain the decisions and actions of their private lives or to address the larger issues of public life, words that expressed the shared meanings of a distinct cultural tradition—the language of individualism. The problem, according to the researchers, was at root cultural, not solely personal. Thus: "The primary focus of our research was not psychological, or even primarily sociological, but rather cultural. We wanted to know what resources Americans have for making sense of their lives, how they think about themselves and their society, and how their ideas relate to their actions."[26]

At the time that he was interviewed, Brian Palmer at the age of forty-one had undergone a significant change in his personal life: from being a hardworking businessman whose main goal in life was material success (a goal that left little time for sharing life with his wife and their three sons), which brought about a divorce after almost fifteen years of marriage, to being a devoted family man, now sharing his life in a fuller, deeper way with his new wife, also divorced, and her four children along with his three children who had chosen to live with him. When asked by the interviewer why his present life that gives priority to attending to his newly formed family is better than his former life that was devoted almost exclusively to his business career, Brian could only say that in his present life he is happier. He referred to his present life as having new priorities and different values, but it became evident in the interview that what now is of value and a priority to him was based not on a wider, substantive view of what is the good life, but only on his present personal preferences. If his preferences should change, so will Brian's conception of the good. He acknowledged that the values of one person may conflict with the values of another and for this reason, having no other way to justify his values, he stressed that for him a fundamental principle for living life well is to maintain honest and clear communication with others. Likewise, a therapist who was interviewed, Margaret Oldham, emphasized the importance of having a clear sense of one's values, and she particularly stressed the necessity for each individual to take personal responsibility for living according to the values that they have chosen. Herein lies the basis of individual fulfillment for her—self-understanding and self-reliance. These convictions, moreover, she brings to her work as a therapist. Her role, as she sees it, is not to solve the problems of her clients, but to be their guide, helping them to understand and to give concrete form to their personal preferences. But, like Brian, she could offer no broader justification for the values that she has chosen or for those of her clients, and like him she emphasized the need for clear communication between people when their individual values lead to conflict; she also emphasized the importance of toleration when holding different values separates people. The self-understanding and self-reliance of individual fulfillment encouraged

---

breed selfishness but in fact is compatible with altruism. See Marsh, "We Aren't as Selfish as We Think."

26. Bellah et al., *Habits of the Heart* (1985 ed.), x.

by Margaret, the rewards of family life pursued by Brian, are laudable, personal attributes to be emulated by all. But, self-reliance devoid of a social context, family life as a little society formed to one's taste apart from the larger society, results in social isolation. That one's commitments to others rests only on one's personal preferences gives to these commitments a fragile foundation. The limitations evident in the ways Brian and Margaret thought about and articulated the reasons for their decisions and actions were not simply limitations of individuals, but limitations of our common culture, the researchers concluded. Shaping the way Brian and Margaret thought and spoke about their personal lives was the cultural language of individualism.[27]

At first glance, the responses of two others interviewed by the researchers—Joe Gorman and Wayne Bauer—present a striking contrast to the responses of Brian and Margaret. The responses of Joe and Wayne were chosen by the researchers, as were those of Brian and Margaret, as representative examples of the ways Americans make sense of their private and public lives. But, whereas for Brian and Margaret meaning and purpose were found primarily in private life, for Joe and Wayne their private lives gained meaning and purpose through their involvement in public life.

Joe Gorman was living and working in Suffolk, Massachusetts, a suburb outside of Boston, when he was interviewed. He had recently organized and executed with great success a celebration of the town's 250th anniversary. He worked for a large corporation that is located in Suffolk as the director of public relations, which means that civic work was part of his job. Yet, inspiring his efforts in bringing about the nine-month celebration was, more deeply, his love of Suffolk—its traditions, its families, its community life. Joe had grown up in Suffolk; his father had started the athletic program at the high school; to Joe Suffolk was home. Unlike Brian, who saw in his new family a way to realize his own individual goals in life, Joe found personal fulfillment in helping his community achieve its goals. Like Joe, Wayne Bauer sought personal fulfillment through public service, but unlike Joe's participation, Wayne's civic involvement took the form of political activism, this following a chaotic period in his young life that included a break with his family and a move across the country. In political activism he found a way to put the broken pieces of his life back together. His activism began in a tenant-landlord dispute that erupted in his neighborhood in Santa Monica, California. He experienced in the dispute the unfair advantage that the wealthy landlord had over the tenants, who were poor, Spanish-speaking immigrants. His organizing efforts with the tenants against the landlord led to his joining the Campaign for Economic Democracy (a political action organization based in California) and then being elected to the Rent Control Board of Santa Monica. For Wayne civic involvement such as this was rooted in the moral imperative of justice that gave coherence to his life. But, despite the priority that both Joe and Wayne gave to their commitment to public service, how they thought about and acted on this commitment was limited by the language of individualism that shaped their lives and their civic work.

27. Bellah et al., *Habits of the Heart* (1985 ed.), 3–8, 13–17; see also 44–48.

Joe's commitment to Suffolk was rooted in nostalgia, the desire to reconnect Suffolk to its traditions and to rekindle the community spirit of close-knit families that is the charm of a small town. In Joe's eyes, Suffolk was a little society formed to his own taste. In fact, three-quarters of the town's population had moved to Suffolk only within the past twenty-five years, most for reasons of convenience, such as Suffolk's proximity to Boston and its employment opportunities, and for its affordable housing. That Suffolk exists in the shadow of Boston, that life in Suffolk cannot avoid being affected by the complexities and problems of its metropolitan neighbor, this Joe's vision of Suffolk did not bring into view, and thus he could not provide the resources necessary for effectively integrating Suffolk with the larger society of which it was inescapably a part. Wayne Bauer's organizational work to empower tenants in their dispute with their landlord suffered a similar limitation. That the voices of the tenants be heard, that their claims against the landlord be fully represented in the dispute, this was a fundamental matter of justice in Wayne's view. But, when he was asked what would be a successful resolution to the dispute, that is, what would be an outcome that would be just for both the tenants and the landlord, Wayne had difficulty finding an answer. His view of justice was limited to defending the rights of the powerless in society and lacked a wider substantive view of what a just society is and how the goods of a society ought to be distributed in a way that is fair to all. Both Joe and Wayne were caring, generous individuals. But, the way they thought about and acted on the civic matters before them limited the effectiveness of their public service. The limitation did not lie in them as persons, but in the cultural language that shaped their civic involvement, this being the dominant language of individualism.[28]

Despite the differences between these four representative characters, they were profoundly similar in one respect—their "first language," according to the researchers, was the language of individualism, while their "second language," which distinguished them from one another, was derived from one of the distinct cultural traditions that make up American life. The individualism that shaped Brian's early life was a "utilitarian individualism," a devotion to economic success. (A historical example of this tradition, in the view of the researchers, was the life of Benjamin Franklin.) But, the individualism that marked Brian's life in his second marriage and the personal life and therapeutic work of Margaret was an "expressive individualism," an individualism centered on a life devoted to cultivating one's own values. (A historical example of this tradition is the life and writings of the poet Walt Whitman.) The public service of Joe and Wayne evoked a very different cultural tradition, one that fosters the civic and political participation of citizens as being necessary to the well-being of the republic. This is the cultural tradition of civic republicanism (exemplified historically in the political life of Thomas Jefferson). Others who were interviewed by the researchers drew upon the tradition of biblical religion, the cultural tradition shaping American life from the colonial period to the present day, this to explain the ethical and spiritual

---

28. Bellah et al., *Habits of the Heart* (1985 ed.), 8–13, 17–20.

meaning to their involvement in matters pertaining to their local community and the wider society (the life of the Puritan John Winthrop, the first governor of the Massachusetts Bay Colony, being a historical example). Yet, whether the individualism that was utilitarian or expressive in form, or the individualism that motivated civic and political participation, or the individualism that took shape in and through ethical and religious commitments, these differences, given voice by those who were interviewed, all shared a common presupposition (the basis of their first language)—the presupposition that the goals that we pursue in life as goods are at root arbitrary, based only on our individual preferences.[29]

But, these different forms of American individualism, when viewed broadly in the context of the traditions from which they come, also reveal a core value, Bellah and his associates emphasize, that runs through American history and that defines who we are as Americans—the intrinsic worth of the individual. "Whatever the differences among the traditions and the consequent differences in their understandings of individualism, there are some things they all share, things that are basic to American identity. We believe in the dignity, indeed the sacredness, of the individual," they state. What they intend through their study of the culture of individualism, then, is not to persuade Americans to abandon individualism as such, but rather they intend to address the tendencies within individualism that threaten the value that stands at its center. As cultural traditions, both civic republicanism and biblical religion have provided resources for sustaining the relationship between the individual and the larger society and thus the basis for integrating private life with public life, this to the well-being of the individual. With the dominance of utilitarian and expressive individualism in the present day, however, the countervailing influence of the cultural traditions of civic republicanism and biblical religion has been lost, in which case even they exhibit utilitarian and expressive forms of individualism, this made apparent in the more than two hundred interviews that the researchers conducted. Here religion readily becomes a private matter. Civic and political participation devolves into the pursuit of self-interest. But, if the bond between the individual and society is weakened or broken, then the well-being not only of the society but the individual is threatened. Thus, according to Bellah and his associates: "The question is whether an individualism in which the self has become the main form of reality can really be sustained. What is at issue is not simply whether self-contained individuals might withdraw from the public sphere to pursue purely private ends, but whether such individuals are capable of sustaining either a public *or* a private life."[30] Echoing in these words is Tocqueville's warning of despotism.

The rise of utilitarian and expressive individualism in the present day corresponds with the ascendancy of the market. But, in this correspondence, the culture of individualism is faced with a seemingly intractable problem: "Indeed, one of the

29. Bellah et al., *Habits of the Heart* (1985 ed.), 20–22, 27–35.
30. Bellah et al., *Habits of the Heart* (1985 ed.), 142–43.

conundrums of contemporary individualism is that it can combine an absolute belief in the freedom of individual choice with market determinism," Bellah and his associates point out. "But we believe this determinism is an ideological delusion: neither the global economy, nor the stock market, nor the profit margin can determine our institutional choices unless we as citizens let them. But the capacity to make institutional choices rests on cultural resources that are, along with material and social resources, seriously depleted."[31]

What fosters the two-pronged "ideological delusion" that, firstly, the market ultimately decides how we approach the institutional choices we face as a society, and, secondly, that this market determinism is nevertheless compatible with the freedom of the individual, is the understanding of individual freedom presupposed in the ideology of the market. Here freedom of choice is understood as a freedom *from*—freedom from the demands of others, whether from the demands of individuals or from social and institutional constraints. But a freedom such as this is in the end isolating, its power being only to this—to be ourselves, to choose our own values, to determine our own destiny, to live in the moment outside of the forces of history or present-day institutional expectations. In exercising a freedom such as this, we in effect separate ourselves from others and from the larger society. Herein lies the basis to Tocqueville's warning. If the value of individual freedom, which stands at the heart of American democracy, is understood and lived simply as a freedom from the demands imposed on us by others and by the larger society, this leading to self-isolation or to our withdrawing into little societies shaped to our taste, leaving the concerns of the larger society to others, then in matters both social and economic the market indeed decides. Missing in this understanding of freedom is a wider view of what freedom is *for*—the power we have for cooperating with one another to build a better life together; for putting in place the social means to realize collective goods; for acquiring the ability and summoning the desire to propose, debate, and negotiate collectively conceptions of the good life and the good society. To relinquish the exercise of this freedom for the sake of a purely private freedom was, in Tocqueville's eyes, the loss of freedom itself. Leaving the larger society to itself by breaking the bond between private life and public life eventuates only in the rise of some form of despotism. Bellah and his associates agree. But, in present-day American life the cultural resources needed to strengthen the bond between private and public life, this particularly through the traditions of civic republicanism and biblical religion, are overshadowed and weakened by the dominance of utilitarian and expressive individualism. Rather than having a foundation for dialogue about the good that we as a society seek in common or a harm that we collectively seek to avoid, we are left only with the possibility to communicate our preferences to one another, whether as individuals or as groups, in a manner that

---

31. Bellah et al., "Introduction to the Updated Edition" xxx.

is clear and honest, but having no other basis on which to come together in mutual understanding and practical agreement.[32]

Here is the basic reason for our inability as individuals to be moved to act collectively either in response to a harm that threatens us all or for a social good that requires on our part collective action for the well-being of all—the limitation that is inherent in the dominant cultural viewpoint that shapes what we see and how we act as a society—this as portrayed variously by the historian Rodgers and the sociologist Bellah and his colleagues. The limitation of this cultural viewpoint lies in our inability to see society as a cohesive whole through this dominant lens. Here we see society only in terms of its aggregated parts—the individual desires, decisions, and actions that make up the whole—thus giving us no way to establish a basis for shared understanding and for the willed cooperation of all within the society, either to realize a good in common or to avoid an evil that threatens us all. We experience the limitation of the dominant viewpoint acutely when as a society we are faced with the threat of harm that requires the cooperative actions of all within the society, but lack the cultural and institutional resources necessary to facilitate cooperation other than through governmental coercion. The dilemma intensifies when the threat of harm requires our willed cooperation not only on a societal level but on a global level as well. The threat of climate change presently facing us as a world population provides an illustrative example.

Climate Change as an Example

In 1988 climate change (also referred to as global warming) became a controversial issue, not in the halls of science where the reality of climate change was being investigated, but in the realm of public opinion and public policy. In that year, James Hansen, a climate scientist at NASA, appeared before a US congressional committee on climate change, there to declare that according to current scientific research the earth is warming at a significant rate, and that one cause of the increase in global warming is human activity, specifically the burning of fossil fuels that releases carbon dioxide (CO_2) into Earth's atmosphere, which prevents atmospheric heat from passing into the stratosphere, thus creating a greenhouse effect. The probability that global warming is simply the result of natural occurrences, Hansen thought, is no more than 1 percent. "The global warming is now large enough that we can ascribe with a high degree of confidence a cause and effect relationship to the greenhouse effect," Hansen stated.[33] Hansen's bold statement, reported widely by the media, brought climate change to the forefront of the public's attention. Indeed, that year *Time* magazine, rather than

---

32. Bellah et al., *Habits of the Heart* (1985 ed.) 23–25, 210–11.

33. Quoted in Oreskes and Conway, *Merchants of Doubt*, 184.

present an individual as "Person of the Year," presented "Endangered Earth" as "Planet of the Year."[34]

Also, that year, for the purpose of establishing an ongoing, productive relationship between the scientific community and the policymakers of the world's governments regarding climate change, the United Nations formed the Intergovernmental Panel on Climate Change (IPCC). The purpose of the panel is to assess and present the current state of the science on climate change to governmental policymakers and more broadly to the people of the world. The panel's first assessment was presented in 1990, with subsequent assessments in 1995, 2001, 2007, and 2014. The IPCC's sixth assessment will be completed in 2022. The work of the IPCC combines two disparate endeavors—science (knowledge) and policy formation (action)—for the sake of achieving an outcome that requires both, the goal of the collaboration between climate scientists and the world's governments being a science-based set of international policies that control the harmful effects of climate change. Each IPCC assessment report is the result of hundreds of climate scientists from many nations working together: first some collaborate in writing teams, each team reporting on a particular aspect of climate change; then other climate scientists are given the work of each team for critical review (peer review); finally, the assessment report is presented to the world's governments for review. To facilitate this last step in the assessment process, the report concludes with a "Summary for Policymakers," which presents the main conclusions of the assessment in a form that is accessible to the nonexpert. Because the Summary is the place in the assessment where scientists and policymakers meet, those representing the world's governments have the opportunity to contribute to the shape of the final version of the Summary by voting on each sentence of the Summary to either accept it or alter it or eliminate it. Unanimous agreement is required for each sentence as written to remain in the Summary.[35]

One sentence in the Summary of the Second Assessment (1995), for example, provoked a sharp dispute during the voting process. The topic of concern had to do with attributing the cause of climate warming to human activity. The specific matter in question was the adjective that the lead author of the chapter on the detection and the attribution of the causes of climate change in the body of the report had used to describe the human influence on climate change: there is an "appreciable" human influence, he had stated. This assertion was then restated in the Summary. The delegate from Saudi Arabia strongly objected to the use of the word "appreciable," its implication being that the evidence of human influence was clearly perceptible and measurable. One of the lead scientists of the second assessment agreed with this objection. Of the several alternative words that were then considered, "discernible" was finally judged to be the most appropriate. Thus, the sentence that appeared in the Summary

---

34. Dessler, *Introduction to Modern Climate Change*, 220–21.

35. Dessler and Parson, *Science and Politics*, 62–63; Dessler, *Introduction to Modern Climate Change*, 8–10.

was as follows: "The balance of evidence suggests that there is a discernible human influence on global climate."[36]

This dispute over one word in one sentence in the Summary of the 1995 Second Assessment of the IPCC provides for us a window into the way that climate science, indeed all science, works. In the resolution of this dispute, we have on display two key characteristics of science—the desire to know that drives scientific investigation and the caution that science employs in its advance of knowledge. Minimizing the claim of human influence on climate change from "appreciable" to "discernible" was a cautious move on the part of the climate scientists that reflected the state of the science at the time, but also expressed the tendency in science to be conservative in its claims to knowledge.[37] An advance in scientific knowledge takes place only on the basis of evidence, this derived from scientific observation and experimentation, not simply the work of individual scientists but the collective work of the scientific community. Thus, an advance in scientific knowledge requires consensus within the relevant community of working scientists. The five assessment reports on the current state of the science of climate change that the IPCC has produced thus far, from 1990 to 2014, demonstrate just such an advance in scientific knowledge. Moreover, the IPCC's assessment reports, insofar as they reflect the consensus of the community of climate scientists, are regarded by the scientific community and by the world's policymakers as authoritative statements on the current state of knowledge regarding climate change.[38] Thus, that the IPCC's statements regarding the attribution of the cause of climate change on human activity, based on growing evidence, grew stronger with each assessment was indeed notable.

The First Assessment in 1990 had made no definitive statement regarding human activity as a cause of climate change; this came in the Second Assessment of 1995 (a "discernible" human influence). The Third Assessment in 2001 offered a stronger statement, but with a note of uncertainty: the cause of global warming is "likely" to be human activity (a 66 percent chance of being the case). With the Fourth and Fifth Assessments came far stronger statements: according to the Fourth Assessment (2007), the chance of human activity being the cause of climate change is "very likely" (a 90 percent chance); according to the Fifth Assessment (2014), that human influence is the cause of global warming is "extremely likely" (a 95 percent chance). Yet, in these strong, definitive statements, there is still a note of caution. Scientific conclusions based on strong evidence, although definitive, remain provisional in the eyes of the scientific community. New evidence might appear that would challenge the present state of the science. But, in 2014, in the eyes of the worldwide community of climate scientists, such an occurrence was considered highly unlikely. James Hansen's bold declaration regarding the cause of global warming in 1988 to a congressional

36. Quoted in Oreskes and Conway, *Merchants of Doubt*, 204–5.
37. Oreskes and Conway, *Merchants of Doubt*, 206–7.
38. Dessler and Parson, *Science and Politics*, 40–51, 60–63.

committee on climate change, although perhaps lacking in scientific caution, nevertheless demonstrated remarkable foresight.[39]

Climate change became a controversial issue in the aftermath of Hansen's congressional testimony, but only outside the halls of science. The controversy was ignited and fueled by various incendiary means: denying global warming outright; acknowledging that the earth was warming but denying that the warming was anthropogenic (human-caused); and attacking individual climate scientists directly, either by misrepresenting their work or by questioning the intentions underlying their work. Some of the protagonists opposing the empirical claims of climate science regarding the causes of global warming were themselves scientists, but these scientists were not climate scientists engaged in current research. Their oppositional views were expressed, not in the peer-reviewed science journals, but in the opinion section of newspapers and through other media outlets. Their oppositional voices blended with other oppositional voices coming from a wide variety of sources—think tanks, institutes, blogs, websites, speeches on the floor of the US House and Senate, the Twitter account of the former US president—all reflecting the interests of and with funding from the fossil fuel industry. The historians of science Naomi Oreskes and Erik Conway point out that by the 1990s the fossil fuel industry was facing a problem generated by climate science much like the problem that science created for the tobacco industry in the 1960s. In both cases, advances in scientific knowledge, based on evidence, enabled science to address directly the issue of causality regarding the harm that smoking and the harm that the burning of fossil fuels causes, thus giving science the capability to demonstrate in the 1960s that smoking causes cancer and in the 1990s that burning fossil fuels causes climate change. To deal with this threat to its market profitability, the fossil fuel industry adopted the same strategy that had been employed by the tobacco industry—sow doubt about the causal claims of science. "Doubt is our product" stated a memo issued by an executive of the tobacco industry in 1969, to be sold along with its primary product, which is tobacco. Such a strategy is highly effective in shaping public opinion because outside of the scientific community most people do not have a clear understanding of how science works, particularly of how science makes causal claims. This strategy of obfuscation, furthermore, is abetted unwittingly by the news media that seek to give fair representation to all sides of a controversy, thus presenting the claims of a climate scientist alongside the oppositional claims of a scientist who is not a climate scientist in such a way that each view is given equal weight. But this is a false equivalence. The claim of the climate scientist represents the consensus of the worldwide community of climate scientists, whereas the opposing claim represents the view of one, a claim based on no current peer-reviewed climate research, a claim that stands apart from the scientific consensus. That the controversy is given public expression by the news media, however, is to the benefit of the fossil fuel industry, because the controversy sows doubt in the mind of the public and such

---

39. Dessler, *Introduction to Modern Climate Change*, 220–28.

doubt breeds inaction.[40] In which case, this question presents itself: Is the present-day controversy regarding climate change really about science at all? If not, what is the controversy about?

In the eyes of climate scientists, the controversy over climate change that is taking place in the realms of public opinion and public policy is not about science—the controversy is not a legitimate scientific debate regarding the nature and causes of climate change. But this point is not readily apparent to the public for two reasons. The first has to do with the scientists themselves who are doing the work of climate science. Oreskes and Conway point to the reluctance on the part of scientists to engage in public controversy regarding the matters of science. Scientists see the primary purpose of their work to be advancing scientific knowledge, not disseminating it to the wider public or defending it against attacks coming from outside the scientific community. Moreover, insofar as the advance of scientific knowledge is the result of a collective effort on the part of scientists, there is a reluctance on the part of individual scientists to take on the challenge of informing the public regarding the truth of climate science.[41] One notable exception to this tendency within the scientific community to be silent in the face of denial regarding climate change is the prominent voice of the climate scientist Michael Mann, who has wholeheartedly engaged in what he calls "the climate wars." His motivation, he states, is this: "Scientists who study climate change and its potential impacts understand better than anyone the nature of the climate change threat. It would, in my view, be irresponsible for us to silently stand by while industry-funded climate change deniers succeed in confusing and distracting the public and dissuading our policy makers from taking appropriate actions."[42]

The second reason that the public fails to see the controversy regarding climate change for what it is—a controversy that is in fact not about the science of climate change—has to do with the nature of scientific knowledge itself. Scientific knowledge is based on evidence. The stronger the evidence, the stronger the claim made by science to know the truth. The strongest claim science can make is a causal claim—the claim that science has demonstrated the truth of the matter (smoking causes cancer). However, that the causal claim made by science is based on statistical evidence (in which case, words such as "likely" or "very likely" are used) can make the truth claim of science seem unsettled in the eyes of the nonscientist (smoking causes cancer, but not all who smoke contract cancer). Accordingly, the public's lack of understanding of how science works, particularly with regard to making a causal claim, gives those who deny the fact of climate change, or those who deny that climate change is caused by

40. Oreskes and Conway, *Merchants of Doubt*, 5–9, 32–35, 197–215, 240–43.

41. Oreskes and Conway, *Merchants of Doubt*, 262–65.

42. Mann, *Hockey Stick and the Climate Wars*, 254; see 53–58. See also Mann and Toles, *Madhouse Effect*; Mann, *New Climate War*.

human activity, the ability to sow doubt regarding the conclusions of climate science and thus keep the controversy alive.[43]

Consider the distinction that climate scientists make between weather and climate. That Portland, Oregon, registered a temperature of 116°F on June 29, 2021, is an example of weather—the condition of the atmosphere in that place and at that time. Was this weather event in the Pacific Northwest simply an anomaly, or was it an indication that the climate is changing—climate being stable weather patterns statistically observed over a long period of time, at least for several decades? For the scientist to demonstrate that the climate is changing, some element of the climate of a specific region, such as temperature, is measured and recorded in one period of time, to then be compared with the statistical data on temperature from a different period or periods of time of the same region. A change in the statistical data regarding temperature indicates a change in the climate. A long-term change in the global average temperature, furthermore, would provide evidence that Earth's climate overall is changing. This has indeed been the case—the global average temperature has risen throughout the twentieth century and continues to rise in the twenty-first century. That today's global climate is changing, that Earth is warming, is "unequivocal," the IPCC states. The extreme heat in Portland, Oregon, was not simply an odd weather event but a stark warning of our changing climate. But, could this period of global warming simply be episodic, that is, a natural variation to be followed by a cooling period? A response to this question requires assessing today's global warming in the wider context of Earth's changing climate over an extended period of time.[44]

Michael Mann and his colleagues undertook the task to do just this—to measure and record the surface temperature of the Northern Hemisphere (the part of the earth with the most available data) from the eleventh century to the twentieth century. Since the temperature data of most of this time period predates the use of instruments that measure temperature directly, such as thermometers, temperature data from this period is derived indirectly by observing the imprint that the climate of the past has left as physical, chemical, or biological evidence—for example, in ice cores extracted by drilling deep into glaciers and ice sheets, lake and ocean sediments, corals, and tree rings. As a lead author in the IPCC's Third Assessment (2001), Mann, in conjunction with his colleagues, presented the results of research in the body of the report and then in the form of a graph in the Summary for Policymakers. One scientist observed that the temperature data as presented in the graph resembled the shape of a hockey stick lying on its back with its blade turned upward. The top portion of the handle of the hockey stick, which is the temperature data from the eleventh to the fourteenth century, depicted what has been termed "the medieval warm period," this to be followed by a decline in average temperature from the fifteenth to the nineteenth century (the bottom portion of the hockey stick), a period referred to as "the Little Ice Age." As

43. Oreskes and Conway, *Merchants of Doubt*, 34–35.
44. Dessler, *Introduction to Modern Climate Change*, 1–2, 4–5, 17–21, 28–29.

depicted in the graph, this cooling period ended abruptly with a sharp rise in temperature that runs through the twentieth century (the blade of the hockey stick). When the researchers included instrumental temperature readings for this latter period, the rise in temperature became even more pronounced—the upturned blade of the hockey stick more acute. In the end, the graph depicts a level of climate warming in the twentieth century that far exceeds the warming of the climate in any other period of the past millennium. This finding on the part of Mann and his colleagues that the recent rise in climate warming is anomalous when viewed in the context of the entire millennium suggested, Mann thought, that human activity is involved in the warming. But he added this caution: "We had established correlation—the anomalous warming that we documented coincided with the human-caused ramp-up in greenhouse gas concentrations—but we hadn't established causality." The confidence to make such a causal claim came only a short time later, this based on published research using climate modeling that estimated the causal effects that changes in natural factors would have had on the climate during the millennium—changes such as an increase in the output of solar energy (warming) and the eruption of volcanic gases into the atmosphere that block the light of the sun (cooling). Although natural factors such as these could explain the warming and cooling periods through the nineteenth century, such natural factors could not explain the increase in warming in the twentieth century. Such a sharp rise in global average temperature could only be explained in terms of human influences, particularly the increasing concentration of greenhouse gases in the atmosphere due to the burning of fossil fuels. Thus, according to Michael Mann, "The conclusion was clear: Natural factors could explain the temperature changes of the past millennium through the dawn of the Industrial Revolution, but only human influences could explain the unusual recent warming. Causality was at least tentatively established now."[45]

The causal claim, based on statistical evidence, became only stronger in the Fourth and Fifth Assessments of the IPCC. That Portland, Oregon, registered a temperature of 116°F in June 2021 is a discrete fact; that the IPCC in 2014 (with the Fifth Assessment) judged human activity to be the dominant cause of climate warming in the modern age, a judgment made with 95 percent certainty ("extremely likely"), gave to the causal claim the status of a statistical fact. Whether as a discrete fact or as a statistical fact, once science determines the truth of the matter, science considers the matter settled. In which case, the scientist deems any further debate on the matter fruitless and certainly uninteresting. Unless strong new counterevidence should be ascertained, science moves on.[46] Why, then, does the controversy regarding climate change in the realm of public opinion and public policy continue in the present day? If science considers its judgment regarding the anthropogenic causes of climate change as settled, why does the present-day controversy over climate change continue to

45. Mann, *Hockey Stick and the Climate Wars*, 57–58; see xvii–xx, 53–58.
46. Dessler and Parson, *Science and Politics*, 47.

treat the matter as unsettled? What is the controversy really about? The controversy is certainly not about the scientific knowledge of climate change as such, but it does concern public action and this in relation to public policy regarding climate change.

Doubt breeds inaction. Those who challenge the findings of climate science do so, not to advance the scientific knowledge of climate change, but to foment doubt regarding the findings of climate science and thereby distract and confuse the public regarding the very real threat of climate change. Still, the strategy of sowing doubt takes place under the guise of science. For example, climate scientists have demonstrated that between 1970 and 2013 Earth's surface temperature rose rapidly. Within this long-term warming period, however, there were short-term variations, such as an unusually hot year (the El Niño event of 1998) and an unusually cool year (the La Niña event of 2008). These short-term variations, according to the climate scientists, had no effect on the long-term trajectory of climate warming, and thus they were judged to be natural variations (natural cycles) unrelated to human-caused climate change. But, by highlighting these short-term variations, those who deny the reality of climate change seek to offer a convincing counterargument that either climate warming has stopped (say, since the hot year of 1998) or climate warming is not occurring (given the cool year of 2008). Scientists refer to this strategy as "cherry-picking"—that is, selecting specific data from the whole data set to achieve a desired conclusion, but one that stands at odds with the conclusion that the whole data set would yield. The outcome of such a strategy is that it sows doubt regarding the threat of climate change, which then breeds inaction, both on the part of the public and on the part of policymakers regarding the actions that must be taken to address the global harm that climate change is presently inflicting and will inflict on Earth in the near future.[47]

Of the actions that must be taken to avoid the inevitable consequences of global warming, what action do those who challenge the findings of climate science most oppose? According to Oreskes and Conway, it is this: governmental regulation. That the global harm that is caused by climate warming comes from the use of fossil fuels, and that this source of energy is the primary means by which the world economy moves, links free markets with the global harm of climate change. Indeed, Oreskes and Conway emphasize, the harm that comes from climate change is at root the result of a global market failure. Market exchanges include costs and benefits for the parties involved in the exchange, but if there is a cost that comes from the exchange that is imposed on others who are not party to the exchange, that is, an external cost that lies outside of the market exchange, this represents a market failure (an inefficiency in the market). As we saw in Chapter 4, Milton Friedman referred to such external costs as "neighborhood effects." Climate change is such a neighborhood effect (worldwide), a negative externality that is borne by industrialized nations (the primary source of the problem) and nonindustrialized nations alike—indeed an external cost borne

---

47. Dessler, *Introduction to Modern Climate Change*, 22–23, 116–17. Dessler and Parson, *Science and Politics*, 106–8.

by the whole of planet Earth. Markets alone cannot rectify this failure. Government intervention is necessary. Moreover, given the global nature of this market failure, only the coordinated response on the part of all the world's governments will be sufficient to meet this present and future environmental threat. It is precisely the need for governmental regulation to address the harm of climate change that evokes opposition from the fossil fuel industry and all those who espouse the ideology of free markets. The voices of opposition, however, direct their ire not only at governmental regulation but also at climate science and individual scientists working on climate change. Oreskes and Conway observe: "What this all adds up to . . . is that the doubt-mongering campaigns we have followed were not about science. They were about the proper role of government, particularly in redressing market failures." But, because the findings of climate science regarding the global harm of climate change clearly demonstrate the need for governmental regulation to address this market failure, and this the proponents of the free market are unwilling to accept, Oreskes and Conway point out that "the enemies of government regulation of the marketplace became the enemies of science."[48]

The ongoing controversy regarding climate change is not about what we know or do not know regarding climate change and its causes, but about what we ought to do or not do regarding climate change—the controversy concerns decisions and the actions that result from these decisions, and not only decisions by individuals, but, more importantly, decisions by governments about policy. Science does not make decisions for us. What we gain from science is understanding, the empirical and theoretical knowledge of the world that can inform our decisions. Our decisions and the actions that issue from these decisions are based on our values—what we consider to be important. But our values (hence our normative judgments) need facts (hence science) if our values are to be based on objective reality, and if our values are to be reliable guides for making not only personal decisions but also governmental policy decisions. Those who refute the conclusions of climate science do so, not for reasons of science, but for reasons of value, particularly for the value of protecting the free market, which includes ensuring that the primary energy source that drives the free market—the use of fossil fuels—will continue to do so in an unrestricted manner. This value judgment, however, is made at the expense of the scientific facts regarding climate change.[49]

The political scientist Jennifer Hochschild would understand this strategy. We saw in her study of the connection between values, the perception of facts, and public policy, which we considered above, how the misperception of facts can shape our values (where you stand depends on what you see), which in turn shapes our political attitudes and policy preferences as citizens. Those who distort the facts of climate science know this well. The ongoing controversy regarding the science of climate change

48. Oreskes and Conway, *Merchants of Doubt*, 262; see also 133–35, 236–39, 246–55.

49. Dessler and Parson, *Science and Politics*, 35–40, 51–60.

is at root a conflict brought about by the competing values that fuel the climate wars (the value of protecting the environment versus the value of protecting the free market). But the controversy is also a battle over the representation or misrepresentation of the facts concerning climate change. Can getting the facts right—presenting the facts of climate warming clearly and accurately to the public—end the controversy? Hochschild points out that facts alone do little to change values that are rooted in deep-seated predispositions, this particularly when facts are presented to change deep-seated political attitudes and policy preferences. Only when the facts are seen in a different light—combined with a value that provides an alternative viewpoint—can facts effectively change deep-seated attitudes. The alternative viewpoint (value) widens our view by bringing a different perspective to bear on the facts, thus enabling us to see the facts in a wider context (what you see depends on where you stand).[50] The fact that Portland, Oregon, registered a temperature of 116°F on one day in June is indisputable, but this fact might be seen and dismissed simply as a variable weather event, particularly by one who views the findings of climate science as a threat to economic growth. However, for those who viewed this day of extreme heat with concern for the environment, particularly with concern for what science has demonstrated as the harmful consequences of global warming not only in the present but in the future, this day was seen in a very different light. From the viewpoint of concern for the well-being of the environment, the fact of this extreme weather event had a very different meaning—a foreshadowing of the harm that is to come.

That extreme weather events in the present day are increasing in number and severity throughout the world—during the summer of 2021, for example, there were extreme heat waves in the Pacific Northwest and in Siberia, Russia; massive wildfires in California, Oregon, Greece, and Siberia due to extreme heat and drought; and damaging floods in New York City, western Germany, and China's Henan province due to excessive rainfall—gives climate change an insistence that calls for our attention, and thus makes our being inattentive to or dismissive of the statistical fact of climate change difficult to maintain as a personal conviction. For this reason, the fossil fuel industry has adopted an alternative strategy to breed inaction regarding climate change, a strategy that Michael Mann refers to as "a softer form of denialism"—the strategy of deflection in which attention on climate change, and thus the responsibility to address climate change, shifts from the business practices of corporations to the personal behavior of individuals.[51] For example, in 2004 BP, the multinational oil and gas corporation, introduced on its website a "carbon footprint calculator" to be used by consumers to determine the carbon footprint (CO_2 emissions) of their personal road and air travel. Whether the carbon footprint calculator is simply an attempt on BP's part to raise consumer awareness of the problem of climate change or a strategy to deflect attention from its corporate practices regarding the production and use of

---

50. Hochschild, "Where You Stand," 321–24.

51. Mann, *New Climate War*, 3; see also 63–68.

fossil fuels and thus a strategy to deflect attention from corporate accountability to individual accountability, what is clear is that the model that BP presents to consumers to address the threat of climate change reduces effective action regarding climate change to the individual desires, decisions, and actions of consumers. What BP does not present is a plan for institutional change. In other words, the model for action here regarding climate change is the market. Effective action that addresses the threat of climate change is being viewed through the lens (the value) of what Daniel Rodgers referred to above as the dominant social metaphor of the age—the market. But, effective action to limit climate change requires more than a change in individual behavior. The harm that climate warming is presently inflicting on the global environment, and the greater harm that is certain to come in the future, requires collective action on the part of all—the world's governments, the world's markets, and indeed the individual acts of the people of the world, whose decisions and actions maintain the social institutions that shape our world community.

The IPCC's recent report (from August 2021), which is the first chapter of the Sixth Assessment (the report of Working Group I), presents the present state of climate science regarding the causes and consequences of climate change in the starkest terms yet. The Summary for Policymakers reads like a scene from a doctor's office in which the doctor, sitting before a patient whose health is deteriorating rapidly due to alcohol addiction, tells the patient in clear but disturbing terms that their addictive drinking has thus far caused irremediable damage to their body, something that they must now live with, but by taking decisive action now to stop the drinking of alcohol, the patient can avoid suffering the most severe consequences that will come from continued drinking. Should the patient choose an intermediate response to the diagnosis (say, choosing to drink moderately), harmful consequences will result that will exacerbate the bodily damage that has already occurred and will cause new damage, but the consequences will perhaps not be as severe as taking no remedial action at all. Note: The doctor's proper role here is to inform the patient; the patient is the one who must choose to act or not act in response to this information, this not only in regard to their own health but also with regard to the well-being of their family both now and in the future.

Consider now words from the Summary for Policymakers: "It is unequivocal that human influence has warmed the atmosphere, ocean and land," thus causing "widespread and rapid changes" in the atmosphere and on the Earth's surface (A.1). "Human-induced climate change is already affecting many weather and climate extremes in every region across the globe. Evidence of observed changes in extremes such as heatwaves, heavy precipitation, droughts, and tropical cyclones, and, in particular, the attribution to human influence, has strengthened" since the Fifth Assessment (A.3). In the 2015 Paris Agreement, the outcome of the twenty-first United Nations Climate Change Conference, the world's governments made voluntary pledges to limit their greenhouse gas emissions to keep the global temperature from increasing no more than 1.5°C above preindustrial levels, a goal that sets the limit for the increase in temperature notably lower than the 2.0°C limit set by earlier UN conferences. In the past two decades of the twenty-first century (2001–2020), the global surface temperature has increased by 0.99°C above preindustrial levels (A.1.2). Environmental harm has already occurred. The extent of further harm to the environment depends on the rate at which the world's governments reduce greenhouse gas emissions in the future (even the rise in global surface temperature of a fraction of a degree greatly increases harm to the environment). The Summary predicts: "Global surface temperature will continue to increase until at least the mid-century under all emissions scenarios considered. Global warming of 1.5°C and 2.0°C will be exceeded during the twenty-first century unless deep reductions in CO_2 and other greenhouse gas emissions occur in the coming decades" (B.1). The world community, therefore, is faced with a decision regarding the severity of climate change in the future: By the end of the century, the global surface temperature, averaged over the years 2081–2100, will very likely rise by 1.0°C to 1.8°C above preindustrial levels according to a very low emissions scenario, by 2.1°C to 3.5°C according to an intermediate emissions scenario, and by 3.3°C to 5.7°C according to a very high emissions scenario (B.1.1). With each level of temperature increase, the severity of environmental harm increases proportionally. Moreover, the harm extends indefinitely and irreversibly into the future. "Many changes due to past and future greenhouse gas emissions are irreversible for centuries to millennia, especially changes in the ocean, ice sheets and global sea level" (B.5). What, then, is required of the world's governments in order to limit the harm of global warming? "From a physical science perspective, limiting human-induced global warming to a specific level requires limiting cumulative CO_2 emissions, reaching at least net zero CO_2 emissions, along with strong reductions in other greenhouse gas emissions" (D.1).[52]

Climate science has made clear to the world the threat that the world faces regarding climate warming, the cause of climate warming, and the actions that must be taken to mitigate the present and future harm of climate warming. The actual decisions to limit and eventually to eliminate greenhouse gas emissions and the concrete actions to be taken to accomplish this goal on a global scale, however, lie not with the climate scientists but first and foremost with the world's governments, particularly with the representatives from 197 nations who convened in Glasgow, Scotland, from October 31 to November 12, 2021, at the twenty-sixth UN Climate Change Conference of the Parties (the world's nations) with the purpose of hastening action toward realizing the goals initially set by the 1992 Framework Convention on Climate Change, the first international treaty on climate change, and more recently by the 2015 Paris Agreement. Given the complexity of global warming and the worldwide coordination required to address the crisis of global warming, effective action must begin here in the halls of government. But, insofar as climate change affects us all in comprehensive ways—how

52. Intergovernmental Panel on Climate Change, "IPCC, 2021."

we work, where we live, what we eat, how we construct or modify our houses, how we travel, our health, our recreation, our families, our communities, our place in nature—the crisis of climate change necessarily involves us all in deeply personal ways and thus the crisis calls for effective action from each of us individually, particularly as collective action, as well as from markets and governments, the social institutions that we as individuals must hold accountable for responding effectively to the crisis (the work of civil society). The crisis affects us all. An effective response to what is the undeniable threat of global warming must come from us all, from each as a distinctive part of the whole—civil society, markets, and government.

Is the collective action that is required to address the threat of climate change effectively, this on a societal and global scale, possible? This is the challenge that we face as a world community. Only by finding a basis of shared understanding, one that calls for the willed cooperation of all, will we as a world community respond in effective ways to the threat of climate change. If we approach the threat of climate change on the basis of self-interest alone, this whether as individuals, through markets, or in terms of national interest, we will fail to meet the threat in its enormity. Why?

From the viewpoint of self-interest, the global good (the common good) that would be realized by checking the progress of climate change through collaborative action does not come into view and thus does not move us to act collectively. The challenge of addressing the growing harm of climate change at the international level well illustrates this point. All nations of the world share in the benefit of a stable and habitable climate, but the benefit is realized only if all nations fully cooperate in taking action to attain this goal. Herein lies the challenge facing the world community. If for reasons of national self-interest one nation exempts itself from cooperating in this common endeavor due to the costs involved but at the same time assumes the ongoing cooperation of the other nations, then the effect of its noncooperation will be seen by the one nation as inconsequential to the overall effort to attain the benefit that is shared by all nations, including the noncooperative nation, thus giving the nation a reason to not incur the costs of cooperation and the incentive to be a free rider. On the other hand, in that all nations face the same decision to cooperate or not based on national self-interest (no international authority or world government exists to enforce cooperation), the assumption of global cooperation on the part of all nations may be seen by any one nation as unrealistic and thus a reason and an incentive to not incur the costs of cooperation. Indeed, seeking a beneficial outcome, such as the benefit of a stable and habitable climate, from nations acting on national self-interest alone leads to what the biologist Garrett Hardin described as "the tragedy of the commons." The tragedy lies in the inevitability of a negative outcome when the individual good is pursued at the expense of a shared good that is a free resource available to all—the result being that in the end even the individual good is not attained. Hardin uses the example of a pasture that is open to all herders without restriction to show that the inevitable outcome of the use of this free resource will be the overgrazing of the pasture. "Freedom in a commons brings ruin to all," he concludes.[53] The example that we have before us is the unrestricted use by the nations of the world of fossil fuels that emit carbon dioxide into the atmosphere, this to move a world economy (the benefit), each nation doing so without paying the cost of environmental harm to all (hence a free resource to the emitter), the inevitable outcome being the destructive warming that threatens our common resource—planet Earth.

Taking action to stop climate change involves costs as well as benefits. The task of balancing the costs and benefits of taking action on a global scale, this in terms of each nation's self-interest, falls to the policymakers of the world's governments. But, given the imbalance between the costs and the benefits of taking action to limit greenhouse gas emissions in the present day by the nations of the world, there is little incentive for the world's nations each to take strong action to address climate warming. The reason for the imbalance between the costs and the benefits of taking action to stop climate warming, and thus the reason for inaction on the part of the world's nations, lies in the physics of climate warming. Unlike methane, another potent greenhouse gas, which stays in the atmosphere for about ten years after having been emitted, carbon dioxide once emitted resides in the atmosphere for hundreds of years. Moreover, insofar as the industrialized nations have been emitting carbon dioxide into the atmosphere through the burning of fossil fuels since the dawn of the industrial age, the accumulation of carbon dioxide in the atmosphere is of such a magnitude that the continued use of fossil fuels at the present rate will warm the planet for thousands of years. Even a sharp reduction in the use of fossil fuels now will not slow the increase of the global surface temperature for several decades. Thus, as we saw above, the IPCC states in the Sixth Assessment: "Global surface temperature will continue to increase until at least the mid-century under all emissions scenarios considered" (B.1). Harm from climate change has already taken place and will remain with us to some degree through our lifetime. Therefore, the full benefit of taking decisive action to reduce and then eliminate greenhouse gas emissions in the present day, particularly the burning of fossil fuels, will accrue to those who live in the future age, whereas the cost for fundamentally transforming how we produce and use energy in order to curb climate change will be incurred by those who live in the present age. Herein lies the imbalance between the costs and benefits of taking action now to stop climate change, an imbalance that inhibits a strong cooperative response on the part of the world's nations.[54] Indeed, despite the success of the 2015 Paris Agreement that attained commitments (voluntary pledges) from the world's nations to meet the collective goal of limiting the increase in global surface temperature to 1.5°C, concrete actions taken by the world's nations have not kept pace with achieving this goal or with reducing the overall threat

---

53. Hardin, "Tragedy of the Commons," 1244.

54. Dessler, *Introduction to Modern Climate Change*, 84–85, 90–92, 136–39, 188–90. For an analysis of this cost-benefit imbalance from the viewpoint of an economist, see Tirole, *Economics for the Common Good*, 195–206.

of climate warming. The high cost of taking action now provides a persuasive reason and incentive for inaction.[55]

Inaction in the face of climate change (whether due to individual self-interest, market incentives, or governmental priorities), however, involves high costs as well. The extreme weather events that we are currently experiencing worldwide due to climate warming, and the global sea level that will continue to rise through the twenty-first century, posing a growing danger to all coastal regions of the world, are indications of the costs—the environmental harms—that we face as a world community now, and of the greater costs that we will pass on to future generations if we fail to take decisive action. The question, then, is this: What will move us as a world community to face these environmental costs honestly and to take collective action now to make a substantial down payment toward the elimination of these environmental costs in the future? Fear, suggests the journalist David Wallace-Wells, the emotion that he seeks to evoke in his portrait of "The Uninhabitable Earth" that awaits us and future generations if we do not act now to curb climate warming.[56] The climate scientist Michael Mann disagrees: "An objective assessment of the scientific evidence is adequate to motivate immediate and concerted action on climate. There is no need to overstate it," he asserts. The scientific evidence regarding the growing harm of climate warming presents a disturbing picture, but "recognizing that dangerous climate change is here already is, in an odd way, empowering. For there is no 'danger' target to worry about missing. It is too late to prevent harmful impacts—they're already here. *But how much* additional danger we encounter is largely up to us." An effective response to climate warming entails "both urgency and agency," Mann emphasizes. "Fear," on the other hand, "does not motivate, and appealing to it is often counterproductive, as it tends to distance people from the problem, leading them to disengage from, doubt, or even dismiss it."[57]

The IPCC's recent report reflects this sense of urgency and agency. The Summary states that presently "many weather and climate extremes in every region across the globe" are occurring due to "human-induced climate change" (A.3). The Summary further states: "It is *virtually certain* that global mean sea level will continue to rise over the 21st century" (B.5.3). These factual statements based on scientific evidence are a call for action, not panic. Accordingly, these factual statements are presented along with projections based on climate models regarding possible climate futures. As the rise in global surface temperature will vary significantly by the end of the century, this according to different greenhouse gas emissions scenarios (from very low to very high), as we saw above, so the rise in global sea level by 2100 will also vary significantly according to different emissions scenarios. That the global sea level will rise is virtually certain according to scientific evidence, this due to the melting of

---

55. Dessler and Parson, *Science and Politics*, 176–79, 189–92.

56. Wallace-Wells, *Uninhabitable Earth*, 157.

57. Mann, *New Climate War*, 179–82; see also 205–17.

glaciers and ice sheets and to the warming of the ocean which expands as its waters warm, but the extent of the sea level rise will vary according to the actions taken by the world community now to limit greenhouse gas emissions: The likely rise in global sea level (relative to 1995–2014) will be 0.28–0.55 m according to a very low emissions scenario, 0.32–0.62 m according to a low emissions scenario, 0.44–0.76 m according to an intermediate emissions scenario, and 0.63–1.01 m according to a very high emissions scenario (B.5.3). With each fraction of a meter rise in global sea level comes greater destruction from coastal flooding and powerful storm surges throughout the world. The Florida Keys and most of Miami-Dade County in Florida, for example, will be inundated at high tide with a sea level rise at the level of the intermediate emissions scenario, while the destructive storm surges that New Orleans suffered during Hurricane Katrina will worsen and become more frequent.[58] The future of climate change lies in our hands as a world community. This is made clear in the IPCC's report. The time to act is now.

But, does knowing the facts of climate change and having before us the possible options that might be taken by us to avoid the worst future consequences of climate warming provide sufficient motivation for us, the world community, particularly the policymakers of the world's governments, to take strong actions now—actions that entail taking on high costs now in order to realize collectively the future benefit of a stable and habitable climate? If not, what more is required if the world's nations are to avoid this tragedy of the commons—the tragedy that will surely take place if the nations of the world are not sufficiently moved to act now in collaborative ways to preserve and to nurture the environment that we share in common? A view wider than national self-interest is required—one based on the facts of climate science but that sees the scientific evidence of climate change from an evaluative viewpoint that challenges the dominant market-driven viewpoint currently shaping the ongoing controversy over climate change. What we need is an evaluative viewpoint that both widens our perspective and moves us to act by giving us an alternative way to see the crisis that confronts us as a world community. Michael Mann offers a glimpse of this evaluative viewpoint by reflecting on a vacation that he and his family took in the Florida Keys, this through the eyes of his young daughter:

> My four-year-old daughter was entranced by the Keys—the mangrove forests, the sonorous birds, the leaping dolphins, the coral reefs with their exotic and colorful fish. It was unlike anything she had ever seen. In fact, three generations of my family—my parents, my wife and me, and our daughter—were all sharing this mutual opportunity to enjoy one of Earth's true wonders . . . I didn't have the heart to tell our daughter that this island paradise was under assault—by us. That the warming and increasingly acidic ocean was slowly killing the reefs, that increasingly destructive hurricanes would subject them to further insult, and that projected sea level rise over the next few decades

58. Dessler, *Introduction to Modern Climate Change*, 150, 154.

> under "business as usual" emissions would literally submerge vast regions of
> the Florida Keys, including the wildlife refuges home to so many of its unique
> species . . . I am determined to do whatever I can to make sure that it will be
> possible for us to return decades from now—my wife and me, our daughter,
> her children, and perhaps theirs—to again marvel at these natural wonders.
> While slowly slipping away, that future is still within the realm of possibility. It
> is a matter of what path we choose to follow. I hope that my fellow scientists—
> and concerned individuals everywhere—will join me in the effort to make
> sure we follow the right one.[59]

In this reflection, Mann expresses hope, not simply as an aspiration, but as a
determination to realize what is possible in the future—a hope fired by his experience
of the good that was before him. The environmental good that moved him during
this visit to the Florida Keys he might have seen as the useful good that he strives
to realize as a climate scientist (a stable and habitable climate), but clearly what he
expresses here is that in this setting he was moved (as was his family) by the natural
beauty of the Keys—the intrinsic goodness of this natural wonder ("one of Earth's true
wonders"). In this light, the imbalance between the present costs and future benefits
of curbing climate change dissolves. The future good is valued in light of the present good. The costs required now to protect the future good are willingly assumed
out of love for the present good. ("I am determined to do whatever I can to make
sure that it will be possible for us to return decades from now—my wife and me,
our daughter, her children, and perhaps theirs.") As Mann shows, the environmental
good that he values both for its utility (the good of a stable and habitable climate)
and for its intrinsic goodness (the beauty of this natural wonder) can come to shape
what we see regarding the threat of climate change and, on the basis of what we see,
can move us to act to address the threat of climate warming. To put it another way,
the environmental good provides an alternative viewpoint through which to view the
climate crisis, a viewpoint that throws into bold relief the dominant viewpoint shaped
by market incentives ("business as usual") that rules the policy debates in the halls
of government. (That the fossil fuel industry, according to the Center for Responsive
Politics, contributed $46 million during the 2020 US election cycle to the Republican
Party, the political party most aligned with its interests, highlights the influence that
market interests can have on governmental policymaking about climate change—and
so also highlights Tocqueville's warning of a soft despotism undermining democracy,
here in the form of "the rule of the few," classically termed an oligarchy.[60]) The alternative viewpoint challenges the dominant viewpoint by providing a perspective (the
environmental good) that is wider than the self-interests of markets and nations, thus
enabling us to face with honesty the threat before us of climate warming and to act

59. Mann, *Hockey Stick and the Climate Wars*, 258.

60. Friedman and Davenport, "G.O.P. Shifts on Climate"; see Bellah et al., "Preface to the 2008
Edition."

with hope that by taking decisive action now we will avert the worst outcomes. The alternative viewpoint provides a realistic basis for both urgency and agency regarding climate change.

Still, the question remains: Can the alternative viewpoint in fact provide the basis for a shared understanding among the nations of the world, one that calls forth the willed cooperation of the world's governments (and more broadly the world community) to respond effectively to the global threat of climate warming? Herein lies the challenge that the alternative viewpoint faces: the challenge to change the perspective (where we stand) from the dominant view (here shaped by the market interests of the global economy) to a view shaped by an essential reason for social cooperation regarding climate change (the environmental good). If the new viewpoint can take hold, it would make possible the cooperation of many wills on a global scale, a cooperation based on the understanding of the global common good and the rational desire (will) to realize this global common good. In short, can the alternative viewpoint as an evaluative viewpoint move us to act collectively as a world community?

THE HOPE

The Alternative Viewpoint

The environmental good is one form of the global common good—the good that all human beings share, the good that is realized only in and through the willed cooperation of all, the good that is the hope of the world community in this time of environmental peril. The environmental good is as wide as the biosphere which encompasses the interdependency of all life on Earth—all plants and animals and the physical environment, such as the earth's atmosphere and surface, on which all life depends. Accordingly, the human good depends on and can be realized only in and through the environmental good, and this evaluative judgment calls for the preservation and nurturance of the environment on Earth. That human beings have altered the earth's biosphere in fundamental ways since the dawn of the industrial age—so much so that climate scientists refer to this period in the earth's history as the Anthropocene—raises this question: If human beings have the ability to alter the earth's environment in harmful ways, do we not also have the ability to heal the earth, to restore the environmental good through cooperative action?[61] In which case, we as the world community are faced with the decision—at root, a moral decision—to act collectively in the present to heal the earth, not only for our own sake, but for the sake of all future life on planet Earth. But, the act of healing the earth must be collaborative to be effective: first, at the level of international and national cooperation, but then most basically in the form of individual cooperation, this at the local level (civil society) as well as at the international level (global civil society). Is collaboration such as this,

61. See Mann and Kump, *Dire Predictions*, 50, 68, 212–14.

whether at the institutional level or at the personal level, in fact possible? Or, despite the severity of the consequences from not acting now in collaborative ways to address climate warming, is the world community faced with the inevitability of an outcome that is the tragedy of the commons? Is realizing the environmental good, in other words, a realistic hope?

To be hopeful at a critical time such as this requires more than having a hopeful attitude. Michael Mann would agree—what is required, he states above, is having the determination to do what is necessary to protect and restore the earth's environment. Being hopeful is a feeling, a human emotion that moves us toward a good, specifically a future good that we feel is difficult but possible to attain. Unlike the feeling of fear, which drives us away from what we see as evil, the feeling of hope drives us forward toward a future good, despite the obstacles that stand in our way. (In addressing the danger of climate change, Mann emphasizes: "the most motivating emotions are worry, interest, and hope. Importantly, fear does not motivate."[62]) As we saw in Chapter 3, Thomas Aquinas determines the feeling of hope to be one of the irascible passions. Unlike the concupiscible passions, whose object is a desired, present sensible good, the irascible passions have as their object a future, arduous sensible good—one that is possible to attain but with difficulty. Like the concupiscible passions, the irascible passions need the guidance of reason to attain the good in the right way, this specifically by means of practical reason (the work of prudence) and the guidance of justice, the moral virtue that realizes the good according to a measure that is true to reality. But the good is actually realized concretely only by means of the power that moves the intellect and the passions to act, which is the will (here then is Mann's determination to realize the environmental good). That the passion of hope participates in reason by following the directives of reason enables hope to function as a stable habit of the mind and thus as an acquired moral virtue akin to the virtue of fortitude (courage), the cardinal virtue of the irascible passions; both hope and fortitude, then, bring moral strength to human struggles.[63] So the environmental good that reason knows, and that the will desires to realize concretely—this the passion of hope feels, and thus hope moves us, and when hope moves us to act in accordance with reason, the feeling of hope provides a strength of character that energizes the human struggle to realize the environmental good. But, given the scale and complexity of realizing the environmental good, the moral character of a person or a people, while a necessary cultural resource, is not sufficient. More is required—effective institutions.

Here, precisely with regard to the need for effective institutions, the worldwide struggle to achieve the environmental good faces a significant obstacle. Unlike individual nation-states, in which common purposes are realized, not only through the willed cooperation (hence the moral character) of citizens, but also through government regulations, the nation-states of the world have no world government and thus

62. Mann, *New Climate War*, 182.
63. Thomas Aquinas, *Summa Theologica* I–II.40.1–2; II–II.17.1.

no institution through which to establish enforceable regulatory rules for international cooperation regarding common goals. The starting point of all relations between the governments of the world lies in the inviolable sovereignty of each nation. In which case, absent a central authority to impose rules on the activities of nation-states, their functioning is based on national self-interest, and negotiation between the world's nations regarding common goals relies on the compatibility of the national interests of autonomous states—a condition that the study of international relations refers to as anarchism (where "anarchy" is understood, not as disarray, but as having no rules) or as realism (by which conflicting interests between nations are seen and resolved in terms of mutual benefit, in the context of the balance of power).[64] Does viewing international relations between nation-states in this way—as a system seen only in terms of anarchism or realism—provide an adequate basis for understanding and encouraging the mutual cooperation of nations with regard to a common threat, such as climate warming—a threat that concerns each nation individually, but a threat that requires a cooperative response on the part of all the world's governments?

No, the German social philosopher Jürgen Habermas would argue, his reason being that in the negotiations between nations concerning a common concern, such as climate change, more is at play in the negotiations than the self-interested bargaining between autonomous nation-states. At work shaping the negotiations between nations is a disparate sphere of activity, not as an outside force impinging on the functioning of the nation-state, but as a force deep within its sovereignty and beyond its control—the global economy. Here "global" refers, not to what takes place between nations, but to the global reality that is instantiated in and through the localized decisions and actions of the nation-state. (The sociologist Saskia Sassen, we saw in Chapter 1, refers to cities such as New York and London as global cities in that they are localized spaces of the global, thriving as centers of international finance and immigrant labor.) Habermas terms this new global reality "the postnational constellation." Recognizing this new global reality is the necessary first step on the part of the world's nations toward taking effective action regarding common concerns. What we need as a world community, Habermas argues, is "a politics that can catch up with global markets."[65] Robert Bellah, commenting on Habermas, adds this: "when nations are the sole locations of effective politics and the economy has become global, then the disparity in power between global economy and even the strongest state means that it is the economy that will in the end determine outcomes."[66] Thus, when the political decisions of nation-states are based on national self-interest, but the worldwide cooperation of nation-states is determined by market decisions that make up the global economy, a fundamental disparity in power exists between the self-interests of the world's nations and the overriding interests of global markets. Accordingly, given

64. See Rosenau, "International Relations"; see also Martin, "International Cooperation."
65. Habermas, "The Postnational Constellation and the Future of Democracy," 109.
66. Bellah, "Religion and *The Civil Sphere*," 47.

this disparity, when the interests of nations conflict with the workings of the global economy, global markets ultimately decide the outcome.

When the disparity between national interest and global markets concerns a threat as dire as that of climate warming, the consequences of this disparity of power leads to an outcome that is a worldwide tragedy for all. For example, the international shipping industry, which emits as much carbon dioxide into the atmosphere as do all of the US coal plants combined, operates outside of the control of any one nation and was not a party to the United Nations 2015 Paris Agreement (the agreement to limit carbon emissions made by the world's nations). Yet, the international shipping industry, given the volume of carbon dioxide that it emits into the atmosphere, has the capability to undermine the emission goals set by the Paris Agreement. The International Maritime Organization (IMO), the agency that represents and regulates the industry, furthermore, is secretive regarding its regulatory decisions and has delayed taking decisive action to reduce the carbon emissions of international shipping. Without external, enforceable rules to follow, the IMO operates at will.[67] Here on bold display is the tragedy of the commons. Still, what is played out on a grand scale by one global industry making market decisions based on self-interest to the harm of the environmental whole, is replicated throughout the global economy in the day-to-day individual transactions that move markets—transactions made on the basis of self-interest and without a wider view of the environmental good.

Is there a way to move beyond the impasse resulting from the disparity between the localized interests of nation-states and the globalized interests of markets, this for the purpose of addressing the worldwide threat of climate warming? Yes, Habermas would respond, but to do so requires changing our perspective (where we stand) as a world community from either the localized interests of nation-states or the global interests of markets to a perspective that is global in reach yet at the same time localized in the evaluative judgments (and thus also in the concrete decisions and actions) of those who have taken on this viewpoint. However, the global reach of this viewpoint does not envisage a world government as the way to overcome the impasse between the local interests of nations and the global interests of markets. (Here the local would remain under the tutelage of the global.) Rather this viewpoint envisages, as Habermas describes it, a "world domestic policy," that is, political policy that is global in extent, yet viewed in terms of and enacted in and through the domestic policies of individual nation-states (hence a politics that has the ability to catch up with the global economy). Where is this viewpoint represented? In civil society, outside the halls of government, where the voices of individual citizens, social movements, nongovernmental organizations and institutions engage in normative argument in the public sphere and strive to influence the representatives of government regarding matters of concern that are wider than national interest and global in nature but beyond the interests of global markets, Habermas would answer. Here, in the public sphere that is

67. Apuzzo and Hurtes, "Industry Ducks Efforts."

civil society, building the solidarity that is necessary for human cooperation, not only within nations, but on the world stage, Habermas thinks, is possible. Here effective global governance can be achieved without world government. Indeed, due to the nature of the threats to human well-being that are global in scope (such as climate change), Habermas emphasizes the need for a "compulsory cosmopolitan solidarity" as the necessary condition for effectively responding to these threats.[68]

Bellah agrees, but questions whether such a cosmopolitan solidarity can be built only on the abstract moral principles that Habermas sees as necessary for the work of public civil discourse, principles such as universal human rights. Bellah, for his part, highlights the importance of the world's religions in building global solidarity that is the basis of human cooperation. He states: "It is one thing to believe in abstract principles. It is another to mobilize the motivation to put those principles into institutional practice." Herein lies the contribution that the world's religions can make to realizing an effective world politics. "I am convinced," Bellah asserts, "that religious motivation is a necessary factor if we are to transform the growing global moral consensus and the significant beginnings of world law into an effective form of global solidarity and global governance, in relation to an actually existing global civil society with a spiritual dimension drawing from all the great religions of the world."[69]

We have before us, then, two questions. First, can the alternative viewpoint (here seen in terms of the environmental good) in fact move us as a world community—being a constellation of nation-states in a postnational setting—to collectively take decisive action to address climate warming? Is there empirical evidence that such a change in perspective can in fact engender cooperative action from the world's nations (and more broadly from the world community) in order to realize a global common good, such as the environmental good, if the cooperative action is strengthened by effective institutions created and maintained to sustain it? Is this a hope that is realistic—hope in a future, arduous good, yet one that is possible to attain? Or, are we as a world community faced with the inevitability of the tragedy of the commons? Secondly, if the alternative viewpoint in fact provides the basis for a realistic hope of realizing the environmental good, this viewed in a secular context, what more does the voice of religion bring to this perspective? In consort with the other voices in the global civil society, what is distinctive to religion's contribution to the normative discourse addressing the threat of climate warming? Both questions merit responses. Let us move to the first question.

68. Habermas, "Postnational Constellation," 104–12. See also Habermas, "Learning from Catastrophe?," 53–57.

69. Bellah, "Religion and *The Civil Sphere*," 51, 53.

In the Context of the Immanent Frame

Does the use of a natural resource that is available to all without cost or other limits lead inevitably to a tragic outcome for all? The political scientist Elinor Ostrom raises this question at the beginning of her study on the theory of collective action. She points out that the phrase "tragedy of the commons," while interesting and powerful as a model for highlighting certain problems of collective action, is also dangerous when used as a model for formulating public policy regarding the governance of what Ostrom terms "common-pool resources." Applied metaphorically, the phrase "tragedy of the commons" assumes tragic outcomes as inevitable in the shared use of a commons, but the metaphor maintains this assumption outside of empirical settings. The hazard in using this metaphor as a guide for policy analysis is that the metaphor leaves policymakers with only two options for avoiding tragic outcomes: either governing common-pool resources by means of a central authority through coercion (hence government) or resorting to the privatization of these resources by changing common-pool resources into resources that are held as private property (hence reliance on the market). Despite the difference between the two options, however, Ostrom emphasizes that both options share this in common: "Both centralization advocates and privatization advocates accept as a central tenet that institutional change must come from outside and be imposed on the individuals affected." What is missing in this model of collective behavior is a role for self-governance—the possibility that the individuals themselves, who share the common-pool resource, might negotiate the use of the resource in such a way that all will benefit, this by means of institutional structures that they themselves create and maintain through the mutual agreement of all involved.[70]

To consider the viability of a self-governed commons, both as a theoretical model and as an empirical possibility, Ostrom turns to research conducted in specific field settings to understand what constitutes success and failure in attempts at self-governance. One focal example of success that she cites at the beginning of her study is the binding contract that was the result of the mutual agreement between fishers engaged in commercial fishing off the coast of Alanya, Turkey, in the open waters of the Mediterranean Sea. In response to growing hostility over unrestrained inshore fishing and increasing competition for the most desirable fishing locations, the local fishers themselves devised a system of rotation between the different fishing locations and between the different months of the year for using these locations. Essential to this arrangement was the unanimity of the agreement on which the rotation was based. The plan spells out the rights and duties of each fisher without privatizing the resource and puts in place an institutional structure that monitors the rotation and enforces compliance without relying on an external authority. Indeed, Ostrom emphasizes that the information that was required to devise the rotation plan could

70. Ostrom, *Governing the Commons*, 14; see 1–15.

have come only from the fishers themselves, not a central authority.[71] Yet, the system of rotation, while ingenious in Ostrom's view, is at the same time fragile. The number of fishers involved in the plan was about one hundred, half of whom belonged to the local fishers' cooperative. "Although the rules devised in Alanya provide an elegant way to solve an assignment problem, they do not address the problem of limiting access to the local fishery," Ostrom notes. More individuals seeking access to this common-pool resource, perhaps using different fishing technologies, would create a new and different problem for collective action. "In the past, collective choices were made partly through the facilities of a local co-op and partly through discussions in the local coffeehouse. Without a regular arena for collective choice, it would be difficult for the Alanya fishers to adjust their rules in the future if conditions were to change."[72]

Does Ostrom imply with this observation that as the group of users becomes larger and the issues regarding the use of a common-pool resource become more complex, the possibility of self-governance through collective action diminishes and the need for an external authority to regulate the use of the commons becomes necessary? No, Ostrom would respond: rather the design of the institutional structure of collective action must change to accommodate the new situation. She has focused on relatively small-scale settings for her study of the use of common-pool resources, she states, "because the processes of self-organization and self-governance are easier to observe in this type of situation than in many others. The central question in this study is how a group of principals who are in an interdependent situation can organize and govern themselves to obtain continuing joint benefits when all face temptations to free-ride, shirk, or otherwise act opportunistically."[73] Should the use of the common-pool resource widen by becoming part of a larger system of use, then a different institutional design must come into play if the collective use of the commons is to remain successful, an institutional design that Ostrom refers to as "the use of nested enterprises." Here "the larger organizational units in these systems are built on previously organized smaller units." In which case, if a large influx of other fishers were to take place in the waters off the coast of Alanya, for the successful use of this common-pool resource to continue, the social capital that the rotation plan created, the plan devised by the fishers of Alanya, would be seen and used by all involved as an essential component to the larger, more complex institutional arrangement of collective action that is now required. "Success in starting small-scale initial institutions enables a group of individuals to build on the social capital thus created to solve larger problems with larger and more complex institutional arrangements," Ostrom states.[74] Finally, these nested levels of self-organization and self-governance are "also nested in local, regional, and national governmental jurisdictions," she adds. Accordingly,

71. Ostrom, *Governing the Commons*, 15–21.
72. Ostrom, *Governing the Commons*, 179.
73. Ostrom, *Governing the Commons*, 29, 188–89.
74. Ostrom, *Governing the Commons*, 189–90; see 90–91, 101–2.

the cooperation of government is necessary if the self-governance of the commons is to be successful. That the government recognizes and supports the institutional arrangements of the self-governance of the commons (as does the local government in Alanya) gives legitimacy to these arrangements. "A theory of self-organization and self-governance of smaller units within larger political systems must overtly take the activities of surrounding political systems into account in explaining behavior and outcomes," Ostrom asserts; she draws this conclusion from the empirically based case studies that she has considered. Political systems can either impede or contribute to the self-governed use of the commons. Still, the successful organizing and governance of the commons itself, this at local, regional, and national levels, lies with those using the resource.[75] We are left, then, with this question (a question that Ostrom herself does not ask): Can the self-governance of the commons, as Ostrom portrays it, be extended to a common-pool resource as wide as the environment—a self-governance that can be understood theoretically and observed empirically on a global scale? Is the global governance of the environment without a world government in fact possible?

Ostrom provides empirical evidence from the case studies that she presents (such as the successful self-governance of inshore fishing at Alanya) that the shared use of a common-pool resource need not result inevitably in the tragedy of the commons. Her case studies offer a basis for hope that the shared use of a commons can be successfully accomplished through collective action, whether at the local, regional, or national level. Is there a basis for hope that collective action at the international level can achieve successful outcomes through cooperation as well?

The political scientist Bruce Cronin asks this question, not in regard to the shared use of the natural resources of the environment, but in regard to the protection of foreign populations, such as the protection of refugees, through cooperative action taken by the world's nations and international organizations. Cronin states:

> The recurrence of these practices over time suggests that they constitute a definable form of institutional cooperation, which I call International Protection Regimes (IPRs). IPRs are multilateral institutions designed to protect clearly defined classes of people within sovereign states. They are initiated by either international organizations or coalitions of states, whose members make general commitments to defend the target population against violations either by their governments or other segments of their societies.

The purpose of his study, Cronin states, is to present "a theory of cooperation that is based on a shared normative and political vision of international order" that addresses the anomaly of sovereign states, having as their the primary responsibility the furtherance of their own national interests, nevertheless taking on the obligation to protect the welfare of foreign groups of people, thus taking on a responsibility

---

75. Ostrom, *Governing the Commons*, 102, 190.

outside of their national self-interest.[76] Cronin's study is significant for our purposes because it offers the empirical evidence to demonstrate, firstly, that collective action at the international level from nation-states and international organizations facing matters of common concern does in fact take place in order to realize goals wider than national self-interest and, secondly, that international cooperation such as this can result in successful outcomes. Thus, Cronin's study helps us answer the question before us: Is the global governance of the environment without a world government in fact possible?

Cronin presents his theory of international cooperation in conversation with the dominant theory of international relations—variously termed realism or anarchism (which we considered above)—not in order to refute it, but rather to bring to light an aspect of international cooperation that realism cannot explain, and thus to raise an aspect that is not considered if the theory of realism dominates the study of international relations. The theory of realism (or anarchism) in international relations presupposes an international system in which nation-states cooperate with each other, but only on the terms of national self-interest. That this system of realism can produce unwanted outcomes for all when nations interact with each other only on the basis of national interest led a group of scholars in the field of international relations, referred to as neoliberals, to turn their attention to the importance of international institutions in shaping cooperative behavior between nation-states—the General Agreement on Tariffs and Trade (GATT) being a prime example of such an institution. While the theory of neoliberalism accepts the system of realism as the basis of international relations between states, neoliberals nevertheless maintain that on the basis of strong international institutions ongoing cooperation between nation-states can be achieved. Still, Cronin argues, "in a neoliberal world, states participate in regimes only to achieve *national* objectives in an environment of perceived international interdependence. Governments join the GATT, for example, because they realize that they must trade in order to prosper and their ability to export their own goods depends upon reciprocal reductions in trade barriers." The limitation in neoliberal theory regarding the good of international cooperation, in Cronin's eyes, is this: "The institutionalist emphasis on expected utility and reciprocal benefit eliminates the need to consider questions of obligation or justice. This makes it difficult to apply neoliberal theories to explain any common interest that cannot be reduced to the sum of individual interests."[77] What neither the theory of realism nor the theory of neoliberalism can explain is why nation-states undertake collective action to realize a good that is wider than national self-interest.

When Cronin brings international protection regimes into view, what he sees is collective action on the part of nation-states that is motivated by a shared political

76. Cronin, *Institutions for the Common Good*, 1–3.

77. Cronin, *Institutions for the Common Good*, 8–9. See also Martin, "International Cooperation," 434–36.

interest that transcends national self-interest. Here the stability of the international order takes precedence as a good to be pursued collectively over the good that comes from the power and security that nation-states seek individually. Accordingly, states Cronin, "a desire to promote the cohesion of the international order is the *primary* factor that motivates states to construct IPRs. Stability and order, rather than power and security," are the values that move nation-states to take cooperative action, this "to advance the welfare and principles of the collectivity."[78]

For example, during the period of the two world wars in the twentieth century, the movement of refugees presented a distinct challenge to the system of sovereign nations—the only place refugees fleeing their own country could go was to another sovereign nation—in which case, the fate of refugees was placed in the hands of a sovereign nation that was not their own. The refugee was in fact a person without a state. Moreover, given the nature of sovereignty, the receiving nation had no ability to address the oppressive situation in the sending country, nor did it have a political incentive to admit refugees from another country into its own country. Despite the seemingly intractable problem of the movement of refugees during this time, nation-states responded to the problem by establishing systems of protection for refugees, at first for specific groups of refugees in the wake of World War I, then universally for all refugees fleeing persecution (but not for the many who had been displaced by war) following World War II—this through the United Nations Office of High Commissioner on Refugees (UNHCR). The collective effort to protect refugees that was shaped by the UNHCR was motivated, Cronin emphasizes, not simply out of humanitarian concern for refugees, but more broadly by the desire on the part of the world's nations to realize the good of stability and order in the international community by establishing an international protection regime for refugees.[79] Cronin states: "I consider any regime that is created primarily to promote, preserve and/or extend the principles of a regional or global political order or collectivity (as opposed to providing direct benefits to its members) to be an institution for the common good." Present-day examples, in Cronin's view, would be the International Criminal Court, United Nations peacekeeping missions, and United Nations specialized agencies, such as the UNHCR.[80]

The United Nations Framework Convention on Climate Change (UNFCCC), the first international treaty on climate change, which was negotiated and signed by the world's nations at the Rio Earth Summit in 1992 and then ratified by these nations in 1994, thus making the treaty a legally binding agreement for the nations that signed it, is a further example of what Cronin means by an institution for the common good. The UNFCCC is a general agreement (convention) that was made by the parties (nations)

78. Cronin, *Institutions for the Common Good*, 24.

79. Cronin, *Institutions for the Common Good*, 152–84. See also Harrell-Bond and Shacknove, "Refugees," 776–78.

80. Cronin, *Institutions for the Common Good*, 20; see Riordan, *Global Ethics*, 117–20.

to the treaty that establishes the framework for negotiating and ratifying more specific agreements in subsequent conferences that are held yearly—the first Conference of the Parties (COP1) was held in Berlin in 1995, the most recent in Glasgow (COP26) in 2021. Presently 197 nations are signatories to the treaty. The broad goal of the UN-FCCC is "stabilization of greenhouse gas concentrations in the atmosphere at a level that would prevent dangerous anthropogenic interference with the climate system," but the Framework Convention does not specify what precisely that level must be to prevent catastrophic harm from climate warming. This determination was left to future conferences, most notably achieved in the 2015 Paris Agreement (COP21) in which all nations, both developed and developing, agreed to limit the increase of climate warming to 1.5°C above preindustrial levels, this based on voluntary commitments made by the parties to the agreement, each nation stating its intended course of action and goal to limit carbon emissions. These voluntary national commitments are referred to in the Paris Agreement in its ratified form as "nationally determined contributions" (NDCs). The NDCs both allowed for and reflected the significant differences between the industrialized developed countries and the developing countries, the former being historically the primary contributors to climate change. That the Paris Agreement acknowledged the difference in responsibility between nations in addressing climate change, moreover, gave concrete form to the principle stated in the Framework Convention of "common but differentiated responsibility" that the world's nations have regarding their response to the crisis of climate change. Although each nation has the obligation to address the global harm of climate change, all nations must do so according to their contribution to the harm and their ability to alleviate it. "The developed-country Parties should take the lead in combating climate change and the adverse effects thereof," states the Framework Convention.[81]

The Glasgow Climate Pact—the agreement reached by 197 nations most recently at the United Nations Conference of the Parties held in Glasgow (COP26)—both offers hope and raises alarm regarding the future consequences of climate change. With the goal of the Paris Agreement to limit the rise of climate warming to 1.5°C before them and the heightened awareness of the necessity to do so to avoid catastrophic consequences, the world's nations agreed to intensify their efforts to curb climate change and, as a means to strengthen this resolve, established transparency rules to foster accountability among the nations for meeting their voluntary commitments. At the same time, the voluntary national commitments that have been made fall short of achieving the Paris goal, and the financial aid that the rich nations (those most responsible for climate change) had pledged to help the poor nations adapt to the crisis of climate change (those least responsible for climate change) has not been fully forthcoming (the pledge of $100 billion a year by 2020 was made in the 2009 Copenhagen Accord). Thus, the Glasgow agreement calls for all nations to come to COP27 next year in Egypt with updated pledges, the goal being to collectively reduce

81. Quoted in Dessler and Parson, *Science and Politics*, 27; see 26–33, 175–79.

carbon emissions by 45 percent by 2030 to keep climate warming from rising above 1.5°C, and calls for the rich nations at the minimum to double their financial help to the poor nations for the purpose of climate adaptation by 2025.[82] The strength of the UNFCCC and its implementation through the yearly COPs, such as COP26, is the institutional structure that the Framework Convention has put in place that enables the world's nations to negotiate a collective response to the threat of climate change. Here the global community finds a basis for hope. Yet, that the global average temperature presently has risen 1.1°C above preindustrial levels, that if the pledges made by the world's nations are not strengthened, the climate is projected to warm well above 2.0°C by the end of the century with catastrophic consequences, and that the actions that the world's nations must take to achieve the Paris goal of 1.5°C are voluntary and not enforceable at the international level, is cause for alarm in the global community. The UNFCCC provides the institutional framework to realize the environmental good—the common good—through the collective action of the world's nations, but a successful outcome to the international cooperation that the Framework Convention facilitates depends on more than intergovernmental cooperation. Here a successful outcome requires the active response of the wider global community as well.

A main driver of the human collaboration that is required to address the growing threat of climate change effectively comes from civil society—grassroots mobilization at the local, national, and global levels. Such grassroots mobilization is the concern of the sociologist: "This mobilization has engaged a large number of organizations that range in size from small neighborhood groups to large, formal international organizations with budgets that are in the hundreds of millions of dollars, and millions of members." Although the goals of these groups and the institutional levels at which they operate vary, "a clearly identifiable climate movement in the form of a loose network structure advocating for action to address climate change can be identified. As a result of this mobilization, climate change has become a major political issue across the globe," say the sociologists Beth Schaefer Caniglia, Robert J. Brulle, and Andrew Szasz.[83] Precisely because social movements that originate in civil society operate outside of the institutional purposes of the market and the state, they have the ability to bring a different perspective to bear on the issues of the society as a whole, enabling them to both frame the issues in distinct ways and mobilize the society's citizens by changing hearts and minds, thus engendering social change in effective ways. That this mobilization within civil society extends beyond the local and the national to global civil society gives this mobilization the ability at both the global and local levels to check the power of the global economy, thus shaping "a politics that can catch up with global markets" (to use the words of Habermas quoted above). The climate movement is a case in point. Of interest to the sociologists here is the role that religious communities play in the climate movement, particularly as a force within civil

82. Plumer and Friedman, "Climate Summit Reaches Accord."
83. Caniglia et al., "Civil Society," 235.

society with the potential to promote climate activism through religion's framing of the issue of climate change in religious and moral terms and in its ability to mobilize resources, both institutional and economic, for the purpose of achieving the collective goals of social change.[84]

Michael Agliardo, SJ, points out, however, that from the Catholic community in the United States mobilization for the sake of addressing the present-day threat of climate change has been mixed—a strong response both in terms of voice and action on the part of Catholic universities and the wider theological community, women's and men's religious orders, and Catholic NGOs, but a muted response on the part of the US Catholic bishops. The muted response on the part of the bishops is notable because their overall silence on climate change in the present day stands in sharp contrast to the public, prophetic voice that they brought to bear on the issues of international peace and social justice in the US economy in their pastoral letters of the 1980s (see Chapter 2) and in contrast to the pastoral statements that they made in 1992 (*Renewing the Earth*) and 2001 (*Global Climate Change*) regarding the threat of climate change to the planetary common good. Furthermore, their overall reticence to actively engage the present-day issue of climate change stands in sharp contrast to the strong response to the present and future threat of climate change that has come from Pope Francis.[85]

This interest on the part of the sociologists regarding the place of religion in the climate movement brings us to the second question that was posed above: If religion's role in civil society is formative regarding citizens' beliefs and practices, then what is the distinctive contribution that religion makes to the global collective effort to address the threat of climate change—this both in terms of normative argument and the concrete mobilization of collective action? The political scientists that we considered above demonstrate empirically that collective action for the purpose of realizing a common good is in fact possible, not only at local and national levels (Elinor Ostrom), but at the international level as well (Bruce Cronin). What more does the viewpoint of religion bring to collective action for the common good? Bellah, as we saw above, points to the contribution that the world's religions make to building global solidarity, this by engendering a moral consensus that values and thus encourages a sense of global membership, which is foundational to global governance and a source of motivation to mobilize for the sake of the global common good. Here the contribution that religion makes to global concerns lies in the distinctiveness of its perspective. Whether through normative argument or concrete mobilization, when religion engages global concerns, such as climate change, it does so necessarily in a secular context (what Charles Taylor terms "the immanent frame," as we saw in Chapter 2), yet it does so from the perspective of transcendence. Herein lies the distinctiveness of

---

84. See Caniglia et al., "Civil Society," 236–62.

85. Agliardo, SJ, "Reception of *Laudato si'*," 44–60; see United States Catholic Conference, *Renewing the Earth*; United States Conference of Catholic Bishops, *Global Climate Change*.

religion's contribution—its perspective of transcendence. Hence, we pose the second question: given the distinctiveness of religion's perspective, what more does religion's viewpoint of transcendence contribute to the collective response of the global community regarding the threat of climate change? What we see and how we act collectively as a global community depends on where we stand—what we value. From the perspective of transcendence, what do we see and how are we moved to act in response to the global crisis of climate change, this as a world community? Here we ask this question specifically in the light of Catholic social teaching.

Yet from the Perspective of Transcendence

On June 18, 2015, six months prior to the UN climate summit in Paris (COP21), Pope Francis published his encyclical *Laudato si'* (*On Care for Our Common Home*).[86] The title of the encyclical comes from words of praise in *Canticle of the Creatures* composed by Saint Francis of Assisi in the thirteenth century in the Italian language, "*Laudato si', mi' Signore*"—translated into English as "Praise be to you, my Lord." The encyclical is pastoral in intent, offering guidance to Christians facing the present ecological crisis by promoting ecological education (nos. 209–215) and by fostering, in the pope's words, "an ecological spirituality grounded in the convictions of our faith, since the teachings of the Gospel have direct consequences for our way of thinking, feeling and living. More than in ideas or concepts as such, I am interested in how such a spirituality can motivate us to a more passionate concern for the protection of our world. A commitment this lofty cannot be sustained by doctrine alone, without a spirituality capable of inspiring us" (no. 216). What the present-day ecological crisis requires on the part of Christians, Francis emphasizes, is an "ecological conversion," a change of heart in Christians "whereby the effects of their encounter with Jesus Christ become evident in their relationship with the world around them. Living our vocation to be protectors of God's handiwork is essential to a life of virtue; it is not an optional or a secondary aspect of our Christian experience" (no. 217). Such a change of heart, however, cannot simply be the concern of individual Christians. Given the nature of the ecological crisis, Francis points out, "the ecological conversion needed to bring about lasting change is also a community conversion" (no. 219). Thus, Pope Francis addresses the encyclical not only to Christians worldwide, but to "every person living on this planet," this being our common home. Indeed, as Francis begins his pastoral letter, he makes this proposal: "In this Encyclical, I would like to enter into dialogue with all people about our common home" (no. 3).

Our common home—its natural goodness, its beauty, its rhythms, its bounty—this is the setting for the dialogue that Francis initiates, not only with Christians, but with all people, all who share this common home. In undertaking this dialogue, Pope Francis takes as his model the saint whose name he chose when he was elected pope

86. Pope Francis, *Laudato si'* (*On Care for Our Common Home*).

of the Roman Catholic Church—Saint Francis of Assisi. In the words and life of St. Francis, Pope Francis finds the guidance and inspiration that we all need to address the ecological crisis that threatens our common home (no. 10). "Praise be to you, my Lord, through our Sister, Mother Earth, who sustains and governs us, and who produces various fruit with colored flowers and herbs," *Canticle of the Creatures* intones. "St. Francis of Assisi reminds us that our common home is like a sister with whom we share our life and a beautiful mother who opens her arms to embrace us," Pope Francis comments (no. 1). The significance of the words of *Canticle of the Creatures* lies in their power to awaken in us a deep sense of belonging to the earth in all its fullness, calling us to an awareness of the relationships that we have with all creatures of the earth and above the earth and the relation that we have in and through these creaturely beings with the One who is their Creator. "Praised be you, my Lord, with all your creatures, especially Sir Brother Sun, who is the day and through whom you give us light . . . Praised be you, my Lord, through Sister Moon and the stars . . . through Brother Wind . . . through Sister Water . . . through Brother Fire, through whom you light the night, and he is beautiful and playful and robust and strong" (no. 87). That St. Francis gives praise to God through God's creatures highlights that for St. Francis the goodness and beauty of God the Creator is manifested in and through all that God has created. Indeed, comments Pope Francis, St. Francis "invites us to see nature as a magnificent book in which God speaks to us and grants us a glimpse of his infinite beauty and goodness" (no. 12). Moreover, seeing the world in this light, St. Francis was moved to celebrate in joyous song the common bond that we humans have with all that exists—all creatures that make up our common home. "His response to the world around him was so much more than intellectual appreciation or economic calculus, for to him each and every creature was a sister united to him by bonds of affection. That is why he felt called to care for all that exists," says Pope Francis (no. 11). This way of seeing the world that St. Francis celebrates in his canticle of praise, the sensibilities that this vision evokes, Pope Francis brings to the dialogue that he initiates with the peoples of the world concerning the ecological crisis that we face as a world community. This vision provides the perspective through which Pope Francis views the ecological crisis that threatens our common home and, in its light, the motivation to act—to care for our common home.

But, can this perspective, given the particularity of its viewpoint which is rooted in the distinct faith tradition of Christianity, function in a meaningful and effective way as both guide and inspiration in a dialogue that includes, not only this particular faith community, but all who share our common home? "I urgently appeal," states Francis, "for a new dialogue about how we are shaping the future of our planet. We need a conversation which includes everyone, since the environmental challenge we are undergoing, and its human roots, concern and affect us all." That Francis undertakes this dialogue from the distinct perspective of the Christian faith, he does not see as impeding the human cooperation that is required on a worldwide scale to address the ecological crisis; nor does he see the contributions of other distinct viewpoints shaping the dialogue as being a hindrance to collective action. "All of us can cooperate as instruments of God for the care of creation, each according to his or her own culture, experience, involvements and talents," the pope maintains (no. 14). Indeed, as we saw in our consideration of the pastoral letters of the US Catholic bishops on peace and the US economy in Chapter 2, when the church enters the public sphere to address a matter of common concern, it does so for the purpose of bringing the distinctiveness of its faith perspective to bear on the public matter at hand, but at the same time, to speak meaningfully and effectively in this public sphere, the church addresses the public matter in terms that are shared by all involved regarding the matter of common concern. Here there are not two discrete discourses represented—one expressed in the form of rational, normative argument which is addressed to the public; the other expressed in the form of the particularity of faith which is addressed to the community of faith. Rather, when the church speaks publicly, the distinctiveness of its faith perspective is mediated in and through the terms of the argument at hand. In the church's public voice, both the particularity of faith and the universality of reason are represented, the one informing the other. Moreover, that the church's use of rational argument is motivated by and presented in the light of its faith commitment enables the church's public voice both to avoid the abstractness that can undermine the effectiveness of rational argument (the statement of principles without context) and to provide motivation to carry out the actions that rational argument calls for. Thus, Pope Francis seeks to foster "an ecological spirituality grounded in the convictions of our faith," one that "can motivate us to a more passionate concern for the protection of our world," this being his primary intention, as he stated above, more than an interest in the formulation of "ideas or concepts as such." Still, the ecological crisis that threatens us all, in order to be addressed meaningfully and effectively by the world community, requires both a shared understanding and evaluation that can only be expressed in the universal terms of normative rational argument. This Francis does in undertaking a dialogue with the peoples of the world regarding care for our common home—he presents the ecological crisis in terms that are common to all, yet from the perspective of Christian faith. In what way, then, does the distinctiveness of the Pope's perspective of transcendence contribute to the dialogue concerning the ecological crisis that we face as a world community? Here we ask this question specifically with the ecological threat of climate change in view.

"The climate is a common good, belonging to all and meant for all," Francis declares (no. 23). With this assertion Francis expands our view of the common good beyond its traditional formulation in Catholic social teaching, which portrays the common good as the good that is realized in and through the mutual relations that make up society, this for the purpose of achieving the human fulfillment of all in the society. Moreover, insofar as human interdependence has increasingly become global in scale, the common good has come to be viewed in the tradition of Catholic social teaching in the form of the global common good. As we saw in Chapter 4, the Second

Vatican Council's *Pastoral Constitution on the Church in the Modern World* defines the common good in these terms: "Because of the increasingly close interdependence which is gradually extending to the entire world, we are today witnessing an extension of the role of the common good, which is the sum total of social conditions which allow people, either as groups or as individuals, to reach their fulfillment more fully and more easily. The resulting rights and obligations are consequently the concern of the entire human race." Here the reach of the common good as a moral norm is envisaged in terms of "the human family as a whole," states the *Pastoral Constitution* (no. 26). Pope Francis, for his part, widens the scope of the common good as a moral norm to include planet Earth as a whole. That the climate is seen by Francis as a common good that belongs to all and is meant for all brings into view the intrinsic goodness of all creatures of the earth and above the earth. Here Francis widens the focus of the common good from an anthropocentric viewpoint (the good of the human family as a whole) to an ecocentric viewpoint (the good of planet Earth as a whole). Here the common good of the human family as a whole is neither bypassed nor de-emphasized but rather seen in a new light—what Catholic theologian Daniel Scheid terms "the cosmic common good." Here, in this light, we humans see our good as interdependent, not only with one another in settings ranging from the local to the global, but as interdependent with all creatures of the earth and above the earth. The human good is realized only in and through a mutual relationship with the whole—the good of Earth. "The cosmic common good," says Scheid, "is an essential component of our human identity. We are incomplete without the cosmos, without Earth, just as the cosmos is incomplete without our full participation."[87]

But, our full participation as a world community in realizing the good of Earth—our common home—is lacking. Based on what Pope Francis describes as "a very solid scientific consensus," he draws upon the findings of climate science to portray in stark terms the warming of the climate and the environmental harm that this is causing, harm for which we humans are responsible, and harm that we humans have yet to address fully and effectively. In light of these scientific findings, Francis calls upon the world community to act in constructive, healing ways to address this environmental harm, such as by substituting the use of fossil fuels with forms of renewable energy (nos. 23–26). Our collective response as a world community to this environmental threat, however, requires more than the development of alternative technology. To focus only on technological remedies to address the threat of climate warming is to miss seeing the deeper roots of the problem, Francis maintains: "It would hardly be helpful to describe symptoms without acknowledging the human origins of the ecological crisis. A certain way of understanding human life and activity has gone awry, to the serious detriment of the world around us. Should we not pause and consider this? At this stage, I propose that we focus on the dominant technocratic paradigm and the place of human beings and of human action in the world" (no. 101).

87. Scheid, *Cosmic Common Good*, 25, 43.

In the technocratic paradigm shaping our lives we find the deeper roots of the ecological crisis that we face as a world community. The problem does not lie in the use of technology as such, but in "the way that humanity has taken up technology and its development *according to an undifferentiated and one-dimensional paradigm.* This paradigm exalts the concept of a subject who, using logical and rational procedures, progressively approaches and gains control over an external object," states Francis (no. 106). Here human interaction with the natural world, when undertaken wholly from a technological perspective, renders nature only as an object to be controlled. Here human interaction with the natural world takes place only on humanity's terms, in the mode of instrumental use, driven by humanity's self-interests. The unrestricted use of fossil fuels is a case in point. Francis declares: "There needs to be a distinctive way of looking at things, a way of thinking, policies, an educational program, a lifestyle and a spirituality which together generate resistance to the assault of the technocratic paradigm" (no. 111). What is this distinctive way of seeing the world, what will it show us about the world, and how will this distinctive view of the world move us to act?

The distinctive way of seeing the world that Pope Francis calls for requires a change of perspective on our part—from what Francis calls "a misguided anthropocentrism" in which "human beings place themselves at the center," giving absolute priority to humanity's immediate interests, thus making all else relative to these interests (no. 122), to a way of seeing the world that places human beings in a living relationship with the whole that is Earth. Here, from this perspective, human well-being is seen in the context of the relations that exist between all living organisms and the relation that these organisms have with the physical environment in which they exist. Francis states: "It cannot be emphasized enough how everything is interconnected" (no. 138). Human beings cannot thrive independently of the balance of life that occurs in the ecosystem of which they are a part; the community of life that consists of the interdependencies that exist between microscopic organisms, such as bacteria, and the vegetative and animal life that make up the ecosystem, including human life, and the relation of this community of life with its physical environment, will not thrive if the balance is distorted, this due to human activity. Earth is a complex whole, a planetary community of life made up of diverse, interconnected relationships, both human and nonhuman, both biotic and abiotic. For Francis, an effective response to ecological crisis, such as the threat of climate warming, requires a vision of the whole, thus "an *integral ecology*" (no. 137). From this viewpoint, nature and society cannot be held apart as if they are separate realities. "We are part of nature, included in it and thus in constant interaction with it," states Francis. Thus, regarding an ecological threat such as climate change, "it is essential to seek comprehensive solutions which consider the interactions within natural systems themselves and with social systems. We are faced not with two separate crises, one environmental and the other social, but rather with one complex crisis which is both social and environmental" (no. 139). For this reason, Francis emphasizes, "a true ecological approach *always* becomes a social approach; it must integrate questions of justice in debates on the environment, so as to hear *both the cry of the earth and the cry of the poor*" (no. 49).[88]

The disparity between the rich and poor nations of the world in regard to the causes and effects of climate change, both in terms of the relative contribution of each to the degradation of the climate and in terms of the relative consequences suffered by each due to climate warming, underscores Francis's point that the ecological crisis that we face as a world community is at once environmental and social, both a matter of Earth healing and effecting social justice. At the UN climate summit in Glasgow (COP26), Sonam P. Wangdi, speaking as chair of the bloc of forty-seven nations listed by the United Nations as "the least developed countries" (the majority of which are countries in Africa), declared in reference to the role that this bloc of poor countries plays in regard to climate warming: "We have contributed the least to this problem, yet we suffer disproportionately . . . There must be increasing support for adapting to impacts,"[89] this support as a matter of justice coming from the rich, industrialized nations whose wealth and power have been built on the use of fossil fuels that now degrade life for all on planet Earth. Pope Francis would agree: "A true 'ecological debt' exists, particularly between the global north and south . . . The warming caused by huge consumption on the part of some rich countries has repercussions on the poorest areas of the world, especially Africa, where a rise in temperature, together with drought, has proved devastating for farming" (no. 51). Indeed, at the Glasgow summit, the environment minister from Kenya, Keriako Tobiko, pointed out that the UN goal of limiting the increase in the global average temperature to 1.5°C will still entail a 3°C rise in temperature in Africa, causing erratic patterns of excessive rainfall and then severe drought that will only intensify, increasing the harm that these weather patterns are presently causing for farming in Africa. "In Kenya and Africa, we cry, we bleed," Tobiko noted. "We bleed when it rains. We cry when it doesn't rain. So for us, ambition, 1.5 is not a statistic. It is a matter of life and death."[90] The affliction that this African cry of pain expresses calls for an active response by all the nations of the world to the environmental and social harm caused by climate change. As we saw above, the United Nations Framework Convention on Climate Change (UNFCCC) called for a shared but differentiated response from the world's nations to address climate change, this according to the principle of "common but differentiated responsibility." In his response to the cry of the world's poor who are suffering the effects of climate change, Pope Francis echoes this principle, but states it with a distinctive emphasis on the place of the poor in the climate crisis: "regarding climate change, there are *differentiated responsibilities*. As the United States bishops have said, greater attention must be given to 'the needs of the poor, the weak and the vulnerable, in a debate often

88. The words of Pope Francis reflect the influence of the Brazilian Catholic theologian Leonardo Boff. See Boff, *Cry of the Earth, Cry of the Poor*.

89. Plumer and Popovich, "Figuring Out Who Bears the Most Responsibility."

90. Sengupta et al., "Deadline Passes."

dominated by more powerful interests.' We need to strengthen the conviction that we are one single family" (no. 52).[91]

The cry of the poor and the cry of the earth are interconnected. Seeing this interconnectedness is necessary if we are to address the threat of climate change fully and effectively. Although the poor nations of the world have contributed to the harm of climate change the least, they suffer the consequences of climate change the most and have the fewest resources to adapt to the growing harm of climate change. The rich nations of the world, on the other hand, have contributed the most to causing climate change, yet they are lacking in their response to address fully and effectively both the causes of climate change and the consequences of climate change suffered by the poor countries. Francis warns: "The human environment and the natural environment deteriorate together; we cannot adequately combat environmental degradation unless we attend to causes related to human and social degradation. In fact, the deterioration of the environment and of society affects the most vulnerable people on the planet" (no. 48).

Thus, as a world community, if we are to address the threat of climate warming fully and effectively, we must hear both the cry of the earth and the cry of the poor— both the moral call for Earth healing on the part of the world's nations, and the moral call for just relations between rich and poor nations regarding their shared but differentiated response to the environmental harm of climate change as well as for just relations between this generation and future generations regarding the harmful effects of climate change. Concerning the issue of justice between generations, Francis observes: "Once we start to think about the kind of world we are leaving to future generations, we look at things differently; we realize that the world is a gift which we have freely received and must share with others" (no. 159). Our lack of attention to the consequences of present-day environmental harm for future generations is linked to the lack of attention on the part of the rich nations to the suffering of the poor nations from climate change, Francis maintains: "our inability to think seriously about future generations is linked to our inability to broaden the scope of our present interests and to give consideration to those who remain excluded from development. Let us not only keep the poor of the future in mind, but also today's poor, whose life on this earth is brief and who cannot keep on waiting" (no. 162).

A full and effective response to the environmental crisis that we face as a world community will come only if we collectively widen our vision to see the common good of the whole—the planetary good that can be realized only in and through the interdependent relationships that make up the whole that is our common home. But, while seeing the interconnectedness in the relationships that make up the whole that is planet Earth is a necessary step in addressing climate change, it is not sufficient. More is needed if we are to act—to care for our common home. What moves us to act in response to the cry of the poor and the cry of the earth?

91. See United States Conference of Catholic Bishops, *Global Climate Change*, 3.

The cry of pain from another moves us. Our response to the cry presumes that we have both a relationship with the source of the cry and an understanding of the reason for the cry—as a parent does, responding to the cry of a sick baby; as a citizen does, responding to a request for help from one who is homeless. Being moved by the cry of another indicates that the suffering of the one has become the suffering of the other. That your suffering moves me means that your suffering has become mine, as your good then becomes my good if your suffering is alleviated. In my being moved by your cry, our relationship becomes one of mutuality, a bond based on the feeling of pain that we share in common. But, the mutual feeling of pain alone is insufficient to move the one to act on behalf of the other who suffers. We may have sympathetic feelings for the other's suffering (compassion), but what moves us to act on behalf of the one who suffers is the good that must be restored to the sufferer (justice). Yet, our acting for the good of the other is shaped by what we feel—our compassion. As moral virtues, justice and compassion (mercy) strengthen each other. Our compassion finds rational guidance in justice; our acts of justice are empowered by our compassion.

We saw this relation between compassion and justice in our consideration of the parable of the good Samaritan in Chapter 3. The Samaritan is moved with compassion at the sight of the victim by the side of the road, but the Samaritan's actions in response to the victim's suffering are impelled by the Samaritan's willed determination to restore the victim to health and to enable the victim to return to society and to realize the victim's own good, which is now the Samaritan's good as well. At the same time, the Samaritan's actions are fueled by his compassion (mercy) for the victim, which affectively shapes the Samaritan's actions on behalf of the victim. "Who is my neighbor?" the lawyer had asked Jesus, prompting the telling of the parable that illustrates what being a neighbor entails—a relationship of mutuality, indeed friendship, that in this situation is solidified through an act of compassion. Who was neighbor to the victim? "The one who showed mercy on him," the lawyer answers. Rather than answer the question that the lawyer asked regarding who is my neighbor, the parable presents us with a portrait of the love that makes us a neighbor to another.

This dynamic between compassion and justice is at play in Pope Francis's entreaty to the world's nations that as a world community we must collectively care for our common home. The term "care" connotes feeling (I care for you) and commitment to another's good (I will care for your well-being). A commensurate term used in Catholic social teaching is the term "solidarity." As we saw in Chapter 3, Pope John Paul II in his 1987 encyclical *Sollicitudo rei socialis* (*On Social Concern*) views the fact of interdependence between the peoples of the world as a value, a good to be realized by us, and thus a moral good. "When interdependence becomes recognized in this way, the correlative response as a moral and social attitude, as a 'virtue,' is *solidarity*," states John Paul. The virtue of solidarity, John Paul emphasizes, "is not a feeling of vague compassion or shallow distress at the misfortunes of so many people, both near and far. On the contrary, it is *a firm and persevering determination* to commit oneself to the *common good*; that is to say to the good of all and of each individual, because we are *all* really responsible *for all*" (no. 38, italics original). The virtue of solidarity seeks to realize the good of justice for all; importantly, John Paul II adds, it does so by fostering an attitude of care and respect for the other as neighbor: "*Solidarity* helps us to see the 'other'—whether a *person, people, or nation*—not just as some kind of instrument, with a work capacity and physical strength to be exploited at low cost and then discarded when no longer useful, but as our 'neighbor'" (no. 39, italics original). In this light, the neighbor is seen and treated by us as possessing intrinsic worth, thus deserving our care and respect. Here, in the eyes of Pope John Paul II, the virtue of solidarity fosters both justice for our neighbor and love of our neighbor.

Pope Francis likewise calls our attention to the importance of fostering the virtue of solidarity, but he extends the reach of solidarity to include the good, not only of persons, peoples, and nations, but of all creatures of the earth and above the earth, including the human creature. Here Francis widens our vision of the good, enabling us to see the good of the whole as the cosmic common good, thus fostering in us the virtue of "earth solidarity."[92] The interdependence that makes up our common home is viewed by Francis in light of the common good of all creatures and their interrelationships that constitute the whole that is planet Earth. In the face of global injustice, whether environmental or social, "the principle of the common good immediately becomes, logically and inevitably, a summons to solidarity and a preferential option for the poorest of our brothers and sisters" (no. 158), Francis states. Our response to the summons to solidarity (justice) binds us to the whole in such a way that the good of the whole becomes our good and the cry from the whole—the cry of the earth, the cry of the poor—becomes our cry, expressing our compassion for the suffering of the other. In the face of environmental degradation, "we can feel the desertification of the soil almost as a physical ailment, and the extinction of a species as a painful disfigurement," observes Francis (no. 89). Hence our response as a world community to "what is happening to our common home" must be our response to the call to solidarity, both as a collective commitment to the common good of the whole, and as a collective willingness to be moved, "to become painfully aware, to dare to turn what is happening to the world into our personal suffering and thus to discover what each of us can do about it" (nos. 17, 19). For Francis, care for our common home entails both justice and compassion for the neighbor who suffers—the neighbor here being all creatures subject to environmental degradation. The love that the Samaritan showed the victim by the side of the road models for us the love that makes us a neighbor to another—the neighbor who is moved by the suffering of planet Earth and who is committed to acting for its common good.[93]

92. The term is that of Daniel Scheid. See Scheid, *Cosmic Common Good*, 82–100; see also Scheid, "*Laudato si'* and the Development," 186–88.

93. The Catholic theologian Elizabeth Johnson reads the parable of the good Samaritan in this way. See Johnson, *Ask the Beasts*, 281.

What moves us to act in response to the ecological crisis that we face as a world community? Love for the earth that is victim to the environmental harm that we humans have inflicted on the earth and love for the peoples of the earth that suffer the environmental harm disproportionately, Francis would answer. Love such as this is a deeply human response to the natural goodness of Earth's beauty and bounty, and to the goodness of justice that insures well-being for all the peoples of the earth. At the same time, in the eyes of Christian faith, the love that moves us to act for Earth healing and to act for social justice is more—it is our response to God's love as well, the divine love that is experienced by us in and through God's creation: "In the Judeo-Christian tradition, the word 'creation' has a broader meaning than 'nature,' for it has to do with God's loving plan in which every creature has its own value and significance." Here, from the distinctive perspective of faith, the natural world is seen by us as God's creation, and thus as "a gift from the outstretched hand of the Father of all, and as a reality illuminated by the love which calls us together into universal communion" says Francis (no. 76). The ecological conversion that Francis calls for is shaped by attitudes of "gratitude and gratuitousness" that come from our "recognition that the world is God's loving gift, and that we are called quietly to imitate his generosity in self-sacrifice and good works." Moreover, Francis points out, ecological conversion "also entails a loving awareness that we are not disconnected from the rest of creatures, but joined in a splendid universal communion. As believers, we do not look at the world from without but from within, conscious of the bonds with which the Father has linked us to all beings" (no. 220).

That, in this light, human beings see themselves as sharing the goodness of God's gift with all creatures of the earth corrects the distorted interpretation of God's words in Gen 1:28 giving human beings "dominion" over the creatures of the earth as meaning that God imparts to human beings the privilege to dominate the earth. Rather, Francis emphasizes, "our 'dominion' over the universe should be understood more properly in the sense of responsible stewardship" (no. 116). Furthermore, that God gives to human beings the task to "till and keep" the garden in Gen 2:15 implies, not a relationship of domination, but "a relationship of mutual responsibility between human beings and nature," Francis maintains: "'Tilling' refers to cultivating, ploughing or working, while 'keeping' means caring, protecting, overseeing and preserving" (no. 67). Here in these images from Genesis we see the place of humans in the garden of God's creation as one of interrelationship with all creatures of the earth ("joined in a splendid universal communion," says Francis), and we see the role that humans are called to play in response to God's gift of creation as one of responsible care. In the light of faith, we are moved to act—to care for our common home in a time of ecological crisis—in response to our experience of creation as God's gift of love that calls us to love God and all of God's creatures in return.

From the perspective of transcendence, the eyes of faith see the natural world as the gift of God's love, but the eyes of faith also see the God of love in and through the gift of creation.[94] Earth—the "reality illuminated by the love which calls us together into universal communion"—manifests the God who is love, the eternal communion of the three persons of God: Father, Son, and Holy Spirit. Francis states: "For Christians, believing in one God who is trinitarian communion suggests that the Trinity has left its mark on all creation." Referring to Bonaventure, the thirteenth-century Franciscan theologian, Pope Francis elaborates this point: "The Franciscan saint teaches us that *each creature bears in itself a specifically Trinitarian structure*, so real that it could be readily contemplated if only the human gaze were not so partial, dark and fragile. In this way, he points out to us the challenge of trying to read reality in a Trinitarian key" (no. 239). By reading reality in this light, we see that the good (fulfillment) is realized only in and through relationship. "The divine Persons are subsistent relations, and the world, created according to the divine model, is a web of relationships. Creatures tend toward God, and in turn it is proper to every living being to tend toward other things, so that throughout the universe we can find any number of constant and secretly interwoven relationships," states Francis. The human person, accordingly, finds fulfillment in solidarity with others, that is, "to the extent that he or she enters into relationships, going out from themselves to live in communion with God, with others and with all creatures. In this way, they make their own that trinitarian dynamism which God imprinted in them when they were created" (no. 240). Here the Trinity—the eternal communion of the three persons—stands as the supreme model of solidarity for Christians, thus providing both meaning and motivation to our human striving to achieve solidarity with one another and with all creatures of the earth and above the earth.

We find a helpful illustration of the Trinity as the supreme model of solidarity in the fifteenth-century Russian icon of Andrei Rublev. The German theologian Jürgen Moltmann first made reference to the icon in the 1980 preface to *The Trinity and the Kingdom*, the first volume of his systematic theology. (The icon since then has been widely used as an image of the Trinity.) For Moltmann the significance of the icon for the study of the Trinity was its portrayal of mutuality: "Anyone who grasps the truth of this picture understands that it is only in the unity with one another which springs from the self-giving of the Son 'for many' that men and women are in conformity with the triune God." Where we as the human community become most like God is in the unity (solidarity) that we achieve with one another through acts of self-giving love, a love that reflects the unity of love that exists between the Persons of God—Father, Son, and Holy Spirit—and a love that is modeled on God's love for us, expressed in "the surrender of the Son on Golgotha." This unity Moltmann sees portrayed in the icon.[95]

The icon is based on a scene in Gen 18 in which three travelers approach Abraham, who is sitting before his tent. Abraham offers hospitality to the three by giving

94. Donal Dorr makes this distinction. See Dorr, *Option for the Poor and for the Earth*, 420–21.

95. Moltmann, *Trinity and the Kingdom*, xvi. To view the icon, go to: Trinity (Andrei Rublev) https://en.wikipedia.org/.

them a place to rest and a meal that he and Sarah prepare. In the telling of the story in Genesis we come to see the three as God (Yahweh) and two angels—a divine appearance. At the hands of Rublev, the three come to represent the persons of the Trinity—Father, Son, and Holy Spirit. The icon depicts the three sitting at a table, each one of their heads inclined toward the other creating the appearance of circular movement. The distinctiveness of their garb, one from the other, emphasizes the uniqueness of each one, but the inclination of their heads expresses the mutuality that they share with one another. Their mutuality forms a circle, but the circle is open, not closed. The positioning of the figures in the icon is such that there is an opening in the circle—an invitation to the one meditating on the icon to enter the circle. The cup of wine at the center of the table Moltmann interprets as a sign of God's self-giving love for us in the cross that "stands from eternity in the centre of the Trinity."[96] The late Catholic theologian Catherine LaCugna interprets the cup at the center of the table as the eucharistic cup, "the sacramental sign of our communion with God and with one another." She finds it fitting that this divine encounter takes place in the setting of hospitality: "One has the distinct sensation when meditating on the icon that one is not only invited into this communion but, indeed, one already is part of it. A self-contained God, a closed divine society, would hardly be a fitting archetype of hospitality."[97] What both interpretations of the icon share in common is this: the mutual love that binds the persons of the Trinity together as a unity includes us as well, humankind. Abraham invited the visitors to share in his household, but in the end he and Sarah came to share in God's household. So it is with us and all creatures of the earth and above the earth.

In Rublev's icon we see portrayed but one household—our common home seen through the eyes of faith. The figures seated at the table portray the communion of the three persons—Father, Son, and Holy Spirit—but the cup of wine at the center of the table widens the communion of the Three to include, not only humankind, but all of creation. Whether seen as representing God's self-giving love for us in Jesus' death on the cross (Moltmann) or as the Eucharistic sign of our communion with God and with one another (LaCugna), the cup of wine at the center of the table symbolizes all creation being part of the circle—the communion of the Three—and thus having a place at the table. That the Son of God became incarnate—embodied in the world (the Word of God "became flesh") and thus a very real part of the world as the definitive, concrete sign of God's love for the world and all that it holds—means that all that is matter is lifted up and brought into the divine circle, embraced in the communion of the three. Rublev's icon indicates that all creation has a place in God's household, and that the destiny of all creation is to partake in the fullness of God's household—this symbolized in the cup of wine at the center of the table, representing both the death of Jesus on the cross (his identity with all creatures of the world) and the hope that comes from God's raising Jesus from death to the fullness of life. In the death and

96. Moltmann, *Trinity and the Kingdom*, xvi.

97. LaCugna, "God in Communion with Us," 84.

resurrection of Jesus the Christ, God's household becomes our household—the common home of all creation—and God's promise of the fullness of life becomes the basis of our hope.

Pope Francis would agree: "In the Christian understanding of the world, the destiny of all creation is bound up with the mystery of Christ, present from the beginning: 'All things have been created through him and for him' (Col 1:16)." Francis draws our attention to the words of the Prologue of the Gospel of John: "In the beginning was the Word, and the Word was with God, and the Word was God . . . And the Word became flesh and dwelt among us" (John 1:1, 14). Francis comments: "One Person of the Trinity entered into the created cosmos, throwing in his lot with it, even to the cross. From the beginning of the world, but particularly through the incarnation, the mystery of Christ is at work in a hidden manner in the natural world as a whole, without thereby impinging on its autonomy" (no. 99). That the Word of God became flesh joins God with the natural world in a material way, enabling all creatures, human and nonhuman, biotic and abiotic, to participate in the divine communion, and thus to be part of God's life forever. That the Son of God became incarnate is indeed a cosmic event, comments Catholic theologian Elizabeth Johnson, one in which all creatures of the earth and above the earth come to share in the promise of new life manifested in Jesus' resurrection to new life.[98] "This leads us to direct our gaze to the end of time, when the Son will deliver all things to the Father, so that 'God may be everything to every one' (1 Cor 15:28)," says Francis: "Thus, the creatures of this world no longer appear to us under merely natural guise because the risen One is mysteriously holding them to himself and directing them toward fullness as their end. The very flowers of the field and the birds which his human eyes contemplated and admired are now imbued with his radiant presence." (no. 100).

In the eyes of faith, the fullness (goodness) that all creatures seek, including the human creature, is bound up with the fullness (goodness) of God—the loving communion of the Three—this in and through "the mystery of Christ." In this light, the destiny of all creation is seen to be the new creation: "a new heaven and a new earth" (Rev 21:1), indeed, "new heavens and a new earth in which righteousness dwells" (2 Pet 3:13). Here, in God's promise of new life, the eyes of faith find the basis for hope in this time of environmental peril. Our hope is "hope . . . against hope" (Rom 4:18)—a hope that stands apart from all human expectations—much like Abraham's hope that was based on God's promise given to Abraham and Sarah as God and the two angels were departing their hospitality—the promise that Sarah old and childless would bear a son. The basis for Abraham's hope was not a belief in the possibility of bodily regeneration, but his trust in the faithfulness of God. With Abraham's hope came no clear picture of the future, but the courage to move forward into the future which Abraham saw as God's future. The hope that comes from God's promise of new life enables us to face the present and future threat of climate warming directly with a clear-eyed

98. Johnson, *Ask the Beasts*, 197.

assessment of the harm that results from environmental degradation, this based on the evidence of science, and at the same time to respond to the environmental threat with courage and the resolve to act, this based on the conviction of our faith that all creation, from its origin in God's love to its consummation in the fullness of the new creation, exists in the loving embrace of the three persons of God. In the eyes of faith, our actions to address the threat of climate warming are seen both as practical, effective steps toward healing the earth, and as acts that express in concrete ways our love for God's gift of creation and our hope in God's promise of the fullness of life—the new creation. Here our hope-inspired actions that address the harm of environmental degradation participate in and thus make present, albeit in a proleptic manner, the fullness of life that is God's promise, the new creation that is the object of our hope. In this light, to use the words of Francis quoted above, "The creatures of this world no longer appear to us under merely natural guise because the risen One is mysteriously holding them to himself and directing them toward fullness as their end." Our lives are finite; they will end. From modern science we know that our universe is finite; in some form, it too will end. Yet, in the eyes of faith, we see the natural world in a distinctly different light. In the light of the risen One—in the truth that God raised Jesus of Nazareth from death to the fullness of life—we see all creation as destined to share in the fullness of life that is the life of God. Herein lies the basis of Christian hope that moves us to act in this time of environmental peril.[99]

The virtue of hope inspires action. With hope we undertake actions to attain a future (possible) but arduous good, moved to act by our love for the good that we see, however dimly. That our common home—planet Earth—is threatened by climate warming that we humans have caused, this since the dawn of the industrial age, calls for immediate, decisive action on our part to not only adapt to the consequences of climate change, but more importantly to mitigate and then eliminate the emissions of all greenhouse gases, especially carbon dioxide. To this task all peoples of the earth— as individuals, as local communities, as nation-states, as the global community—are called to respond through collective action. What will move us to act collectively? How we act is determined by what we see, and what we see depends on where we stand— our viewpoint: that is, what we value. The dominant viewpoint that undermines all efforts at collective action has been presented under various semblances throughout our study—the financialization of the US economy, the dominance of market ideology, the culture of individualism, the technocratic paradigm—but all semblances of the viewpoint center self-interest and sideline the interests of the whole—from local and familial spheres to regional, to national, to global arenas, to planet Earth itself. Here the good of the whole is seen only in terms of the aggregate of individual goods, thus giving primacy to the individual good as the dominant value. Only an alternative viewpoint that envisages the good of the whole as a common good that is shared by all, and that requires the participation of all to be realized, can provide meaning and

---

99. See Johnson, *Ask the Beasts*, 219–27.

motivation to all who make up the whole in order to act collectively to address a harm that affects the whole, such as the environmental harm of climate change. That such an alternative viewpoint in fact effectively challenges the dominant viewpoint and provides a realistic basis for the hope inspiring collective action (from the local area to the national landscape to the global space), we have seen in the context of the immanent frame (the secular world) and from the perspective of transcendence—specifically from the perspective of Catholic social teaching that envisions the common good as the good shared by all and further in the light of Christian faith as the good shared by all that is the fullness of God's own life. Still, an alternative viewpoint, such as the viewpoint of Catholic social teaching, is a partial viewpoint, as is the dominant viewpoint. To effectively provide meaning and motivation for collective action for the common good, an alternative viewpoint must bring before society, indeed the world community, its vision of the good in such a way that other partial viewpoints come to see what it sees but through their own lens—the good that we share in common. Herein lies the struggle that we must undertake if we as a community are to act collectively for the common good.

The Next Step

Acting for the common good entails struggle, this primarily between different institutional viewpoints. When we as a society or the global community are faced with a contentious social issue, particularly one that concerns a matter of social justice, the voices that speak to the matter at hand are first and foremost institutional voices. Recall the words of the anthropologist Mary Douglas stated in Chapter 3: "The most profound decisions about justice are not made by individuals as such, but by individuals thinking within and on behalf of institutions."[100] Different institutional viewpoints provide distinct yet complementary approaches to social issues, the intended outcome being one of social equilibrium. Here, in the interplay between social institutions, the logic of one institutional viewpoint relativizes the logic of the other viewpoints, preventing any one institution from absolutizing its own viewpoint, thus providing a dynamic balance between society's institutions. The sociologist Robert Bellah and associates, we saw in Chapter 4, underscore the benefit of this institutional interplay for society: "We advocate taking advantage of society's institutional pluralism to escape from the logic of one kind of institution (for example, the market) by looking at it from the standpoint of another (for example, the church)."[101] But contentious social issues elicit conflict and competition, not harmony, between institutional viewpoints, one viewpoint endeavoring to engage the other viewpoints in the light of its own logic, thus translating the logic of other viewpoints into its own. Herein lies the struggle between institutional viewpoints that constitutes public argument, a struggle we saw

100. Douglas, *How Institutions Think*, 124.
101. Bellah et al., *Good Society*, 292.

played out in the extended examples that we have considered throughout our study—the financial crisis of 2008, gender inequality in the family and in the workplace, raising the minimum wage, and climate change. For public argument (dialogue) to be vital all relevant institutional viewpoints must be represented in the argument on their own terms; for public argument to proceed toward a practical, beneficial resolution the argument must have a common point of agreement that all the disputants share (a shared meaning, a common understanding) despite their deep disagreements; for the public argument to end in concrete action the consensus on which the argument is based and the argument itself that holds the disputants together in a common effort must be seen by them as a good to be realized—a good that they share in common. The resolution of the argument, the decision to act for the good on the part of the disputants, is indeed the result of individuals thinking within and on behalf of institutions, but the action itself that is taken is the work of the individuals themselves. Here the good that the disputants share in common exists in the end only in the concrete actions that they take collectively to realize the common good.

The common good exists in concreteness and anticipation. The common good is realized only in and through the concrete acts of individuals that make up social groups, whether they be small and intimate, such as the family, or local, national, or global in scale. The good that these acts seek to realize serves the interests of the individuals who perform them, but at the same time the good is seen and pursued by the individuals as having a meaning and a validity that transcends particular self-interest. Recall the example of Meeder's Restaurant presented in Chapter 4: The actions taken collectively by the restaurant's owners, workers, and customers in response to the State of New York's raising the minimum wage above the federal level (the restaurant being in close proximity to Pennsylvania, which had retained the federal level) were motivated by an awareness of the social good that was shared by all (a good-for-many), but a social good that could be realized only through the cooperative efforts of all, hence a social good that was more than the aggregate good of the individuals involved (a good distributed to many). This particular social good was experienced by the owners, workers, and customers in the concreteness of their decisions and actions, but this social good would have been seen by them more broadly as an instance of human flourishing—the good of being a community—if an explanation of the meaning and motivation of their actions was elicited from them in response to the wider public argument concerning the state government's raising the minimum wage. In this light, the social good would have been seen by them in terms of the end or purpose to be realized in and through their decisions and actions. Here the social good—the common good—stands before them as an idea, as a good to be realized, thus as an anticipation.

As an idea (an ideal), the common good leads us, giving purpose to our concrete decisions and actions without itself being concrete. The process of realizing the common good the Catholic philosopher Patrick Riordan describes as a process that is heuristic, a process that is an open-ended endeavor of discovery, "naming that which is sought, but which is not yet attained." In the process of being a community, the common good is identifiable (able to be named) but not fully specifiable (not having concrete form). In this process, Riordan states, "the end is not yet grasped in its entirety, but is sufficiently identifiable so that the process is directed and focused. The common good of the community names that which is to be realized in the process of pursuing the good life."[102] What gives specificity to the common good then is the actual process of pursuing the good life—the concrete acts that realize, albeit partially, the good of being a community, such as the acts of social justice.

Viewing the pursuit of the common good in the light of faith yields a similar insight. "Placing the common good in this theological horizon," the Catholic theologian Dennis McCann emphasizes, highlights a point that is latent but present throughout the tradition of Catholic social teaching: "the common good is an eschatological concept."[103] Here the common good is seen through the eyes of faith in its ultimate form as the good that is the fullness of life which is life in God—the end or purpose (*eschaton* in Greek) of all creation. The anticipation for Christians that the destiny (consummation) of all creation is life in God points to the future reality that is grounded in God's promise, yet this future reality is made present (given specificity) in the concrete practices of Christian living—in the lived virtues of faith, hope, and love; in the sacramental life of the church—and more broadly in the very existence of the church itself as the believing community. Just as the good is sought in common within the immanent frame, so through the eyes of faith the good that is the fullness of life in God is discovered in and through the embodiments of faith—in the actual process of living the Christian life, in being the community of faith.

What moves us to act for the common good is not the idea of the common good, but the rational desire to realize the common good concretely. The source of moral action, as well as faith action, lies not in the intellect, but in the will. (This we considered in Chapter 3, in Aquinas's account of the moral virtue of justice.) The good that the intellect knows and the passions feel, this the will desires. The will both is moved by the good apprehended by the intellect and moves the self to act in order to realize the good, the object of desire. In being moved by the good to act, we see that the good for us as the object of desire does not lie wholly beyond us, but exists in us first in the form of love for the good, which is the cause of our desire for the good. The will's desire for the good, being moved by the good, begins in love. Recall that the Samaritan's desire to come to the aid of the victim by the side of the road begins in his love (compassion) for the victim, but the parable does not end there. Moral action, as well as faith action, begins in love (love of neighbor, love of God) but ends only in concrete acts that realize the good. In our struggle to realize the common good, then, the common good—"that which is sought, but which is not yet attained" (to borrow Patrick Riordan's words)—is present to us affectively in the form of love and desire,

102. Riordan, *Grammar of the Common Good*, 27.
103. McCann, "Common Good in Catholic Social Teaching," 143.

and rationally in the form of the intellect's apprehension of the common good and in the instrumental reasoning of the practical intellect: all this for the purpose of realizing the common good as the end or purpose not only of the human community but of planet Earth. But the common good exists in actuality only in the concrete acts that we as the human community, individually and collectively, will to undertake in order to realize the good that is social and cosmic justice. For this reason, our study of the common good necessarily remains unfinished. Acting for the common good—this is the next step.

Bibliography

Admati, Anat, and Martin Hellwig. *The Bankers' New Clothes: What's Wrong with Banking and What to Do about It.* Princeton: Princeton University Press, 2013.

Agliardo, Michael, SJ. "The Reception of *Laudato si'* in the United States in Secular and Sacred Arenas." In *All Creation Is Connected: Voices in Response to Pope Francis's Encyclical on Ecology,* edited by Daniel R. DiLeo, 44–62. Winona, MN: Anselm Academic, 2018.

Alexander, Jeffrey C. *The Civil Sphere.* Oxford: Oxford University Press, 2006.

Anderson, Elizabeth. *Value in Ethics and Economics.* Cambridge: Harvard University Press, 1993.

Appiah, Kwame Anthony. *Cosmopolitanism: Ethics in a World of Strangers.* Issues of Our Time. New York: Norton, 2006.

Apuzzo, Matt, and Sarah Hurtes. "Industry Ducks Efforts to Set Climate Rules." *New York Times,* June 4, 2021. https://www.nytimes.com/2021/06/03/world/europe/climate-change -un-international-maritime-organization.html/.

Aristotle. *Metaphysics.* Translated by W. D. Ross. In *The Basic Works of Aristotle,* edited by Richard McKeon, 689–926. New York: Random House, 1941.

———. *Nicomachean Ethics.* Translated by W. D. Ross. In *The Basic Works of Aristotle,* edited by Richard McKeon, 935–1112. New York: Random House, 1941.

———. *Politics.* Translated by Benjamin Jowett. In *The Basic Works of Aristotle,* edited by Richard McKeon, 1127–316. New York: Random House, 1941.

Augustine. *The Confessions of St. Augustine.* Translated by John K. Ryan. Garden City, NY: Image, 1960.

———. *The Trinity.* Translated by John Burnaby. In *Augustine: Later Works,* edited by John Burnaby, 37–181. Library of Christian Classics. Philadelphia: Westminster, 1955.

Bane, Mary Jo. "Public Policy and the Common Good." In *Empirical Foundations of the Common Good: What Theology Can Learn from Social Science,* edited by Daniel K. Finn, 64–90. New York: Oxford University Press, 2017.

Barber, Benjamin R. *A Place for Us: How to Make Society Civil and Democracy Strong.* New York: Hill & Wang, 1998.

Barker, Kim. "When 'Renovations' Lead to Relocation." *New York Times,* May 21, 2018. https://static01.nyt.com/images/2018/05/21/nytfrontpage/scan.pdf

Barker, Kim, et al. "How Courts Became Landlords' Crowbar." *New York Times,* May 22, 2018. https://static01.nyt.com/images/2018/05/22/nytfrontpage/scan.pdf/.

Barrera, Albino. *Economic Compulsion and Christian Ethics.* New Studies in Christian Ethics. Cambridge: Cambridge University Press, 2005.

Bartels, Larry M. *Unequal Democracy: The Political Economy of the New Gilded Age.* 2nd ed. Princeton: Princeton University Press, 2016.

Bell, Daniel. *The Coming of Post-Industrial Society: A Venture in Social Forecasting.* New York: Basic Books, 1973.

Bellah, Robert N. "Religion and *The Civil Sphere*: A Global Perspective." In *Solidarity, Justice, and Incorporation: Thinking through "The Civil Sphere,"* edited by Peter Kivisto and Giuseppe Sciortino, 32–56. Oxford: Oxford University Press, 2015.

Bellah, Robert N., et al. *The Good Society.* New York: Knopf, 1991.

Bellah, Robert N., et al. *Habits of the Heart: Individualism and Commitment in American Life.* Berkeley: University of California Press, 1985.

———. *Habits of the Heart: Individualism and Commitment in American Life.* Updated ed. Berkeley: University of California Press, 1996.

———. *Habits of the Heart: Individualism and Commitment in American Life.* With a new preface. Berkeley: University of California Press, 2008.

———. "Introduction to the Updated Edition: The House Divided." In *Habits of the Heart: Individualism and Commitment in American Life,* vii–xxxix. Updated ed. Berkeley: University of California Press, 1996.

———. "Preface to the 2008 Edition." In *Habits of the Heart: Individualism and Commitment in American Life,* vii–xi. Berkeley: University of California Press, 2008.

Benedict XVI, Pope. *Charity in Truth: Caritas in Veritate.* Washington, DC: United States Conference of Catholic Bishops, 2009.

Benestad, J. Brian. *Church, State, and Society: An Introduction to Catholic Social Doctrine.* Catholic Moral Thought. Washington, DC: Catholic University of America Press, 2011.

Berger, Peter L. *Invitation to Sociology: A Humanistic Perspective.* Anchor Books. Garden City, NY: Doubleday, 1963.

Bernardin, Joseph. "Religion and Politics: The Future Agenda." *Origins: NC Documentary Service* 14.21 (November 8, 1984) 321, 323–28.

———. "Toward a Consistent Ethic of Life: Address at Fordham University." *Origins: NC Documentary Service* 13.29 (December 29, 1983) 491–94.

Blank, Rebecca M., and William McGurn. *Is the Market Moral? A Dialogue on Religion, Economics, and Justice.* The Pew Forum Dialogues on Religion and Public Life. Washington, DC: Brookings Institution, 2004.

Blau, Francine D., and Lawrence M. Kahn. "The Gender Pay Gap: Going, Going . . . But Not Gone." In *The Declining Significance of Gender?,* edited by Francine D. Blau et al., 37–66. New York: Russell Sage Foundation, 2006.

Blinder, Alan S. *After the Music Stopped: The Financial Crisis, the Response, and the Work Ahead.* New York: Penguin, 2013.

Boff, Leonardo. *Cry of the Earth, Cry of the Poor.* Translated by Phillip Berryman. Ecology and Justice. Maryknoll, NY: Orbis, 1997.

Boushey, Heather. *Finding Time: The Economics of Work-Life Conflict.* Cambridge: Harvard University Press, 2016.

Brighouse, Harry. *Justice.* Key Concepts. Cambridge: Polity, 2004.

Brown, Peter. *Augustine of Hippo: A Biography.* Berkeley: University of California Press, 1967.

Byrnes, Timothy A. *Catholic Bishops in American Politics.* Princeton: Princeton University Press, 1991.

Calhoun, Craig. "Introduction: Habermas and the Public Sphere." In *Habermas and the Public Sphere*, edited by Craig Calhoun, 1–48. Studies in Contemporary German Social Thought. Cambridge: MIT Press, 1992.

———. "Series Introduction: From the Current Crisis to Possible Futures." In *Business as Usual: The Roots of the Global Financial Meltdown*, edited by Craig Calhoun and Georgi Derluguian, 9–42. Possible Futures Series 1. New York: New York University Press, 2011.

Calvez, Jean-Yves, SJ, and Jacques Perrin, SJ. *The Church and Social Justice: The Social Teaching of the Popes from Leo XIII to Pius XII.* Translated by J. R. Kirwan. London: Burns & Oates, 1961.

Campbell, John L. *Institutional Change and Globalization.* Princeton: Princeton University Press, 2004.

Caniglia, Beth Schaefer, et al. "Civil Society, Social Movements, and Climate Change." In *Climate Change and Society: Sociological Perspectives*, edited by Riley E. Dunlap and Robert J. Brulle, 235–68. New York: Oxford University Press, 2015.

Carruthers, Bruce G., and Sarah L. Babb. *Economy/Society: Markets, Meanings, and Social Structure.* Sociology for a New Century Series. 2nd ed. Los Angeles: Sage, 2013.

Casanova, José. *Public Religions in the Modern World.* Chicago: University of Chicago Press, 1994.

Chafe, William H. *The Paradox of Change: American Women in the 20th Century.* New York: Oxford University Press, 1991.

Cohen, Jean L. "Interpreting the Notion of Civil Society." In *Toward a Global Civil Society*, edited by Michael Walzer, 35–40. International Political Currents 1. Providence, RI: Berghahn, 1995.

Cohen, Jean L., and Andrew Arato. *Civil Society and Political Theory.* Studies in Contemporary German Social Thought. Cambridge: MIT Press, 1992.

Coleman, John A., SJ. "Retrieving or Re-Inventing Social Catholicism: A Transatlantic Response." In *Catholic Social Thought: Twilight or Renaissance?*, edited by J. S. Boswell et al., 265–92. Bibliotheca Ephemeridum Theologicarum Lovaniensium 157. Leuven: Leuven University Press, 2000.

———. "The Future of Catholic Social Thought." In *Modern Catholic Social Teaching: Commentaries and Interpretations*, edited by Kenneth R. Himes, OFM, 522–44. Washington, DC: Georgetown University Press, 2005.

Copleston, Frederick, SJ. *A History of Philosophy.* Vol. 1, Part 2, *Greece and Rome.* Rev. ed. Garden City, NY: Image, 1962.

———. *A History of Philosophy.* Vol. 5, Part 2, *Modern Philosophy: The British Philosophers.* Garden City, NY: Image, 1964.

Cronin, Bruce. *Institutions for the Common Good: International Protection Regimes in International Society.* Cambridge Studies in International Relations 93. Cambridge: Cambridge University Press, 2003.

Curran, Charles E. *Catholic Social Teaching 1891–Present: A Historical, Theological, and Ethical Analysis.* Moral Traditions Series. Washington, DC: Georgetown University Press, 2002.

———. *The Development of Moral Theology: Five Strands.* Moral Traditions Series. Washington, DC: Georgetown University Press, 2013.

———. "Relating Religious-Ethical Inquiry to Economic Policy." In *The Catholic Challenge to the American Economy: Reflections on the U.S. Bishops' Pastoral Letter on Catholic Social*

Teaching and the U.S. Economy, edited by Thomas M. Gannon, SJ, 42–54. New York: Macmillan, 1987.

Dahl, Robert A. *On Democracy.* Nota Bene. New Haven: Yale University Press, 2000.

Davis, Gerald F. *Managed by the Markets: How Finance Reshaped America.* Oxford: Oxford University Press, 2009.

DeFleur, Melvin L., et al. *Sociology: Human Society.* 2nd ed. Glenview, IL: Scott, Foresman, 1977.

Dembinski, Paul H. "Toward a Financial Education Geared to Common Good: Some Preliminary Proposals." In *Finance and the Common Good: Placing People at the Center of the Economy and Society*, 33–47. Mahwah, NJ: Paulist, 2016.

Derenoncourt, Ellora, and Claire Montialoux. "Raise the Minimum Wage." *New York Times*, October 26, 2020. https://www.nytimes.com/2020/10/25/opinion/minimum-wage-race-protests.html/.

Desmond, Matthew. *Evicted: Poverty and Profit in the American City.* New York: Crown, 2016.

Dessler, Andrew. *Introduction to Modern Climate Change.* 2nd ed. New York: Cambridge University Press, 2016.

Dessler, Andrew E., and Edward A. Parson. *The Science and Politics of Global Climate Change: A Guide to the Debate.* 3rd ed. Cambridge: Cambridge University Press, 2020.

Donahue, John R., SJ. *The Gospel in Parable: Metaphor, Narrative, and Theology in the Synoptic Gospels.* Philadelphia: Fortress, 1988.

Dorr, Donal. *Option for the Poor and for the Earth: From Leo XIII to Pope Francis.* Rev ed. Maryknoll, NY: Orbis, 2016.

———. "Solidarity and Integral Human Development." In *The Logic of Solidarity: Commentaries on Pope John Paul II's Encyclical "On Social Concern,"* edited by Gregory Baum and Robert Ellsberg, 143–54. Maryknoll, NY: Orbis, 1989.

Douglas, Mary. *How Institutions Think.* The Frank W. Abrams Lectures. Syracuse: Syracuse University Press, 1986.

Dulles, Avery, SJ. *The Reshaping of Catholicism: Current Challenges in the Theology of Church.* San Francisco: Harper & Row, 1988.

Dworkin, Ronald. *Taking Rights Seriously.* Revised, with a new appendix and a response to critics. Cambridge: Harvard University Press, 1978.

Edwards, Michael. *Civil Society.* 3rd ed. Cambridge: Polity, 2014.

Elsbernd, Mary, OSF, and Reimund Bieringer. *When Love Is Not Enough: A Theo-Ethic of Justice.* Collegeville, MN: Liturgical, 2002.

Elshtain, Jean Bethke. *Augustine and the Limits of Politics.* Catholic Ideas for a Secular World. Notre Dame: University of Notre Dame Press, 1995.

England, Paula. "Toward Gender Equality: Progress and Bottlenecks." In *The Declining Significance of Gender?*, edited by Francine D. Blau et al., 245–64. New York: Russell Sage Foundation, 2006.

Falwell, Jerry. "Future-Word: An Agenda for the Eighties." In *The Fundamentalist Phenomenon: The Resurgence of Conservative Christianity*, edited by Jerry Falwell et al., 186–223. Garden City, NY: Doubleday, 1981.

Ferguson, Charles, dir. *Inside Job.* Written by Charles Ferguson et al. Starring Matt Damon et al. Sony Pictures Classics, 2010.

Financial Crisis Inquiry Commission. *The Financial Crisis Inquiry Report: Final Report of the National Commission on the Causes of the Financial and Economic Crisis in the United States.* Authorized ed. New York: Public Affairs, 2011.

Finn, Daniel K. *The Moral Ecology of Markets: Assessing Claims about Markets and Justice.* Cambridge: Cambridge University Press, 2006.

Fiorenza, Francis Schüssler. "The Church as a Community of Interpretation: Political Theology between Discourse Ethics and Hermeneutical Reconstruction." In *Habermas, Modernity, and Public Theology*, edited by Don S. Browning and Francis Schüssler Fiorenza, 66–91. New York: Crossroad, 1992.

Fleischacker, Samuel. *A Short History of Distributive Justice.* Cambridge: Harvard University Press, 2004.

Francis, Pope. *Laudato si'* (*On Care for Our Common Home*). Washington, DC: United States Conference of Catholic Bishops, 2015.

Frankena, William K. *Ethics.* 2nd ed. Prentice-Hall Foundations of Philosophy Series. Englewood Cliffs, NJ: Prentice-Hall, 1973.

Freeman, Samuel. *Rawls.* Routledge Philosophers. New York: Routledge, 2007.

Friedman, Gillian. "Base Wage of \$15 Gains in Popularity across U.S." *New York Times,* January 1, 2021. https://www.nytimes.com/2020/12/31/business/economy/minimum-wage-15-dollar-hour.html/.

Friedman, Lisa, and Coral Davenport. "G.O.P. Shifts on Climate, but Not on Fossil Fuels." *New York Times,* August 14, 2021. https://www.nytimes.com/2021/08/13/climate/republicans-climate-change.html/.

Friedman, Milton. *Capitalism and Freedom.* With the assistance of Rose D. Friedman; with a new preface by the author. 40th anniversary ed. Chicago: University of Chicago Press, 2002.

Gallagher, David M. "The Will and Its Acts (Ia IIae, qq. 6–17)." In *The Ethics of Aquinas,* edited by Stephen J. Pope, 69–89. Moral Traditions Series. Washington, DC: Georgetown University Press, 2002.

Godøy, Anna, and Michael Reich. "Minimum Wage Effects in Low-Wage Areas." *Institute for Research on Labor and Employment.* Working Paper No. 106–19 (July 2019). https://irle.berkeley.edu/publications/working-papers/minimum-wage-effects-in-low-wage-areas/.

Goldin, Claudia. *Career and Family: Women's Century-Long Journey toward Equity.* Princeton: Princeton University Press, 2021.

Gould, William J. "Father J. Bryan Hehir: Priest, Policy Analyst, and Theologian of Dialogue." In *Religious Leaders and Faith-Based Politics: Ten Profiles,* edited by Jo Renee Formicola and Hubert Morken, 196–223. Lanham, MD: Rowman & Littlefield, 2001.

Gula, Richard M., SS. *Reason Informed by Faith: Foundations of Catholic Morality.* New York: Paulist, 1989.

Habermas, Jürgen. *Between Facts and Norms: Contributions to a Discourse Theory of Law and Democracy.* Translated by William Rehg. Studies in Contemporary German Social Thought. Cambridge: MIT Press, 1996.

———. "Learning from Catastrophe? A Look Back at the Short Twentieth Century." In *The Postnational Constellation: Political Essays,* 38–57. Translated, edited, and with an introduction by Max Pensky. Studies in Contemporary German Social Thought. Cambridge: MIT Press, 2001.

———. "The Postnational Constellation and the Future of Democracy." In *The Postnational Constellation: Political Essays,* 58–112. Translated, edited, and with an introduction by Max Pensky. Studies in Contemporary German Social Thought. Cambridge: MIT Press, 2001.

———. *The Structural Transformation of the Public Sphere: An Inquiry into a Category of Bourgeois Society.* Translated by Thomas Burger with the assistance of Frederick Lawrence. Studies in Contemporary German Social Thought. Cambridge: MIT Press, 1989.

Hacker, Jacob S., and Paul Pierson. *Winner-Take-All Politics: How Washington Made the Rich Richer—and Turned Its Back on the Middle Class.* New York: Simon & Schuster, 2010.

Haight, Roger, SJ. *An Alternative Vision: An Interpretation of Liberation Theology.* Mahwah, NJ: Paulist, 1985.

Haldane, John. *Faithful Reason: Essays Catholic and Philosophical.* London: Routledge, 2004.

———. "Natural Law and Ethical Pluralism." In *Faithful Reason: Essays Catholic and Philosophical,* 129–51. London: Routledge, 2004.

———. *Practical Philosophy: Ethics, Society and Culture.* St. Andrews Studies in Philosophy and Public Affairs. Exeter, UK: Imprint Academic, 2009.

Hamel, Ronald. "*Justice in the World.*" In *The New Dictionary of Catholic Social Thought,* edited by Judith A. Dwyer, 495–501. Collegeville, MN: Liturgical, 1994.

Harak, G. Simon, SJ. *Virtuous Passions: The Formation of Christian Character.* Mahwah, NJ: Paulist, 1993.

Hardin, Garrett. "The Tragedy of the Commons." *Science* 162 (1968) 1243–48.

Harrell-Bond, B. E., and Andrew Shacknove. "Refugees." In *The Oxford Companion to Politics of the World,* edited by Joel Krieger, 776–78. New York: Oxford University Press, 1993.

Hehir, J. Bryan. "Principles and Politics: Differing with Dulles." *Commonweal* 114 (March 27, 1987) 169–70.

———. "The Right and Competence of the Church in the American Case." In *One Hundred Years of Catholic Social Thought: Celebration and Challenge,* edited by John A. Coleman, SJ, 55–71. Maryknoll, NY: Orbis, 1991.

Heilbroner, Robert, and Lester Thurow. *Economics Explained: Everything You Need to Know about How the Economy Works and Where It's Going.* Newly rev. and updated. New York: Touchstone, 1998.

Herbert, David. *Religion and Civil Society: Rethinking Public Religion in the Contemporary World.* Religion, Culture, and Society Series. Aldershot, UK: Ashgate, 2003.

Hewlett, Sylvia Ann, and Carolyn Buck Luce. "Off-Ramps and On-Ramps: Keeping Talented Women on the Road to Success." *Harvard Business Review* 83 (March 2005) 43–54.

Heyer, Kristin E. "Catholics in the Political Arena: How Faith Should Inform Catholic Voters and Politicians." In *Catholics and Politics: The Dynamic Tension between Faith and Power,* edited by Kristin E. Heyer et al., 61–72. Religion and Politics Series. Washington, DC: Georgetown University Press, 2008.

———. *Prophetic & Public: The Social Witness of U.S. Catholicism.* Moral Traditions Series. Washington, DC: Georgetown University Press, 2006.

Himes, Michael J., and Kenneth R. Himes, OFM. *Fullness of Faith: The Public Significance of Theology.* Isaac Hecker Studies in Religion and American Culture. New York: Paulist, 1993.

Himes, Kenneth R., OFM. "Commentary on *Justitia in Mundo (Justice in the World).*" In *Modern Catholic Social Teaching: Commentaries and Interpretations,* edited by Kenneth R. Himes, OFM, 333–62. Washington, DC: Georgetown University Press, 2005.

Hirschman, Alber O. *Exit, Voice, and Loyalty: Responses to Decline in Firms, Organizations, and States.* Cambridge: Harvard University Press, 1970.

Hobbes, Thomas. *Leviathan: Authoritative Text, Backgrounds, Interpretations.* 1651. Edited by Richard E. Flathman and David Johnston. A Norton critical Edition. New York: Norton, 1997.

Hochschild, Jennifer L. "Where You Stand Depends on What You See: Connections among Values, Perceptions of Fact, and Political Prescriptions." In *Citizens and Politics: Perspectives from Political Psychology*, edited by James H. Kuklinski, 313–40. Cambridge Studies in Political Psychology and Public Opinion. Cambridge: Cambridge University Press, 2001.

Hoffmann, Tobias. "Prudence and Practical Principles." In *Aquinas and "The Nicomachean Ethics*,*"* edited by Tobias Hoffmann et al., 165–83. Cambridge: Cambridge University Press, 2013.

Hollenbach, David, SJ. "Afterword: A Community of Freedom." In *Catholicism and Liberalism: Contributions to American Public Philosophy*, edited by R. Bruce Douglass and David Hollenbach, 323–43. Cambridge Studies in Religion and American Public Life. Cambridge: Cambridge University Press, 1994.

———. "Commentary on *Gaudium et spes* (*Pastoral Constitution on the Church in the Modern World*)." In *Modern Catholic Social Teaching: Commentaries and Interpretations*, edited by Kenneth R. Himes, OFM, 266–91. Washington, DC: Georgetown University Press, 2005.

———. *The Common Good and Christian Ethics.* New Studies in Christian Ethics 22. Cambridge: Cambridge University Press, 2002.

———. "A Communitarian Reconstruction of Human Rights: Contributions from Catholic Tradition." In *Catholicism and Liberalism: Contributions to American Public Philosophy*, edited by R. Bruce Douglass and David Hollenbach, 127–50. Cambridge Studies in Religion and American Public Life. Cambridge: Cambridge University Press, 1994.

———. *The Global Face of Public Faith: Politics, Human Rights, and Christian Ethics.* Moral Traditions Series. Washington, DC: Georgetown University Press 2003.

———. "Modern Catholic Teachings Concerning Justice." In *The Faith That Does Justice: Examining the Christian Sources for Social Change*, edited by John C. Haughey, 207–31. Woodstock Studies 2. New York: Paulist, 1977.

Hume, David. *A Treatise of Human Nature.* Edited by L. A. Selby-Bigge. Oxford: Clarendon, 1888. Reprint, Oxford: Clarendon, 1968.

Intergovernmental Panel on Climate Change. "IPCC, 2021: Summary for Policymakers." In *Climate Change 2021: The Physical Science Basis. Contribution of Working Group I to the Sixth Assessment Report of the Intergovernmental Panel on Climate Change.* Cambridge: Cambridge University Press, forthcoming.

Jacobs, Jerry A., and Kathleen Gerson. *The Time Divide: Work, Family, and Gender Inequality.* The Family and Public Policy. Cambridge: Harvard University Press, 2004.

Jayachandran, Seema. "A Raise for Workers Can Be a Win for All." *New York Times*, June 21, 2020. https://www.nytimes.com/2020/06/18/business/coronavirus-minimum-wage-increase.html/.

Jefferson, Thomas. "Letter of January 1, 1802, to the Danbury Baptist Association." In *The Papers of Thomas Jefferson*, Vol. 36, *1 December 1801—3 March 1802*, edited by Barbara B. Oberg, 258. Princeton: Princeton University Press, 2009.

Jeremias, Joachim. *The Parables of Jesus.* Translated by S. H. Hooke. Rev. ed. New York: Scribner, 1963.

John Paul II, Pope. *Centesimus annus (On the Hundredth Anniversary of Rerum novarum)*. In *Catholic Social Thought: The Documentary Heritage*, edited by David J. O'Brien and Thomas A. Shannon, 439–88. Maryknoll, NY: Orbis, 1992.

———. "Pope John Paul II: Opening Address at the Puebla Conference." In *Puebla and Beyond: Documentation and Commentary*, edited by John Eagleson and Philip Scharper, 57–71. Translated by John Drury. Maryknoll, NY: Orbis, 1979.

———. *Sollicitudo rei socialis (On Social Concern)*. In *Catholic Social Thought: The Documentary Heritage*, edited by David J. O'Brien and Thomas A. Shannon, 395–436. Maryknoll, NY: Orbis, 1992.

John XXIII, Pope. *Mater et magistra (Christianity and Social Progress)*. In *Catholic Social Thought: The Documentary Heritage*, edited by David J. O'Brien and Thomas A. Shannon, 84–128. Maryknoll, NY: Orbis, 1992.

Johnson, Elizabeth A. *Ask the Beasts: Darwin and the God of Love*. London: Bloomsbury, 2014.

Johnson, Luke T. *Sharing Possessions: Mandate and Symbol of Faith*. Overtures to Biblical Theology. Philadelphia: Fortress, 1981.

Johnson, Simon, and James Kwak. *13 Bankers: The Wall Street Takeover and the Next Financial Meltdown*. New York: Pantheon, 2010.

Karris, Robert J. *Invitation to Acts: A Commentary on the Acts of the Apostles with Complete Text from the Jerusalem Bible*. Doubleday New Testament Commentary Series. Garden City, NY: Image, 1978.

Keenan, James F., SJ. *Goodness and Rightness in Thomas Aquinas's "Summa Theologiae."* Washington, DC: Georgetown University Press, 1992.

Kent, Bonnie. "Habits and Virtues (Ia IIae, qq. 49–70)." In *The Ethics of Aquinas*, edited by Stephen J. Pope, 116–30. Moral Traditions Series. Washington, DC: Georgetown University Press, 2002.

———. "Losable Virtue: Aquinas on Character and Will." In *Aquinas and "The Nicomachean Ethics,"* edited by Tobias Hoffmann et al., 91–109. Cambridge: Cambridge University Press, 2013.

Keys, Mary M. *Aquinas, Aristotle, and the Promise of the Common Good*. Cambridge: Cambridge University Press, 2006.

Kirk-Duggan, Cheryl A. "A Rose by Any Other Name? Deconstructing the Essence of Common." In *In Search of the Common Good*, edited by Dennis P. McCann and Patrick D. Miller, 190–210. Theology for the Twenty-First Century. New York: T. & T. Clark, 2005.

Kleinfield, N. R. "Pleading for Their Homes, in Sea of Chaos and Grime." *New York Times*, May 27, 2018. https://www.nytimes.com/images/2018/05/27/nytfrontpage/scan.pdf/.

Kraut, Richard. *Aristotle: Political Philosophy*. Founders of Modern Political and Social Thought. Oxford: Oxford University Press, 2002.

———. *What Is Good and Why: The Ethics of Well-Being*. Cambridge: Harvard University Press, 2007.

Krippner, Greta R. *Capitalizing on Crisis: The Political Origins of the Rise of Finance*. Cambridge: Harvard University Press, 2011.

Krugman, Paul. *End This Depression Now!* New York: Norton, 2012.

———. "Why Weren't Alarm Bells Ringing?" Review of *The Shifts and the Shocks: What We've Learned—and Still Have to Learn—from the Financial Crisis*, by Martin Wolf.

New York Review of Books 61 (October 23, 2014) 41–42. https://www.nybooks.com/articles/2014/10/23/why-werent-alarm-bells-ringing/.

LaCugna, Catherine Mowry. "God in Communion with Us: The Trinity." In *Freeing Theology: The Essentials of Theology in Feminist Perspective*, edited by Catherine Mowry LaCugna, 83–113. San Francisco: HarperSanFrancisco, 1993.

Leo XIII, Pope. *Rerum novarum (The Condition of Labor)*. In *Catholic Social Thought: The Documentary Heritage*, edited by David J. O'Brien and Thomas A. Shannon, 14–39. Maryknoll, NY: Orbis, 1992.

Lewis, Michael. *The Big Short: Inside the Doomsday Machine*. New York: Norton, 2010.

Lindblom, Charles E. *The Market System: What It Is, How It Works, and What to Make of It*. Yale ISPS Series. New Haven: Yale University Press, 2001.

Locke, John. *The Second Treatise of Government*. In *Two Treatises of Government*, edited by Mark Goldie, 113–240. Everyman's Library. London: Dent, 1993.

Lopez, Steve. "A Total Abdication of Leadership." *Los Angeles Times*, June 5, 2019. https://www.latimes.com/local/california/la-me-lopez-06052019-story.html/.

Los Angeles Times Editorial Board. "Can a City with 58,000 Homeless Still Function?" *Los Angeles Times*, March 1, 2018. https://enewspaper.latimes.com/infinity/article_share.aspx?guid=b323a5d0-ced0-4137-8002-8c6117b05018/.

Lowenstein, Roger. *The End of Wall Street*. New York: Penguin, 2010.

MacIntyre, Alasdair. *After Virtue: A Study in Moral Theory*. 2nd ed. Notre Dame: University of Notre Dame Press, 1984.

———. *Dependent Rational Animals: Why Human Beings Need the Virtues*. The Paul Carus Lecture Series 20. Chicago: Open Court, 1999.

Madison, James. "Letter of September 1833 to the Reverend Jasper Adams." In *Religion and Politics in the Early Republic: Jasper Adams and the Church-State Debate*, edited by Daniel L. Dreisbach, 117–21. Lexington: University Press of Kentucky, 1996.

Madrick, Jeff. *Age of Greed: The Triumph of Finance and the Decline of America, 1970 to the Present*. New York: Knopf, 2011.

Maguire, Daniel C. *Ethics: A Complete Method for Moral Choice*. Minneapolis: Fortress, 2010.

Mann, Michael E. *The Hockey Stick and the Climate Wars: Dispatches from the Front Lines*. New York: Columbia University Press, 2012.

———. *The New Climate War: The Fight to Take Back Our Planet*. New York: PublicAffairs, 2021.

Mann, Michael E., and Lee R. Kump. *Dire Predictions: Understanding Climate Change*. 2nd American ed. New York: DK, 2015.

Mann, Michael E., and Tom Toles. *The Madhouse Effect: How Climate Change Denial Is Threatening Our Planet, Destroying Our Politics, and Driving Us Crazy*. New York: Columbia University Press, 2016.

Mantzavinos, C. *Individuals, Institutions, and Markets*. The Political Economy of Institutions and Decisions. Cambridge: Cambridge University Press, 2001.

Marsh, Abigail. "We Aren't as Selfish as We Think." *New York Times*, May 27, 2021. https://www.nytimes.com/2021/05/26/opinion/individualism-united-states-altruism.html/.

Martin, Lisa L. "International Cooperation." In *The Oxford Companion to Politics of the World*, edited by Joel Krieger, 434–36. New York: Oxford University Press, 1993.

May, Larry. *The Morality of Groups: Collective Responsibility, Group-Based Harm, and Corporate Rights*. Soundings. Notre Dame: University of Notre Dame Press, 1987.

McBrien, Richard P. *Catholicism*. Minneapolis: Winston, 1981.

———. *Caesar's Coin: Religion and Politics in America*. New York: Macmillan, 1987.

McCann, Dennis P. "The Common Good in Catholic Social Teaching: A Case Study in Modernization." In *In Search of the Common Good*, edited by Dennis P. McCann and Patrick D. Miller, 121–46. Theology for the Twenty-First Century. New York: T. & T. Clark, 2005.

Mich, Marvin L. Krier. *Catholic Social Teaching and Movements*. Mystic, CT: Twenty-Third Publications, 1998.

Miller, Claire Cain. "Race and Class Define Men Who Take 'Women's Jobs.'" *New York Times*, March 10, 2017. https://www.nytimes.com/2017/03/09/upshot/more-men-are-taking-womens-jobs-at-least-certain-men.html/.

Miller, David. "Complex Equality." In *Pluralism, Justice, and Equality*, edited by David Miller and Michael Walzer, 197–225. Oxford: Oxford University Press, 1995.

———. *Principles of Social Justice*. Cambridge: Harvard University Press, 1999.

Moltmann, Jürgen. *The Trinity and the Kingdom: The Doctrine of God*. Translated by Margaret Kohl. 1981. Reprint, 1st Fortress ed., with new preface Minneapolis: Fortress, 1993.

Mooney, Christopher F., SJ. *Boundaries Dimly Perceived: Law, Religion, Education, and the Common Good*. Notre Dame Studies in Law and Contemporary Issues 3. Notre Dame: University of Notre Dame Press, 1990.

———. *Public Virtue: Law and the Social Character of Religion*. Notre Dame Studies in Law and Contemporary Issues 2. Notre Dame: University of Notre Dame Press, 1986.

Murray, John Courtney, SJ. *We Hold These Truths: Catholic Reflections on the American Proposition*. Kansas City, MO: Sheed & Ward, 1960.

———. *We Hold These Truths: Catholic Reflections on the American Proposition*. New ed. Sheed & Ward Classic. Lanham, MD: Rowman & Littlefield, 2005.

National Conference of Catholic Bishops. *The Challenge of Peace: God's Promise and Our Response; A Pastoral Letter on War and Peace*. Publication of the United States Catholic Conference 863. Washington, DC: United States Catholic Conference, 1983.

———. *Economic Justice for All: Pastoral Letter on Catholic Teaching and the U.S. Economy*. Publication of the United States Catholic Conference 101. Washington, DC: United States Catholic Conference, 1986.

Nozick, Robert. *Anarchy, State, and Utopia*. New York: Basic Books, 1974.

Nussbaum, Martha C. *Cultivating Humanity: A Classical Defense of Reform in Liberal Education*. Cambridge: Harvard University Press, 1997.

———. "Patriotism and Cosmopolitanism." In *For Love of Country: Debating the Limits of Patriotism*, edited by Joshua Cohen, 3–17. Boston: Beacon, 1996.

———. "Rawls and Feminism." In *The Cambridge Companion to Rawls*, edited by Samuel Freeman, 488–520. Cambridge Companions to Philosophy. Cambridge: Cambridge University Press, 2003.

O'Brien, David J., and Thomas A. Shannon, eds. *Catholic Social Thought: The Documentary Heritage*. Maryknoll, NY: Orbis, 1992.

O'Connell, Timothy E. *Principles for a Catholic Morality*. San Francisco: Harper & Row, 1978.

Okin, Susan Moller. *Justice, Gender, and the Family*. New York: Basic Books, 1989.

Oreskes, Benjamin, and Doug Smith. "County Homelessness Increases 12%." *Los Angeles Times*, June 5, 2019. https://enewspaper.latimes.com/infinity/article_share.aspx?guid=ef291ef3-20e0-4ae2-b209-669e60446edf/.

Oreskes, Naomi, and Erik M. Conway. *Merchants of Doubt: How a Handful of Scientists Obscured the Truth on Issues from Tobacco Smoke to Global Warming.* New York: Bloomsbury, 2010.

Ostrom, Elinor. *Governing the Commons: The Evolution of Institutions for Collective Action.* The Political Economy of Institutions and Decisions. Cambridge: Cambridge University Press, 1990.

Pappas, Nickolas. *Routledge Philosophy Guidebook to Plato and "The Republic."* Routledge Philosophy Guidebooks. London: Routledge, 1995.

Pasnau, Robert. *Thomas Aquinas on Human Nature: A Philosophical Study of Summa Theologiae Ia 75–89.* Cambridge: Cambridge University Press, 2002.

Paul VI, Pope. *Octogesima adveniens* (*A Call to Action*). In *Catholic Social Thought: The Documentary Heritage*, edited by David J. O'Brien and Thomas A. Shannon, 265–86. Maryknoll, New York: Orbis, 1992.

Perkams, Matthias. "Aquinas on Choice, Will, and Voluntary Action." In *Aquinas and "The Nicomachean Ethics,"* edited by Tobias Hoffmann et al., 72–90. Cambridge: Cambridge University Press, 2013.

Phillips, Kevin. *Bad Money: Reckless Finance, Failed Politics, and the Global Crisis of American Capitalism.* New York: Viking, 2008.

Piaget, Jean. *The Moral Judgment of the Child.* Translated by Marjorie Gabain. 1932. Reprint, 1st Free Press paperback ed. Psychology. New York: Free Press, 1965.

Pieper, Josef. *The Four Cardinal Virtues: Prudence, Justice, Fortitude, Temperance.* Translated by Richard and Clara Winston et al. Notre Dame: University of Notre Dame Press, 1966.

———. *Leisure the Basis of Culture.* Translated by Alexander Dru. New York: Pantheon, 1952.

Pinckaers, Servais, OP. *The Sources of Christian Ethics.* Translated by Sr. Mary Thomas Noble, OP. Washington, DC: Catholic University of America Press, 1995.

Pius XI, Pope. *Quadragesimo anno* (*After Forty Years*). In *Catholic Social Thought: The Documentary Heritage*, edited by David J. O'Brien and Thomas A. Shannon, 42–79. Maryknoll, NY: Orbis, 1992.

Plato. *The Republic of Plato.* Translated by Francis MacDonald Cornford. Oxford University Press paperback. London: Oxford University Press, 1941.

Plumer, Brad, and Lisa Friedman. "Climate Summit Reaches Accord amid Contention." *New York Times*, November 14, 2021. https://www.nytimes.com/2021/11/13/climate/cop26-glasgow-climate-agreement.html/.

Plumer, Brad, and Nadja Popovich. "Figuring Out Who Bears the Most Responsibility for Climate Change." *New York Times*, November 13, 2021. https://www.nytimes.com/interactive/2021/11/12/climate/cop26-emissions-compensation.html/.

Porter, Jean. *Justice as a Virtue: A Thomistic Perspective.* Grand Rapids: Eerdmans, 2016.

———. *Nature as Reason: A Thomistic Theory of the Natural Law.* Grand Rapids: Eerdmans, 2005.

———. "The Virtue of Justice (IIa IIae, qq. 58–122)." In *The Ethics of Aquinas*, edited by Stephen J. Pope, 272–86. Moral Traditions Series. Washington, DC: Georgetown University Press, 2002.

Rahner, Karl, SJ. "Reflections on the Unity of the Love of Neighbor and the Love of God." In *Theological Investigations*, 6:231–49. Translated by Karl-H. and Boniface Kruger. 14 vols. Baltimore: Helicon, 1969.

Rawls, John. *Collected Papers.* Edited by Samuel Freeman. Cambridge: Harvard University Press, 1999.

———. "The Idea of Public Reason Revisited." In *Collected Papers*, edited by Samuel Freeman, 573–615. Cambridge: Harvard University Press, 1999.

———. "Justice as Fairness: Political Not Metaphysical." In *Collected Papers*, edited by Samuel Freeman, 388–414. Cambridge: Harvard University Press, 1999.

———. *Justice as Fairness: A Restatement*. Edited by Erin Kelly. Cambridge: Belknap, 2001.

———. *Political Liberalism*. John Dewey Essays in Philosophy 4. New York: Columbia University Press, 1996.

———. *A Theory of Justice*. Cambridge: Belknap, 1971.

Reich, Robert B. *The Common Good*. New York: Knopf, 2018.

Reiss, Ira L. *Family Systems in America*. 2nd ed. Hinsdale, IL: Dryden, 1976.

Riordan, Patrick. *Global Ethics and Global Common Goods*. Bloomsbury Studies in Global Ethics. London: Bloomsbury, 2015.

———. *A Grammar of the Common Good: Speaking of Globalization*. Continuum Studies in Religion and Political Culture. London: Continuum, 2008.

———. *A Politics of the Common Good*. Dublin: Institute of Public Administration, 1996.

Rodgers, Daniel T. *Age of Fracture*. Cambridge: Belknap, 2011.

Rosenau, James N. "International Relations." In *The Oxford Companion to Politics of the World*, edited by Joel Krieger, 455–60. New York: Oxford University Press, 1993.

Roubini, Nouriel, and Stephen Mihm. *Crisis Economics: A Crash Course in the Future of Finance*. New York: Penguin, 2010.

Sacks, Jonathan. *The Home We Build Together: Recreating Society*. London: Continuum, 2007.

Sassen, Saskia. *Sociology of Globalization*. New York: Norton, 2007.

———. *Territory, Authority, Rights: From Medieval to Global Assemblages*. Updated ed. Princeton: Princeton University Press, 2006.

Scheid, Daniel P. *The Cosmic Common Good: Religious Grounds for Ecological Ethics*. New York: Oxford University Press, 2016.

———. "*Laudato si'* and the Development of Catholic Social Teaching." In *All Creation Is Connected: Voices in Response to Pope Francis's Encyclical on Ecology*, edited by Daniel R. DiLeo, 182–94. Winona, MN: Anselm Academic, 2018.

Schubeck, Thomas L., SJ. *Love That Does Justice*. Maryknoll, NY: Orbis, 2007.

Schuck, Michael J. "Modern Catholic Social Thought." In *The New Dictionary of Catholic Social Thought*, edited by Judith A. Dwyer, 611–32. Collegeville, MN: Liturgical, 1994.

———. *That They Be One: The Social Teaching of the Papal Encyclicals 1740–1989*. Washington, DC: Georgetown University Press, 1991.

Scott, A. O. "Who Maimed the Economy, and How." Review of *Inside Job*, directed by Charles Ferguson. *New York Times*, October 7, 2010. https://www.nytimes.com/2010/10/08/movies/08inside.html/.

Selznick, Philip. *The Communitarian Persuasion*. Washington, DC: Woodrow Wilson Center Press, 2002.

———. *The Moral Commonwealth: Social Theory and the Promise of Community*. Berkeley: University of California Press, 1992.

Sen, Amartya. *The Idea of Justice*. Cambridge: Belknap, 2009.

Sengupta, Somini, et al. "Deadline Passes, but Climate Plan Remains Elusive." *New York Times*, November 13, 2021. https://www.nytimes.com/2021/11/12/climate/glasgow-climate-cop26.html/.

Shelley, Bruce L. *Church History in Plain Language*. 2nd ed. Dallas: Word, 1995.

Shiller, Robert J. *Finance and the Good Society*. Princeton: Princeton University Press, 2012.

Smialek, Jeanna "As Push for Higher Wages Grows, New York Offers a Test Case." *New York Times*, November 13, 2019. https://www.nytimes.com/2019/11/13/business/economy/minimum-wage-new-york-pennsylvania.html/.

Smith, Adam. *An Inquiry into the Nature and Causes of the Wealth of Nations*. Great Books of the Western World 39. Chicago: Encyclopaedia Britannica, 1952.

———. *The Theory of Moral Sentiments*. Great Books in Philosophy. Amherst, NY: Prometheus, 2000.

Sowell, Thomas. *Basic Economics: A Citizen's Guide to the Economy*. Rev. and exp. ed. New York: Basic Books, 2004.

———. *The Housing Boom and Bust*. Rev. ed. New York: Basic Books, 2010.

Spicq, Ceslaus, OP. *Agape in the New Testament*. Vol. 1, *Agape in the Synoptic Gospels*. Translated by Sister Marie Aquinas McNamara, OP, and Sister Mary Honoria Richter, OP. 3 vols. 1963–1966. Reprint, Eugene, OR: Wipf & Stock, 2006–2007.

Stiglitz, Joseph E. *Freefall: America, Free Markets, and the Sinking of the World Economy*. New York: Norton, 2010.

———. *Globalization and Its Discontents*. New York: Norton, 2003.

———. *The Price of Inequality*. New York: Norton, 2012.

Synod of Bishops. *Justitia in Mundo (Justice in the World)*. In *Catholic Social Thought: The Documentary Heritage*. Edited by David J. O'Brien and Thomas A. Shannon, 288–300. Maryknoll, NY: Orbis, 1992.

Taylor, Charles. "Irreducibly Social Goods." In *Philosophical Arguments*, 127–45. Cambridge: Harvard University Press, 1995.

———. *A Secular Age*. Cambridge: Belknap, 2007.

———. "Western Secularity." In *Rethinking Secularism*, edited by Craig Calhoun et al., 31–53. Oxford: Oxford University Press, 2011.

Taylor, John B. *Getting Off Track: How Government Actions and Interventions Caused, Prolonged, and Worsened the Financial Crisis*. Hoover Institution Press Publication 570. Stanford, CA: Hoover Institution, 2009.

Tenbrunsel, Ann, and Jordan Thomas. *The Street, The Bull and The Crisis: A Survey of the US & UK Financial Services Industry*. Presented by the University of Notre Dame and Labaton Sucharow LLP (May 2015). https://secwhistlebloweradvocate.com/pdf/Labaton-2015-Survey-report_12.pdf/.

Thiemann, Ronald F. *Religion in Public Life: A Dilemma for Democracy*. Washington, DC: Georgetown University Press, 1996.

Thomas Aquinas. *Commentary on Aristotle's "Physics."* Translated by Richard J. Spath, et al. Rare Masterpieces of Philosophy and Science. New Haven: Yale University Press, 1963.

———. *Commentary on Aristotle's "Politics."* Translated by Richard J. Regan. Indianapolis: Hackett, 2007.

———. *Commentary on "The Metaphysics" of Aristotle*. Translated by John P. Rowan. 2 vols. Library of Living Catholic Thought. Chicago: Regnery, 1961.

———. *Commentary on "The Nicomachean Ethics."* Translated by C. I. Litzinger, OP. 2 vols. Chicago: Regnery, 1964.

———. *Summa Theologica*. Translated by Fathers of the English Dominican Province. 3 vols. New York: Benziger, 1947.

———. *Truth*. Translated by Robert W. Mulligan, SJ, et al. 3 vols. Library of Living Catholic Thought. Chicago: Regnery, 1952–1954.

Tirole, Jean. *Economics for the Common Good*. Translated by Steven Rendall. Princeton: Princeton University Press, 2017.

Tooze, Adam. *Crashed: How a Decade of Financial Crises Changed the World*. New York: Viking, 2018.

Turner, Bryan S. "Civil Sphere and Political Performance: Critical Reflections on Alexander's Cultural Sociology." In *Solidarity, Justice, and Incorporation: Thinking through "The Civil Sphere,"* edited by Peter Kivisto and Giuseppe Sciortino, 57–80. Oxford: Oxford University Press, 2015.

United States Catholic Conference. *Renewing the Earth: An Invitation to Reflection and Action on Environment in Light of Catholic Social Teaching*. Publication of the United States Catholic Conference 468-6. Washington, DC: Office for Publication and Promotion Services, United States Catholic Conference, 1992.

United States Conference of Catholic Bishops. *Global Climate Change: A Plea for Dialogue, Prudence, and the Common Good*. Publication of the United States Conference of Catholic Bishops 5-431. Washington, DC: United States Conference of Catholic Bishops, 2001.

Vatican Council II. *Gaudium et spes (Pastoral Constitution on the Church in the Modern World)*. In *Vatican Council II: The Basic Sixteen Documents; Constitutions, Decrees, Declarations*, edited by Austin Flannery, OP, 163–282. A completely revised translation in inclusive language. Northport, NY: Costello, 1996.

Verstraeten, Johan. "Re-Thinking Catholic Social Thought as Tradition." In *Catholic Social Thought: Twilight or Renaissance?*, edited by J. S. Boswell et al., 59–77. Bibliotheca Ephemeridum Theologicarum Lovaniensium 157. Leuven: Leuven University Press, 2000.

Wadell, Paul J., CP. *The Primacy of Love: An Introduction to the Ethics of Thomas Aquinas*. New York: Paulist, 1992.

Wallace-Wells, David. *The Uninhabitable Earth: Life after Warming*. New York: Duggan, 2019.

Walzer, Michael. *Spheres of Justice: A Defense of Pluralism and Equality*. New York: Basic Books, 1983.

Weigel, George. *Tranquillitas Ordinis: The Present Failure and Future Promise of American Catholic Thought on War and Peace*. Oxford: Oxford University Press, 1987.

Williams, Rowan. "Knowing Our Limits." In *Crisis and Recovery: Ethics, Economics and Justice*, edited by Rowan Williams and Larry Elliott, 19–34. Basingstoke, UK: Palgrave Macmillan, 2010.

Wolf, Martin. *The Shifts and the Shocks: What We've Learned—and Have Still to Learn—from the Financial Crisis*. New York: Penguin, 2014.

Wolfe, Alan. *Whose Keeper? Social Science and Moral Obligation*. Berkeley: University of California Press, 1989.

Yuengert, Andrew M. "What Can Economists Contribute to the Common Good Tradition?" In *Empirical Foundations of the Common Good: What Theology Can Learn from Social Science*, edited by Daniel K. Finn, 36–63. New York: Oxford University Press, 2017.

Zahn, Gordon C. "Social Movements and Catholic Social Thought." In *One Hundred Years of Catholic Social Thought: Celebration and Challenge*, edited by John A. Coleman, SJ, 43–54. Maryknoll, NY: Orbis, 1991.

Index

Printed in the USA
CPSIA information can be obtained
at www.ICGtesting.com
LVHW061515040424
776428LV00006B/140